For Ken Harwood -- one of the great gentlemen of the world,

With the hope the promise of the New Frontier will be reawakened in the 1990s...

Your friend and admirer,

MaryAnn Watson

# The Expanding Vista

# THE EXPANDING VISTA

## American Television in the Kennedy Years

MARY ANN WATSON

New York   Oxford
OXFORD UNIVERSITY PRESS
1990

## Oxford University Press

Oxford   New York   Toronto
Delhi   Bombay   Calcutta   Madras   Karachi
Petaling Jaya   Singapore   Hong Kong   Tokyo
Nairobi   Dar es Salaam   Cape Town
Melbourne   Auckland

and associated companies in
Berlin   Ibadan

## Copyright © 1990 by Mary Ann Watson

Published by Oxford University Press, Inc.,
200 Madison Ave., New York, New York 10016

Oxford is a registered trademark of Oxford University Press

Library of Congress Cataloging-in-Publication Data
Watson, Mary Ann.
The expanding vista : American television in the Kennedy years
/ Mary Ann Watson.
p.   cm.   Includes bibliographical references.   ISBN 0-19-505746-5
1. Television—United States—History.
2. Television and politics—United States—History—20th century.
3. Kennedy, John F. (John Fitzgerald), 1917–1963.
I. Title.   PN1992.3.U5W4
1990 791.45′0973′09046—dc20
90-31266

2 4 6 8 9 7 5 3 1

Printed in the United States of America
on acid-free paper

# Preface

Few eras of American history are as forthrightly fascinating as the New Frontier. The period's colorful and emotional appeal to human interest, however, its evocative potential, does not diminish its instructive value. Recurring themes of the American experience surface throughout the story of this republic in the early 1960s as we encounter American aspirations and ideals, as well as mistakes and failures. .

In examining television as a social force, no more revealing time exists than the New Frontier. The pronounced cultural consequences of the medium's introduction into American life were being felt most potently in the Kennedy years. An exploration of television during the early 1960s is rife with reference points for present-day concerns.

The saga of the civil rights movement, for instance, so fully bound in television—the story of people committed to justice, fighting like fury with nonviolent tactics—nourishes the hopes of those who believe that great social movements resulting in great social changes are still possible.

During the 1970s and 1980s, President Kennedy's legacy was buffeted with various revelations of personal transgressions—true or otherwise. Harsh historical evaluations supplanted the effusively glowing chronicles that were published in the years just after his assassination. Yet, despite the lowering of President Kennedy's reputation in the academic world, his mythic stature outside the Ivory Tower has not been reduced. Public opinion polls reveal he is a cherished American president.

One of the lures of history, even though it will never disclose its alternatives, is the provocation to ponder "What if?" It is probably a safe assumption that more speculation has been invested in the question of how different the world would be had John Kennedy survived and been reelected in 1964 than in any other intrigue of recent American history.

A study of television in the Kennedy years obviously offers no more answers than scholarship with any other focus. It does provide, however, a different and widely overlooked set of clues. The account of John Kennedy's attempts to exploit the full potential of television as a new tool for effective governance adds a stratum of texture to the existing record of his administration.

The Kennedy years were, perhaps, America's best chance to truly integrate the public interest standard of broadcast regulation with the freedoms of the First Amendment. The Kennedy administration engaged in civil thinking about the significance of popular culture. It was understood that not everything of genuine importance can carry its weight in the marketplace.

The contemporary debate—the arguments pro and con for government intercession in programming practices—sounds very much like the discourse of the early 1960s. Today, as thirty years ago, opponents of broadcast regulation offer the "on-off switch" solution as if it were a trump card of reason. Yet, it will remain as useless an observation in the 1990s as it was in television's formative years.

Despite how any citizen interprets our constitutional protection of free expression, no genuinely rational person can deny in his or her heart that there is some connection between what happens on American TV screens and what happens in American streets. A reckoning cannot be put off forever.

In recent years there have been some important additions to the literature of television history, though scholars undertaking such studies have often been made to feel like academic stepchildren—encountering hostility from an old guard resistant to an encroachment of the mass media into the humanities. But, slowly, an enlightened perspective of the liberal arts is becoming perceptible.

The appropriateness and the need for educated men and women to consider the historical, aesthetic, and cultural aspects of television is exceedingly apparent. Television as an agent of socialization has long ago earned its place alongside family, church, and government—institutions that are studied in a variety of departments through a variety of methodologies at every university.

The technique of social history is unpretentious. The gathering and analysis of evidence, however, are only preparatory to the social historian's true objective—to produce a story of veracity that is meaningful to human experience. It is the presentation of a scholarly investigation as a readable narrative that is the goal. For only then can it matter at all.

*Ann Arbor, Mich.*                                                                          M.A.W.
*January 1990*

# Acknowledgments

The award of a Rockefeller Fellowship in the Humanities, which allowed for a semester in residence immersed in the archival collections of the Wisconsin Center for Film and Theater Research at the State Historical Society in Madison, was the critical vote of confidence in the value and importance of this research project. Though the work was arduous, it was a luxurious time of complete involvement with a single academic enterprise—facilitated by a support staff of the highest caliber and caring colleagues with insight to spare.

The Research Department of the John F. Kennedy Library, under the guidance of E. William Johnson, and the library's Audiovisual Archive, directed by Allan Goodrich, were central to the completion of this undertaking. Each of many visits to Boston deepened my respect for the professionalism of government archivists and heightened my appreciation for the scope of their responsibilities.

A large portion of the travel and photo expenses for *The Expanding Vista* was underwritten by the Howard R. Marsh Center for the Study of Journalistic Performance and the Department of Communication at the University of Michigan. Only through the skillful administration and bookkeeping of Louisa van Der Kooy, however, did every account balance.

I am indebted to many friends in the field of media history for their input and encouragement over the past years. Lawrence W. Lichty, from the start, understood the need I hoped to fill with this book. He generously made available to me his own considerable collection of resources on television history while his beautiful family made me feel welcome and comfortable on numerous visits to their frolicsome household.

As a student assistant, Matthew Katzive was as enterprising as he was dependable. He has my gratitude for his countless library trips and the uncomplaining way in which he undertook the especially tedious chore of transcribing hour after hour of audiotaped interviews.

Dennis Watson, my beloved, willingly shared every sacrifice required to bring a long-term endeavor such as this one to closure. His sardonic humor was an elixir for disappointment and discouragement.

The students in my broadcast history seminars in the Department of

Communication at the University of Michigan provided a steady stream of inspiration. Though most were born after the death of John Kennedy, as young people they instinctively felt connected with the New Frontier.

Norman Corwin, one of America's greatest writers, who is my hero, offered moral support that eroded self-doubt. It would be impossible to overstate the thrill of his kindness.

To publish under the imprint of Oxford University Press has been an ideal since first reading and being moved, as an undergraduate, by Erik Barnouw's magnificent trilogy on broadcast history. I am grateful for the opportunity of working with an exceptional publishing house—and especially for the sagacity of my editor, Rachel Toor.

It was my extreme good fortune to have Tom Mascaro agree to work with me as a research associate on *The Expanding Vista*. His formidable editorial skills and probing intellect, along with his guaranteed forbearance in difficult times, permitted me to write the book I wanted to write. My debt to Tom is deep and enduring.

# Contents

# The Expanding Vista

# PROLOGUE

# The Kennedy-Television Alliance

It is impossible to separate the major events of American history in the early 1960s from the development of American television. They are inextricably intertwined. The Kennedy years stand out as an era bracketed by TV milestones. In the years between the Great Debates and the network coverage of the assassination and funeral of the President, television became truly central to American life.

The New Frontier was a time in which traditions were being established in the young medium. Its resonance has not yet faded. It was a time when our broadcast heritage was emerging. Viewing patterns would be set; fundamentals of TV production ordained.

John Kennedy's overriding campaign theme in 1960 was the need "to get America moving again." After the seeming stillness of the Eisenhower years, the promise of a society in motion, however vague, was exhilarating. And television, itself making technological strides, was the perfect medium to chronicle movement. But the currents of change would be stronger and swifter than anyone could have imagined.

During the Kennedy years, so crowded with occurrences of critical consequence, television kept pace in a way that newspapers and magazines could not. Radio's inability to convey the images of motion rendered it incapable of adequately capturing the temper of the times. The dynamics of the era propelled television's development and, in turn, the force of the medium shaped the social landscape.

For students of history, using a new decade to delineate one historical period from another is a device that imposes neatness, but rarely true accuracy. In broadcast history, though, 1960 is a genuine turning point, a natural dividing line. Television's ascendancy to the most dominant position among the mass media had already been realized by the mid-1950s. As the new decade approached, there was a growing sense of expectancy about the capabilities and responsibilities of the medium. There was a palpable change in mood.

The sinister increase in Soviet accomplishments led to an American search for national purpose. Intellectual discourse was preoccupied with the question of how the United States should face the future. To whatever heights we would rise in the remainder of the century, television would be a key player in our uplifting.

In 1960 the television industry had something to prove. Like the nation, it was trying to overcome a malaise. Television too had suffered a decline in prestige brought on by a complacency with material success. Social critics pointed to the self-indulgent values reflected in popular television programming as a symptom of a deep moral ill-being in the United States. Television critics pointed to the rigging of quiz shows and the use of excessive violence in programming as symptoms of pernicious greed and contempt for viewers. Both the television medium and American society were victims of the embarrassment of riches. In troubled tandem they entered the sixties.

The presidential election of 1960 was to be a barometer of a new era. It represented a shift in American political technique and underscored the forcefulness of television in the formation of public opinion. The medium's ability to convey the human dimensions of political figures, however— whether reliably or not—was far from a virgin issue in 1960. The factor of television performance was introduced in the elective process eight years earlier.

Richard Nixon's melodramatic Checkers speech, his well-known attempt to restore his reputation and position as the 1952 Republican vice-presidential candidate in the wake of slush fund allegations, has entered American folklore. Nixon, who felt he had been seriously mistreated by the Republican hierarchy, savored the sweetness of success as letters began to pour in demanding his retention on the GOP ticket. But the incident also instilled in him a confidence about his efficacy as a television performer that would hurt him in 1960. Before long, as the novelty of television diminished, his speech would be regarded as cloying and transparent.

Dwight Eisenhower's decision in 1952 to become the first presidential candidate to appear in television commercials raised eyebrows, but the inevitability of the situation was soon apparent. During the first four years of the Eisenhower administration, the Chief Executive had come to appreciate the changes television was imposing on the presidency and on the process of campaigning for the Oval Office. He willingly honed his skills and talents as an electronic communicator. His warm, avuncular image flourished and his re-election in 1956 seemed certain.

Eisenhower's Democratic opponent, Adlai Stevenson, rejected the notion of developing a TV technique. He was a man of eloquent words. In stark contrast to the incumbent, he was an intellectual. Television could not transmit the complexity of his erudition. To the frequent frustration of many of those closest to him, Stevenson refused to adapt his style to the demands of time and simplicity made by television. To him, television felt like a gimmick. Whether the reason was integrity or myopia, Stevenson was quickly becoming a political anachronism.

By 1956 John Kennedy, who had already made a rapid rise in national politics, was growing more aware of the danger in underestimating the magnitude of the medium and the benefits of catering to it. His TV appearances in the early 1950s on news panel discussion shows, such as *Meet the Press*, while not flawless, displayed enviable ease. In October 1953, shortly after his highly publicized high-society wedding, Senator Kennedy and his bride were on Edward R. Murrow's *Person to Person*, a live interview program broadcast, in part, from the homes of the guests. The conversation could charitably be referred to as stilted, which, in many ways, was a hallmark of the times and the series.

Just as Kennedy was about to explain his position on the Taft-Hartley law, a ringing in the background distracted him. He looked over his shoulder, flashed an endearingly sheepish grin and said, "Perhaps somebody could answer my phone." The senator then continued his well-planned answer just where he'd left off. It was a fleeting instant of naturalism, engaging but insignificant. Yet, in retrospect, it foreshadowed a contemporary style of both politics and television the American public would soon come to embrace.

Kennedy was one of several men Stevenson was considering for his running mate in 1956. The nominee decided, however, to let the convention select the vice-presidential candidate. It was Senator Kennedy's good fortune to narrowly lose the vice-presidential nomination to Senator Estes Kefauver of Tennessee, which meant Kennedy escaped any blame for Stevenson's loss to Eisenhower. He was remembered instead for his delivery of the speech nominating Stevenson. It transfigured Kennedy into the party's brightest star. Television viewers were favorably impressed with the slender and winsome senator from Massachusetts. He was very soon the most sought after speaker in the Democratic party and clearly a strong contender for 1960.

Kennedy's re-election to the Senate in 1958 was a romp. His 1957 Pulitzer Prize for *Profiles in Courage* anointed him a statesman and an intellectual. His elevated status made him all the more attractive as a guest on national public affairs programs, where he was treated as a presidential candidate well before his announcement.

The readers of *TV Guide* found the by-line of Senator John F. Kennedy in the magazine's November 14, 1959, issue. In his article, "A Force That Has Changed the Political Scene," he gracefully anticipated some of the criticism that would be directed his way in the following year. Television image, he argued, is not simply a counterfeit measure of a candidate's capacity to govern and lead. Rather, it is a substantive factor. "Honesty, vigor, compassion, intelligence—the presence or lack of these and other qualities make up what is called the candidate's 'image,' " he wrote. "My own conviction is that these images or impressions are likely to be uncannily correct."

On January 2, 1960, John Kennedy formally announced what even the most casual observer already knew was fact—he was running for the Democratic presidential nomination. The following day he appeared on *Meet the Press* and made it very clear he would not settle for the vice-presidential spot. In 1960, he said, the American public would "presume that the presidential candidate is going to have a normal life expectancy." He felt, therefore, the second name on the ticket was not going to be of critical importance to American voters. Kennedy said he was not interested in spending the next eight years of his life "breaking ties (in the Senate) and waiting for the president to die."

As the 1960 primary season unfolded, Kennedy's Catholicism promised to be a damaging circumstance. The West Virginia primary was the turning point on the issue. And it was a television appearance that was the turning point in the primary.

Against the advice of many seasoned politicians, the candidate decided to confront religious prejudice straightaway instead of sidestepping it. For almost two weeks before the vote in West Virginia, Kennedy boldly and emotionally referred to his religion in personal appearances. "Nobody asked me if I was Catholic when I joined the United States Navy," he said. "And nobody asked my brother if he was Catholic or Protestant before he climbed into an American bomber plane to fly his last mission."

The Sunday before election day, the Kennedy campaign purchased thirty minutes of television time. The format of the discussion program had Franklin Roosevelt, Jr., asking the questions the candidate would answer. Within the first few minutes of the program, as planned, the question of religion was raised. Kennedy did not direct his answer to Roosevelt or focus on him. He looked directly into the lens of the camera, into the eyes of the voters, as he delivered an impassioned statement of principle on the separation of church and state. He was deeply persuasive.

Kennedy had been trailing Hubert Humphrey—who had a far more active Senate record—in the polls throughout the primary, though he was gaining momentum. Following the Sunday night program Kennedy took a slim lead. When Tuesday's votes were counted, though, the Massachusetts senator's victory in West Virginia was not even a close call. He captured more than 60 percent of the vote. Later, during the general election, network television's generous coverage of Kennedy's eloquent remarks on religion addressed to the Greater Houston Ministerial Association finally put the matter to rest.

Kennedy's polished use of television in West Virginia was enhanced by the ineptitude and naivete of his opponent. Humphrey foolishly challenged

Kennedy to a televised debate, resulting in the senator from Minnesota being upstaged by Kennedy's aplomb. Both candidates shared similar views on the federal government's responsibility to the impoverished families of West Virginia. Kennedy, however, brought with him to the TV studio a government-distributed food package that included the daily ration of powdered milk made available to the unemployed poor. He *visually* underscored his concern.

The night before the West Virginia election Humphrey participated in an ill-advised telethon. Not understanding the importance of controlling all the factors of a telecast over which one has control, the Humphrey campaign devised a program of true spontaneity, not one that simply gave the illusion of spontaneity.

The Humphrey broadcast was a fiasco. The senator from Minnesota sat at a desk with a telephone and answered unscreened questions coming in over two phone lines. Callers insulted him, asked long questions taking circuitous routes to get to their points, and during one call the operator broke in demanding the line be cleared for a medical emergency. The Kennedy forces were already far too sophisticated about television to make such an elementary mistake. Kennedy later joked that had he known about the acceptance of unscreened calls he would have had his brother Bobby phone in a question or two for Humphrey. The presidential campaign trail in 1960 was no place for someone who had not yet learned to manipulate television to his advantage.

John Kennedy believed that nonpolitical talk to the unconvinced was better than political talk to the already convinced. Television expedited the impact of his logic. His appearance on Jack Paar's *Tonight Show* in June 1960 demonstrated Kennedy's ability and willingness to use TV for personality projection.

In Paar's introduction of the candidate, he welcomed him to the "relaxed atmosphere" of the late-night talk show and said, "I think Mr. Kennedy came here tonight because he feels he can reach people who would not ordinarily watch news programs." Their conversation, which included actress Anne Bancroft and comedienne Peggy Cass, was pleasantly jocular. Kennedy seemed altogether accessible.

At the first commercial break, Paar deferentially apologized for the interruption, but Kennedy responded, "No, don't apologize—that's how it all operates." When telling a campaign anecdote, Kennedy alluded to the many popular prime-time western series on the air. "I was made an honorary Indian," he said. "And now I cheer for our side on TV." As the lengthy interview came to a close, Kennedy told Paar, "In campaigning through Wisconsin and West Virginia I ran into a lot of people who sat up nights watching you. And I think anytime it's possible for those of us in public life to have a chance to communicate, I think we ought to take it. Therefore, I regard it as a privilege to appear on this program."

The Democrats were scheduled to meet in Los Angeles; the Republicans were convening in Chicago. But long before the summer arrived, the TV networks were planning to cover the 1960 nominating conventions with all the pageantry that the panoply of new electronic marvels would allow. Miniaturization, transistorization, and videotape were changing the whole picture. And the machinery of government was increasingly adapting to the machinery of television.

Print journalists sensed that television was making inroads into their sphere of influence. They were distressed, for instance, to find that broadcasters were given preferential treatment by the Democratic National Committee in the allotment of premium working space at the convention hall. Most newspaper reporters actually found themselves and their typewriters housed in a tent outside the Los Angeles Sports Arena. The heat, though unpleasant, was not their major problem. Many of the key figures of the convention preferred to give exclusive interviews to broadcasters. Newspaper reporters realized they needed to monitor the television networks to keep abreast of the news. It would become a familiar frustration in the months and years ahead.

In 1960, 87 percent of American homes, more than 46 million, were equipped with television—at least 25 percent more TV households than existed in 1956. The rivalry among the networks to capture the growing audience was more intense than ever. The conventions would be a showcase for a new look and feel in television reporting.

Smaller, lighter, more sensitive TV cameras and walkie-talkie radios allowed correspondents greater mobility on the convention floor. Because of videotape, the natural drama and spectacle of the political conventions could be embellished by the ability to record simultaneous events and structure them through editing. The desultory could be eliminated; the tedious abbreviated. Improvements in synchronizing TV signals from various sources permitted live remote feeds from outside the convention hall and increased the use of graphic inserts and split-screens. The tremendous expense, with appropriate fanfare, was chalked up to public service.

The 1960 Democratic Platform, entitled "The Rights of Man," directly addressed some of the skeletons in the closet of the broadcasting industry that made public service such an important commodity. "We have drifted into a national mood that accepts payola and quiz scandals," the document proclaimed. It also pointed to "the exploitation of sadistic violence as popular entertainment." The platform intimated that government had a legitimate role in such matters. "For eight long critical years," it read, "our present leadership has made no effective effort to reverse this mood. The new Democratic Administration will help create a sense of national purpose and higher standards of public behavior."

In the Los Angeles Sports Arena, a tremendous, emotional floor demonstration for Adlai Stevenson concluded his career as a presidential hopeful. Later, Kennedy watched his first-ballot nomination on television. The subsequent messy business of selecting a vice-presidential candidate was an exhausting ordeal for the Kennedy team. But the weariness of the Democratic nominee was not as easily detected by the 60,000 people in the Los Angeles Coliseum assembled to hear his acceptance speech as it was by the 35 million people watching it on television.

Box seats around the immediate area of the podium were sold for ten dollars each. Shortly before Kennedy was to begin speaking, campaign manager Robert Kennedy was disturbed that many of the reserved seats had not yet been taken. "He had them opened up to the public," Walter Cronkite reported during CBS's convention coverage, "so those stands would be filled and the television picture would be a little more impressive."

Richard Nixon, watching on TV, was unimpressed as he listened to the quick delivery of the address which christened Kennedy's candidacy. "The old era is ending," Kennedy said, "the old ways will not do." Though his sentiments were surely more global that evening, he could have easily been referring to the campaign ahead.

The vice-president was proud of his skill and reputation as a first-class debater, but the long-discussed proposal of a series of television debates between the candidates gave him pause. Now, hearing Kennedy, he felt a little more favorably inclined to the notion. He said to his viewing companions, including Attorney General William P. Rogers, "I can take this man."

The complex needs of the electronic media in 1960 made the logistical management of the Democratic convention a daunting responsibility. The challenge was confidently met, however, by J. Leonard Reinsch, whose contemporary communication talents had long been put to use by Democratic candidates. Presidents Franklin Roosevelt and Harry Truman had both benefited from his understanding of the principles of broadcasting. In 1960 Reinsch had taken a leave of absence from his post as executive director of the Cox group of broadcast stations. Under his direction, the convention coverage never faltered. His expertise in television and his impressive administrative skills were valuable assets to the Democratic party.

Shortly after winning the nomination, Kennedy asked Reinsch to join his campaign strategy team. Reinsch recalled the candidate saying, "Television may be the most important part of the campaign. It may decide the election. Will you handle my TV arrangements?"

Within forty-eight hours Reinsch was in the Kennedy home in Hyannis Port discussing television strategy over clam chowder. The issue of television debates was raised and the candidate wondered what format they might take. "I'm not really concerned about the program," Reinsch told Senator Kennedy. "All I want is a picture of you and Nixon on the same television tube. We'll take it from there."

In Chicago, the in-fighting of the Republican party, though bitter, was relatively discreet. It was not shared with the television audience. When the dust settled, Richard Nixon was unanimously nominated. His choice of Henry Cabot Lodge as a running mate produced little dissension. Nixon's acceptance speech was, he felt, as did many others, one of the finest of his career. It was an address imbued with what was called "theatrical intensity."

And so the stage was set—a hackneyed phrase that is consummately appropriate here—for a general election of intense national interest. To the envy of popular dramatists, the compelling dissimilarity of the players kept the public eager for the action to continue. One man was privileged and handsome, his character tempered by family tragedy and personal pain. The other, accustomed to hard work throughout his youth, had common features and a patina of defensiveness about his ordinary roots. In the months that followed, the television networks capitalized on the inherent drama in the hard-fought contest that was filled with conflict and plot twists leading to a cliff-hanger ending.

From Labor Day to election day, Kennedy adhered to a relentless schedule of personal appearances, with an emphasis on swing states, fully aware of the dividends of local and national television coverage. An associate professor of voice and speech at Boston University—a former opera singer—was retained to help the candidate maintain his vocal timbre through relaxation techniques used by professional performers.

His campaign also secured the services of a new kind of business, Mobile Video Tapes, to record every stop in its entirety. The idea of video documentation was an appealing one to Kennedy. It was not as important to the Nixon team, though. The company received no reply from the Republicans when it offered the same videotaping service.

As a candidate, and later as president, Kennedy shunned silly hats and kissing babies. Looking presidential mattered. Kennedy also jettisoned conventional wisdom about the rhetoric of campaign stumping. He didn't make homespun references to the town he was in or pretend to be interested in the winning season of the local football team. His hand waves of greeting were tentative, rarely above shoulder height. Kennedy held back; he didn't give himself to a crowd. He was in control even when passionate. On television, a medium that magnifies personalities and mannerisms, Kennedy's reserve translated into a dignified, statesmanlike persona.

Nixon, who pledged to visit all fifty states, was an old-fashioned campaigner. He was always well briefed on local color, particularly football scores. He used this information to structure "applause points" into his speeches. Nixon's movements were broad, his facial expressions verged on mugging. And the hand wave that in later years would become a sad trademark and final salute to his country, was vigorous and exaggerated. His style was successfully geared to live campaign appearances. It was guaranteed to rouse a crowd. But Nixon too understood that free exposure of film clips on the evening news had to be exploited. This added to his frustration when campaign time was lost in the early weeks of September due to his hospitalization with a serious knee infection.

The most monumental degree of free exposure for both candidates came, of course, with their series of four televised debates. The largesse of the television networks in coordinating and producing the joint appearances, in addition to making the approximately $6 million worth of commercial-free time available, was also part of a calculated attempt to improve public and governmental relations.

As soon as broadcasters were freed from the burden of affording equal access to all legally qualified presidential candidates by a Congressional suspension of Section 315 of the Communications Act in August 1960, preparations began in earnest for the long-awaited video confrontations.

All three networks extended formal invitations to the candidates, though NBC was the first. The very night Nixon was nominated, Chairman of the Board Robert Sarnoff sent wires to the two men. Sarnoff is credited with coining the title "The Great Debates" in his invitation.

Kennedy accepted without hesitation. He had everything to gain. The debates would magnify his status and would be his best chance to close the "maturity gap," the lingering perception that the senator was simply too young and inexperienced for the position he sought.

A week before the first debate, on the CBS program *Presidential Countdown: Mr. Kennedy, A Profile*, Walter Cronkite asked the candidate, "Do you ever wish that you looked older?" Kennedy believed his youthfulness would ultimately work to his advantage. Concerning Kennedy's hairstyle, the reporter asked if "getting away from the forelock" was "a considered political opinion." "Well," Senator Kennedy replied with good-natured irritation, "I've been cutting it the same way for six or seven years—or even longer. But, it's a—unfortunately when you run for the presidency, your wife's hair or your hair or something else always becomes of major significance. I don't think it's the great issue, though, in 1960."

Nixon had more to lose than to gain by participating in the debates. He was urged by many, including President Eisenhower, to avoid a forum that would put Kennedy on seemingly equal footing. But the prospect of looking like he was chickening out of a fair fight was unacceptable to the vice-president. It was a matter of personal pride.

The logistics and the debate formats were sorted out in careful negotiations, fifteen meetings in all, among the networks and representatives of the candidates. By mid September all parties had agreed to four one-hour programs that would air simultaneously on all three television networks and all four radio networks. In precise terms, the joint appearances were not debates; they were closer to news conferences. Nevertheless, the coverage was focused on the idea that there would be a winner and a loser.

Thoughtful volumes have been written on the Great Debates and exhaustive research studies undertaken. The impact of the first debate, which took place at Chicago's CBS affiliate, WBBM, on September 26, 1960, is well documented. It ushered in, if not in actual practice, surely in public thinking, a new way to gauge the worthiness of those vying to be the chief executive. And for print journalists, it was yet another sign of an eclipse in progress. Despite cries of foul from many of them, the moderator and four-man panel for the first telecast came from the broadcast industry. The first and most important debate belonged to television.

A myriad of factors converged that evening for a hapless Richard Nixon. Not yet completely recovered from his serious and painful hospital stay, his wan appearance looked even worse when juxtaposed with Kennedy's sun-tanned countenance. This, of course, was beyond Nixon's control, but Nixon was less aggressive than Kennedy in controlling what he could.

Kennedy displayed greater astuteness about the process of television production and paid closer attention to detail. The day before the first debate Kennedy himself and his broadcast strategist, J. Leonard Reinsch, met with Don Hewitt, the CBS director of the telecast, to discuss set design and shooting patterns. The same invitation was extended to Nixon but was not accepted. The vice-president declined the valuable opportunity to familiarize himself with the venue of a performance that would be critical for him.

The day of the first debate, Kennedy kept a light schedule, only a short meeting at noon with a labor group. The rest of that Monday was spent studying, with the phone off the hook, from a stack of index cards and a notebook labelled "What Nixon Said." After dinner he took a short nap. It was going to be a big night.

The dramatic tension of the first debate was enhanced by the latest Gallup poll, which indicated an even split of 47 percent of the electorate for each man, with 6 percent of the voters undecided. A hint of true acrimony between the candidates added interest.

Both candidates were offered the services of a professional make-up artist brought in by the network from New York. Both refused. Kennedy needed no make-up. Nixon did, but he was touched up questionably by a member of his own staff. It was a regrettable folly that has become a permanent footnote in American political history.

When the studio lights were being checked shortly before airtime, Hewitt commented that Kennedy's white shirt caused an unattractive glare. An aide to the senator was promptly sent to bring one of Kennedy's blue shirts back to the station. Combined with his dark blue suit, Kennedy would look crisp and stand out from the neutral gray background. In comparison, Nixon's recent eight-pound weight loss caused his shirt collar to sag ever so slightly and his light gray suit blended blandly into the set.

Moments before air Robert Kennedy was looking at the image of the candidates on the monitor. He was surprised at Nixon's peaked appearance.

When Nixon spotted him checking the screen, he asked what the younger Kennedy thought. "Dick," the candidate's brother said, "you look great."

Throughout the campaign, and especially in regard to the debates, John Kennedy sought out and respected the expertise of media professionals. Nixon had savvy media advisors on his staff and at his disposal as well, but he did not make good use of their knowledge. Nixon's style was insular. He dismissed the advice of men who had impressive credentials and track records in the broadcast media. He misjudged what mattered most.

Whether or not Nixon and Kennedy were substantively peers that evening—as the research on the radio audience indicates they were—hardly mattered. It was the combination of sight and sound that determined the winner. And Kennedy outdistanced the vice-president by furlongs. In the jargon of pollsters, Kennedy created a "victory psychology" and Nixon precipitated a decline in his "enthusiasm quotient."

Russell Baker, covering the story for *The New York Times*, recalled listening to but not watching a TV monitor at the Chicago studio: "I thought Nixon had a slight edge in what little argument there had been but as I talked to more and more people it was clear they thought Kennedy had won a great victory. . . . I missed it completely because I had been too busy taking notes and writing to get more than fleeting glimpses of what the country was seeing on the screen. That night television replaced newspapers as the most important communications medium in American politics."

In the days that followed, Kennedy's crowds grew noisier and television's critics quieter. The medium emerged with a greater aura of respectability. Television also became a bigger part of the story of the campaign. Through standard news reports the public was getting acquainted with the behind-the-scenes considerations of television. The fact that television mediated reality was discussed not only in college classrooms, but around the office water cooler and over the back fence.

The image gulf between Nixon and Kennedy was not as wide in the following three debates. The vice-president took precautions not to look "sick and weak and mean," the way his own staff told him he did after the first round. More sleep, more calories, and more carefully applied make-up softened his appearance.

Kennedy was not lax in his preparation for the remaining encounters. He continued to warm up by listening to audiotapes of Nixon's speeches and ad-libs. The sound of the vice-president's voice reportedly helped put Kennedy in an aggressive mood.

J. Leonard Reinsch believed the vice-president was a "psychosomatic sweater." Nixon's visible perspiration in the reaction shots of the first debate delighted Reinsch since the Republican candidate's perceived nervousness could only reflect favorably on Kennedy. It was just the kind of television image he had hoped for.

When the TV advisor entered the NBC studio from which the second debate was about to be broadcast, the temperature was only about sixty-four degrees in an apparent concession to Nixon. Reinsch was determined to optimize conditions for Kennedy. "I finally located a janitor in the second basement below the studio," Reinsch recalled, "and with a series of threats got him to locate the key to the thermostat buried in the bottom drawer of a desk. We turned the temperature up as high as we could."

After his bad experience with reaction shots in the first debate, Nixon asked that the tally lights on the cameras be visible for the second so he could better know when to safely use the handkerchief he kept in front of him on the podium. Reinsch remembered about the second debate: "The first half hour produced no reaction shots. . . . I got quite concerned. I was in the control room and threatened the producer and director if we didn't get reaction shots." About forty minutes into the program Reinsch got what he was after—a shot of Nixon rubbing his brow in nervousness. "To the Democrats," Reinsch believed, "this picture was most important."

The final two debates were produced by ABC News. The network offered each candidate full use of studio facilities for rehearsal in the day-and-a-half before the telecasts. According to an ABC spokesman, Tom Moore, who subsequently became president of the network, Kennedy rehearsed more than seven hours before each of the final broadcasts. The Kennedy team also engaged the services of Fred Coe, the renowned theater and television producer, to supervise the ABC rehearsals. Nixon did not avail himself of the network's offer. The vice-president, according to Moore, arrived at the studio twenty-four minutes before the third debate and nine minutes before airtime for the fourth.

The proposal by a group of Democratic senators for a fifth debate in the week before the election failed to materialize. Kennedy pushed hard for the idea, though, and vigorously challenged Nixon to accept. The vice-president, understandably, was reluctant to participate unless the format was amended. He would not again debate face-to-face.

Kennedy made the most of the vice-president's avoidance. "The networks were willing to give time for this debate," Kennedy said in a statement the Democratic National Committee sent out as a press release. "The American people wanted this debate. Only Mr. Nixon stands in the way."


In 1960 the Democrats made wider use of five-minute paid political programs on network television. Forty-eight such purchases were made for Kennedy, while the Republicans made only nineteen. This shorter format proved to be more effective in reaching viewers than the more typical thirty-minute Nixon program. The five-minute programs followed shortened versions of regularly scheduled entertainment shows and naturally inherited their audiences. The longer political programs preempted popular shows and disrupted viewing routines. And they were, of course, more expensive to air.

Kennedy's paid political coverage was an intentional blend of image and substance, while the Nixon campaign made little use of impressionistic advertising. Nixon preferred commercial spots laden with issues presented in an unadorned manner.

To reinforce voters' recollections of Kennedy's impressive performance in the Great Debates, a sixty-second spot featuring debate footage was produced and entitled "Historic Moment." In another commercial, Eleanor Roosevelt praised Kennedy's grasp of history, an attribute essential in great statesmen, such as her late husband. Jacqueline Kennedy recorded a television message in Spanish for selected areas of the country. Shyly, she declared, "Viva Kennedy."

Nixon's failure to appreciate the potency of stylized television imagery did not wane—even in the home stretch. His media staff had prepared a film called *Ambassador of Friendship*, which depicted "a rousing hero image of Dick Nixon." It was to be nationally televised following *The Ed Sullivan Show* the Sunday night before election day. But the candidate nixed the presentation and instead chose to go on the air himself and make his positions on the issues perfectly clear.

On election eve, NBC president Robert Kintner told his assembled news staff, "Men, you may think this election is a contest between Kennedy and Nixon. It's not. It's a race between NBC and CBS." While NBC would emerge victorious by a wide margin, the political contest between Kennedy and Nixon came to a close just the way any TV producer would have scripted it. It was a horse race with a photo finish. The all-night election vigil broke the viewership records of the first debate. More than 90 percent of the television sets in American homes were tuned in for some part of the coverage.

Kintner recalled how the news desk at his network received an unexpected telephone call that election night. "When you run down the board, could you keep the figures on the screen a little longer?" the caller from the Associated Press asked. "You're going so fast we can't copy them."

The significance of television in the outcome of the election became the subject of wide discussion in the mass media. Most people came to the same conclusion the president-elect did—television was indeed the edge in his narrow margin of victory. And J. Leonard Reinsch was heralded as "the architect of a triumph on television."

"Kennedy happens to look like a composite picture of all the good stereotypes television has created," wrote one political science professor in his assessment of Campaign '60. And, as one senior citizen told an interviewer conducting survey research on the campaign for the University of Michigan, she did not vote for Nixon because she "didn't like the look in his eyes—especially the left one."

The television industry calculated that from the conventions through election day, roughly July 1 through November 8, $20 million had been spent delivering the story to the homes of the American public. According to the trade press, that figure was the result of "the most conservative and reliable business estimates." The industry hoped its investment would amount to considerable goodwill in Washington.

On the morning of November 9, 1960, an unprecedented sense of familiarity and proprietary interest on the part of the American public toward a U.S. president and his family would begin to develop because of television. In a press conference at the National Guard Armory in Hyannis, President-elect Kennedy, with pregnant Jacqueline at his side, dedicated himself to the cause of freedom around the world and then took his leave by saying, "So now my wife and I prepare for a new administration and a new baby." It was a heartwarming and exciting story that television was only too happy to convey.

The transition from the Eisenhower administration to the New Frontier unfolded on TV screens everywhere as JFK's every move was followed. The television networks competed to cover the Kennedy Inaugural and associated events in the most spectacular, and at the same time, most intimate way. In the fifteen hours between his attendance at morning Mass and his leaving the Inaugural Ball, TV technicians scrambled in the snow along with secret service agents to keep up with the indefatigable John Kennedy.

A lover of poetry, Kennedy understood symbolism. He wanted to use, in the words of British journalist Henry Fairlie, "images of excellence to adorn his Presidency." And he did so exquisitely on the first day. The cultural sheen of his Inaugural was meant to be a harbinger of an uplifting of the American social imagination.

It was a day of striking imagery. The touching sight of Robert Frost blinded by the glare of the sun as he attempted to read from his manuscript; the reserve of Kennedy's wife and the exuberance of his sisters; the gracious and familiar smile of a now former president who suddenly looked old.

Television pictures provided a wonderfully paradoxical portrait of President Kennedy. He was both exalted and personalized. It was the new leader of the free world who punctuated the lofty rhetoric of his inaugural address with emphatic hand motions and pointed finger; but it was a regular kind of guy who got caught running a pocket comb through his generously endowed head of hair when he thought no one was looking.

The New Frontier was off and running, but television would do more than simply follow dizzily from the speed. An unspoken alliance had been formed, a symbiotic bond between Kennedy and the medium. The telegenic new President's affinity for television was going to alter the nature of the relationship between the public and the chief executive. It was also going to define the nature of the relationship between the chief executive and the medium.

American television in the Kennedy years was so different from what had come before—it felt modern, more immediate and sophisticated, sharper than TV in the 1950s. And yet, American television in the Kennedy years was so different from what was to come soon after—long before decade's end it would seem quaint and modest, and so very black and white.

The New Frontier is a time set apart in our national memory and in the personal memories of those who lived through it. Recollections of the era are inevitably rich with video images. The consideration of television in transition in the early 1960s is far more than a nostalgic sojourn, however. The medium is an element inseparable from a pivotal period in the history of the United States.

# CHAPTER 1

# There'll Be Some Changes Made

## A NEW REGULATORY SPIRIT

It was an odd name. Not many average citizens were familiar with it when President-elect Kennedy decided Newton Minow should be chairman of the Federal Communications Commission. That would soon change.

As the excitement surrounding the inaugural festivities mounted in Washington, television was being hailed as a profound new factor in the way Americans governed themselves. It was the way television was to be governed in this democratic society, however, that would become one of the most visible domestic issues of the Kennedy administration—and a key change from the recent past.

During the 1950s the broadcast industry had grown comfortable in the expectation of nothing more than moderate regulation from the federal government. The FCC grappled with technical issues, but was little involved in the programming responsibilities of broadcasters. This passive stance was not entirely a matter of legal limitations, but, rather, philosophy. A suggested motto for the commissioners' activity during this time was, "The agency that regulates least is the agency that regulates best."

John Kennedy, however, was coming to the Oval Office with a different philosophy. The liberal activism of his campaign rhetoric was translated into action in his plans for regulatory agencies. The public interest would be paramount. Kennedy's special assistant, historian Arthur Schlesinger, Jr., recalled, "This naturally outraged businessmen, who, in earlier years had grown used to regarding regulatory agencies as adjuncts to their own trade associations."

Such coziness between the Commission and the broadcast industry was epitomized in the relationship of FCC chairman John Doerfer and the Storer Broadcasting Company. Already publicly exposed for double billing the government on official trips, Doerfer accepted, apparently without qualms, the hospitality of the Storer Broadcasting Company, which owned twelve broadcast stations. In February 1960, Storer's private airplane took Doerfer to Miami, where he spent six days on *Lazy Girl*, the Storer yacht.

Doerfer, who felt broadcast licenses should be granted in perpetuity, was well liked by industry lobbyists. The scandal in which he found himself embroiled was annoying. The favors he received were, according to his own description, "the usual amenities." But President Eisenhower could no longer abide such egregious malfeasance and asked for the chairman's resignation. Shortly thereafter, Doerfer became professionally involved in Storer business deals and eventually assumed the position of counsel and vice-president for Storer Broadcasting.

Kennedy's choice for FCC chairman was not someone who would fit into the hip pocket of broadcasters. Not long after his appointment, Newton Minow explained his qualifications for the job: "I'm here to do what I think needs to be done and I've got two big assets—I'm not interested in being reappointed and I don't want a job in the industry."

The appointment of an activist regulator was largely unexpected. Television had been good to John Kennedy in the 1960 campaign and some in the industry thought, perhaps, a reward was in order. But Kennedy's action shouldn't have been a surprise. The Democratic platform adopted in Los Angeles the summer before couldn't have been more clear. "The Democratic party promises to clean up regulatory agencies," it declared. In an obvious reference to former FCC chairman Doerfer, it said, "The acceptance by Republican appointees to these agencies of gifts, hospitality, and bribes from interests under their jurisdiction has been a particularly flagrant abuse of public trust." The document promised that government agencies in a Democratic administration would be headed by "men of ability and independent judgment."

Kennedy's first appointment to a regulatory agency was Newton Minow. For broadcasters, Minow's Senate confirmation hearing in early February 1961 was a portent of trouble ahead. He was clearly an idealist. To his interrogators he said, "I do think that the Commission has a role in encouraging better programs, and I am determined to do something about it."

Newton Minow was characteristic of the New Frontier image. He served his country at the end of World War II as a signal lineman in India, and then went to school on the GI Bill. He was one of the best and the brightest. And he was young—just thirty-five when sworn in.

His legal background was truly impressive. After graduating first in his class from Northwestern Law School, where he was editor of the *Law Review*, Minow became law clerk to Chief Justice Fred Vinson of the U.S. Supreme Court. Two years later he became an administrative assistant to the governor of Illinois, Adlai Stevenson. Within a few years, Minow and Stevenson were law partners and Minow was deeply involved in national Democratic politics. For John Kennedy, who had an uneasy relationship with Adlai Stevenson, Minow was one of many who served as a bridge between the two men.

An FCC chairman's starting salary of $20,500 was a considerable drop in income for an attorney of Minow's caliber. In private practice his annual income was more than double that amount. He made it clear in various interviews he was making the financial sacrifice for a limited period of time because of a deep respect for John Kennedy and a belief in his policies.

"You've got to look at the period of American history that it was," Minow recalled. "It was the Kennedy era. It was the young people who had served in World War II, for the most part in the Army, who were now taking on the public responsibility, who had a sense of idealism and who cared about the country, who felt that public service was an honorable thing to do."

Minow's work in the presidential campaigns of 1952 and 1956 acquainted him with many broadcast issues. But still, it was a limited exposure. As one reporter put it, "Minow comes to television armed with a background of no experience." Familiarity with the industry, though, was not the reason Minow was brought to the Commission. It was integrity, more than experience, that would be needed to overcome the residue of scandal lingering at the FCC. With this quality Minow came well equipped. Even his harshest opponents had to admit—after scrutinizing his record—he was above reproach.

"I think Robert was the basic reason I was appointed to the FCC," Minow recalled. "Robert (Kennedy) and I got to know each other in the fifties. And in the '56 campaign, most specifically, we got to know each other very, very well. We travelled with the Stevenson campaign and a couple of times we ended up as roommates on the road, sharing a hotel room. He and I were the same age; we had children the same age. And we were very inclined to talk about the effect of television on children and the lack of good programming for children."

Minow said of John Kennedy, that by 1960, "I knew him well. I think I was familiar with his philosophy and his thinking." Putting aggressive pressure on the broadcasting industry to improve its performance is what Minow believed the President had in mind.

Unlike Chairman Doerfer, Minow had no inclination toward fraternizing with broadcasters and took great care to avoid even the suggestion of a conflict of interest. When *Better Homes and Gardens* magazine offered Minow a routine complimentary subscription upon his arrival in Washington, he refused it. Meredith Publications, publisher of the periodical, also owned five television stations.

In the spring of 1961 Minow was preparing his first address as FCC chairman. The speech was to be delivered to the thirty-ninth annual convention of the National Association of Broadcasters in early May, which would be meeting in Washington, D.C. For weeks before the address, rumors were circulating that he was going to take an especially hard line. "Unless he makes an eleventh hour switch," the industry was warned in the trade press, "FCC Chairman Newton N. Minow will tell the NAB convention that if broadcasters don't want to be regulated and mind their manners, they had better get out of the broadcasting business." "Big Brother is indeed watching," they were told.

While final preparations for the meeting were being made, the attention of most Americans was directed heavenward. On May 5, Alan Shepard was launched 115 miles beyond the surface of the earth. Though Shepard was only in space for fifteen minutes, he was the first American to be there and the mission went off without a hitch. President Kennedy was ebullient. All Americans had the opportunity to share in the triumph through live television coverage.

On Monday, May 8, at 10:00 A.M., President Kennedy presented Commander Shepard the Distinguished Service Medal in a Rose Garden ceremony. At 11:00 A.M. Kennedy was scheduled to be the opening speaker at the NAB convention. Spontaneously, the President decided to take America's newest young hero along. "We have with us today the nation's number one television performer," the President said in introducing his surprise guest.

Kennedy's remarks to the broadcasters were a lofty paean to a system of free choice and democracy. In an open society, he said, even an enterprise as risky as manned space flight is allowed to be shown live on television. "You are the guardians of the most powerful and effective means of communication ever designed," he said. A few broadcasters might have taken a premature measure of comfort in the President's glowing words. Freedom of expression sounded better than more regulation. But the convention was far from over.

## The Promulgation of Newton's Law

The NAB had a new president in 1961, LeRoy Collins, the former governor of Florida. He was chosen by the trade association because of his political visibility and Washington connections. Following President Kennedy's speech Collins spoke to the convention. But his first formal address to his constituents had most of them questioning the wisdom of his being selected. Collins's reform-oriented speech calling for "broadcasting to measure up to the full stature of its mighty potential," though elegantly delivered, felt uncomfortably like a public spanking.

Minow was the luncheon speaker on Tuesday afternoon, May 9. About two thousand broadcasters were assembled for the event. "When the New

Frontiersmen rode into town," he said to open the showdown, "I locked myself in my office to do my homework and get my feet wet. But apparently I haven't managed to stay out of hot water. I seem to have detected a certain nervous apprehension about what I might say or do when I emerged from that locked office for this, my maiden station break."

The bespectacled, slightly pudgy chairman first offered flattering words: "It may also come as a surprise to some of you, but I want you to know that you have my admiration and respect. Yours is a most honorable profession. Anyone who is in the broadcasting business has a tough row to hoe."

The tension in Sheraton Hall started rising, though, as the young bureaucrat quickly got to the heart of the matter. "I admire your courage—but that doesn't mean I would make life any easier for you. Your license lets you use the public's airwaves as trustees for 180 million Americans. The public is your beneficiary. If you want to stay on as trustees, you must deliver a decent return to the public—not only to your stockholders." These were ominous words.

The most controversial aspect of Minow's address that afternoon—the day dubbed Black Tuesday—was his direct commentary, both favorable and critical, on television programming. Minow's specific references to programs he felt were "eminently worthwhile," such as *The Twilight Zone*, *CBS Reports*, and *The Fred Astaire Show*, would provide some ammunition for his critics who charged the Number One regulator was attempting to impose his idea of good taste on millions of American viewers.

It was what Minow *didn't* like on TV, however, that fueled the paranoia: "A procession of game shows, violence, audience participation shows, formula comedies about totally unbelievable families, blood and thunder, mayhem, violence, sadism, murder, western bad men, western good men, private eyes, gangsters, more violence, and cartoons. And, endlessly, commercials—many screaming, cajoling and offending."

It sounded like the threat of pure censorship to defensive ears, particularly when he added, "I want to say to you now: Renewal will not be pro forma in the future. There is nothing permanent or sacred about a broadcast license."

Not only the devastating content, but the perceived pontifical tone of Minow's forty-minute message was offensive to broadcasters. The chairman invited those in his audience to watch their own TV stations for one full day. "I can assure you," he warned, "that you will observe a vast wasteland."

According to one analyst of American rhetoric, Minow's pattern of speech helped create an especially threatening mood. Critical sections of his ultimatum were delivered "in cold, measured tones with downward inflections." This, combined with Minow's "youthful appearance and boyish sounding voice," led many in the audience to regard the speech as an unforgivable act of effrontery.

The top executives from all three networks were in attendance and about mid-way through the speech, Minow addressed himself to an issue that caused them much distress. "What I've been saying applies to broadcast stations," said Minow. "Now a station break for the networks. . . . " The chairman proceeded to indicate his support of Congressional legislation that would give the FCC the responsibility and power to oversee the networks more directly.

Minow's promise of stiffening enforcement of license renewal procedures and increased scrutiny of network operations "left his broadcaster audience stunned and indignant," according to *Broadcasting*, the major trade journal of the industry. Other publications described the audience reaction in more colorful terms. "They resembled refugees from an atomic bomb blast," one magazine reported of those in the audience. *Newsweek* readers were told, "The speech produced an instant panic, like a small stone thrown among pigeons." Another writer claimed, "Minow left TV people fish-eyed."

In the hallway after the speech the reactions were personal and harsh. Minow, it seemed, was proud of the fact he was an outsider and the insiders didn't like him much. He was described by one in the audience as "a naive young man who has read all the books but hasn't had to meet the payroll." "A young smart alec," was another assessment. A station manager from Indiana summed up the situation succinctly. Minow managed, he said, "to alienate the whole goddam broadcast industry."

The 1961 NAB convention came to a close with the usual banquet for the delegates. The mood was not as festive as in years past, but the entertainment was top-notch. Those who weren't too busy drowning their sorrows might have noticed the final number of the evening had a prophetic ring. Anna Moffo of the Metropolitan Opera, accompanied by Count Basie and his orchestra, sang "There'll Be Some Changes Made."

Minow's speech was widely and favorably covered in the non-trade press. The popular *Chicago Sun-Times* columnist Irv Kupcinet playfully suggested that Minow was the "greatest boon for broadcasting since Marconi." Well-known TV critic Harriet Van Horne of the *New York World-Telegram* correctly predicted that the name Newton Minow might very well be "enshrined in TV history." In a personal letter to Minow she wrote, "I don't know how your mail runs, but my readers love you. . . . you ARE their advocate!" His mail was running the same way.

The public reaction to the address was quick, abundant, and overwhelmingly positive. Of the first four thousand letters Minow received, fewer than a hundred were not supportive. Within six weeks, six thousand letters, lopsidedly favorable, flooded the Commission offices.

The young chairman was suddenly a genuine celebrity. Not before or since has an FCC chairman been a household name. The phrase "vast wasteland," inspired by the T. S. Eliot poem, immediately entered the American vocabulary.

The likely impact of the "two-word bomb" was not entirely appreciated by Minow. Twenty-five years after the speech he recalled, "There were many drafts. The most helpful came from John Bartlow Martin. And my recollection is that he had 'vast wasteland of junk.' . . . And I remember that I struck off 'of junk' and I paid zero attention to that phrase. I didn't think anything of the significance of the phrase."

Many observers noted, however, that the term "vast wasteland" had figured prominently in FCC press releases prepared prior to the delivery of the speech. Minow's administrative assistant, Tedson J. Meyers, a former ABC attorney, who also contributed to the text of the speech, wrote the press release. According to Minow, Meyers "probably thought more of the phrase than I did."

John Bartlow Martin—the prominent journalist, author, and professor, who would become Kennedy's Ambassador to the Dominican Republic— began developing his concept for Minow's NAB speech as early as March. He wrote to the Chairman, "I am getting some ideas and will pass them along in a few weeks. . . . Meanwhile, I suggest that you not talk to Jack Gould (*The New York Times* television critic) or to anyone else for attribution. I suggest you store everything up until May then drop the bomb."

Early in April, Martin sent Minow his draft. In the accompanying letter he wrote, "At present, the broadcasters' main concern is that there is too much mayhem and sadism on TV. They also bear a great guilt burden because of the quiz-payola scandals. . . . I would like to see you enlarge enormously the whole context of the TV controversy." On the pivotal point of network licensing, Martin counseled the regulator, "In my judgment their fear of being licensed acts as a more effective restraint on them than would actual licensing." It was sage advice.

Minow was accused of deliberately creating anti-TV copy for eager print journalists. The industry feeling was that his speech was intended more for public than broadcaster consumption. "He wanted to hit the front pages and he did," a trade journal complained, "because the speech was calculated to pander to the competitive press."

Shortly after the speech, Minow said, "There was a much larger public reaction than I had anticipated. . . . the press coverage and editorials about it have surprised me." He did not deny, however, that the speech was intended for an audience beyond the broadcast industry. With a reference to the Kennedy-Nixon encounters, he said, "I certainly have succeeded in doing one thing I wanted to do, and that was to start another Great Debate on the role of television and its future." With two-and-a-half decades of retrospect, Minow said, "I didn't mean to be hostile or belligerent or nasty. I was speaking to the country."

A few days after the Vast Wasteland address—which would come to be known in broadcast circles as just "the speech"—Minow was asked by a reporter if he had cleared his remarks with President Kennedy before delivering them. Minow said he did not and then reminded the questioner that the FCC is an independent agency. "But I have since heard from the President," the chairman added, "that he enjoyed the speech very much."

Minow also heard from the President's father. Ambassador Joseph Kennedy—who, legend has it, once told his son that businessmen were sons of bitches—phoned Minow to say the Vast Wasteland speech "was the best speech since January 20 (JFK's inauguration)—give 'em hell—hit 'em again." The senior Kennedy added, "If anybody starts to give you any trouble, you let me know and I will help you. . . . And I've told Jack it was a terrific speech."

The President's sister, Eunice Shriver, also gave Minow positive feedback. "Heard you on the Huntley-Brinkley Report," she telegrammed, "You were marvelous." The President's special assistant, Arthur Schlesinger, sent a laconic note. It simply said, "Magnificent!"

Some pieces of mail in the flood of correspondence were especially rewarding. And one was particularly relevant to Minow's venturesome position. Clarence Dill, a principal architect of American broadcast regulation, wrote and provided the young chairman with a history lesson he undoubtedly already knew well. "I, together with former Congressman Wallace White of Maine wrote the first radio law," the old man wrote, "and as chairman of the Senate Committee on Interstate Commerce I rewrote the radio law into the Communications Act of 1934."

Dill made it clear that the framers of the legislation had a vision of American broadcasting different from what it had become: "So many abuses of the intent of Congress in passing that act have grown up that I had about given up hope of seeing any reform."

The director of the U.S. Information Agency for the Kennedy administration, Edward R. Murrow, was a luminous veteran of many broadcast industry battles. The day after the Vast Wasteland speech he wrote to Minow to assure him that "certain vice-presidents of networks will remain in a state of shock for weeks to come." He then warned of the inevitable, "The counter-attack will of course develop in due course. . . . I think you are engaged in a real battle and the outcome will be much more important to this country than even you realize at this point."

NAB President LeRoy Collins would have been the logical person to lead the counterattack, but instead he attempted to downplay the rift. "I believe Mr. Minow is earnestly dedicated in a mission to help get the quality of programming improved," he said in response to the Vast Wasteland speech. "I think he overstated his case to a degree but I think it was due to his zeal and not any official animosity toward broadcasters." Collins's carefully chosen words did not assuage the anger felt in the industry. The battle lines had been drawn.

Disappointed broadcasters accused Collins of taking Minow's threats "lying down" and even being a "collaborator" with Minow. Many of Collins's early public statements were painful to broadcasters who thought their spokesman didn't speak for them. "Some assert that the FCC has no proper or lawful concern with programming," Collins said. "I shall be candid and say I disagree with this position." Collins's unique approach to his job started talk of defections from the NAB by members who wanted to set up a new trade association, although no one actually seceded.

During his almost four-year tenure in the NAB presidency, Collins grew more unpopular. He was handsomely paid to be a defender, but as a man of conviction he saw his role somewhat differently. He believed there was an inspirational dimension to his duties. "I was trying to give leadership among broadcasters to the proposition that their best interest was the public interest," Collins recalled, "and that when broadcast practices impinged on the public interest, while they might obtain some temporary gain from it, in the long run they would lose."

Broadcasters resented his prodding of them to set higher goals. "I was never anti-Minow the way a great many broadcasters were," Collins remembered years later. "I openly and publicly said on many occasions that I thought what Minow had done was helpful to broadcasting and not hurtful. . . . And I praised him to the President many times."

After the young chairman "seized television broadcasters by the scruff of their collective necks, shook them vigorously and redeposited them in their seats," the trade press urged solidarity. "To us it is evident," *Broadcasting* editorialized, "that he is attempting to circumvent the First Amendment. We believe he cannot sustain his campaign if broadcasters—and that means the NAB—will close ranks."

Though the industry did quickly lobby to defeat an FCC reorganization plan in Congress, which would have given the chairman greater powers in delegating the work load of the agency, in the weeks and months after the NAB convention, no formal or unified industry rebuttal to Minow was offered. Without strong opposition to Minow's philosophies at the top, the industry counterattack remained uncrystallized.

Meanwhile, Minow's image as a protector of the public interest grew stronger and more glowing. He was a supremely popular New Frontiersman. By the end of his first year on the job, Minow made more radio and TV appearances that any other member of the Kennedy administration, except the President himself. He was a media darling long before the term was used.

The Associated Press Annual Poll of editors voted Minow the Top Newsmaker for 1961 in the field of entertainment. The runners-up were Jack Paar, Gary Cooper, and Elizabeth Taylor. The award winners in past years included Marilyn Monroe, Grace Kelly, and Elvis Presley.

Minow enjoyed the limelight. He endeared himself to the public with a charming, self-deprecating sense of humor. He kidded about his own vast waistline and never displayed self-righteousness about his work. When, on a local talk show in South Bend, Indiana, he was likened to the hero in a white hat on TV westerns, he agreed: "Yes, and I might get shot in the back, too."

Political cartoonists capitalized on the chairman's unusual name and easily caricatured looks. Minow cartoons were not limited to the editorial pages, however. The proof positive of his accession to celebrity was that the funny pages frequently carried cartoons that used his name or cause in their gag lines.

Minow understood the value of public opinion. It was not unusual for columnists who questioned his motives or means in print to receive a cordial letter from the chairman offering to clarify his position. For instance, Richard K. Doan, TV and Radio editor for the *New York Herald Tribune,* was told after writing an unflattering column: "As a silent admirer I wish you would let me know some time when you are in Washington, as I'd very much like to have a talk with you. I have the feeling from some of your recent columns that perhaps I am not communicating my views very well and I welcome a chance to talk things over."

The chairman was also an active writer himself. He frequently accepted offers to write columns and editorials in various publications. Some had large circulations such as *The New York Times Magazine* and the *Chicago Sun-Times.* But he did not overlook publications with more limited readerships to express his views on American television. To the amusement of some of the chairman's friends, the Minow by-line appeared in the Spring 1962 issue of *Sweep,* the journal of the Department of Sanitation for the City of New York.

After the Vast Wasteland speech a lot of writers turned to the subject of television. Beginning in the summer of 1961 there was an obvious new wave of criticism of television in the print media. It was especially apparent in mass circulation magazines. Cover stories offering critical views of TV dotted newsstands.

Minow and print journalists were accused of entering a "matrimony of convenience." *Television Magazine* pointed out what broadcasters believed was the sour grapes motive: "Many publications are ready, willing and able to give him a horse, a lance, and a handsome shove in a repetitious and purposeful series of articles telling how television is gnawing away at the vitals of the American Way of Life. Mr. Minow's latest indignation appears in the *Saturday Evening Post,* a magazine that before the advent of television was passed hotly from hand to hand around the American hearth."

Book publishers too were considered by broadcasters to be adversaries. Critical opinions of television were surfacing in works of nonfiction as well as novels. By 1962 there were five books on the market that were particularly galling to industry partisans: *TV in America: The Morality of Hard Cash* by

Meyer Weinberg, *Coast-to-Coast* by Walter Ross, *Face-to-Face* by Edward Rogers, *The Television Writer* by Erik Barnouw, and *The Great Time-Killer* by Harold Mehling. "What these books have in common," lamented the trade magazine *Television Age*, "is a condemnation of the American system of commercial TV. One can only hope the excesses of these books themselves will give their readers pause to think."

The growing public consciousness about television was not a trend welcomed by the industry since the questioning of station and network policies seemed to follow. Letters of complaint to the FCC and broadcasters were estimated to have increased at least three-fold. "The public," a trade magazine observed, "has gotten the message that it 'owns the airwaves.' " With characteristic flippancy, *Variety* reported that the reason for the "hail of mail" was clearly the "promulgation of Newton's Law."

Throughout Minow's tenure on the Commission, the television industry maintained a defensive posture and a hypersensitivity to criticism. Minow was credited with unleashing a torrent of anti-TV sentiment. Because of him, the insiders felt, television had become "America's most popular scapegoat since the Indian."

Critics of television, whether they were associated with the government, higher education, or the print media, were characterized by the broadcast trade press as naive do-gooders out of touch with the pulse of mass taste. These critics seemed to be blaming television for all social ills. Minow's Vast Wasteland speech was seen as "an official endorsement of a critical attitude that has become fashionable with intellectuals." The chairman's views were, according to a *Television Quarterly* essay, "seized upon and held up as official verdict."

In lieu of a concerted effort of industry opposition, the trade press served as an outlet for the bitterness that accompanied the heat of increasing public scrutiny. In the pages of industry publications intellectuals took a beating. They were depicted as self-appointed guardians of public taste and morality hell-bent on forcing their own predilections on the masses.

In the eyes of broadcasters, Jack Gould represented everything wrong with misguided intellectuals. The highbrow columnist for *The New York Times* regularly rankled TV industry loyalists. *Television Age* accused the *Times* of being "close to carelessness" in its reporting and reviewing of television programs. "It is probable that Jack Gould will despise anything that is popular," it was asserted. "He doesn't understand the work he is doing, nor understand the needs of the people for whom the bulk of programming is built. He doesn't give a damn for the public."

There is a touch of irony in the fact that at the same time intellectuals were being harangued in the trade press, the industry was publicly courting them. The Television Information Office (TIO) was created by the NAB in October 1959 as a public relations arm. One of the organization's top priorities was launching a goodwill campaign targeted toward "eggheads." The agency believed intellectuals were the most "vociferous critics" of the medium "able to influence far out of proportion to their number." Direct contact by broadcasters with "highly intellectual opinion makers," to emphasize television's service to the public, was encouraged by the TIO as a way to "turn criticism away from TV."

Baneful adversaries seemed to be expecting too much of the medium. Television's brief history was a point often raised in the trade press. "We would remind Mr. Minow," opined *Broadcasting*, "that progress does not come overnight in television any more than it does in newspapers or in the development of a lawyer or the education of an FCC chairman."

*Television Magazine* pointed out that in approximately one dozen years TV had become the tenth largest industry in the United States, growing three times faster than the automobile industry: "With this kind of growth, a certain amount of growing pains certainly can be expected. But television's detractors insist, nevertheless, that even in this astoundingly short period of time, the medium should be doing greater things than it *is* doing."

The amount of programming material needed in comparison to other forms of entertainment was another frequently discussed issue in the industry's noncohesive attempts to refute Minow. In testimony before the FCC, variety show host Ed Sullivan remarked: "There will always be, of necessity, a TV Wasteland. The three networks must produce 10,950 hours of entertainment per year, in contrast to only 600 hours demanded by the entire moving picture industry of our country and the 125 hours per year demanded by the Broadway theater." A commentary in *Television Magazine* stated the familiar idea simply—"Television is the hungriest monster that ever devoured script."

The industry found solace in the undeniably voracious appetite the American public had for television. The plain facts of viewership were offered as evidence that the medium was performing its function successfully. Roy Huggins, producer of several hit series, including *77 Sunset Strip*, commented: "Nearly 50 million Americans have purchased television sets, spending some 25 billion dollars in sets and service. Many researchers have asked them why they bought those sets, and no American has ever been known to reply that he did so out of devotion to the public convenience, interest and necessity."

A sentiment shared by most in the business and creative worlds of commercial television was that ratings success indicated the choice of the majority of American viewers and therefore was a legitimate gauge of program worth. Minow was often portrayed in the trade press as a threat to a sacred democratic system, as a "cultural czar." "It is possible," *Television Magazine* snidely speculated, "that Minow believes that a majority endorsement of television programming is invalid as a measure of television values. If so, he must be ill at ease in his present job. He was appointed to it by a President who was elected by the narrowest margin in Presidential voting history."

## An Ideological Tussle

Many years later, thinking back on the criticism of his policies, Minow recalled, "I am very thin-skinned. . . . The thing that stung me so was the argument that we were interfering with the First Amendment; we were censoring. What I felt we were trying to do was the opposite. . . . I didn't convey that somehow. I didn't get across to my satisfaction the answer to the First Amendment argument."

In the late summer of 1961, Minow's alma mater, Northwestern University, sponsored a symposium designed to clarify the legal interpretations of the First Amendment issue. The chairman attempted to define the scope and limits of the Commission's authority in the broadest sense. A renowned broadcast attorney, W. Theodore Pierson, took the opportunity to attack the FCC's new zeal. There was danger, Pierson believed, that television under Newton Minow could become a medium of "governmentally induced conformity."

As that summer drew to a close, Minow seemed ubiquitous. Reacting to the chairman's unyielding determination, comedian Jimmy Durante opened an NBC special by saying, "Da next hour will be dedicated to upliftin' da quality of television. . . . At least, Newt, we're tryin'."

By autumn broadcasters were beginning to be a little bolder in challenging Minow directly. In October, Frank Shakespeare, Jr., the vice-president and general manager of WCBS-TV, delivered the keynote address to the annual meeting of the American Women in Radio and Television. *Variety* noted "it was one of the few instances of a broadcaster talking back publicly to Federal Communications Commission chairman Newton Minow." Shakespeare told his audience that television was, above all, a mass medium and only secondarily a medium which serves the needs of minority groups. "Broadcasters are now increasingly faced by specific program suggestions publicly made by the very commissioners who will decide his fate," he said. "We in broadcasting must speak out to safeguard the freedoms in which we believe."

As 1961 drew to a close, industry leaders were singing from the same hymnal, but not loudly or in unison. In the short history of broadcasting, networks and stations traditionally conducted their defenses unilaterally. On December 7, NBC and CBS finally offered individual replies to Minow.

NBC chairman Robert Sarnoff addressed network affiliates in Beverly Hills. "Even if the government could force programs to its prescription," he said, "it could not force the public to watch the prescribed programs." Dr. Frank Stanton, president of CBS, presented his concerns on the preservation of freedom in broadcasting at the University of Pennsylvania. "If we liken the mass of people and their ability to make their own decisions to unsupervised children and their desire for a constant diet of sweets," he said in reference to an analogy Minow used in the Vast Wasteland speech, "we are striking at what the heart of democracy is all about—the people, whatever their temporary errors or inadequacies, are, in the long run, the best judges of their own interests."

In the week following the Sarnoff and Stanton statements, Minow received a White House memo regarding their speeches from Kennedy's special assistant, Arthur Schlesinger, Jr. The message illustrates the support Minow was getting from the White House and how carefully Schlesinger was following the controversy of increasing governmental controls over broadcasting.

Schlesinger noted that simply accepting or rejecting the offerings of commercial television was not the only way the public could register opinions on broadcasting. "The holding of public hearings on the renewal of franchises is just as legitimate a form of public expression," he wrote. Parenthetically he added, "Indeed, increased control through legislation would be another valid expression of the public decision."

According to Schlesinger, Minow was just as willing to adhere to "the verdict of the people" as Stanton and Sarnoff, but Minow wanted "to make the verdict active and informed." The fractious nature of the debate was characterized by Schlesinger's closing remark: "In Sarnoff's speech, I loved his definition of the 'two major challenges for the years ahead.' They are, as you will recall, preserving broadcasting from government and making more money for the networks. Apparently the content of programs is not a major challenge."

The early months of 1962 brought FCC hearings concerning network program practices. Complaints and cries of outrage continued to come from the trade press, and, increasingly, individuals spoke out publicly about their concerns, taking delayed blasts at Minow's Vast Wasteland charges. John S. Hayes, president of the Post-Newsweek broadcast chain, for instance, in an address to the Advertising Federation of America, lambasted "autocrats who would set up cultural tyranny within the framework of democracy."

At his press conference of January 31, 1962, President Kennedy was asked about the apprehension being generated by the FCC hearings. Ray Scherer of NBC queried:

> Mr. President, two network chiefs recently have expressed fear of government supervision of the television networks. The FCC has denied any such intention. Can you foresee circumstances under which FCC supervision of television programming might become necessary or useful?

The President responded in part by saying:

> Mr. Minow has attempted not to use force, but to use encouragement in persuading the networks to put (on) better children's programs, more public service programs. I don't know of anyone—and Mr. Minow has already denied—changing the basic relationship which now exists.

The next day Minow sent Kennedy's press secretary, Pierre Salinger, a letter to clarify his position on network regulation. The correspondence indicates that Minow believed much of the industry defense was being undertaken in bad faith: "The President's answer to the particular question yesterday was fine. However, the trade press, I know, will misinterpret it for technical reasons, and that's why I thought I'd better explain."

The chairman then pointed out that in the summer of 1960, following the quiz show scandals, the FCC—under the interim chairmanship of Frederick Ford—did in fact formally recommend to Congress legislation providing for direct regulation of certain network practices. Minow continued to endorse the legislation. It was a "very technical and complicated" matter, said Minow. But, since the President was likely to be asked about it again, Minow stressed that "none of this involves getting into the content of a program or saying what should or should not be on the air." "To confuse the issue," the chairman continued, "some people in the industry have tried to equate network regulation with program censorship, and it is here that the argument rages."

The pall of government pressure was growing heavier in the early months of 1962. The results of a public opinion survey favorable to the television industry, therefore, were naturally heralded as a moral victory by the Television Information Office. The study, conducted for the TIO by Elmo Roper and Associates, surveyed a representative cross section of two thousand adults. Seven out of ten did not agree with the wasteland characterization of television. They were of the opinion that television did, in fact, offer a balanced schedule of programming.

A *Broadcasting* editorial invited Minow to ponder the significance of the Roper study. "It might be too late to keep 'vast wasteland' out of the catechism of great catch-phrases of American history," the periodical chided. "If public opinion counts for anything, however, the Minowism will find a modest place in this enshrinement—somewhere about the level, say, of those immortal words of Stephen Foster: 'doo-da.' "

The 1962 Peabody Awards brought out the worst in many of Minow's industry foes. Established in 1940, in honor of New York banker and philanthropist George Foster Peabody, the award had long been regarded as the most prestigious in broadcasting. Traditionally it was awarded in recognition of distinguished and meritorious broadcast programming in the public service. The decision of the Peabody Committee to bestow the honor on the FCC chairman "didn't rest too well within high respected places." "Key industryites," the trade press reported, "who have gotten wind of the contemplated award are registering vigorous opposition to such an accolade."

Minow personally accepted his Peabody, the first ever given to a federal official, at the presentation ceremonies in New York. The citation he received said of the chairman, "He has reminded broadcasters of their responsibilities and has put new heart in the viewers." Minow said he believed the award was not being given to him personally, "but as recognition of the role of government in broadcasting."

By acknowledging Minow, *Broadcasting* fumed, the Peabody Awards Committee "defiled its purpose and defamed those it sought to honor." It was felt that the worthiness of "legitimate winners" was besmirched by the implication that Minow was responsible for the good work they had produced. *Broadcasting* declared, "The implication is slanderous nonsense."

But President Kennedy was delighted. "I have always thought of the George Foster Peabody radio and television special awards as proud marks of the highest attainment in service to the public interest," read his wire of congratulations to all the winners. With specific reference to Minow, he continued, "and as President, I am glad one of our boys made it."

The television industry could not afford to display such ill temper toward the popular Minow outside the pages of the trade press, however. In fact, the same week the stinging *Broadcasting* editorial appeared in print, Minow's assistant, Ted Meyers, received a letter from Robert F. Lewine of CBS on behalf of the National Academy of Television Arts and Sciences. He requested that Minow appear on the 1962 Emmy Awards show. "Having Mr. Minow's support is of incalculable value to the Academy," Lewine wrote.

Minow agreed to appear on the telecast as a special guest. The director of the live program, Charles O. Jones of NBC News, sent the chairman a letter concerning production details of the broadcast. Intimating the reason for Minow's appearance was a conciliation of tensions, Jones reminded the chairman, "We met last under slightly different circumstances, while I was directing NBC's coverage of the FCC hearings. There does seem to be a link, however."

The producers of the May 22 Emmy Awards show could not overlook the fact that the industry was in the midst of a crisis provoked by Minow. The chairman was afforded gracious treatment, however, at the biggest public relations event of the year.

The program originated from three cities. Johnny Carson was the primary emcee in New York. Bob Newhart presided over the segments from Los Angeles. And David Brinkley hosted from Washington, D.C. In his opening monologue, Carson made a pointed reference to the times: "Incidentally, there will be no violence on this evening's telecast, with the possible exception of when the award for the best comedy writing is presented." After a long and somewhat tedious introduction of the presidents of the twenty-six Academy chapters around the country, Carson quipped sarcastically, "How they could call it a vast wasteland with dialogue like that, I'll never know."

Later in the broadcast, when the news and public service awards were to be presented from Washington, the host announced, "I'm David Brinkley and this is the unfunny part of the program." He introduced Minow to the viewers in this way:

> BRINKLEY: This is Washington, the home of the FCC. And if anything, this was the year of the FCC. This government agency was more active than it has been before. One result last February was very heavy traffic between network headquarters in New York and a cavernous government hearing room in Washington.
>
> CUT TO: VIDEOTAPE FCC HEARINGS (NETWORK PRESIDENTS TESTIFYING)
>
> BRINKLEY (VOICE OVER): Heads of the three networks appeared. As in any government hearing, the results were subject to all kinds of interpretation, but two things did seem clear. First, television must acknowledge its tremendous responsibility to the public. Second, the FCC in its eagerness to see this responsibility is met, must not curtail television's freedom of expression. . . .
>
> The chairman of the FCC is now quite a star. And here he is, a very courageous public servant—Mr. Newton Minow. . . .
>
> MINOW: As the Academy bestows its prized Emmys tonight, the Academy itself deserves recognition too. The six thousand Academy members all over the country, who voted these awards, include stagehands, cameramen, engineers, writers, directors, stars—plus all those network vice-presidents. All have joined in a common cause to advance higher standards in the arts and sciences of television.
>
> Although we can't give an Emmy to the Academy, we do pay tribute to its high purpose. We hope that next year and every succeeding year the Academy will have an even greater number of qualified contenders for Emmys, and that your choices in rewarding this excellence will become ever more difficult.
>
> Not everyone can win an Emmy. But by encouraging distinguished achievement in television, the Academy well serves a nation which must be first in its journey to the moon and first-rate in its electronic journey to the hearts and minds of man.

The year between the Vast Wasteland speech and Minow's appearance on the Emmy Awards telecast was a period of unrelenting headaches for the broadcast industry. The proverbial rubber stamp used in the past for FCC renewal applications was getting dusty from disuse, seemingly replaced with a fine-toothed comb. In that time, fourteen broadcast stations were put on probation with short-term renewals and local hearings were scheduled in eight renewal cases. It was a sharp reminder of Minow's promise to exercise the disciplinary powers of the FCC.

While the industry preached, in its own defense, that public opinion should be regarded as a sacrosanct entity, Minow's public support was unflagging. Broadcasters feared it was strong enough to have an impact on Congress. If a legislator was not affected by Minow's popularity, a trade journal reported, "there's cause to doubt his political acumen."

Minow had the backing of an attractive and popular president as well as the solid, active support of the "second most important man in Washington," the Attorney General. "Whenever I need anything," Minow said of his idealistic kindred spirit, "I just call Bobby."

Broadcasters would just have to learn to live with Minow "the way you do with a shrewish wife." The chairman was not loved, but his demands could not be ignored. So, at the same time that the trade press and various industry leaders were attempting to show the FCC's new ardor was inherently wrong, was in fact unconstitutional, television programming was being adjusted to meet new standards. Attempts of appeasement to ward off government regulation were conspicuous.

After a rough year, the television industry braced itself for the long haul. There was no public indication Minow would leave the Commission before his seven-year term expired. And surely John Kennedy would be in the White House until 1968.

# CHAPTER 2

# The Cultural Democracy

## PRIME-TIME ENTERTAINMENT

In 1960, in so many aspects of American life, the old was giving way to the new in such discernible ways. On television, *Playhouse 90* ended its original programming that spring. And so the curtain fell on an era of TV history.

Though a handful of live anthology series lingered for another season or two, *Playhouse 90* on CBS had come to symbolize the Golden Years, the 1950s, when television drama was bound by the limitations of the studio, yet magnificent scripts and inspired directing could transcend physical restrictions.

In the halcyon days of live television drama, great young writers emerged. Their plays most often focused on the intimate lives of unremarkable men and women. In these tender examinations of human problems, the development of character was emphasized, while plot and action were subordinate.

For a short time, television's potential as a dramatic art form was electrifying. Not long after his 1954 masterpiece *Marty* moved the television audience, Paddy Chayefsky wrote, "the word for television is depth, the digging under the surface of life for the more profound truths of human relationships." Television, he believed, by offering the drama of introspection, "may well be the basic theater of our century." By the end of the decade, though, westerns and crime series were replacing what Chayefsky called "the marvelous world of the ordinary."

Fall 1960 brought a prime-time show that represented the new decade—*Route 66* spoke to the restlessness of a younger generation. Searching for purpose as much as adventure, the two disparate lead characters crisscrossed the country in a Corvette convertible. The location shooting of *Route 66* resulted in an expansive production style with an emphasis on motion. The tone of the show was aptly labeled by one critic as "purely new-American."

But few shows appearing that season were as literate as *Route 66* or presented characters as complex as Tod Stiles and Buz Murdock. Rather, it was a bloody season, what *Time* magazine called "the worst in the 13-year history of U.S. network television."

The decline of prime time, many observers believed, began in the mid-1950s. Advertisers grew increasingly determined to exert their control over dramatic anthology scripts. The censorship, related to controversial issues, such as racism, as well as the forced enhancement of commercial products within the stories, made the creative work more frustrating. A great number of scriptwriters, producers, directors, and performers who had honed their talents in television ultimately left the medium and found greater artistic freedom in feature films.

By the late 1950s, new recording techniques were also contributing to a changing prime-time climate. Videotape and film had many advantages over live production. Recorded episodic series replaced anthologies and Hollywood replaced New York as the major TV production center. The relationship between the TV networks and the Hollywood movie studios, once arch enemies, grew less antagonistic.

The film industry, so wounded by television, found a new source of income in the production of TV programs. At the same time, a philosophical change regarding programming was taking place at the networks. Executives from the earliest days of television, primarily creative people, were being replaced with businessmen, many of whom had come up from the ranks of sales departments. The new guard at the networks understood that with soaring production costs it was cheaper to let outside agencies assume the financial risks necessary for developing new programs.

Filmed series produced by independent studios such as Desilu, Screen Gems, Ziv-United Artists, and MCA-Revue became the staple of network prime time. *Playhouse 90's* John Frankenheimer, one of the greatest of the Golden Age directors, felt television had evolved from an art form into a supermarket: "It exists to sell cigarettes, gas, lipstick. . . . I don't think any of us left television for financial reasons. What we all wanted to do was good things. They wouldn't let us. They told us, 'We don't want you guys. We want film situation comedies.' "

Beginning with the 1959–60 television season, ABC was, for the first time, a genuine competitor in the prime-time ratings race. The network continued its commitment to the hour-long action-adventure format. The introduction of *The Untouchables* generated a clatter of criticism, but high ratings and profits as well. Based on the life of Eliot Ness, a Treasury Department agent in Chicago during the Prohibition days of the 1930s, each episode of *The Untouchables* featured multiple shootout scenes in which victims were sprayed with bullets. Grisly mob murders were also part of the formula.

With such Hollywood telefilms ABC was actively pursuing the younger audience of postwar families, which were most attractive to advertisers. The next season, 1960, NBC and CBS followed suit and added several action-adventure series to their schedules. Shows like *Michael Shayne*, *Dante*, *Tall Man*, *Dan Raven*, *The Witness*, and *Checkmate* prompted cries of Gresham's Law—the bad drives out the good. Comedian Fred Allen's charge that "imitation is the sincerest form of television" rang very true.

The studios producing the stereotypical TV series came to be known in the industry as "sausage factories." By 1960 live studio drama was considered an experimental and risky form of television. An ABC programming executive claimed the action shows on his network required a different kind of writer than one who had worked in television in the 1950s. The new TV writer of the 1960s should be, he said, "one who doesn't have a burning desire to make an original statement."

A report entitled "The Quality of American Life" prepared for President Eisenhower's Commission on National Goals was released in the autumn of 1960. Its assessment of popular culture found the state of American broadcasting to be "the single most obvious cause for concern." The author of the study, August Heckscher—who would become President Kennedy's special consultant on the arts—wrote: "The temptation to let fourth-rate material replace the better shows seems all too often to be irresistible to the merchandiser. . . . At the very least our society should make sure that the citizen has a real choice among qualities and types of programming and that the standard of excellence is somewhere maintained. . . . Government, moreover, has an ultimate responsibility for maintaining the constructive use of a resource so valuable and so scarce as the TV channels."

Against this backdrop, the Kennedy administration prepared to take office with the belief that government could play a part in the development of a democracy's cultural life. Robert Kennedy particularly found gratuitous television violence offensive and dangerous to the republic. A society bombarded with inferior, escapist entertainment, he felt, was bound to weaken.

A disenchantment among serious television scriptwriters about their profession was surfacing in the early months of 1961. A report prepared for the Television Branch of the Writers Guild by Gene Rodenberry, who later in the decade would create the *Star Trek* series, concluded that members of the Guild were faced with "crippling artistic restrictions." Television had become a "gold-plated ghetto" providing comfortable incomes to "bench-workers." Dramatic programming that allowed writers to maintain self-respect as creative artists was disappearing at an alarming rate.

"The writer has no obligation to grapple with eternal truths every time he approaches the typewriter," Rodenberry wrote to his colleagues. But, "if he does write a script purporting to mirror life, but instead, writes to the prejudices and merchandising needs of his sponsor-patron, that writer is simply a liar. If he compounds this by rationalizing that he bears no responsibility for his act he is also a hypocrite. If he refuses to speak out because he fears it may imperil his income, he is a coward. And if he thinks that his crime is only a misdemeanor, that the torrent of images and thoughts being televised has no effect or bearing on the shape, direction, and security of his family, his nation and mankind, he is a fool."

The 1961–62 prime-time schedules at all three networks were off the drawing boards earlier than any previous season in TV history. By the end of March 1961 the lineups were set. "More of the same" is the way the season was characterized by the trade press. More private-eyes, mysteries, police shows, foreign intrigue—more action-adventure all around. "In a business too expensive for radical experimentation," an industry observer wrote of the new season, "the gambles will be on the safe side."

But, before long, the TV industry would find that, in the Kennedy years, playing it safe might be risky. As network executives were working on the 1961–62 program schedule, *Television Magazine* warned of developments going on in Washington that could have some bearing on their plans. "A new Chairman of the Federal Communications Commission took office with a mandate from President Kennedy to do something to improve TV quality," the periodical advised. "Minow has never said so, but it is authoritatively known that President Kennedy has told him to move in on programs."

Minow made his first move on May 9. The formulaic violence of the action-adventure genre was one of the major targets of the Vast Wasteland speech. "Is there one person in this room who claims broadcasting can't do better?" the chairman asked. "Well, is there at least one network president who believes that the other networks can't do better? Gentlemen, your trust accounting with your beneficiaries is overdue. Never have so few owed so much to so many."

The "Newton shootin'," as *Variety* put it, came too late to have any real effect on the 1961–62 season. The networks had painted themselves into a corner. The schedules that seemed so right in March looked dismal in May. Naturally, the networks were in a better position to make changes in programming produced in-house, such as news and fringe-time offerings. And these changes came quickly. Public affairs programming mushroomed. Large-scale changes in prime time, though, would have to wait until the 1962–63 season. But even with "the rain check in the mail," each network made some minor adjustments in prime time 1961 as they prepared to weather the storm.

For instance, ABC, the network perceived as the culprit in initiating the action-adventure trend, replaced two thirty-minute filmed series, *Rebel* and *Yank*, with a new run of *The Steve Allen Show,* a live variety program that had been on the network since 1956. "In one fell post-Minow swoop," the trade press noted, "ABC took a big step to 'live' it up."

NBC dropped an action show, a Civil War drama called *The Americans*, from its Monday night lineup. Instead, the network returned *National Vel-*

*vet* to the schedule, a gentle family series based on the 1944 Elizabeth Taylor film.

CBS was considering the elimination of *Eyewitness to History,* a half-hour in-depth analysis of a major current news story, which aired on Friday nights in the 1960–61 season. But the Minow speech changed the plan. "If there were any doubts or hesitancies about CBS-TV's *Eyewitness to History* returning in the fall," it was reported the week after the NAB convention, "they were dispelled in the brief 50 minutes it took Minow to unburden himself of his utterances."

All three networks also made an effort to eliminate excessive violence from action-adventure shows to which they were already committed. "Violence is being met with violence at the networks," the trade press observed. They were "hacking away at offending shows with bold strokes" in order to "stay within the dictum of the FCC against excessive violence." More than a dozen programs were re-edited, reshot, or refused permission to air.

In the summer of 1961 *Broadcasting* magazine noticed: "A self-imposed nationwide effort to lessen violence on the television screen is underway. It is principally at work at production studios in Hollywood and network offices in New York." The first signs of "a truly overall policy," the periodical reported, "began last June, a month after the now famous 'wasteland' speech by Newton N. Minow at the NAB convention."

If new programming was not in the action-adventure genre, that fact might be exploited promotionally. Herbert Hirschman, the producer of *Dr. Kildare*, for example, said in promoting his show, "Because we are dealing with matters of life and death, our series will have a maturity of theme and treatment which should be a welcome change from programming which attempts to excite emotion but overlooks the mind and soul."

Even though *Dr. Kildare* was in the NBC lineup before the Vast Wasteland speech, Hirschman felt compelled to relate the two: "*Dr. Kildare* fulfills all of Mr. Minow's requirements: it is adult, literate, free of sadism and violence—a distinguished and at the same time, dramatically engrossing drama. For the first time since *Playhouse 90* I am associated with a show of which I am truly proud."

The swiftness of the response to Washington's vibrations prompted one observer to declare the industry was "stepping blithely to the 'Minow Minuet.'" Independent program producers let it be known to the networks that they could "easily adapt" to the "Minow Pattern." Before the 1961–62 season even made its debut, new projects were in development that were, in the words of one TV executive, "in line with the New Frontier views of FCC Chairman Newton Minow." As another producer explained, "During the 1961–62 selling season the webs were hot for action-adventure. Now you couldn't give a straight action-adventure format away."

## TV Takes It on the Chin

The summer of 1961 was an extremely difficult time for the networks. Beginning in June, in the wake of the Vast Wasteland speech, came the probe of the Senate Subcommittee to Investigate Juvenile Delinquency—commonly referred to as the Dodd hearings. The issue to be examined was the relationship between young people and the crime and violence portrayed on television. The flamboyant Democrat from Connecticut, Senator Thomas Dodd, who headed the subcommittee, conducted the hearings with a crusading zeal.

The format for the investigation consisted of a formal opening, introductory remarks, and then a screening of an episode or clips from a network series. Studio and network executives responsible for the screened program were then interrogated by the subcommittee staff. Much of the questioning was of the "have-you-stopped-beating-your-wife?" variety. Witnesses were hard pressed to defend video brutality when asked something along the lines of "Do you think this scene would give a child of five the proper picture of what family life should be like?"

The subcommittee's grappling with TV's crime wave was also getting a big play in the daily press. Frank Shakespeare, who was general manager of WCBS-TV in New York in 1961, recalled about the Dodd hearings: "It was almost a staged affair. . . . Newspapers would run tremendous publicity on anything that said in effect that television was destroying the young or was not cultural enough. . . . It was an enlightenment to see the rather pompous attitude of the political figures who were then involved, and it became very apparent to me that while there was perhaps some degree of genuineness in their concern, it was overlaid with a great deal of awareness of the publicity benefits and the page oneness of it all."

At the same time the Dodd hearings were going on, in June 1961, the FCC was also engaged in a formal inquiry into TV practices. The emphasis of the examination was the demise of live programming and original drama. And, again, the networks were portrayed as the bad guys—as the ones allowing ratings and advertisers to debase popular entertainment. The most damaging testimony in the FCC hearings came from several of the most successful "prestige" producers and writers in the medium, men with roots in the Golden Age, including Robert Saudek, Worthington Miner, Erik Barnouw, Ernest Kinoy, and Tad Mosel.

On the stand for four hours, David Susskind, executive vice-president of Talent Associates Ltd., explained to the FCC what he believed contributed to making the 1960–61 season "the nadir of television." He recounted his frustrations with the networks' "death grip on programming." Even with advertiser support, Susskind said, a dramatic series he proposed to CBS was dismissed because the network felt "more action" was needed to compete with the other networks.

As a result of his critical testimony, Susskind ended up on the receiving end of the festering bitterness the networks felt toward being put in the defensive position. Within days after his appearance before the Commission, Susskind called the FCC to report an unsettling phone call he had received from Jim Aubrey, president of the CBS Television Network. Aubrey told Susskind that the producer was "completely out" from dealing with the networks. Susskind deduced his blackballing was the result of his testimony before the Commission. He felt he had been branded a traitor.

Early in July 1961, Congressman Abner Mikva wrote Minow a personal letter. He told the chairman he was spending his vacation time "watching crime television programs." "They oughta pass a law," Mikva joked. Minow's playful reply revealed a touch of the snobbism he was accused of by network defenders: "Now I know who is watching westerns and crime shows: I knew that the rating samples depended on relative cultural illiterates but I wasn't sure you were part of the sample."

The TV industry's depression in the summer of '61, the season of trial, was the subject of a *Television Magazine* editorial: "The best thing that could happen to television right now would be a summer hiatus in the dispute over program quality. . . . During recent months the critics have become more and more vociferous and less and less rational. In response, the broadcasters have retreated into an official silence that borders on sullenness while privately reassuring one another that they are giving the people exactly what the people want."

The 1961–62 prime-time schedule debuted in a climate of network anxiety. "Even before all the TV shows have premiered," the trade press reported, "they're pushing the panic button up and down Madison Ave. . . . Seldom have so many new shows been in trouble at such an early date."

If producers felt their programming was new and different, they wanted to bring it to Minow's attention. Roland Kibbee, the producer-writer of *The Bob Newhart Show*, did so without subtlety. He sent the FCC chairman the following telegram: "Respectfully invite you to view the Bob Newhart Show premiering NBC 10pm Wednesday Oct. 11. We believe it to be adult, enlightened social satire, unprecedented on TV. We also think it's very funny and so did a live audience. Your comments would be carefully considered."

Minow's assistant, Ted Meyers, responded to the request with what had become a standard reply: "It is our practice here not to comment upon the qualities of proposed or current programming—however much we may appreciate the value of such a series."

## Benchmarks of the 1961–62 Season

New Frontier Character Dramas

Although most of the network schedule fulfilled the low expectations of critics, some inspired and memorable programming did appear in the 1961– 62 season. The success of *The Defenders, Dr. Kildare*, and *Ben Casey* that fall started a trend of series that could be called New Frontier character dramas. They were programs based on liberal social themes in which the protagonists were professionals in service to society. This new breed of episodic TV hero struggled with occupational ethics and felt a disillusionment with the values of the past.

By the end of the Kennedy years, this group of character dramas would grow to include *The Nurses*; *Channing*, which was a series set on a college campus; the psychiatric dramas *The Breaking Point* and *The Eleventh Hour*; *East Side/West Side*, dealing with the cases of a New York social worker; and *Mr. Novak*, a series about a rookie high school teacher.

Unlike the action-adventure series in which heroes settled their problems with a weapon, the problems of New Frontier character dramas were not always resolved. Poverty, prejudice, drug addiction, abortion, capital punishment, and other issues of public policy did not lend themselves to tidy resolutions. The loose ends of the plot might get tied together, but the world was not necessarily a better place at the end of the story.

There was a wide range of sophistication in the scripting and execution of these programs, but *The Defenders* was clearly the jewel of New Frontier character dramas. The series about a father and son who practice law together was based on a drama originally presented on the *Studio One* anthology series in 1957.

When the television project was first offered to CBS in 1960, the president of the network, Jim Aubrey, was not enthusiastic about the unique cerebral tone of the show. Ernest Kinoy, a regular scriptwriter for the series, recalled Aubrey's reaction: "I wanted *Perry Mason*, and instead you give me this garbage!"

But the network's desire to ease governmental pressure ultimately secured *The Defenders* a place on the schedule. Kinoy said that after the project had been shelved, CBS chairman William Paley was "called to testify before the FCC in Washington." Kinoy related the nature of the exchange this way: " 'Why are you doing such dreadful things on television?' remarked the commissioners. 'I'm glad you asked me that,' replied Paley. 'We have a new show we're putting on by the same people who did *Studio One* and *Playhouse 90*. You'll just love it. It's called *The Defenders*.' "

CBS scored a public relations coup with *The Defenders* and enjoyed a Nielsen success as well. Those who lamented the death of television's Golden

Age saw *The Defenders* as a compromise between *Playhouse 90* and action-adventure. It was serious drama that dealt with delicate subjects. The network engaged the most outstanding production, performance, and writing talent in the medium. Though the episodic style of the program necessitated some reliance on established patterns, *The Defenders* was as close to original anthology drama as a series could be.

By mid-season it was clear that television viewers were accepting episodic character drama as a popular TV genre. *Variety* remarked, "FCC chairman Newton Minow can take some measure of comfort from the fact that, of all the new shows that 'made it' and achieved hit status on the tv networks' '61-'62 schedules, not a single one is in the crime-adventure category." In the two seasons to follow, New Frontier character drama would evolve into a potent vehicle for social criticism and would reflect the deepest concerns of the Kennedy administration.


## Situation Comedies

Two situation comedies of the 1961–62 season stand out for their distinctive and instinctive connection with the new decade. Just as *I Love Lucy* symbolized the 1950s, many social critics have observed how *The Dick Van Dyke Show* symbolized the early 1960s by "perfectly capturing the feeling and sense of the Kennedy years."

Rob and Laura Petrie were a modern husband and wife. They were not a bickering duo with a comic union based on duplicity. Rather, they were stylish and fun loving. He was a comedy writer for a hit TV series; she took care of a suburban home and a young son. But unlike most TV mothers, housework was not Laura's *raison d'etre*. She had interests in the world beyond her front door and talents in which her husband took pride. *The Dick Van Dyke Show* on CBS portrayed the American middle class in the early 1960s in the most attractive and hopeful of terms.

The prominence of television in the Petrie household also set the series apart. *The Dick Van Dyke Show* acknowledged the medium in an unself-conscious way. And television situations often propelled the plot. In one episode, for example, Rob appears as a guest on a television interview show. The wily host gets Rob to admit many of his comic ideas for *The Alan Brady Show* come from his wife. Laura soon starts receiving phone calls from the talk show's viewers to find out if she's really as kooky as Rob described.

*The Dick Van Dyke Show* presented television as a given of American life. When the Petries attend a high-society party, Rob is greatly offended when a bookish matron snootily claims, "I don't own a television machine." The blanket indictment of the medium is presented as ridiculous. Rob and Laura, presumably like the viewers at home, display a far more democratic outlook.

*Car 54, Where Are You?* was a camp spoof. Longtime partners on the

New York City police force, officers Gunther Toody and Francis Muldoon are total schlemiels. And total opposites. Toody is short and dim-witted; Muldoon is tall and well-read. Fortunately, no serious crime ever seemed to occur on their beat.

Though the situations presented in the series were based on standard, comic plotting devices, NBC's *Car 54* presented the changing texture of urban America in an inadvertent way and subtly promoted a tolerance and respect for diversity. In the vanilla world of most TV sitcoms of the era, lines of dialogue like "O'Hara's going to a bar mitzvah" just wouldn't be spoken.

Although race or nationality was never a story issue in *Car 54*, the precinct house was an ethnic melange. Side by side in the locker room, black officers and Hispanics, Poles, Irish, and Jews put on the same uniform and were, quite literally, members of the same fraternal order.

Actor Ossie Davis, who appeared regularly on *Car 54, Where Are You?* with black comedian Nipsey Russell, recalled that even though theirs were not leading roles in the series: "We were permitted to do things in a different manner than in the old days. We were sort of accepted as ordinary human beings. We did not have to scratch our heads or prove to the white man how noble or nice we were. It was just that ordinary everyday American acceptance that made the difference."

In this series too, like *The Dick Van Dyke Show*, television was a major thematic element. Characters were seen watching the TV set and plots were built around TV programs. For example, one episode of *Car 54* called "Catch Me On the Paar Show" involves a cop from the 53rd Precinct who Toody thinks is the funniest man in the world. When Toody and Muldoon pull over TV personality Hugh Downs for a traffic violation, the celebrity—playing himself—agrees to put their buddy on the air. Downs happens to be guest hosting *The Jack Paar Show*. The friend's performance is a predictable disaster, but Toody is a hit when he tries to rescue his stage-frightened colleague and Downs invites him back for an encore. This time, however, Toody gets butterflies and the usually reserved Muldoon steps in and scores big laughs.

Even the FCC gets lampooned in *Car 54*. When it's discovered that crooks are copying crimes seen on the TV show *Crimebusters*, a nervous network president cancels the series: "The way the FCC feels about these crime programs, this is all we need. What can I tell them, that we're doing educational TV!?" Frantic, he orders the Programming Department to yank the *Crimebusters* episode scheduled for that night. "Put anything in its place," he says, "find the simplest, most insipid, clean, wholesome show in our film library."

In the Petrie's upscale suburb of New Rochelle and at the 53rd Precinct in the heart of the Bronx, TV comedy was broadening the view of the American mix and revealing the pervasiveness of television's grasp.

## Sports

In the fall of 1961, ABC introduced a technical innovation that would revolutionize sports telecasting. The Videotape Expander, called VTX by the engineers who developed it, permitted live action to be played back, almost instantaneously, in slow motion.

ABC's vice-president in charge of TV programming explained the network's amazing plans for the invention: "We can show our viewers a touchdown run or other thrilling play immediately after it occurs." During the halftime intermission, he boasted, ABC could "highlight plays of the first half in slow motion." And at the conclusion of the game "we will recap the contest with slow motion of key plays." Viewers first saw the process demonstrated on Thanksgiving Day 1961 when ABC broadcast an NCAA football game between Texas and Texas A&M.

It was during the Kennedy years that televised football, both college and professional, took firm hold of American leisure rituals. In the short time between 1961 and 1963, for instance, the TV audience for NFL football games increased by 50 percent. By 1963 the top ten rated television programs of all time included four football events.

Accordingly, the amount of money the networks paid for the rights to broadcast the games went through the roof. When NFL Commissioner Pete Rozelle negotiated with the television networks in the early 1960s, franchise owners were reportedly "thunderstruck by the dollar amounts they were offered," later acknowledging "it was beyond their wildest dreams."

An important element of the chemistry between football and television was that football was a sport adaptable and willing to take television time outs. Despite the high price of football sponsorship, advertisers found it was a cost-per-thousand bargain. No other form of television duplicated such a decidedly male audience. Messages for gasoline, beer, tobacco, lawn care products, life insurance, and men's toiletries were reaching, according to *Sponsor* magazine, "emotionally involved viewers whose intense interest is generally well-sustained during commercials."

The slow-motion capability, or slo-mo as it was soon called, enhanced the TV presentation of every type of athletic competition. And no program introduced American viewers to more variety than ABC's *Wide World of Sports*, also premiering in 1961. Events that had not previously received wide television coverage, such as figure skating, gymnastics, auto racing, and track and field competitions, fascinated newly converted fans.

The improved vision of skill and athletic prowess, however, was not the sole formula for the amazing growth of sports telecasting that began in the Kennedy years. *Wide World of Sports* became a model for imaginative and satisfying sports coverage because it so pointedly emphasized "the human drama of athletic competition." Sporting events were not merely spectacles, they were stories. Athletes were the players, facing stumbling blocks and disappointments as well as opportunities and sheer luck. Home viewers were drawn to these metaphors of their own lives. The pull of the vicarious experience offered by sports broadcasting was expressed simply and eloquently in the *Wide World of Sports* promise to provide viewers with "the thrill of victory and the agony of defeat."

## Movies on TV

By 1961, more than 11,000 feature films had been released into television distribution, most of them produced before 1948. The Hollywood movie was a cheap programming essential for every local station. Morning, afternoon, and weekend films were often introduced by a studio host who might also conduct contests or answer call-in questions from viewers. Late shows and late-late shows rounded out the programming day.

Feature films were not considered prime-time network fare, however, until the premiere of NBC's *Saturday Night At the Movies.* The first offering of the series on September 23, 1961, was *How to Marry a Millionaire,* starring Lauren Bacall, Betty Grable, and Marilyn Monroe.

The broadcast, which was a tremendous success, began a major shift in network programming strategy for the remainder of the decade. The other networks quickly recognized, as did Hollywood studios, the appeal of movies in prime time. Post-1948 films became a pricey commodity. But, nonetheless, within five years American viewers could watch a feature film on network prime time every night of the week.

While Hollywood executives looked ten years to the future and pondered the possibility of pay-TV as a market for first-run movies, Hollywood directors were not happy with the way commercial television was treating their films at that moment. The president of the Directors Guild of America wrote to Newton Minow with the complaints of his membership:

> When a member such as John Ford watches one of his memorable films on television and finds that approximately 40 minutes of that movie have been cut out haphazardly to allow time for the insertion of commercial messages, he realizes that his reputation as a creator must inevitably be irreparably damaged. The mutilated films make no sense at all, and many times bear very little relation to the original.

> Our Directors' Council and Board of Directors feel that, in addition to this wanton disregard of a Director's creative accomplishments, the public is being hoodwinked and grossly misled when it sees an advertisement for a great film being shown on television, when what it actually sees is a highly abridged version which is practically unrecognizable even to the man who made it.

The Directors Guild hoped Minow would take the lead in a campaign to maintain the integrity of feature films shown on television. But with so many other pressing matters on his administrative calendar, it was not a cause Minow had the time or inclination to champion.

## "A Lion Walks Among Us": A Public Relations Time Bomb

ABC hoped that *Bus Stop*, a new filmed anthology series in the 1961-1962 lineup, just might deflect some of the criticism of the network's bent toward action-adventure. The series was based on the William Inge play of the same name and borrowed the established characters. Each week in the small town of Sunrise, Colorado, a young sheriff, a romantic teenage girl, and the woman who ran the bus stop restaurant awaited the arrival of the guest star at the depot, then the story would unravel.

"*Bus Stop*," explained one of the producers shortly before the season began, "is directed toward a mature audience." Ideally, the network wanted the series to be perceived as contributing to an increasing sophistication in prime-time entertainment.

The series was a ratings disappointment for ABC—and ultimately a public relations disaster. An episode entitled "A Lion Walks Among Us" aired on December 3, 1961. It starred Fabian, the pop singer and teenage heartthrob. And, it was directed by Robert Altman—who, within three years, would turn his back on television because of creative restrictions.

A synopsis of the story discloses: "Fabian was cast as a degenerate drifter capable only of deceit, betrayal, and murder. To win acquittal of one charge of murder in the town, he had an affair with the D.A.'s alcoholic wife, and then used that to blackmail the D.A. Once released, he killed his own lawyers. In a perverse 'balance of justice,' the D.A.'s wife then killed him."

"A Lion Walks Among Us" was based on a novel by noted *New York Times* journalist Tom Wicker. The executive producer of *Bus Stop*, Roy Huggins, elaborated: "The premise of the novel was that evil is insidious, not easy of recognition, not subject to effortless defeat. . . . Like the novel, the show was shocking and disturbing. If it had not been, it could not have been honest. But its violence served an aesthetic purpose."

The produced episode was so "uncompromising and stark," according to Huggins, that the agency representing the sponsor believed the programming environment "might negate the economic purpose of their sponsorship." The advertiser's withdrawal of support drew attention to the program and, in no time, a scandal was brewing.

The rumors were that ABC cooked up a sensational episode to bolster low ratings. But, "A Lion Walks Among Us" was shot and edited before the season began, when the mission of *Bus Stop* to be stimulating and provocative still seemed like a good idea.

Twenty-five ABC affiliates declined to clear the program for broadcast on their stations. Also contributing to the controversy was the NAB code committee's attempt to prescreen the episode before it aired in order to render a judgment. But, despite the pressure, ABC president Oliver Treyz would not pull the episode from the network lineup and would not allow "A Lion Walks Among Us" to be viewed by the industry trade association. They were decisions that would come back to haunt him.

As 1961 drew to a close, Minow acknowledged that many of the changes taking place on television were to his liking. "The trends are pretty good," the chairman said. "Progress is being made when 20-odd stations refuse to clear a network program they believe to be objectionable." Roy Huggins, noting that Minow had on frequent occasions indicted television for avoiding "the new, the creative, the daring," wrote that "Minow may have a few hobgoblins, but consistency is clearly not one of them."

Though prosperous, 1961 was not the kind of year the networks wanted to go through again. At a New Year's Eve party, one network executive raised his glass and proposed a hopeful toast: "To a mellow Minow in '62." But the new year would bring little relief.

## The Creative Chill of 1962

In January, the Dodd hearings resumed in Washington. The senator announced that in the second phase of the probe testimony would focus on the creative development of prime-time series. Dodd was determined to prove that network programmers were the most persistent source of demands for crime, sex, and violence in the shows they aired.

The senator noted that network spokesmen who had testified before the subcommittee in June 1961 denied culpability. Instead, he said, they assigned the blame to the tastes of the American people and the lack of imagination on the part of television writers and producers. After those June hearings, the subcommittee subpoenaed working papers from the networks and major producers.

Dodd launched the January proceedings with a promise of trouble: "We have on file documents which show that direct instructions have been given at various times by network officers to inject more sex and more violence into television to boost or maintain ratings." To the networks' dismay, the introduction of in-house memos, never intended for public consumption, added a sensational dimension to the hearings.

One of the most titillating revelations found in the private correspondence that had been subpoenaed came from the files of *Route 66*. It documented the power CBS wielded over Screen Gems to alter the mood and direction of the series. Evidence showed that Jim Aubrey protested the show was too downbeat and that the lead characters needed normal rather than neurotic romantic involvements. Adjustments were made by Screen Gems. But they apparently were not enough to satisfy the network. Upon reviewing four episodes of *Route 66*, produced after the suggestions were made by Aubrey, a CBS West Coast official wrote a memo stating, "As a one-line critique of the stories, I should like to say they are a far cry from Jim Aubrey's dictum of 'broads, bosoms, and fun.' "

Aubrey denied using those words and called the expression a "Hollywood paraphrase" of his instructions to lighten up the show. His message, however, clearly registered. Shapely sexpots began to appear on *Route 66* with embarrassing regularity.

Herbert Leonard, the co-creator of the series, complained that Aubrey was trying to make the program "nothing more than an hour situation comedy or an ordinary action show." But Aubrey warned that discontinuation of *Route 66* might result from a disregard for the network's "repeated and emphatic suggestions on the proper approach for this series." Senator Dodd's case emerged all the stronger.

The real fireworks of the hearings, however, came with the interrogation of Oliver Treyz concerning the notorious Fabian episode. The ratings of the *Bus Stop* series were flagging when the program aired. Evidence was introduced by the subcommittee showing that the network employed special arrangements in the promotion of "A Lion Walks Among Us." The record indicated a substantially higher Arbitron rating followed. A significant increase in viewership of children under the age of thirteen was most troublesome. "Were you not aware," Treyz was asked, "of Fabian's special appeal to ten- to fourteen-year-olds?"

Senator Dodd also pressed the point of ABC's defiance of the NAB in the *Bus Stop* incident. "At our earlier hearings," Dodd told Treyz, "you insisted if we would give you a chance, you would police your own industry. But here you are, confronted with a request from the NAB to screen one of your programs and you turn them down." ABC was truly in the hot seat.

In what was described as a "high noon" atmosphere, the FCC also resumed its programming inquiry in January 1962. Just two weeks after his appearance before the Senate subcommittee, Oliver Treyz was again answering government questions about his network's schedule. The Commission focused primarily and intensely, some said savagely, on *The Untouchables* and "A Lion Walks Among Us."

While Treyz was uncompromising before the Dodd Committee about his determination to make programming decisions without interference, before the FCC he admitted he had been guilty of poor judgment. If he had the *Bus Stop* decision to make over again, Treyz said, he would not have broadcast the program.

Within a matter of weeks, Oliver Treyz was relieved of his duties at ABC. Though his position at the network was precarious before his testimony, in the industry, his dismissal was considered a case of walking the plank. The five-year reign of Oliver Treyz over the network's schedule was closely associated with the rise of action-adventure programming, and now, after losing face in Washington, it appeared he had outlived his usefulness.

The close of the FCC hearings brought a great deal of speculation on the future of the government-industry relationship. The Commission's itch for authority seemed to be intensifying. *Television Age* offered a pessimistic perspective: "The program hearings before the FCC reveal one alarming but nevertheless dramatic fact: the agency does not intend to stop, slow down, modify, or even define its incursion into tv programming."

For the television industry, the spring of 1962 began what was called the "post-FCC hearing era" and program planning was undertaken with special care by the networks. "With a posse of wildly galloping New Frontiersmen breathing down their necks, and the shadow of the hanging tree lengthening over the land," a trade journal metaphorically noted, "the television industry's own sheriffs are intensifying their efforts to bring law and order to some of the wilder domains of the medium."

Each network had a different name for its internal housekeeping office. At ABC they used the title Continuity Acceptance. NBC's department was called Broadcast Standards and Practices. And at CBS it was simply Program Practices. But, mostly everyone knew them as the "network censors." And by the spring of 1962, they had become among the most powerful individuals at the networks.

A network and station jitteryness about program content was evident. "Television's impulse toward slow but steady improvement has never faltered until today," Roy Huggins, of the lambasted *Bus Stop* series declared. "Now for the first time in that medium's brief history, a decline in quality and spirit is underway, and the abrupt reversal is largely the result of Newton Minow's policies as Chairman of the Federal Communications Commission. . . . Imagination does not flourish in a climate of coercion."

*The Untouchables,* criticized at the FCC hearings because of violent content, underwent major changes for the 1962–63 season. The executive producer of the series for Desilu explained, "The pressure is on us because it's a marked series." After the FCC workover, dialogue was substituted for action whenever possible. Only motivated violence was permitted. "There will be less violence in the series," the *Untouchables* producer promised. "We have stories in which no killings occur."

At NBC, in the spring of 1962, producers working on network series were summoned to a meeting. The vice-president of Standards and Practices and the vice-president of Programming discussed the "various sensitivities of Washington." Hoping to prevent the need to reedit completed programs in the fall, the producers were told the network would not accept excessive violence or stories about sexual deviates. After the guideline meeting, one producer who declined to be identified, told a reporter he was instructed to "be careful"—but not told what to be careful about.

As an independent program packager, Mark Goodson of Goodson-

Todman Productions was in a unique position to recognize the impact of the FCC on the formulation of new program ideas. Addressing the 1962 convention of the American Women in Radio and Television, he summarized his recent experiences:

> When a presentation of a new show lands on my desk, I flip open the folder, look at the title, and then let my eye move down the page to scan the contents, trying to digest the material as rapidly as possible. . . . My attention is flagged somewhere down the page by a name. That name is Minow. And while the verbiage surrounding the name differs from presentation to presentation, the reason for its being put in—the intent of its inclusion—is invariably the same. I have even developed a pet name for this usage. With no disrespect intended, I call it the "Minow Paragraph."
>
> A crude translation might be "You may not like this show. The public may not like it—but *he will*."
>
> . . . The program material of these shows is generally antiseptic, somewhat didactic, slightly dull, offensive to no one and above all else "justifiable." The words "entertainment" or "pleasure" are seldom, if ever, mentioned. Like Latin and spinach, these shows are supposed to be good for you.

As the first Minow Season evolved during the spring and summer of 1962, the innovations in programming the industry had promised after the Wasteland speech failed to materialize. Old stars and old formats appeared on tentative prime-time schedules. Television critic Hal Humphrey believed fear of the unknown precluded breaking new ground. "It's as if the program vice-presidents had decided to find safety by re-living their past," the critic said. Big doses of crime and sex had to go. And, Humphrey pointed out, "nobody ever beefed about Jack Gleason or Lucy Ball, did they?"

At the fortieth annual NAB convention in Chicago in April 1962, the issue of industry self-regulation surfaced with bitter disagreement. The president of the trade association, LeRoy Collins, insisted that the only way to ward off increased government regulation was by stricter industry adherence to the NAB radio and television codes, which, like the Cub Scout Oath, were ethical standards routinely violated with impunity.

Collins offered a plan in which each network would submit descriptive information on entertainment programs to the NAB Code Authority before broadcast. Questionable shows, upon the request of the Director of the Code Authority, would be pre-screened and a judgment rendered. NBC took the position that such an arrangement would be better than government censorship, but ABC and CBS firmly opposed the plan. Minow let it be known that he favored some assertion of the pre-screening prerogative by the NAB.

When the CBS affiliates held their annual meeting in the spring of 1962, network president Frank Stanton expressed disdain for the proposal: "I am persuaded that this is a bad deal for the broadcaster because it is a bad deal for the public. With the programming veto power centralized, you can't help but get a drastic watering down of programming content. You end up with nothing but a great big bowl of Junket. . . . Creative television would die a slow and agonizing death. The tendency to produce what would 'get by' would be irresistible. . . . Experimentation, innovation, all chance-taking would cease as a group of timid, well-meaning men took over the responsibility of deciding what was to be shown on 50 million receivers." Ultimately, the pre-screening provision was never enacted, but nonetheless, a distinct chill continued to run through the creative community.

When the 1962–63 season finally aired, comedy shows stole the limelight from westerns and action series. Seven of the top ten programs were comedies, with *The Beverly Hillbillies,* a surprise ratings blockbuster, as number one. Most critics were appalled. They regarded the program about a back-country Ozark family striking oil and moving to California as corn pone burlesque and felt its phenomenal success was sad proof of the level to which American taste had fallen. A few defenders, however, felt *The Beverly Hillbillies* was a refreshingly zany satire on American class society, a meaningful absurdity that illustrated the pretentious phoniness and shallow snobbery of the monied upper crust. Either way, a chain of imitations was to follow.

The lackluster performance of the hour-long action series was blamed on the need to appease Washington. *Variety* reported, "Producers do feel strongly that the networks have gone overboard in their ban on violence, that when it's not permitted even though a situation requires it, it limits them in story-telling."

Action series were stripped of the elements that appealed to their viewers, and, as a result, they suffered in the ratings. *The Untouchables,* particularly, felt the blow. Regular viewers tuned out when Eliot Ness began engaging in more conversations than gunfights. Minow felt these were signs of progress, "The blood on the living room floor isn't as deep as it was a year ago."

Midway through the season, the news that Newton Minow had decided to leave government service became public. As he prepared to depart the Commission, the results of a survey conducted by the research firm of Trendex, Inc. were released. It concluded Minow "exerted a definite influence" on the thinking of leading television producers in New York and Hollywood. Close to 50 percent of the forty-three producers surveyed said the Chairman's public statements influenced their program ideas.

Minow found satisfaction in the report that his presence was felt in the workaday world of entertainment programming. He sent a clipping from *Variety* which detailed the Trendex study to his friend, the Attorney General. The article, which began, "Television programming has been completely Minowized . . . ," stated: "Minow's pronouncements, especially criticism of undue violence, has had direct and sharp effect on tv programming. A majority of execs admit they have consciously tailored shows to conform with FCC recommendations. An overwhelming percentage of programming policy-makers are resigned to the government's role as a program influencer." The memo the chairman attached to the article said simply, "Dear Bob—Just in time!"

## The Kennedy Craze

There was no escaping the Kennedy influence on popular culture—rocking chairs, fifty-mile hikes, touch football, pill box hats, and Boston accents were all the rage. The mass marketing of Kennedy-inspired amusements was inevitable . . . coloring books, paper dolls, photo albums, and, of course, *The First Family,* the phenomenally successful phonograph record featuring Kennedy-impersonator Vaughan Meader, which spawned a slew of copy cats.

Vaughan Meader first came to the public's attention in July 1962 through an appearance on the CBS television show *Talent Scouts.* The studio audience erupted in amazed laughter when Meader, who physically resembled President Kennedy, started his impression of the Chief Executive conducting a press conference. At the close of the routine, the President announces he has a final statement. Meader then stepped away from the podium and said: "I would like to make that final statement as myself, Vaughan Meader. That is, to say thank you to the United States—a country where it is possible for a young comedian like myself to come out on television before millions of people and kid its leading citizen."

However dyspeptic the regulatory policies of the New Frontier might have left network executives, television didn't shy away from indulging the American public's obvious enjoyment of the President and his infinite relations.

Meader's career was launched into a short-lived orbit with numerous appearances on variety programs, such as *The Steve Allen Show* and *The Ed Sullivan Show.* So popular was the impersonator that Meader himself was parodied on *The Dick Van Dyke Show.* When Rob, Laura, and the gang arrive at a Catskill hotel, which has fallen on hard times, the house comic, assuming the Presidential character, conducts a mock press conference. Sally finally asks, "Mr. President, can you do an impersonation of a bellboy taking our bags up to our room?" "Let me make a judgment on that," the Meaderesque funnyman responds. "If you will all lift up your own bags with courage and vigor, and follow the Kennedy of your choice, we'll move onward to the New Frontier and your rooms."

The Kennedys became a boundless source of gag material for other TV comics too. Political nepotism became a well-worn joke idea prompted by Robert Kennedy's appointment as Attorney General and Edward Kennedy's entry into the race for the U.S. Senate in 1962. Red Skelton, for instance, recalled on his show the days when politicians promised a chicken in every pot, but the new slogan from the White House was "a Kennedy in every office." Continuing in the same vein, Skelton told of the President's conference with his father, the former Ambassador to Great Britain, to complain about his kid brothers—"Ted and Bobby are playing with my country." But, despite the quantity of Kennedy material, the parodies were rarely barbed and the satire seldom stinging—it was, more often, the humor of endearment.

On *The Garry Moore Show* in December 1961, Carol Burnett, Julie Andrews, and Gwen Verdon performed an energetic song and dance production number, a physical fitness tribute called "Everybody's Doing It for JFK." On another Garry Moore broadcast, in reference to Jacqueline Kennedy's much publicized athletic talents, the host quipped that he'd recently come across a magazine so old that it showed "Bess Truman waterskiing."

In the 1962 season opener of *The Jack Benny Show,* a bright-eyed little girl interrupted the star's monologue. Her name, she told the comedian, was Caroline Kennedy. Her Dad lived in Washington and she had an Uncle Bob who worked there too. The still-skeptical Benny finally appeared convinced that the precocious child was indeed the daughter of the President when she rushed back to her empty seat, which was next to a remarkable Jacqueline Kennedy look-alike. But the skit ended with the Caroline double identifying another woman in the audience as her mother. It was thoroughly innocuous fare, but, at the time, the injection of the Kennedys into the program made it seem bright and funny, and very contemporary.

The first lady didn't appreciate the takeoffs, which had become legion. According to the memoirs of her personal secretary, "There were very few things that got Jackie as excited as the subject of Vaughan Meader." The President, though, understood the advantage of being a good sport. At his press conference of December 12, 1962, he was asked about the "heavy barrage of teasing and fun-poking" and whether it produced "annoyment or enjoyment?" "Annoyment? No," Kennedy responded. And then going for the laugh himself the President said, "actually I listened to Mr. Meader's record, but I thought it sounded more like Teddy than it did me—so he's annoyed."

"What's Goin On Here?" was an occasional satirical comedy segment featured on *The Ed Sullivan Show* in the fall of 1963. The comedy team of Bob and Ray appeared as the hosts of a news program. One of their stories was a confused analysis of the situation in Laos. This was directly followed by a film clip of President Kennedy providing a similar perspective during one of his news conferences. The comic effect was at the expense of the President. Ed Sullivan explained to those in the audience who might take offense at the gag that the White House had gone along with the skit and had okayed the use of the film.

In situation comedies of the early 1960s, frequent references to the Kennedys satisfied the public's desire to believe the family in the White House was really not all that different from themselves. When Beaver Cleaver plans on going away to boarding school in one episode of *Leave It to Beaver*, father Ward likens his feelings to "the way Joe Kennedy must have felt when he sent his first son to Washington." In an episode of *Dennis the Menace*, the Mitchells visit the nation's capital. Standing in front of the White House the family contemplates how very similar they are to the occupants of the mansion, especially Dennis and Caroline.

But, despite the projections of normalcy on the Kennedys, they were far from typical. They were American nobility. It's been said Americans want their presidents to be like them—and better than them. Television fulfilled this desire as well.

In the episode of *Car 54, Where Are You?* entitled "Hail to the Chief," officers Toody and Muldoon are chosen to be President Kennedy's drivers during a brief presidential visit to New York. The story, which incorporates actual news footage of the President and Jacqueline Kennedy, revolves around Muldoon's fainting every time the President's name is mentioned. The officer explains his condition this way: "It's just that, well, the President has always been such a great hero to me. I have his pictures all over the walls of my room. He's the greatest man alive today. And to think that I, insignificant Francis Muldoon, have been chosen to drive him from the airport to the U.N. . . . . Oh imagine, sitting behind me, the fate of the Free World!"

The tranquilizer Muldoon is given to steady his nerves puts him to sleep, the stimulants taken to counteract the tranquilizers make him giddy. Of course, the assignment gets bungled. The Secret Service agent in charge of the motorcade is a nervous wreck. He's told he'll be put on some light duty to recuperate—"Like watching Caroline's pony for a few weeks."

Such a widespread presence of a chief executive in entertainment television as during the Kennedy years was a singular trend. No other administration has been the object of so much attention in television fiction. In some instances the President himself was set in the story. For example, a 1962 situation comedy, *Mr. Smith Goes to Washington*, which was based on the 1939 James Stewart movie, starred Fess Parker as the small-town idealist who gets elected to the U.S. Senate. The premiere episode included a teasing glimpse of an actress portraying the first lady, and a repeated routine on the series involved the voice of President Kennedy in high-level discussions.

More commonly, though, characters indicated the popularity of President Kennedy through everyday conversations. In a typical reference, Shirley Booth, as the lead character in *Hazel*, tells her boss that Abraham Lincoln was "way ahead of his time." The 16th President, Hazel says, "had a rockin' chair in the White House a hundred years ago."

## Prime-Time Parables: The Drama of Civil Rights

Corresponding with TV's de-emphasis of action-adventure in the Kennedy years was an increase in character drama. As one producer put it, "The guns of the gangsters, policemen, and western lawmen were replaced by the stethoscope, the law book, and the psychiatrist's couch."

The mature subject matter of these series was often borrowed from headlines of the day. In some cases, the networks exhibited courage in allowing thematically controversial programs to run despite sponsor and affiliate objections. For instance, an April 1962 episode of *The Defenders* entitled "The Benefactor" dealt compassionately with a doctor devoted to the cause of legalizing abortion. Though CBS was facing "Bible-belt resistance" and considerable losses in advertising revenue, the network would not back down. The program aired as scheduled.

Up to and including the 1962–63 season, however, storylines concerning issues of civil liberties for blacks were still considered daring and generally required script revisions to satisfy timid network executives. It was not unusual for black lead characters in proposed stories to be changed into Hispanic characters, for example, to avoid controversy, or for aggressive black characters to be toned down and their anger diffused in final drafts. The networks still believed prime-time audiences, in the North and the South, would not easily accept the integration of entertainment television.

Yet TV scriptwriters could not help recognizing the inherent dramatic value in the fight for desegregation in American society. It encapsulated every element of effective plot structure—the attainment of tangible goals rested on a path laden with formidable obstacles. Matters of heart and conscience collided with the letters of the law.

In the late spring of 1963, as plans for the fall season's series were in the works, a desegregation case in Alabama pitted the Kennedy administration against Governor George Wallace. It was a highly publicized and dramatic confrontation. In a futile, but carefully orchestrated show of defiance, Wallace "stood in the schoolhouse door" at the University of Alabama to prevent the registration of Vivian Malone and James Hood, two black students determined to exercise their educational rights.

The governor understood the inevitability of his defeat. The National Guard, federalized by the President, was not a force that could be repelled by Southern bravado. The young man and woman were registered without the violence and bloodshed that occurred when James Meredith enrolled at the University of Mississippi the year before.

On the night the Kennedy administration prevailed in Alabama, June 11, 1963, the President chose to address the nation on television. His poignant remarks that evening are considered a turning point in the civil rights movement, called by some the Second Emancipation Proclamation or the Kennedy Manifesto. The President officially elevated the civil rights struggle above the realm of politics. "Law alone cannot make men see right," he said. "We are confronted with a moral issue. . . . It is as old as the scriptures and as clear as the American Constitution."

Though Kennedy's early, halting performance in the area of civil rights was disappointing to supporters of the movement, on this night the President personally committed his administration to the goal of integration. The potential of devastating damage to his voter support in the South in 1964 did not dilute his message. It was moral leadership Kennedy offered as he asked his countrymen to share his vision of a pure democracy: "This nation for all its hopes and all its boasts will not be free until all its citizens are free."

It was a sadly prophetic pragmatism he offered as Kennedy warned that militancy would result from the rising tide of discontent: "Those who do nothing are inviting shame as well as violence. Those who act boldly are recognizing right as well as reality."

Less than two weeks after President Kennedy's TV appeal on civil rights, *The New York Times* TV critic, Jack Gould, devoted a column to "negro participation in television." Gould lamented the timidity of the entertainment industry for not creating television scripts "dealing in compelling terms with the agonies of living outside of white democracy." The critic echoed the President by calling civil rights "the most dramatic moral issue to face the country since the Civil War."

The short-sightedness of entertainment television concerning the lives of black Americans underwent a rapid remission in the crucial summer of 1963. Although writers were still cautioned by the networks to avoid stories that might be inflammatory in character, scripts were being prepared that only months before would have been unthinkable. It was as if, when President Kennedy firmly aligned himself with the righteousness of the cause, prime-time television did too. The voices of black advocates who had been agitating for increased media respresentation now fell on more attentive ears.

By the end of July, CBS issued a statement to its own staff producers and outside packagers emphasizing the network's policy that "Negroes should be adequately and accurately" portrayed in programming appearing on CBS. During the same week the New York Chapter of the National Academy of Television Arts and Sciences reminded its membership of their responsibility to "reflect the realities of the American scene by employing and truthfully representing all facets of our population . . . this applies especially to the Negro."

In late August 1963, as the networks were finalizing plans for the 1963–64 season, the March on Washington represented the zenith of the nonviolent civil rights movement. There could be no doubt American life was on the brink of a major change. Thousands of signs were carried in Washington that day. One banner—referring to the long-running series *Lassie*—read,

"LOOK MOM! Dogs Have TV Shows. NEGROES DON'T!!" Whoever painted the message on that sign intuited the potency of entertainment in shaping values and attitudes. The integration of prime-time television was as important as the integration of public transportation and education. Television would be an acculturating force of great magnitude.

The television season that debuted in the fall of 1963 was remarkable because the change in what was possible in storylines came so quickly. Although the number of black characters had increased slightly during the previous two seasons, they were most often victims of circumstance or their own ineptitude. But now, all at once, competent black characters were cast with greater frequency. Beginning in 1963, many series featured blacks as running characters, for instance, Cicely Tyson as Jane Foster, the office secretary in *East Side/West Side*; Ossie Davis as the District Attorney in *The Defenders*; and Vince Howard as Mr. Butler, the history teacher in *Mr. Novak*.

Most important, though, the 1963 season introduced stories in which blacks were the victims of white bigotry. These were characters who could express anger toward white society with justification. And the networks, though not all the affiliate stations, were willing to accept tales of prejudice that pricked the conscience of the viewer.

Before the 1963–64 season ended, at least one racial story appeared on each major network dramatic series. But it was a comedy show that gave viewers the first indication of just how much the times were changing. The September 25th season opener of *The Dick Van Dyke Show*, entitled "That's My Boy," ended with a memorable plot twist.

After a dinner party, Rob tells the story of his son's birth. When he and Laura brought little Ritchie home from the hospital, they noticed he bore no resemblance to either parent. They recalled a series of mix-ups in the hospital between Laura and another new mother, a Mrs. Peters. Food and toys meant for the Peters baby were delivered to Laura's room. Rob, convinced the babies too had been switched, phones the Peters and invites them over to discuss their children's fate.

The doorbell rings; Rob answers. Unable to mask his shock, he freezes in a moment of brilliant comic timing, then ushers an attractive, well-dressed young couple into the living room—a black version of the Petries. The studio audience, stunned for an instant, spontaneously applauds not only the skillful execution of the gag, but its conspicuous benevolence as well.

In the storylines of dramatic series, though, racial harmony did not come so effortlessly. All white Americans were not as welcoming as the Petries and all black Americans were not as forgiving as the Peters. In New Frontier character dramas, as in real life, the process of integration demanded soul-searching.

Actor Greg Morris, who played Mr. Peters on *The Dick Van Dyke Show*, appeared the next week in an episode of *Ben Casey* entitled "Allie." It was the story of a black baseball star, portrayed by Sammy Davis, Jr., who loses an eye during a freak accident on the diamond. His adjustment to the condition is complicated by his eye surgeon, played by Morris, who is filled with hatred toward white society.

Other programs included "Who Is to Say How the Battle Is To Be Fought?" on *The Eleventh Hour*. The episode, which featured Barbara McNair and Brock Peters, dealt with a black couple who clashes over their differing views on integration. On *Channing*, James Earl Jones starred as a brilliant author who disagrees with a matronly professor over a student's capabilities for a fellowship.

The series *The Lieutenant*, set in Camp Pendleton, California, lasted just one season on NBC. But during this 1963–64 season, the issue of civil rights, specifically prejudice in the Marine Corps, was dealt with passionately. In an episode entitled "To Set It Right," racial tensions surface between two recruits who had been high school adversaries. Though the strong language of the dialogue was shocking, it gave the story a disturbingly realistic edge. The white marine taunts his foe by calling, "You black monkey." After a scuffle, the black marine tells his commanding officer the animosity between himself and the other marine came about because, "I was just another nigger who didn't know his place." In the story, the black marine tells his girlfriend, who urges him to purge his anger before it destroys him, "I'm nobody's Uncle Tom. . . . My father, your father, all of us before, we wouldn't fight back. We took it, but what did it get us?"

That season, even a series set in the late 1800s, *Bonanza*, was compelled to comment on racial issues of the early 1960s. When Thomas Bowers, a world-famous opera singer, arrives in Virginia City to perform a benefit concert, many of the town's citizens are surprised and upset to learn he is a black man. Unable to secure a room at the hotel, Bowers is offered the hospitality of the Ponderosa by the Cartwrights—and ultimately refuge from an angry mob.

Of the many shows with civil rights themes that were broadcast in the 1963–64 season, four in particular deserve closer attention for their boldness and their impact on viewers.

"A Single Isolated Incident"
*Mr. Novak*, October 22, 1963

NBC's *Mr. Novak* series debuted in the fall of 1963. The setting of the show was urban Jefferson High School. The title character was a first-year English teacher played by James Franciscus. The actor's handsome features and familiar haircut prompted one viewer to write to the producer of the show to ask, "Is Mr. Novak's resemblance to JFK accidental?" (Eighteen years later, James Franciscus would, in fact, be cast as President Kennedy in a made-for-TV movie.)

In its first season, several *Mr. Novak* stories were based on events and issues of the day, including sex education, anti-Semitism, escape from East Germany, Russian defection, and the rights of the disabled. To characterize the show as somewhat pontifical in tone does not seem unfair. One letter of complaint to the series said, "After a hard day's work we want entertainment, not lectures." But what the audience really got when it tuned in to *Mr. Novak* and the other character dramas were not lectures, but parables.

A columnist, commenting on the new trend in TV drama for *The New Yorker* in the fall of 1963, reported, "virtue is popping up all over the TV screen." The "firmly established moral position" of the character dramas, the critic believed, generated a tone of "moderate evangelism."

The producer of *Mr. Novak*, E. Jack Neuman, wrote the first draft of the script for "A Single Isolated Incident" in July 1963 and shooting began the last week in August. The story revolves around Jefferson High's first racial incident. A black student, Marcy Desmond, is bombarded with garbage and warned to stay away from school. She's told that "her kind" is not wanted. Soon it is learned that other black students have received the same threatening phone calls and the local newspapers jump on the incident to create sensational headlines.

As the schoolday begins at Jefferson High, the Stars and Stripes are raised on a flagpole, a bugle plays, and the entire student body recites the Pledge of Allegiance. When the final words are spoken, "with Liberty and Justice for all," the faculty must begin to cope with the tension and fear generated by the morning's racial incident.

After homeroom is dismissed, Mr. Novak helps the administrative staff phone the absent black pupils. They urge those who had been threatened to return to school. With the grim task completed, a frustrated Principal Vane claims, "It's obvious that somewhere along the line, someone has failed—parents or teachers." "Or both," Novak replies. "I know this much Mr. Vane, no child is born *with* prejudice."

The victimized student finally decides to identify her attackers—one girl and three boys, who show no contrition for their acts when probed by Vane and Novak. "They lower our standards," is one response, "I think we'd be better off without them."

The climax of "A Single Isolated Incident" comes when Principal Vane addresses a specially called student assembly—the high school equivalent of a special television address by the President. "I'm confident," Vane says, "that all of you know how our constitutional government operates." And just as Kennedy pledged to use the authority of his office to uphold the law, the principal tells his young audience: "My job is to keep Thomas Jefferson High School running. When trouble comes I have the authority to suspend trouble-makers. . . . I have the right to recommend expulsion. . . . That is as severe a measure as I can take. But I *will* recommend expulsion for any individual who is responsible for any more incidents such as happened around here this morning." And just as President Kennedy ultimately framed the issue as a moral one, Principal Vane says with staunch conviction, "Every student has the right to an education and the right to walk with dignity on this campus."

As the year 1963 was beginning to fade into history, President Kennedy's more vigorous support of the civil rights movement alienated a great many Americans afflicted with the deep malignancy of racism. Not surprisingly, "A Single Isolated Incident" touched a raw nerve in many viewers, as evidenced by the score of vitriolic letters sent to the *Mr. Novak* series in the days and weeks following the broadcast. The correspondents seemed to fear the capacity of television entertainment to influence public perceptions.

For those to whom integration was anathema, the potential power of TV to homogenize American society was getting out of control by late 1963. A newspaper article datelined Rayville, Louisiana, was sent anonymously to the *Mr. Novak* series. The clipping reported, "A Ku Klux Klan official called on some 5,000 to 7,000 hooded klansmen gathered around three huge flaming crosses Saturday night to join a letter writing campaign against 'national television shows that exaggerate the use of Negroes.' "

It is possible that some of the letters regarding "A Single Isolated Incident" were the result of Klan efforts. Most, however, appear self-initiated. The thoughts these viewers committed to paper represent an indigenous heritage of bigotry:

> I don't like it when a NIGGER is shoved down my throat on the program so please leave them out of it.

> You show too many negroes in the background and the one about the negro girl was disgusting. I see no reason to appease negro actors or include them with white people so intimately. Let them create their own "all negro" shows and keep them separate—please.

> I am sick and tired of tunning [*sic*] in my television and watch those phony symthay [*sic*] stories about negroes.

> White people are getting a little tired of so many Coons being shown on their, usually, favorite programs. I am sure it is not necessary for you or any other producer to hire so many colored people and throw them out to the public via TV.

The program's fan mail also provides some insight on the season:

> Since Mr. Novak is taught in an intergrated [*sic*] school, our local T.V. station has stopped showing the program. The station had no right to junk my next-to-favorite program. What can I do to get to see Mr. Novak? I suppose I could move away from Alabama.
>
> Sincerely,
> An Angry Alabama Adolescent

> The "Mr. Novak" show is GREAT! This type of show certainly helps to put green pastures in Mr. Minnow's [*sic*] "wasteland."

"Who Do You Kill?"
*East Side/West Side*, November 4, 1963

Despite the bad blood between David Susskind and CBS over his testimony before the FCC in 1961, the network decided to take a chance when Susskind and co-producer Daniel Melnick pitched a project called *East Side/West Side* for the 1963–64 season. The timing was right for an experiment in meaningful drama.

The series about a New York social worker won instant acclaim. The program appealed to sophisticates because, according to Laurence Laurent of *The Washington Post*, it violated "every sacred tenet for television success." Typical TV heroes, for instance, all had a similar look, said Laurent, "Short straight noses, direct from a plastic surgeon, gleaming smiles courtesy of a dental laboratory." But Neil Brock, the lead character in *East Side/West Side*, played by George C. Scott, observed Laurent, was "hooknosed and disheveled."

The stark realism of the series was discomforting. Most viewers didn't know what to make of a hero who was often dazed by moral complexities. For CBS the series was a bust. One-third of the advertising time remained unsold. A few years later Susskind reflected on the ratings problem of his show: "A gloomy atmosphere for commercial messages, an integrated cast, and a smaller Southern station lineup, all of these things coming together spelled doom for the show. I'm sorry television wasn't mature enough to absorb it and like it and live with it."

But before *East Side/West Side* ended its one-season run, the series would present two of the most compelling civil rights dramas in television history. The stories, powerfully written and artistically produced, stunned audiences.

In August 1963, Executive Producer Arnold Perl got the OK from CBS to develop his draft of a script about a black couple in their early twenties living in a Harlem tenement, and how they face the death of their infant daughter from a rat bite. Perl wanted the episode to be a love story rather than a tract. And he succeeded in creating an affection and intimacy between black characters that had never been seen before on television.

Diana Sands played Ruth Goodwin, the mother who works in a neighborhood bar to support the family. Her husband Joe, played by James Earl Jones, frustrated by unemployment, grows more bitter each day. Helping professionals like social worker Neil Brock are of no use. The system is immovable. The community activism espoused by the reverend in the storefront church offers no immediate relief to the young man's psychological suffering.

With the death of the child Ruth withdraws completely. She won't get out of bed, drinks in an attempt to ease the pain, and refuses to attend the funeral of the baby. Unable to reason with her, Joe, in desperation, turns to those he had earlier rejected.

Neil Brock has no answers. "I don't know what to say to you, Joe." Touching his own white skin, Brock says, "I don't know what anyone can say who looks like I look. What white man knows what it's like—the life of a Negro?"

"Love is the only real answer," says Reverend Williams in counseling Ruth about why she should carry on. And in the end, for the sake of her husband, she finds the wherewithal to persevere.

Through the story of two individuals, "Who Do You Kill?" humanized the struggle for better jobs, better housing, and human dignity. And in doing so, it was bound to elicit strong reactions.

"Last night," wrote one crude viewer in response to the show, "we fully expected to see those slobbering social workers get down on their knees and kiss the negroes' behind." "What nauseous propaganda," said another, "even the 'reverend' was made up to look like that rabble rouser, Martin Luther King."

But, perhaps because *East Side/West Side* had a smaller and, presumably more liberal audience than *Mr. Novak*, the viewer mail concerning "Who Do You Kill?" was overwhelmingly positive and expressed similar sentiments to those of this viewer: "I'm sorry every white person in the country could not see it, with an open mind and an open heart. I'm sorry every Negro person could not see it, to assure them that there are those of us who at least try to understand their feelings and thoughts, as well as their social predicament."

In an attempt to publicize the broadcast of "Who Do You Kill?," the producers, the scriptwriter, and star George C. Scott sent a letter of invitation to view the program, along with a copy of the script, to one hundred people they described as "outstanding Americans in all walks of life, of all political persuasions, and of all races." Robert Kennedy, who was at the vortex of the civil rights struggle, was among those who received the correspondence. "Who Do You Kill?" was described in the letter as "neither sensational nor exploitive of the plight of a people. Rather, we believe, it is an honest reflection of one of the terrible realities of our time which too many people still face."

The week after the broadcast, Senator Jacob Javits, a liberal pro-civil rights Republican, moved that two newspaper articles be entered into the Congressional Record. One was from the *New York Herald Tribune* and carried the headline "A CBS Show Stars Two Negroes: Atlanta Blacks It Out." The other, from *The New York Times*, was entitled "TV: A Drama of Protest." Javits told his Senate colleagues that CBS displayed courage in airing "Who Do You Kill?" and he was distressed that not all Southern viewers had the opportunity to see the drama. The program, Senator Javits said, "dealt honestly and sensitively with the vital problems of job discrimination, housing conditions and the terrible cancerous cleavage that can exist between the Negro and the white community." "Who Do You Kill?" was "shocking in its revelations of what life can be like without hope."

"No Hiding Place"
*East Side/West Side*, December 3, 1963

In creating *East Side/West Side*, it was the wish of David Susskind and Daniel Melnick to bring to television the work of many outstanding writers who had not been active in the medium because of its limitations on subject matter. One of these was to be Millard Lampell.

In the early 1940s, Lampell toured the country with Woody Guthrie, Pete Seeger, and Lee Hayes as the folk-singing group the Almanac Singers. During this time he began his writing career as a contributor to *The New Republic* magazine and soon achieved success as a radio dramatist. While serving in the U.S. Army Air Force, Lampell continued to write radio plays. His most famous work, "The Lonesome Train," the classic cantata about the journey of the funeral train of Abraham Lincoln, was produced on the prestigious *Columbia Presents Corwin* series in 1944.

In the late forties and early fifties, Lampell added screenplays and novels to his prolific output. But his career faltered when, called before the House Un-American Activities Committee, he refused to name names. For years he was forced to write under a pseudonym. Finally, in 1960 he was able to begin writing for theater using his own name. The power of the blacklist lingered in broadcasting, however. Lampell could not work in television until *East Side/West Side* provided the opportunity.

His story, "No Hiding Place," was completed in September 1963. It traced the events in an all-white Long Island neighborhood when a black family moves in. The script revealed the "block-busting" tactics of unscrupulous real-estate agents. Creating panic and tension in the community, the businessmen convince white residents to sell their houses to the realty company, below the market value, for cash. "Couple of months from now," a home-owner is told, "it'll only be worse. What with our dark brothers pushing in here." The agents then re-sell the homes at inflated prices to black families eager to get out of the ghetto. The block buster's big profit is made on the turnover.

In "No Hiding Place," the Marsdens—played by Ruby Dee and Earle Hyman—are a middle-class, professional black couple. They move next door to Chuck Severson, a liberal public relations executive who is a friend of Neil Brock. His wife, Anne, a native of Louisiana, is sensitive about carrying the mantle of Southern racism.

Hoping to avoid a panic situation in the neighborhood, the Seversons plan to host a welcoming party for the Marsdens. Marilyn Marsden cooly declines the invitation. She tells her husband, "I know what they're like.

And I know what the party'll be like. There'll be ladies who keep asking me what I think of James Baldwin. And men who keep telling you how much they admire Jackie Robinson." Mr. Marsden, more congenial and easygoing, responds in exasperation: "You don't give them a chance. I know you. You got on that phone, and you heard that magnolia accent, and you froze."

The Marsdens finally do attend the get-together, and, as expected, there are many moments of awkwardness and tension. In the following days, the real-estate agents work overtime throughout the neighborhood as a genuine friendship begins to develop between Marilyn and Anne.

The impending sale of a nearby home to a successful, but unrefined, black man in the construction business puts Chuck Severson's professed principles in conflict with his concern over property values and other deep-seated fears. Neil Brock sizes up Severson's misgivings about the sale succinctly, "You were expecting a white Negro. And you got a black one."

Rationalizing his position, Chuck says, "I'm telling you, he's not the type for this community." But Brock doubts Severson would object to a rough-edged, uneducated, white man who made it the hard way. Savagely the social worker confronts his friend: "There's another yardstick when it comes to measuring a Negro! If he went to Harvard, if he plays golf, and talks like a Boston gentleman, and looks like a Philadelphia lawyer—then fine, let him have brown skin. Only not too brown! Sure. Chuck believes in equality, *but . . .*"

The story ends without optimism. For Sale signs spring up along the block. Chuck Severson wants in his heart to make a stand and stay in Maple Gardens, but he reminds his wife: "Everything we own in the world is tied up in this house. We can't afford to take a beating, we can't *afford* it." Their tormented decision, however, remains undisclosed.

Again, a provocative television drama prompted some viewers to express disgust with what they perceived to be liberal propaganda. But the program garnered awards and praise for its realistic depiction of families caught in the crosscurrent of social change. "As I looked at the teleplay that you wrote for *East Side/West Side*," a black junior high school principal wrote to Millard Lampell, "my mind kept repeating the question: How does he *know* so much of the *truth*? The story rang so *true*. . . . How in the world do you come to possess such truth?"

"No Hiding Place" aired the first week that regular broadcasting schedules resumed after the assassination of President Kennedy. "In view of the tragic events of last week," one viewer wrote to David Susskind, "the need for re-examination of our beliefs is apparent. . . . Further soul searching is needed if we are to retain the values of democracy we hold so dear." The day after the telecast Harriet Van Horne wrote in her review of "No Hiding Place" in the *New York World-Telegram*, "Of all the mass media, perhaps television is best equipped to light a candle of understanding in this country's confused heart."

## "The Non-Violent"
*The Defenders*, June 6, 1964

In the spring and summer of 1963, the NAACP staged construction-site demonstrations in several Northern cities to protest discrimination in labor hiring practices. An episode of *The Defenders* based on such a protest was one of the most compelling of the series.

Ernest Kinoy's treatment for "The Non-Violent" was written in October 1963—in the final weeks of the New Frontier. It was the story of a college-aged white boy from a wealthy family and a young black minister. The two are arrested for obstructing traffic during a civil rights demonstration at the construction site of a new hospital.

The program, produced in the spring of 1964, after the death of President Kennedy, was unsettling because it forced an acknowledgment of the potential danger in the civil rights movement. "Look, we're talking about a genuine revolution going on in this country," lawyer Ken Preston tells his father. "Blood's being spilled. There're millions of people fighting for their freedom."

The opening scene of "The Non-Violent" is shot to look like news footage, adding to the realism of the episode. As picketers carry signs that say "Jobs and Freedom" and sing "We Shall Overcome," a concrete mixer drives up and is forced to stop because the roadway is blocked by Alton Pell and Reverend Bonham. The clergyman is played by James Earl Jones.

The pair is warned that they are in violation of several city ordinances and asked calmly to leave. When they refuse to move, they are threatened with arrest. Still they don't budge. And when finally they are placed under arrest, they won't walk and their limp bodies must be carried to the waiting police wagon.

The Prestons are engaged to represent Pell by his parents, liberal and respected members of the community, and, in fact, contributors to the NAACP. But they don't want their son mixed up in protests and feel that Reverend Bonham has taken advantage of Alton's immaturity. The parents want the boy out of jail. Alton, however, is determined to remain behind bars with the reverend as a form of passive, nonviolent resistance. "It's funny," his father says, "I don't think Alton ever knew a Negro in his life, except maids and elevator boys. Next thing you know he's going to jail for them."

The Prestons arrange to meet with Bonham's young black attorney, John Bird, to discuss a possible joint strategy in the case. Lawrence and Ken arrive at a spirited gospel church service and fund-raising meeting for Reverend Bonham's defense. The two white attorneys are visibly uncomfortable, but awkwardly participate, when hands are joined and the congregation sings "We Shall Overcome."

The conference with Bird takes place in the Sunday school classroom. He explains to the Prestons that he is not merely an advocate in this case, but a participant: "When I act in an issue like this, it is *my* case. I too am on trial." As Bird explains that he represents the rights of millions of people to be free and equal, a framed portrait of President Kennedy hanging on the wall behind Bird becomes apparent in the shot. The image of the President, slightly above shoulder level, appears to be looking over him as a guardian angel would.

Ken Preston and John Bird plan to mount a defense based on a new interpretation of the First Amendment guarantee of free speech: if all conventional channels of protest, such as speeches, petitions, or picketing, are ineffective over an extended period of time, and the grievance is not even considered, then a protest that gains notice is a legitimate exercise of the First Amendment—which would include sitting in the pathway of a truck. When the script for "The Non-Violent" was written, a similar legal concept was being developed by Freedom Rider attorney William Kunstler.

The case moves to trial. The judge, a city magistrate, is unaccustomed to deliberating on points of constitutional law and prefers not to stir up a hornet's nest. He decides the case on a technicality which benefits both sides, but is not a clear-cut victory for either.

Alton Pell believes agreeing to such a compromise is an abandonment of principle. The boy is shocked that Reverend Bonham is ready to concede— an idol has fallen. But Bonham explains that they were in jail not to prove their own courage or purity, but to get action from the city on jobs for black workers. It was a practical goal. The city now has been pressured into negotiation and progress has been made.

During the Freedom Summer of 1964, as hundreds of college students prepared to go to Mississippi to register black voters, "The Non-Violent" depicted the mechanics and strategy of the civil rights movement—not as a noble abstraction, but as a pragmatic struggle that welcomed the efforts and commitment of white citizens.

In the mythology of the American West, the frontier was a place of moral regeneration. And so it was that the New Frontier was a time in which the climate was right for popular television entertainment to question American values. Though it is impossible to quantify, it is also impossible to deny that the society grieving for its President in late 1963 was endowed with a heightened sense of justice that was transmitted in large measure through glowing television screens.

The early 1960s were a period of ferment for entertainment television as the raised eyebrow of government became the flexed muscle. The paternalistic approach of the FCC and Congressional committees in attempting to guide the direction of the medium violated the networks' creed that prime-time schedules represented a cultural democracy in action.

Though the accuracy of the Nielsen ratings was vigorously discussed in regulatory and legislative quarters, there was no evidence that they misrepresented the distribution of tastes in the nation. The networks could say, quite properly, "Every night is election night on TV."

The issue, then, was framed by those in government authority as one of network responsibility. There were duties inherent in the position of elected representative. They had an obligation to provide programming that was not harmful to the common good, and to serve minority as well as majority tastes. The networks couldn't completely counter the reasonableness of that logic and were forced to adjust their offerings.

A lessening of violence and an emphasis on comedy were two reactions to the regulatory spirit of the New Frontier. Another was the development of character drama, which, particularly in the 1963–64 season, evolved into a forum for the examination of social injustice.

When Minow left the FCC in May 1963, the broadcast industry found little reason to rejoice. The new appointments promised no relief from programming pressures. The same day Kennedy regretfully accepted Minow's resignation, he named commissioner E. William Henry to replace the chairman. Kennedy also disclosed his intention to nominate Lee Loevinger, an assistant attorney general, to fill the vacancy left by Henry's promotion. With the recently appointed Kenneth Cox replacing conservative commissioner T.A.M. Craven, the FCC looked extremely dangerous from the industry point of view. The three men—Henry, Loevinger, and Cox—were expected to be "the toughest trio in FCC history."

The thirty-four-year-old Henry, who had been a valuable campaign aide to Robert Kennedy in 1960, was, like Minow, known as "one of Bobby's boys." He was almost a New Frontier caricature, said one trade journal—Ivy League school-educated, bright, hardworking, pragmatic, athletic, lean, and good looking. And his daughter attended kindergarten in the White House with Caroline Kennedy. A *Variety* headline told the whole story—"OH HENRY (THAT AIN'T CANDY)."

Minow's successor was to continue the hard line and lead the FCC into the "Second Wave of the New Frontier." But it never happened. Henry didn't capture public attention the way Minow did, and, as a result, was less of a catalyst for reform. Loevinger turned out to be far more conservative than anticipated. "If I am to err," he said at his confirmation hearings, "I would rather err on the side of restraint."

The big change in the direction of the FCC, however, came with the change of presidential administrations at the end of 1963. The industry took comfort in the fact Lyndon Johnson assumed office with an estimated $8 million worth of broadcast holdings. It signalled a welcome change of pace. Aggressive broadcast regulation—what network executives perceived to be the interfering hand of government in entertainment television—was not to be on the agenda of the Great Society.

# CHAPTER 3

# A Ringside Seat on History

## THE NEWS EXPLOSION

Charles Van Doren was the perfect quiz show contestant. In the fall of 1956, the young English instructor from Columbia University made his first appearance on *Twenty-One*, one of the most intellectually challenging of the many game shows on the air. Week after week his winnings grew as Van Doren, son of the Pulitzer Prize-winning poet, Mark Van Doren, displayed his well-rounded education. He was interrogated on the subjects of history, science, literature, and art. Some questions he answered with ease; others he struggled with.

Van Doren's inevitable loss came in March 1957, after a series of dramatic showdowns with his final opponent—a "lady lawyer." But the nation's favorite egghead left *Twenty-One* with $129,000 in prize money and a valuable celebrity status. Within weeks he accepted a $50,000 per year contract with NBC to deliver five-minute educational commentaries on the *Today* show each morning.

But rumors of large-scale quiz show rigging started circulating in the summer of 1958. A standby contestant on the show *Dotto* found evidence of foul play while looking through the notebook of a winning player. Once the issue captured public attention, the earlier claim by one of Van Doren's opponents that his loss to the English teacher was pre-arranged could no longer be dismissed as sour grapes.

Denials by all involved were issued. And, while a grand jury investigated the matter, the networks could legitimately claim they had no control over the quiz programs since the shows were produced by advertising agencies representing the sponsors.

Scores of people were involved in the fraud, but it was Charles Van Doren's admission of guilt in the fall of 1959 that ignited the debate over television's role in a decaying American morality. The producers claimed they just wanted to infuse their shows with solid entertainment values. Van Doren claimed he felt his success would have a positive effect on the national attitude toward education. But the duplicity and greed at the heart of the trickery induced an examination of the public conscience and an act of contrition from the broadcast industry.

The networks, while not perpetrators of the quiz show riggings, ultimately came to accept responsibility. In December 1959, FCC chairman John Doerfer announced a plan to help the networks regain the confidence of opinion leaders. There is irony, of course, in Doerfer prescribing the penance needed for television's absolution. He called for each network to present a weekly one-hour prime-time public affairs series and asked that the programs not be placed in competing time slots. Though this precise arrangement did not occur, the networks' prompt increase in informational programming was considered in large part attributable to the Doerfer Plan.

That fall, while the FCC chairman was devising his proposal for atonement, Senator John F. Kennedy addressed the Radio-Television News Directors Association. Though not yet officially a candidate for the presidency, he knew he was standing in front of a group of people who would be critically important in the next year of his life, and, he hoped, many years beyond that. The young politician opened with a reference to the raging scandal by joking about a game show trademark, "You see here today a fugitive from an isolation booth known as the United States Senate. . . ."

Kennedy massaged the self-esteem of his audience: "The greatest days of the television industry are just ahead; its service to the public interest just beginning. And, in time, we will look back to the present difficulties as merely a misstep in a long climb to usefulness in the public interest."

Of informational programming the senator said: "I know there are a good many Americans who would rather watch the fastest gun in the West. . . . But, nevertheless, all you can do in the television industry is to make it available. If people will not watch it—you've met your responsibility. They haven't met theirs."

By the time John Kennedy won the presidency, he certainly could not complain that television hadn't met its responsibility in covering the elective process. When asked at his press conference the day after the election if he felt he could have prevailed over Nixon without the benefit of the medium, he said without hesitation, "I don't think so."

Not only in campaigning, but in holding office, John Kennedy would depend on television to meet his needs while fulfilling its obligations. Though it would not be true for his successors, for the 35th President of the United States, no more mutually beneficial arrangement could have been developed than the live television press conference.

The idea originated with Press Secretary Pierre Salinger. According to his account, he approached the president-elect shortly after the election and said, "What do you think of opening up your press conferences to live television? I don't think there's any doubt you can handle it. You proved that against Nixon in the debates."

Kennedy considered the disadvantages of the forum before agreeing with Pierre Salinger it was in his best interest. The president-elect knew that overexposure on the airwaves was a possibility and the result could be citizen disinterest. Kennedy understood that vexing print journalists—the Gutenberg boys, as they were called—by appearing to favor television could be damaging.

He did not, however, buy the arguments made by sincere critics, some on his own staff, who believed that "off-the-cuff" government was hazardous. The thinking was that a slip of the presidential tongue could easily embarrass the United States or its allies. "The stakes are too high," believed David Lawrence, chief editor of *U.S. News and World Report*. Kennedy was sure enough of his own rhetorical and intellectual capabilities, however, to take the uncushioned chance.

As early as November 29, 1960, *The New York Times* reported that Kennedy was considering "occasional live telecasts of news conferences." The official announcement came on December 27, 1960, at Salinger's daily transition-period briefing in Palm Beach. Salinger recalled the assembled reporters broke into "a storm of protest." But he would not entertain their opinions on the matter. Salinger remembered informing the group with stridency, "It was the President's news conference—not theirs—and he would run it his own way. The decision was final. They could take it or leave it."

While New York TV consultant Bill Wilson worked with the White House on the staging of the sessions, the networks worked out their plans for covering them. The arrangement devised was that each conference would be broadcast through a pool feed to all three networks. ABC, CBS, and NBC would rotate originating the pool. The broadcasts would also be available to independent stations that wanted to tap in to the nearest affiliate.

Only five days after he took the oath of office, Kennedy conducted the first live televised presidential press conference. It took place in the spacious State Department auditorium, which was a huge difference from the cozy setting of Eisenhower news conferences held in the Indian Treaty Room of the Executive Office Building.

More than four hundred reporters were present at the Kennedy debut. One of them, CBS correspondent Robert Pierpoint, recalled, "The President stood on stage, which gave him a psychological advantage, much like a judge seated above the rest of the courtroom."

*Chicago Daily News* reporter Peter Lisagor remembered that "in Eisenhower's time we were up close to him. . . . we could see his temper flair. We could almost feel like we were shoving a hypodermic needle into him." But, with Kennedy, he said, a nearsighted reporter might have a problem seeing the man. Lisagor complained that conducting the conferences in the mammoth auditorium, with its thick beige carpeting and orange and black seats, was like "making love in Carnegie Hall—and that ascribes to it an intimacy it doesn't have."

While the reporters in the room were not sitting as close to the Chief Executive as they would have preferred, the home viewers did have ringside seats. They could not have been much closer to John Kennedy if they were making love. They could examine his face and observe his expressions and gestures freely.

The 6 P.M. broadcast of the first live press conference was a ratings success, capturing almost 34 percent of the total available television audience. It also prompted a spate of telegrams and letters from citizens who felt the reporters were not treating the President with appropriate deference. One viewer wrote to David Brinkley to ask for some clarification. He explained to the NBC newsman that he had watched the first press conference with a group of friends:

> To say it mildly we were all somewhat amazed at the following:
> (1) While they were asking questions a few of the reporters had their hands in their pockets while addressing the President. A non-commissioned officer would not permit this and all of us thought it was disrespctfull [sic] to the President.
> (2) One of the reporters was making a speech, and not asking a question.
> (3) The president had to question a reporter as to what he was talking about.
> But the "Hands in the pocket" shocked everybody in our party. Is this really permitted?

Brinkley assured his correspondent from Cleveland that while the courtesy of the gesture might be questionable, there were no restrictions on reporters placing their hands in their pockets. In years to come, viewers of presidential press conferences would grow accustomed to grandstanding by reporters and questioning in harsh tones. But in 1961, the novice television audience still expected politeness toward a president.

After the first three live press conferences, *Television Magazine* felt safe in declaring "television has proven about as hazardous for Kennedy as water for a fish." Even early skeptics could not deny that the President's grace under pressure and capacity to retain information were remarkable.

As one student of American political rhetoric observed, Kennedy demonstrated two stylistic virtues essential to the small screen: he was underexpressive in his bearing and gestures and he employed an economy of language well suited to television. While he could be charmingly evasive, he could also be uncommonly direct, sometimes answering a question with a single word—"No."

While the networks carried the conferences live, a local station in Washington carried them on a delayed basis. Pierre Salinger recalled: "In the early press conferences Kennedy would go back to the White House and watch it. After the first few, he became concerned about how the cameras focused on him and the lighting. That's why we brought Schaffner down. To take a look at our setup." Salinger was referring to the famed TV and film director Franklin Schaffner who had worked on many prestigious television series, such as *Studio One* and *Playhouse 90*.

Kennedy grasped the nuances of television in a way that surprised CBS newsman George Herman. Referring to the press conference of March 23, 1961, he said, "For the first time, I saw a President of the United States do something which was so professional, from a television man's point of view." The President opened the conference with a statement on the advance of communist-backed rebels in Laos, and Herman remembered that when Kennedy spoke "he didn't look at any reporter in the auditorium. . . . He was not trying to give the appearance of a news conference; he wasn't looking around the room. He looked right over all our heads, right into the camera with the red tally light on it, the one he knew was on. It was clear to me at the time that this was a man who was extraordinarily professional and that this was something that was carefully planned. This was to go direct to the people."

In April 1961, Salinger met the membership of the American Society of Newspaper Editors on the occasion of their annual convention. The Gutenberg boys were mad. A panel of critics contended that presidential press conferences were unfair to print journalists. "With the television monster all around," Salinger was told, "the reporters have become little more than props." The press secretary's response was to say cooly, "Television is here to stay." He was not worried by the rancor he encountered: "I think things are going pretty well. The people are getting a closer view of their President and the presidency than they've ever had—and that's just what we wanted."

The TV lessons President Kennedy learned through his press conferences extended to his televised speeches as well. NBC correspondent Ray Scherer was present when Kennedy was about to deliver his first formal televised address to the nation. It was the spring of 1961 and Kennedy had just returned from the summit with Khrushchev in Vienna. The newsman recalled, "The President told the network men he didn't think he looked his best in one of his recent television appearances." Kennedy told them, "These lights sometimes give me a double chin."

Scherer continued: "He had a *New York Times* photographer sit in (his) chair, and he squinted through the viewfinder of one of the TV cameras. He didn't like what he saw." "Too much shadow around the chin," the Chief Executive felt. The technicians suggested the President take a peek at the monitor in the remote truck in the White House driveway and they would adjust the lighting.

"As Mr. Kennedy walked to the truck," Scherer said, "electricians lowered each of seven floodlights in the office six inches. The President peered into the monitor tube and decided this was a vast improvement."

By the end of the first year of the New Frontier, *Life* White House reporter Hugh Sidey believed that because of Kennedy's use of television, "No official face has ever become so much a part of American consciousness." While few would deny that President Kennedy's sixty-four live television press conferences stimulated the interest of American citizens in the affairs of their government, it was also true that his innovation caused an imbalance between the coverage of the presidency and the coverage of Congress and the Supreme Court. During the Kennedy years, because of television, the presidency psychologically became the center of American government.

Live television press conferences allowed John Kennedy to get his ideas to the American public without a middleman. A prime example of the way this principle translated into power occurred on April 11, 1962. Kennedy, certain of formidable newspaper opposition to his pressure on steel companies to reverse price increases, used a press conference to stimulate public opinion to his cause and thereby force the steel companies into a defensive posture. In his opening five-minute statement the President castigated the action of the steel industry in raising prices as an "irresponsible defiance of the public interest." His televised show of anger was a wounding thrust in the duel.

Though the President likened the process of preparing for a press conference to cramming for a final exam every two weeks, he wanted to keep open the channel that allowed his message to be delivered unadulterated. Kennedy once told his friend, journalist Ben Bradlee, "When we don't have to go through you bastards we can really get our story to the American people."

There was, of course, a consequence the executive branch of government had to bear in exchange for this privilege. During the Kennedy years, Americans began to harbor inflated expectations of what a president was capable of doing and what he was empowered to do. When the most critical news story of the nuclear age broke in October 1962, it became as much a showdown of individual personalities as a confrontation between governments. And, again, television did not simply cover the story, it was part and parcel of it.

## Mr. K vs. Mr. K:
### A Game of Thermonuclear Chicken

With the mid-term congressional elections at hand, John Kennedy's track record in foreign affairs was not enviable. He had been humbled by the Bay of Pigs defeat, bullied by Khrushchev in Vienna, and was unable to prevent the construction of the Berlin Wall. Leading the partisan assault on the administration's shortcomings in foreign policy were Republican Senators Kenneth Keating and Earle Capehart. They charged that Kennedy was allowing a dangerous buildup of Soviet military aid to Cuba.

The President's response was to warn the Soviets and Castro that offensive weapons—those able to reach the United States—would not be tolerated, but he offered assurance to the American people that the buildup in Cuba consisted merely of defensive weapons. The distinction was not comforting to many critics and Kennedy was not entirely successful in diverting attention from the growing Soviet military presence on the island. The President was sharply criticized by the conservative press for allowing domestic politics to interfere with national security.

Tuesday, October 16, 1962, was a dismal morning for John Kennedy. Reading the early papers in his bedroom after breakfast, he was interrupted by McGeorge Bundy. The National Security Advisor had urgent news. The night before, the CIA had examined evidence, aerial photographs, which proved conclusively that nuclear missile emplacements were being constructed in Cuba. The warheads were already there and crews were working to make them operational. When completed, they would be capable of hitting targets throughout the southeastern United States. By the President's own definition, the offensiveness of the weapons was undeniable. And Kennedy had pledged to take action if such a situation arose.

The United States, of course, also had intermediate-range missiles on ally soil and claimed them to be for purposes of deterrence—therefore defensive weapons. Some scholars have blamed Kennedy for generating a crisis that didn't need to exist. He could have regarded the missiles as defensive if he so chose. Whether American cities were hit from established long-range missile sites or from newly constructed ones a hundred miles off the United States coast would not be an important distinction to the victims. The missiles in Cuba did not materially alter the strategic nuclear balance—the United States remained in a superior position. The brinksmanship was wholly unnecessary, it has been contended.

But, on that October 16, several theories on the Soviet motives in placing the missiles in Cuba were advanced in the meetings of the President's closest advisors. Whatever might have been true—whether or not the Soviet Union did intend the missiles simply to defend Cuba from an attack by the United States—the theory Kennedy believed was that the missiles were being put in Cuba as a probe of American resolve, that Khrushchev was testing the young President's character. Kennedy had made great claims about the strength of the American will in responding to communism. Now Khrushchev, he felt, was calling his bluff.

During the next week the Executive Committee of the National Security Council, Ex Comm, met unremittingly to debate on the course of action to be taken. The meetings were held in strictest secrecy. Even Ex Comm spouses were not to be advised of the situation. To maintain the appearance of normalcy, the President left Washington on Wednesday to keep his commitments to campaign for Democratic candidates.

On Friday, unusual American troop movements led enterprising news reporters to conclude that another Cuban crisis of some sort was imminent. Pierre Salinger, who knew nothing of the situation, was frustrated as he was beleaguered by demands for comment. "All I can tell you is this," Kennedy's Special Assistant Kenny O'Donnell told Salinger, "the President may have to develop a cold somewhere along the line tomorrow."

On Saturday, after being informed that Ex Comm had reached a tentative decision, the President cut short his campaigning. Salinger informed the press that the Chief Executive had a cold. To make the story more believable, the President appeared in a top coat and hat, a rare occurrence, as he departed Chicago for Washington.

By Sunday, *The New York Times*, *The Washington Post*, and the *New York Herald Tribune* had the substance of the story. At Kennedy's personal intervention, all three papers withheld publication of the facts.

On Monday morning, October 22, Salinger requested that the television networks prepare for a presidential address of "highest national security" that evening. The night before, Salinger had placed a call to Franklin Schaffner asking him to come to Washington. When Schaffner arrived on Monday he detected an unusually high degree of security at the White House. Schaffner's help was needed in making the President look as relaxed and effective as possible on camera. The medication Kennedy took for his painful back condition resulted in a puffiness in his face. Schaffner's advice on lighting and lenses contributed an extra measure of confidence to the President.

Few people knew, including Schaffner, what Kennedy planned to say. But, as the Chief Executive's TV advisor entered the control truck moments before the telecast, he was given a copy of the text. Schaffner recalled being "besieged by a swarm of reporters who wanted advance word on what Kennedy would say."

After giving his hair a final brush stroke, Kennedy took his place at his desk. Viewers at home were hearing announcements like *"Stump the Stars* will not be seen tonight. . . . "

The President got right to the point. There were missiles in Cuba. They were deliberately provocative and unacceptable. "To halt this offensive buildup," he said, "a strict quarantine on all offensive military equipment to Cuba is being initiated." With these words a crisis was officially underway.

In his study of the press and the government during the Cuban Missile Crisis, Professor William LeoGrande of American University wrote of the TV speech: "It represented a landmark in political communication for it was the first time a president had used television in quite this way. . . . Its impact was extraordinary. Over the ensuing days, the entire nation followed the unfolding crisis which Kennedy had sprung upon it with such drama Monday evening."

Of course, the President had not only sprung it on the American people, he also sprung it on the Russians and U.S. allies. Cuban Missile Crisis historian Thomas Paterson believes that what is most telling about Kennedy's response to the missiles in Cuba is that he suspended traditional diplomacy "and chose a television address, rather than a direct approach to Moscow, urged upon him by some of his advisers. . . . The President practiced public rather than private diplomacy and thereby significantly increased the chances for war. . . . The President left little room for bargaining, but instead issued a surprise public ultimatum on television—usually not the stuff of diplomacy."

Once the crisis became public, Professor LeoGrande has documented, the press, both print and broadcast, "acted as a willing partner in the administration's strategy." The American mass media did not constitute a forum for differing opinions.

The TV coverage of the Cuban Missile Crisis was continual but not continuous. The networks offered regular news flashes, plus news specials. Unlike a space flight, the missile crisis was not a story with an expected time of closure. A total preemption of programming made little sense to the networks. Not only would the cost be overwhelming, but what could actually be reported? There was a grave danger, the networks felt, if reporters turned to speculation. As noted in the trade press, "that might unnecessarily inflame an already frightened public to terror."

To some viewers, the juxtaposition of news bulletins with commercials put the modern world into a queer perspective. *The Washington Post* TV critic Laurence Laurent saw a deodorant message announcing, "It's new. It's different." "In a world threatened by thermonuclear holocaust," he wrote, "the commercial announcer's horror over a little honest human sweat was too tragic to be ludicrous."

During the crisis, CBS News displayed some especially resourceful thinking that eluded other news organizations. In the effort to monitor the Cuban television network, CBS chartered a plane and equipped it with two TV monitors and a film camera. About forty miles off Havana, pictures from the Cuban network could be picked up and recorded in the plane. Images from CBS's kinescope-style footage received wide circulation in American newspapers.

On Wednesday, October 24, when Soviet ships changed course rather than make contact with the naval blockade, there was some relief in Washington. New weapons shipments to Cuba were being prevented. But the problem of what to do about those already there was no closer to a solution. Work on the missile sites was continuing and they soon would be fully operational. The possibility of U.S. air strikes on the missile bases loomed larger.

John Scali, ABC's State Department correspondent, received an urgent phone call on Friday afternoon. A high level Soviet diplomat and KGB officer, Alexander Fomin, said to the American reporter, "Let's have lunch right away."

Scali, who was the State Department expert for the Associated Press for fifteen years before joining ABC in 1961, had met with Fomin on other occasions—but never on such odd terms. Fomin knew that Scali was well-respected and trusted at high levels of the U.S. government. And Scali knew that Fomin had direct channels of communication with the Kremlin.

The Russian told Scali that the possibly dire consequences of the Cuban crisis might be averted. The American was astonished to realize that he was being used as a conduit for a proposal to end the standoff. The participation of newsmen and newswomen in diplomatic affairs would become less extraordinary by the end of the next decade. In 1962, however, reporters were not apt to think of themselves as players.

Scali was implored to find out if the State Department would be interested in an agreement by which the Soviet Union would dismantle and remove the offensive missiles in Cuba and pledge not to reintroduce them, if the United States would promise before the world not to invade Cuba.

Back at the State Department, the legitimacy of Fomin's proposal seemed to be authenticated by a conciliatory message sent by Nikita Khrushchev. The top Soviet was pondering, just as the President, the outcome of a failure of diplomacy. There was, finally, an optimistic note on which to cling.

But, Saturday morning another message from Khrushchev arrived. This one contradicted Friday's olive branch. He was insisting the Cuban installations would only be dismantled if U.S. bases in Turkey came down as well. Even though those bases were obsolete and scheduled for dismantling, it was an unacceptable compromise to President Kennedy.

Then an added complication heightened the tension. A U.S. U–2 plane was shot down over Cuba by a surface-to-air missile. It was feared the pace of events might be getting out of control. The United States could not fail to respond to the attack. While Washington was trying to figure out what was going on in the Kremlin, the television networks were bracing themselves to cover a possible U.S. invasion of Cuba.

On that bleak Saturday, Mal Goode was a TV correspondent-in-training at the United Nations. Having been a reporter for the black weekly newspaper, the *Pittsburgh Courier*, and an active radio newscaster, Goode joined the ABC television network in September 1962. He was sent to the UN, usually a fairly slow beat, to get acquainted with the new medium.

But on October 27 he delivered seven network news bulletins to worried viewers. After the crisis, ABC received the following letter from a woman in South Carolina: "I think that was a colored man I saw reporting all day long on the Cuban missile crisis. And although I am white, and although he is a colored man, I want to thank him and I want to thank ABC because this is America, and that's the way it ought to be."

John Scali met with Fomin again on Saturday afternoon to try to find out the meaning of the mixed messages. The Soviet said it was a communications breakdown. The second cable, he claimed, was drafted before the favorable American reaction to his proposal reached Moscow. Scali was angry and told Fomin he thought it was all a "stinking double cross." He advised that the Soviets should not underestimate the determination of the United States to get the missiles out of Cuba—and time was running out.

With the clock ticking, Robert Kennedy devised a strategy beautiful in its simplicity. The United States would respond to Khrushchev's favorable communique of Friday and simply ignore the contradictory message sent on Saturday. The Attorney General himself delivered a letter to Soviet Ambassador Anatoly Dobrynin promising the United States would end the blockade and pledge not to invade Cuba in exchange for the withdrawal of the missiles and a pledge from the Soviets not to reintroduce them.

Early on Sunday morning, CBS correspondent David Schoenbrun was preparing his *Washington Report* program for its noon broadcast. He was reviewing background material in his office to finalize the lead story on the Cuban crisis when he heard bells in the newsroom. An office boy came running to him shouting, "Look at this, look at this!"

Schoenbrun grabbed the Teletype bulletin from the British news agency Reuters and read, "Radio Moscow announces an important message to be broadcast at 9:00 a.m." Soon the follow-up bulletins came: "MOSCOW ANNOUNCES DECISION DISMANTLE MISSILES, CRATE THEM AND RETURN THEM TO THE SOVIET UNION."

The correspondent immediately phoned Pierre Salinger at home. His wife did not want to wake the exhausted press secretary. "Wake him, don't argue," Schoenbrun told her, "It's great news. We've won." Schoenbrun recalled that a few minutes later a sleepy Salinger came on the line and threatened, "David, this better be good or I'll beat the hell out you."

"Pierrot," the Francophile newsman said, "K has backed down. He's pulling out the missiles. Your boss has won." After Schoenbrun read Salinger the lead paragraphs from the major wire service stories, the press secretary realized the President probably didn't even know yet. "Hang up, Dave," he said, "I've got things to do."

"Just a sec, Pierre," Schoenbrun urged, "I gave this to you first and I've got a show coming up at noon. Promise you'll get back to me and give me what you can before noon?" "You've got it," Salinger promised. "And, Dave? Thanks for waking me up, you bastard."

While Schoenbrun began calling and talking to every official he could get ahold of in Washington, the producers of *Washington Report* were reviewing file film for pictures of the streets of Moscow, the Kremlin, and Soviet military parades.

At noon Schoenbrun was on the air. After running through the details that were known, he went to CBS Moscow correspondent Marvin Kalb. At that time there were no direct satellite pictures available. Schoenbrun recalled: "We ran a still portrait of Marvin as he began to broadcast on a radio circuit, then cut back to me at my desk, listening to Marvin on the telephone and taking notes on his report." Kalb's account included a description of the grim faces on the people congregating at the Kremlin as they digested the news of the Soviet defeat.

Within seconds, a red light began flashing next to Schoenbrun's telephone. It was a signal from the control room that something was amiss and he should go to a break as soon as possible. Schoenbrun interrupted Kalb and said he would get right back to him. A public service announcement was then run.

Schoenbrun picked up the phone and Pierre Salinger was on the line: "David, I'm speaking from the Oval Office." He told the newsman that an Ex Comm meeting had been adjourned to watch his program. "The President is right next to me," Salinger said. "Please do not let Kalb run on about Soviet defeat. Do not play this up as a victory for us. There is a danger that Khrushchev will be so humiliated and angered that he will change his mind. Watch what you are saying. Do not mess this up for us."

Kennedy was gracious in victory. He welcomed Khrushchev's "statesmanlike decision." When it was suggested Kennedy might go on television to report on Khrushchev's concession, he said shortly: "I want no crowing and not a word of gloating from anybody in this government."

In the days of relief that followed, the President's heroic stature grew and the Democrats were swept into a historic off-year victory in Congress by an unusually large voter turnout. Through the auspices of the Advertising Council, Inc., a campaign urging citizens to vote in the 1962 election was launched. A light voter turnout, it was suggested, might lead the Soviets to conclude Americans were indifferent about their free system of government. President Kennedy recorded a message that was incorporated in the radio and television spots.

With the crisis over, a frustrated John Scali wanted to tell his incredible story on the air. But the administration did not want it revealed. Kennedy did not want to take the risk that divulging the story might look like a deliberate attempt to humiliate Khrushchev. Against his own instincts, the ABC newsman promised the President he would not reveal his part in the Cuban Missile Crisis until after Kennedy left the White House.

The Holiday season of 1962 was a bright one for the 35th President. His mettle had been tested and proven superior. He did not know that in time respected scholars would pinpoint his actions in the Cuban Missile Crisis as the beginning of an arms race that would make the world a considerably more dangerous place. He did not know it was the last Christmas he would see. What he knew was that he was at the top of his game—and he wanted to talk about it.

## A Conversation with the President

Because of his frequent press conferences, John Kennedy was cautiously selective about other television appearances. He understood that the mystique of leadership could not survive unsparing entry.

CBS correspondent Robert Pierpoint has written that starting with the Kennedy administration "a perceptible favoritism toward television developed. . . . Pierre Salinger started deferring to the networks. He was quicker to answer television correspondents' calls, more accessible to us in his private office, and began a relationship of daily phone conversations and periodic meetings with network Washington bureau chiefs."

Yet, despite this courtship of the medium, the President kept the upper hand in the relationship by playing hard to get. He was available for television interviews only when he needed or wanted to reach the American public. Otherwise, the numerous requests were turned down.

But, in December 1962, Kennedy thought the time might be perfect for the television interview the networks were clamoring for. Each network had individually requested a televised discussion with the President at year's end. Pierre Salinger surprised the news division chiefs when he called them to Washington on December 11 to propose a joint interview.

Although CBS's Dick Salant missed the meeting—due to a delayed flight and a taxi stalled in Washington's bad weather—ABC's Jim Hagerty and NBC's Bill McAndrew heard and agreed to the press secretary's plans. He offered the President's availability for a sixty-minute program with one newsman from each network asking questions. It would be a less formal format than a press conference. But, absolutely mandatory to the plan, was this provision: ninety minutes would be taped and thirty minutes would be edited from the conversation. This way, Salinger explained, slow sections or less-interesting comments could be deleted and a better program would result.

Salant was annoyed by the stipulation and considered pulling CBS out of the venture. ABC and NBC, however, did not protest. When CBS registered its opposition in writing to Salinger, the press secretary advised the network that the White House would in no way interfere with the editing process. A committee composed of one representative from each network would make the editing decisions.

The arrangements were finalized. On December 16 the discussion would take place in the Oval Office. The correspondents would be Bill Lawrence of ABC—a favored golf partner of JFK's whose close association with the President diminished his credibility in some journalistic circles; Sander Vanocur of NBC—Newton Minow's roommate at Northwestern University; and George Herman of CBS.

As Herman, who had been turned down for presidential interviews in the past, prepared for the taping of the broadcast, he asked himself about John

Kennedy: "Why does he want to give this appearance? Why does he want to go before the American people and let them have a look at him at this particular time? What is his aim? What is his purpose in this?"

The correspondent surmised that with the Cuban Missile Crisis over and the President's popularity at a high point, "He wanted to cement this view of himself as a person who was able to handle peace and war.... He was trying to project a smooth, quiet, rather deeper image of himself."

The President sat in his rocking chair and the three men sat just a few feet away in a cozy cluster, unlike the imperial distance of press conferences. After about fifty minutes, Kennedy suggested they all take a coffee break. Then they continued to talk for another half-hour.

The editing committee—Bob Quinn for ABC, Ernest Leiser of CBS, and Reuven Frank for NBC—trimmed twenty minutes from the eighty minutes recorded on videotape. The special news program entitled *After Two Years: A Conversation with the President*, aired the next day, Monday, December 17, 1962. "The Rocking Chair Chat," as it was called, was telecast in the early evening on ABC and CBS. NBC aired the program in prime time. *Variety* noted that NBC would not regret the decision to preempt the most valuable commercial time, because "as they say in Washington 'a Kennedy never forgets.'"

While no broadcast in which he ever participated did anything but enhance John Kennedy, reporter Mary McGrory believed this telecast was "the most effective appearance of his entire presidency.... It was perfectly delightful." Kennedy displayed a range of admirable qualities. He was clever and funny. He was contemplative and charming. He would occasionally interrupt himself and change course in mid-sentence. He was, viewers had to conclude, the genuine article.

The President's graceful command of the English language was the most impressive of traits as he looked back at the first half of his first administration. In referring to the Bay of Pigs, or as he called it "the Cuber of 1961," he said, "Success has a hundred fathers and defeat is an orphan." Reflecting on the office of the presidency, he told the questioners, "It's much easier to make speeches than to finally make the judgments." There was no sense, he said "in having the shadow of success and not the substance." And, in a remarkably perceptive and candid stroke of self-assessment, he claimed, "Appearances contribute to reality."

What viewers couldn't see was the amount of control John Kennedy exercised in the situation he was in. George Herman recalled one of the questions he asked that was deleted from the broadcast. He reminded Kennedy that presidential scholar Richard Neustadt had written that "any president who hopes to be considered great by future historians must be widely accused of subverting the Constitution in his own time." "If that's true," Herman posed, "what have you been subverting lately?" It was a witty and tough question.

"Well, he gave me," remembered the CBS newsman, "I think, the coldest stare that I've ever had from anybody. He really sort of looked at me from my head down to my feet and back up again with a look that sort of put icicles on me. And I thought to myself, 'What did I say? What did I do?' And then he said, 'No, I don't believe that's true.' And then he changed the subject completely."

Only after George Herman was out of the circumstance could he fully understand the President's strategy and the insistence of the White House that more material be taped than used. The newsman realized: "Every time we asked an unfriendly question, he gave the most magnificently dull answer that I have ever heard in my life with the certain knowledge that we were going to have to cut out one-third of the material . . . all his dull answers to these unfriendly questions were almost certain to be dropped. It was a fascinating performance of skill."

As 1962 ended, not only the President, but the television industry too wanted to celebrate its noteworthy accomplishments. It was a year, *Television Magazine* proclaimed, of "shining hours for TV News"—the year the medium "gave the nation a ringside seat on history."

This was the year, said Robert Kintner, that the networks "proved what's right with television." In those months of swiftly breaking events, the networks brought space flights, the Ecumenical Council in Rome, rioting in Mississippi, comprehensive election coverage, and the President of the United States into American living rooms with deceptive ease.

As news budgets and the number of hours devoted to news programming ballooned, the competition among networks gained intensity. Nineteen sixty-three would be the year in which the two major contenders for ratings and prestige engaged in a full-scale war for supremacy.

## The Rivalry

The news leadership CBS established in radio in the earliest days of broadcast journalism carried over into television. For most of the 1950s, CBS had a virtual monopoly on the top-dog status in TV news.

Edward R. Murrow, Walter Cronkite, Douglas Edwards, Harry Reasoner, and Eric Sevareid had no true challengers on the air until 1956. The NBC brass, desperate to carve into the CBS audience, came up with a lucky group decision regarding the network's coverage of the political conventions that election year. The teaming of newsmen Chet Huntley and David Brinkley was an "accident of casting," said their NBC news producer Reuven Frank.

The on-screen marriage of one solemn and one sarcastic personality, one craggy and one smooth face, was an instant success. The duo replaced anchorman John Cameron Swayze on the network's evening news program and the broadcast soon took the name the *Huntley-Brinkley Report*. By 1959, NBC had lured away several of CBS's top news employees in the hope of building a news division with equal prestige. And, by the summer of 1960, NBC was on the verge of succeeding in the endeavor.

The Democratic convention in July brought out the best in the news team. Huntley's political analysis was unobtrusively astute, while Brinkley's cracks were irreverent. "This is the first convention of the space age," he said in his distinctive clipped cadence, "where a candidate can promise the moon and mean it."

When viewers tuned to NBC en masse, CBS panicked. Walter Cronkite was teamed with Edward R. Murrow in what turned out to be an embarrassing copycat move. When the final counting was over, as many people watched NBC convention coverage in 1960 as watched ABC and CBS combined.

With the critical election season unfolding, the *CBS Evening News with Walter Cronkite* was chasing the *Huntley-Brinkley Report*. And it could not be denied that a new factor—celebrity—entered the business of TV journalism in a big way. "This is a phenomenon of show business rather than of the news business," admitted *Huntley-Brinkley* producer Reuven Frank. "We didn't plan it this way, but there's no doubt that the chemistry that comes over when they work together is a show-business thing."

At John Kennedy's Inaugural Gala, Frank Sinatra and Milton Berle amused the audience with a musical tribute to "NBC's Gold Dust Twins." To the tune of "Love and Marriage," the showmen sang, "Huntley Brinkley, Huntley Brinkley. One is glum. The other is quite twinkly. . . . "

A fan letter David Brinkley received from Edna Miller of Lombard, Illinois, in March 1961 conveyed his appeal. The viewer wrote, "I like your sense of humor and the wicked gleam in your eye."

Walter Cronkite didn't appreciate the pressure to jazz up his on-camera demeanor. "Probably if I made a few more acerbic remarks, I might win a few more viewers," he acknowledged, "but I don't feel like being funny with the news; I don't think that's my place."

In 1961, ABC began in earnest to build a news operation with the appointment of James Hagerty, President Eisenhower's press secretary, to head the news department. The early 1960s were considered a "Let's build a cathedral" phase at the struggling network. ABC conceded its third place position and would be patient about vying with the vanguard.

But CBS and NBC were in constant combat. A sign in Reuven Frank's office read, "It's not important how you play the game, but whether you win or lose." NBC president Robert Kintner had a standing order for NBC News—"CBS Plus 30," which meant whenever the two networks were covering the same event, NBC was to provide an additional half-hour of live coverage.

Each evening Chet Huntley anchored the newscast from New York and

David Brinkley from Washington. The program's sign-off—"Good night, Chet." "Good night, David."—alternating night by night, became the stuff of widespread parody and affection.

The evening news ritual dictated particular behavior patterns in homes across the country. David Halberstam reported on the routine at the White House: "The door to Kennedy's office was always open, a surprisingly large number of people could drop in and chat with the President of the United States. But when the Huntley-Brinkley or the Cronkite show was on, everything stopped. No one was to disturb him. . . . He put, aides noticed, more concentration into watching the news than almost anything else. You could watch with him, but you could not talk."

At the home of the President's father, Joseph Kennedy, the news watching ritual had a unique twist. Chet Huntley recalled the ambassador telephoning him "every night or so after the show and saying 'That was beautiful,' or just giving us hell about something."

*Variety*, the journal of record on matters of stardom, announced in mid-1962 that "the Dave Brinkleys, the Chet Huntleys, the Walter Cronkites, et al" were the "new heroes of TV today." "The Crisis Boys," as television newsmen were generically called, were definitely "hot box office."

The rivalry between CBS and NBC was considered the greatest in journalism since Hearst and Pulitzer. Even though CBS enjoyed ratings dominance in the money-making department of entertainment, especially with the introduction of *The Beverly Hillbillies*, it still found NBC's dominance in the money-losing area of news distressing. Status and respect aside, eventually, if left unchecked, the *Huntley-Brinkley Report* would begin to lead viewers in to NBC's prime-time lineup.

As early as 1961, CBS News president Richard Salant was thinking in terms of expanding the nightly newscast from fifteen minutes to a half-hour. The idea was developing through 1962 with the support of CBS president Frank Stanton and board chairman William Paley. In December of that year, the CBS plan to double the daily news in the 1963 season was announced publicly.

NBC, as CBS expected, was forced to adopt the same ambitious scheme. Hoping for a much earlier premier, NBC soon bowed to the realities of sponsorship, personnel needs, and the displeasure of affiliate stations. September 1963 became the target date for NBC as well.

Considerable negotiating—in fact, arm twisting—with affiliate stations was needed by both networks to gain acceptance of the longer newscasts. The stations, which usually ran fifteen minutes of local news to form a half-hour news block, were faced with the burden and expense of doubling their own efforts and offering a full hour of news each night. The tremendous profitability of local news had not yet been realized, but the expansion of network news in 1963 speeded the waiting revolution in local television production.

CBS prepared assiduously for the September expansion. The network's weekly series *Eyewitness to History*—produced by Les Midgley—which covered breaking news stories on short notice, was a helpful primer in organizing crews and producers to generate highly visual stories. (Though the name of the series was officially shortened to *Eyewitness* in the fall of 1960, it continued to be widely referred to and listed as *Eyewitness to History* throughout the Kennedy years.)

CBS also undertook a streamlining reorganization of its regional offices, consolidating control to expand coverage. A half-dozen dry runs of a thirty-minute newscast were conducted by CBS in the two weeks before the first expanded broadcast.

Like boxers before a prizefight, CBS and NBC exchanged pointed insults. "NBC is a fine organization, but all they've got going for them is a pitcher and a catcher," claimed Salant, boasting of CBS's larger contingent of editorial and technical staff. David Brinkley answered, "Mr. Salant is going into an area he knows nothing about. We have a large staff, too." "I don't feel at a disadvantage with two against one," Walter Cronkite claimed, "Let 'em put four in there if they want to."

The CBS anchorman continued to bristle at the "lighten-it-up" school of thought. "The news I have to cover every day isn't very funny," Cronkite said defending his straightforward approach. "We are journalists not entertainers," echoed Salant.

The thirty-minute national newscasts would, in most TV markets, appear in the same time slot, now pitting CBS and NBC in direct competition. And when the *CBS Evening News with Walter Cronkite* aired on September 2, 1963, the first shot in the network battle for the 1964 convention audience had been fired.

"Good evening from our CBS newsroom in New York on this the first broadcast of network television's first daily half-hour news program," Cronkite began. The network requested and received an exclusive interview with President Kennedy for the special occasion.

The prerecorded discussion with Cronkite took place at Kennedy's Hyannis Port home, where the two men were seated outdoors in wicker chairs. "How seriously will civil rights affect your chances in 1964?" Cronkite wondered on that Labor Day which capped an incredible summer of civil rights activity. On the subject of U.S. assistance to South Vietnam, the President concluded, "In the final analysis, it's their war." Kennedy's candid thoughts sent diplomatic ripples throughout the world, "We are prepared to continue to assist them, but I don't think the war can be won unless the people support the effort, and, in my opinion, in the last two months, the government has gotten out of touch with the people." A human interest film package about the success of the play *My Fair Lady* in Japan rounded out and softened the program.

One week later, on September 9, the half-hour *Huntley-Brinkley Report* debuted and David Brinkley acknowledged a telegram from Walter Cronkite wishing them "a reasonable amount of good luck." President Kennedy also appeared on the NBC inaugural broadcast as an exclusive guest, again directing most of his attention to Vietnam.

There was no great upset in the balance of power as the fall of 1963 wore on. NBC maintained a lead it would enjoy until later in the decade. But there was no letup in the ferocity of the competition. All three networks experimented with increasingly sophisticated videotape technology and bolstered human and technical resources.

During the Kennedy years, the nudging of government, the pressure of competition, and the happenstance of major news events forced network news divisions to acquire greater confidence, skills, courage, and integrity—all of which would be needed at once when the New Frontier came to a sudden end in Dallas.

# CHAPTER 4

# The Chosen Instrument
# of the Revolution

## CIVIL RIGHTS

The problems of black Americans in the 1950s held little interest for Dwight Eisenhower. In fact, he had even confided his sympathies for white Southerners whose petite daughters might be forced to sit next to big black youths in integrated classrooms. But, as a good soldier, he put his personal feelings aside in defense of the Constitution.

When the governor of Arkansas, Orval Faubus, announced in September 1957 that he was directing police and National Guard to prevent the desegregation of Central High School in Little Rock, Eisenhower was faced with a dilemma. In 1954, the Supreme Court had declared racial segregation in public schools unconstitutional. The recalcitrance of Governor Faubus and the violence of white mobs gave Eisenhower little choice. However disagreeable, it was the President's duty to see to it that the Little Rock Nine were afforded their constitutional right.

Eisenhower ordered the Army into Little Rock and put authorities and citizens on notice that their resistance was to cease and desist. That night Eisenhower explained his action on television. "Our personal opinions about the decision have no bearing on the matter of enforcement," he said. Southerners, he believed, "like the rest of the nation, have proved in two great wars their readiness to sacrifice for America. And the foundation of the American way of life is our national respect for law."

The drama, extending into the fall, was television's first comprehensive on-location coverage of a racial conflict. Lessons were learned that would be critical in the coming decade. Reporters, for instance, quickly figured out they were prime targets for the wrath of segregationists. The power of moving pictures to convey physical as well as psychological brutality was also underscored by Little Rock. Print and radio accounts could not compare in pathos to the sight of nine grave youngsters walking through a bastion of armed paratroopers protecting them from a pack of antagonists with faces contorted as they screamed hateful insults.

By the end of the 1950s, television ownership among black Americans, though a large percentage were in poverty, had spread with great rapidity. As explained in the pages of *Television Quarterly*, "Television holds for Negroes the advantage of providing entertainment at home, enabling especially the Southern Negro to avoid the indignities of ill-kept, humiliating, separate balconies of segregated movie houses in the Southern border states."

As John Kennedy campaigned for the presidential nomination of his party in the early weeks of 1960, four freshmen from North Carolina Agricultural and Technical School, an all-black institution in Greensboro, walked into the local Woolworth's, sat down at the lunch counter, and ordered coffee. When they were denied service, they refused to leave and inspired a wave of students to follow their lead.

In March 1960, when 120 people participated in sit-ins at nine downtown restaurants in Nashville, Tennessee, the governor of the state, Buford Ellington, charged the sit-ins had been staged for the benefit of a CBS television crew in town to film a documentary. On the primary trail, Senator Kennedy, whose commitment to civil rights was uninspired, was asked about the growing lunch-counter movement. His opinion was favorable: "It is in the American tradition to stand up for one's rights—even if the new way is to sit down."

At the nominating conventions in the summer of 1960, both parties made serious attempts to attract black voters. In some cases, however, their efforts were undermined by the television networks. Rather than risk offending southern stations, the networks cut away from black speakers at the convention podiums.

But civil rights was not an issue that could be ignored in the election— and Kennedy's campaign discourse gave black voters reason to believe he would be an advocate. In the second televised debate with Nixon, the Democrat implied the Republicans did not have a sound understanding of the Supreme Court rulings pertinent to civil rights. In a theme that would become familiar in his presidency, Kennedy said that racial strife at home was an international embarrassment. On the matter of civil rights, he told Nixon, America's democracy was a "goldfish bowl before the world."

In 1960, for the first time in American history, the black electorate played a decisive role in a presidential election. John Kennedy's phone call of concern in late October to a pregnant Coretta Scott King, wife of Martin Luther King, who was distraught over her husband's sentence on a technicality to four months in a Georgia jail, won him the admiration of black citizens—a large number of whom were yet undecided. Kennedy collected approximately 70 percent of the black vote and won the closest election in history.

On Inauguration Day, many black Americans, including an Air Force veteran named James Meredith, found strength and encouragement in Kennedy's words: "Let the word go forth from this time and place, to friend and foe alike, that the torch has been passed to a new generation of Americans . . . unwilling to witness or permit the slow undoing of those human rights to which this nation has always been committed today at home and around the world."

A few weeks after the new president took office, the *Bell & Howell Close-Up!* series on ABC presented a documentary on the 1960 desegregation of a New Orleans elementary school. "The Children Were Watching" captured the reprehensible behavior of mothers and fathers and grandparents opposed to integration as they congregated around the school to taunt black children. It was a lamentable foreshadowing of miles of television footage to be shot in the remainder of the Kennedy years.

The program prompted one viewer to send an emotional letter to *TV Guide*:

> The first time I saw a Negro was when I was seven. In fact, it was my seventh birthday—the day my town was liberated from the Nazis. He gave me the most precious birthday present a person could receive. At the time, I thought the candy he gave me was the best present I ever had. But, of course, now I realize he gave me my freedom, which was by far more precious! So why can't the people in Little Rock and New Orleans give the Negro *his* freedom? I hope programs like "The Children Were Watching" will continue and open the eyes of the people so they can take a good look at themselves. I'm sure they'll be shocked.

Those who knew politics and knew John Kennedy understood he would not be in a hurry to contend with the social intricacies of civil rights. On an NBC broadcast in February 1961, newsmen Ray Scherer and Sander Vanocur discussed their predictions. "He has said he will use his moral authority on civil rights when the time is right," Scherer said while pointing out that the President was loathe to offend the South by quickly introducing legislation. Vanocur's assessment of Kennedy's civil rights plan was accurate: "He's a very pragmatic man—and a very deliberate man. . . . He's proceeding consolidating his political power, building his pressure up on Congress. He's been building up his personal esteem through television appearances and the rest of that—And I think that this is his style going slow on this."

But, in the spring of 1961, the Freedom Rides were a powerful sign that the pace of the civil rights movement was not something that the President could control. His faith in breaking down racial barriers by incrementalism would be challenged on buses travelling through the South and on television screens throughout the country.

In 1960 the Supreme Court struck down segregation in interstate bus terminals. The Congress of Racial Equality, CORE, decided to test the ruling with the Freedom Rides. Groups of black citizens ventured on routes that posed serious dangers.

Mobs harassed and assaulted the riders on every leg of their journey. John Lewis, one of the young people with the Student Nonviolent Coordinating Committee (SNCC), recalled one of his Freedom Ride experiences: "We got to Montgomery on a Saturday morning. Just seconds after the bus stopped, a white mob came out of nowhere and grew to more than two thousand people. It was very angry and hostile—mostly young people. They had baseball bats, lead pipes, chains, bricks, sticks—every conceivable weapon or instrument that could be used as a weapon. I thought it was my last demonstration, really. I'd never seen anything like that. They were looking for blood. First, they jumped on the press. If you had a pencil and pad, or camera you were in real trouble . . . then . . . they turned on us."

In Southern newspapers, network correspondents were branded "propagandists." Editorials charged that racial demonstrating was being undertaken in collusion with TV photographers. Assistant Attorney General Nicholas Katzenbach explained the phenomenon that would confound television coverage of the civil rights movement throughout the New Frontier: "The bitter segregationists' view of this is that demonstrators are following the cameras, not vice versa. To them it is the northern press and television networks which seem to be the motive force in the civil-rights movement. This idea apparently motivated many of the toughs during the 1961 freedom rides in Selma and elsewhere. Almost their first moves were against the cameras."

Cameraman Moe Levy of NBC was one of those attacked and beaten to the ground as he tried to chronicle the progress and fate of the Freedom Riders. Only when a *Life* magazine reporter began to take pictures of Levy's attackers did their attention shift from the television photographer. Levy was able to crawl away, but one of his legs sustained permanent injury.

As President Kennedy was preparing for a summit in Vienna with Nikita Khrushchev, the violence of the Freedom Rides, attracting international publicity, was an embarrassment to him. When the Freedom Riders vowed to continue their pilgrimage despite dangers, the administration was forced to intervene to uphold the law. Federal marshals, dressed in street clothes not uniforms, were dispatched to protect them. In exchange, John and Robert Kennedy hoped, in vain, for a "cooling off period" in civil rights activity.

During his first year in office, the President was intellectually but not yet emotionally dedicated to civil rights. The issue was still one of law, rather than morality. An orderly process of change was how he envisioned a responsible movement. Voter education projects, for instance, were a high priority. Once black Americans achieved political power, Kennedy believed, the other problems they faced would diminish. Though his appointments of black Americans to high office were unprecedented—and in his personal life, John Kennedy declined social invitations to private clubs practicing racial segregation—the President's counsel of patience on civil rights was frustrating and depressing to activists. His cautious approach, his unwillingness to tear at the social fabric, seemed a betrayal of campaign promises, both implied and direct.

In September 1961, another *Bell & Howell Close-Up!* documentary on civil rights projected into the troubled future. "Walk in My Shoes," reported Jack Gould in *The New York Times*, "was nothing short of an unforgettable visit to the world of the Negro in the United States, a work of artistry, courage and power." The program, which was not carried by some ABC affiliate stations in the South, examined the restiveness of younger people in the civil rights movement. It was a warning that extremism would rise with the continued denial of rights and opportunities to black Americans.

Having grown up during the Great Depression, John Kennedy instinctively felt compassion and sympathy for society's underprivileged. Upon assuming the Oval Office, the 35th President of the United States understood the frustrations of intolerance. In earlier decades his family encountered blatant hostility toward their Irish ancestry and as a presidential candidate, Kennedy confronted bigotry toward his Roman Catholicism. But, nonetheless, the zealotry of the civil rights movement was not something the President felt comfortable with. The single-minded advocacy of the movement's leaders was alien to him. In 1962, the President's learning curve on civil rights was only beginning to develop.

The importance of network television to the movement, however, was understood in full measure by those who wanted to keep the pressure on the Kennedy administration—most notably, Martin Luther King, Jr. In the words of Bill Monroe, who was the chief of NBC's Washington news bureau during the Kennedy years and had spent the early years of his career as a newsman in New Orleans, network news became "the chosen instrument of the revolution."

Not only did television force northern viewers to take notice of the struggle for segregation, but it also engendered a solidarity among southern blacks. "With few exceptions," Monroe noted, "Southern newspapers and Southern radio and TV stations carried very little news about Negroes and paid almost *no* attention to news involving racial issues. . . . At twilight Negro families watched network newscasts originating from Washington and New York— in most cases, the only daily news source they trusted."

As a Mississippi cotton planter explained, "You got to understand that every one of those Negroes on my land has a television set in his shack, and he sits there in the evening and watches." And what he saw was a revolution in progress.

## All Eyes on Ole Miss

The day after President Kennedy's inaugural address, January 21, 1961, James Meredith applied for admission to the University of Mississippi. After several months, Ole Miss, as the institution was affectionately called, formally rejected the application of the twenty-nine-year-old black man who had served nine years in the U.S. Air Force and who had already earned twelve college credits. The case slowly proceeded through a legal maze until early September 1962, when a federal court clearly stated Meredith's right to pursue his education at the Oxford, Mississippi, campus—where sororities, fraternities, and football dominated the interests of the majority of students.

The governor of the state, Ross Barnett—whose popularity with voters had suffered by revelations he had squandered taxpayers' money to refurbish the gubernatorial mansion with luxuries like gold-plated bathtub faucet handles—was looking for an issue to galvanize his support. The Meredith case seemed custom made. Barnett made a statewide television address on September 13 asking the people of his state to join him in opposing the federal government. Mississippi was facing, he said, "the moment of our greatest crisis since the War Between the States." "There is no case in history," he warned, "where the Caucasian race has survived social integration."

Dan Rather, who was the correspondent covering the University of Mississippi integration for CBS, had an early clue that he was entering a maelstrom. Driving into Oxford, the crew stopped at the first motel they saw. They were greeted by a hand-lettered sign on cardboard in the window that read: "NO DOGS, NIGGERS OR REPORTERS ALLOWED."

The Kennedy administration wanted to uphold the integrity of federal courts and federal laws without resorting to an armed confrontation as in Little Rock. But, three times the Justice Department attempted to have Meredith registered and three times the action was blocked.

Behind the scenes, Governor Barnett, facing the possibility of a jail sentence and heavy fine for defying federal law, was negotiating with the Attorney General. Barnett knew Meredith's registration was inevitable and was trying to concoct a graceful retreat in which he could save face with his constituency.

On Saturday afternoon, September 29, Barnett spoke directly with the President. Kennedy made it clear he intended to carry out the orders of the court. The governor suggested a plan to sneak Meredith's registration at Jackson, Mississippi, while everyone's attention was on the events at Oxford—but later that night Barnett changed his mind. The President, preparing for the worst-case scenario, signed the documents federalizing the Mississippi National Guard. Meanwhile, Kennedy aides were working on two television speeches—one to be used if Barnett peacefully acceded to federal law and one if the governor kept up his resistance.

On Sunday morning, Robert Kennedy threatened the governor with the possibility the President would, on national television, reveal Barnett's double-dealing—which would surely be a political kiss of death. Barnett, shaken by the prospect of being exposed as a duplicitous segregationist, promised that if Meredith was brought to Oxford that afternoon, the governor would meet his duty to maintain law and order. Barnett had given his word he would make a televised statement indicating Mississippi's intention to comply with Meredith's enrollment. But, still worried about keeping up the front of a Southern hero, Barnett inquired of the Attorney General, "You won't mind if I raise Cain about it?"

The White House originally asked the networks for a 7:30 P.M. time slot for a presidential address that Sunday, but later requested a delay until 10 P.M. The President wanted more time to be certain the governor was managing to keep the peace at Oxford.

As evening fell, the mood on the campus grew ugly. Rowdy crowds of students and outsiders eager to fight began congregating. Rocks and bottles and anti-Kennedy slogans began to fly. "Two-four-one-three, We hate Kennedy!" "Two-four-six-eight, We ain't gonna integrate!"

As promised, Barnett made a statewide television address. He reported that Meredith was on the Oxford campus accompanied by federal officers. Though he asked all Mississippians to "do everything in their power to preserve peace and avoid violence in any form," he fanned the flames by framing the conflict in a Civil War motif: "Surrounded on all sides by the armed forces and oppressive power of the U.S.A., my courage and commitment do not waiver." Directing his remarks to "officials of the federal government," he added: "Gentlemen, you are trampling on the sovereignty of this great state. . . . You are destroying the Constitution of this great nation. . . . May God have mercy on your souls."

President Kennedy, not aware of Governor Barnett's incitement, assumed the state police would maintain order in Mississippi. It was expected that the raucous crowd could be brought under control without the intervention of federal troops.

Just moments before the Chief Executive was to appear on national television and deliver the speech prepared for the peaceful accession contingency, the White House learned the situation at Oxford had grown out of control. As the President spoke, the rioting worsened.

Again, television crews took a beating. Dan Rather recalled that improvisation was needed in covering the domestic battlefield: "Whenever anyone turned on a light—which meant every time we needed to film—one or more bullets would attempt to knock it out. We had to film and move. Film and move. After a while we worked out a pattern: Turn on our battery-powered, portable lights, film for fifteen seconds by actual count, turn off the light—if we didn't get hit—and then run, because we were bound to catch gunfire or bricks or both. We had no way of protecting ourselves, except to avoid the crowds, keep moving and stay low."

The terrible anger and hatred directed toward the medium that surfaced so palpably in Oxford was explained concisely by Bill Monroe: "The first time many Southern whites saw Negroes standing up and talking about their rights was on network television. . . . Network television broke through the magnolia curtain. The segregationist South was shocked. And, of course, men get angry at those who shock them and threaten their cherished illusions."

The President's television speech was a disappointment to the civil rights activists who viewed the broadcast, including Martin Luther King, Jr. It was a discourse on constitutional principles, not a statement of moral leadership. Especially offensive was the conciliatory tone of the message. The responsibility for racial disharmony, the President said, could not be heaped exclusively on the South. It was shared "by every State, by every citizen." The honor of the South, "won on the field of battle and on the gridiron," was stroked with praise. Mississippi, he noted, had a long record of courage and patriotism and had produced heroes who "placed the national good ahead of sectional interest."

Kennedy's words did not produce the intended effect. Instead of savoring a victory of reason, the President and his staff spent an anxious night monitoring the violence. The federal troops, whose use the President hoped to avoid, were ordered in. Finally, at 4:30 in the morning, convinced the worst of the savagery had ended—including the deaths of a French newsman, a bystander, and countless injuries—the President went to sleep.

The networks' commitment to the coverage of the events in Mississippi was not diminished by the fact that the space shot of Wally Schirra was scheduled for the next week at Cape Canaveral and personnel and equipment were strained. CBS began the focus on Oxford with the *Eyewitness to History* program presented on Friday, September 28. "The U.S. Vs. Mississippi" included interviews with James Meredith and Ross Barnett.

On Saturday and Sunday, all three networks presented numerous bulletins and special reports, which disrupted the season premieres of many entertainment shows. Offering kudos, *TV Guide* observed, "NBC didn't hesitate to knock off one of its new and hopeful series, *It's A Man's World*, to make room for an hour long Mississippi news special."

After the President's Sunday night speech, the networks presented commentary and some on-the-scene reports. But a request from Governor Barnett for equal airtime to present his side of the story was denied. The next morning James Meredith was officially registered at Ole Miss and began attending classes with a military police escort.

In the postmortem, the White House and the television networks came to realizations that would color their relationships with the civil rights movement in the monumental year to come. The depth of the racism in the South shocked John Kennedy. His faith in appealing to reason and respect for law as a means of healing racial divisions was undermined.

Network news divisions recognized more clearly their inescapable role in exposing massive injustice. Not every story had two sides with equal merit. Balance was not a journalistic prerequisite in matters of human decency. Villains deserved excoriation and good guys rightfully earned sympathetic coverage.

### 1963: Watching the Republic Quake

"It seems to me that our responsibility in this year of change and hope is to prove that we are equal to this great inheritance," President Kennedy said in January 1963. The occasion was his acceptance of the Anti-Defamation League's "Democratic Legacy Award." CBS televised the festivities in a live prime-time special, *Dinner with the President.*

In accepting the award—a tribute to those closing the gap between democratic principles and democratic action—the President reflected on the meaning of American citizenship: "We are the descendants of forty million people who left other countries, other familiar scenes, to come here to the United States to build a new life—to make a new opportunity for themselves and their children. I think that it is not a burden, but a privilege to have the chance in 1963 to share that great concept which they felt so deeply among all our people—To make this really a new world."

Tangible changes were being felt in the television industry in the early months of 1963. CBS followed the lead of ABC in hiring a black newsman. Ben Holman was promoted from the network's Chicago affiliate to a general assignment reporter in New York. Many local stations, too, wanted to add a black reporter to their staff. Classified ads announcing "Negro Newsman Wanted" could be spotted in the trade press.

This progress of black Americans in the television industry was largely a result of activism by black citizens, not simply the timely benevolence of the networks or ethical suasion by the Kennedy administration. For instance, black actor P. Jay Sidney, who was a bit-part regular on *The Phil Silvers Show*, the series that created the unforgettable character of Sgt. Ernie Bilko, launched his own crusade. Writing to President Kennedy in December 1961 to register his complaints about the American mass media, Sidney said he knew his outspokenness would hurt his career. But, he told the President, "I was black before I was an actor, and I am prepared to go back to being just black and no longer an actor." In January 1962, Sidney wrote to producer David Susskind, "This week, I and friends will be picketing the Theatre Guild, protesting the U.S. Steel Show's exclusion of Negroes except in such roles as a servant named 'George.' "

By the summer of 1962, ABC and NBC were publicizing the fact that they adhered to nondiscrimination policies. NBC conceded, however, "this does not mean that any special effort should be made merely for its own sake to include members of racial minorities in programs that do not logically call for their presence." And ABC offered as proof of its commitment the statistic that "three Negroes have been crowned *Queen for a Day*."

In the autumn of 1962, black Congressman Adam Clayton Powell, Jr., who represented Harlem, presided over five days of hearings before the House Committee on Labor and Education. The focus of the investigation was discrimination against minorities in media employment practices. Sidney Poitier, Ossie Davis, comedian Dick Gregory, and P. Jay Sidney were among those who testified about the difficulties for black performers. "The only television show that hires Negroes regularly," Gregory quipped, "is Saturday Night Boxing." Network spokesmen, while denying bias and citing the progress made in hiring nonwhite employees in creative as well as technical capacities, agreed "much remains to be done."

Perhaps the most vigorous effort, though, undertaken by the NAACP, would come later in 1963. Threatening nationwide demonstrations and boycotts, the organization made demands of program producers and craft unions that included the following: if blacks were shown on a TV program in a menial capacity such as an elevator operator or janitor, a professional black character must also be included in the program; since one-ninth of the American population was black, a one-ninth representation of technical crews working behind the cameras should be black; apprenticeship programs should be set up to train blacks for all types of jobs in television. Although the demands were never formally accepted, the industry was sensitized.

By the beginning of 1963, race was the most heavily covered domestic issue in television documentaries. Though President Kennedy's submission of a new civil rights bill to Congress in February failed to attract widespread public support, the television networks continued to push civil rights to the forefront of American consciousness.

On February 8, a satirical improvisational group called the Premise Players appeared on NBC's *Today* show. They performed a bit that had become a standard in their repertoire. Host Hugh Downs introduced the troupe by explaining that satire was a time-honored device for social comment, dating back to ancient Greece. "I ask you to keep an open mind," Downs emphasized to the audience. Even if someone disagreed with the point, he said, "The important thing is that in this country we are free to do this. I think you have a right to see this." Still, the early morning "sketch on segregation" raised a few hackles:

PLAYER (heavy southern accent): You all know me, I'm the Governor of this here sovereign state. We're gathered here on this campus to iron out a little difficulty.

And before we get started here, I just want to say a few words about higher education.

(Raising his voice to a scream) There's a place for it. Higher education and this fine old university go together like fat back and hominy grits. So much for higher education.

We are gathered on this great campus today to iron out a few of our difficulties. And I just want to say in passing—(again screaming)—I don't think we need any help from any damn Yank Commies coming down here telling us what to do. We don't need any help from the Pope, either.

(Addressing someone off camera) General, it is a pleasure to have you down here with us, sir. But would you take off the white sheet, it don't look good on live TV. Thank ya.

You all know that I'm the best friend a Negro ever had. Now ain't that right? That's right. Ain't I got ten or twelve of them working up there at my mansion, right alongside my own kin folks? And when I'm walking down Main Street, don't I stop and chat with a dear old friend of mine who happens to be a Negro? Don't I sit there and chat with him for maybe five minutes, just like I'm chatting with you, while he shines my shoes? Of course I do.

Been a lot of loose talk in the paper lately about my not wanting the Negro to get an education. You know that's a bald-face lie, don't you? We all know that someday sooner or later maybe, the Negro will get an education. We know that don't we? But you see our point about the matter is—(screaming)—He ain't gonna get it here! He ain't gonna get it here! (Still screaming) Because we're gonna fight him. We'll fight him in the schoolhouses, in the libraries, in the bus station.

WOMAN: That's all right, sonny. Don't you be afraid, just get right on up here. You've died, and you've come to heaven. When I leave you alone with Him, I want you to tell Him your name and what you did back on earth. (Calling) God, ruler of the universe . . .

PLAYER: Lord, my name is Rankin Faubus Barnett, back down on earth I was—

2ND PLAYER: (Mimicking a Negro voice)—Mmmm, I am the Lord.

At the prodding of one of his constituent groups, Women for Constitutional Government, Senator James Eastland of Mississippi asked the FCC to investigate the insult to Governor Barnett and the "blasphemous portrayal of God." After receiving Eastland's telegram of complaint, the FCC requested information on the broadcast from NBC. The network's general attorney and vice-president, Thomas Ervin, responded that the producers of the *Today* show felt the Premise Players sketch was appropriate to the broadcast: "We feel they did not transcend accepted bounds of taste and propriety. In our judgment, this type of performance is wholly consistent with television's right and obligation to encourage free discussion of current issues and affairs and certainly in keeping with our nation's democratic tradition."

During the same month of February, a voter registration drive in Greenwood, Mississippi, was the target of harassment from local officials and violence from white citizens. Arson had destroyed black-owned businesses and SNCC volunteers were terrorized. On the night of February 28, three registration workers were shot at from a passing car. One of the men was seriously wounded. When the project was not abandoned, violent incidents increased and Greenwood became a focal point of national media attention.

In early spring, as 150 demonstrators marched to city hall to protest the lack of police protection for black citizens and volunteers in the voter registration project, a German shepherd was brought out to menace them. The animal was held on a tight leash by a police officer who threatened to turn it loose if people did not go home. When the dog bit the leg of one marcher, the crowd retreated.

The next day, more dogs and officers confronted a group headed for the courthouse in Greenwood. Again demonstrators were terrorized. News photographers were there to witness one of the dogs attack a local pastor. Not all the evidence could be destroyed, but the lawmen confiscated the film of the CBS cameraman on the scene.

Against the wishes of the Attorney General, Birmingham, Alabama, was the next city targeted for a major civil rights protest. The Alabama Christian Movement for Human Rights, headed by Reverend Fred Shuttlesworth, joined forces with Martin Luther King, Jr., and the Southern Christian Leadership Conference in "Project C"—C for *confrontation*.

The protest would be launched just before Easter to disrupt one of the busiest shopping seasons in the year for downtown merchants. The demands by the black citizens were not dogmatic or vague. They simply asked for the right to use the same lunch counters, drinking fountains, and rest rooms as white customers in businesses that profited by black patronage. They also asked that some black sales clerks be employed and that a biracial committee be set up to examine ways in which to desegregate the public school system.

As the largest segregated city in the United States, Birmingham was pivotal to the leadership of the civil rights movement. If change came to Birmingham, no other southern city could hold out for long.

In early April, volunteers began sitting down at lunch counters and picketing in front of stores. As arrests were made, new demonstrators continued to stream into downtown Birmingham. It was a peaceful protest designed for television coverage.

The police chief, the infamous Bull Connor, attempted to cut off media access to Martin Luther King. The hotel in which King was staying was surrounded by Birmingham police. The only way to get past the blockade was to present press credentials issued by the Birmingham police department. Reporters requesting a press pass were likely to be asked, "What the hell you ovah here for, wantin' to give all these niggers mo' publicity?"

On Good Friday, April 12, when King was arrested and thrown in jail, national and world media attention became riveted on Birmingham. Over the next few weeks the drama played out on the evening news and special reports. Every day there were more arrests. As the campaign wore on and morale among some volunteers was sagging, Martin Luther King reminded them that their cause was being seen on the *Huntley-Brinkley Report*. "We are not alone in this," he assured them. "Don't let anyone make you feel we are alone."

The willingness of Birmingham's black citizens to demonstrate and be arrested, baffled and frustrated the segregationist authorities. On May 2, the jails were overflowing when the demonstrations took a new and phenomenally newsworthy turn. For the first time, children joined the protest. Thousands of black children marched. More than nine hundred were arrested.

The ploy to elicit compassion and media attention angered Bull Connor. The following day the Birmingham police department gave up on the arrests and began to physically repel the marchers. Nightsticks, high-pressure fire hoses, and police dogs were their weapons. The violence committed against the demonstrators in Birmingham, so many of whom were children, was captured by news photographers and soon became symbolic of the American struggle for civil rights.

The bared fangs of lunging German shepherds and the overpowering streams of water targeted at terrified women and children was a television sight that reportedly "sickened" the President of the United States. "I can well understand," he said, "why the Negroes of Birmingham are tired of being asked to be patient."

On May 4, Burke Marshall, the assistant attorney general in charge of the civil rights division, arrived in Birmingham to serve as a mediator between the city and the demonstrators. Even staunch segregationists were frightened by the economic catastrophe a prolonged standoff would bring. While a truce was being negotiated, protests continued and violent rioting erupted by black citizens against the police.

But, in the opening statement of his May 8 televised press conference, President Kennedy was able to announce that a tentative agreement had been reached between demonstrators and the city of Birmingham. Of the several questions he was asked on civil rights that afternoon, one concerned a suggestion that Martin Luther King had urged upon John Kennedy. "Mr. President," the reporter said, "on the matter of improving race relations in the United States, do you think a fireside chat on civil rights would serve a constructive purpose?" "Well, it might," Kennedy responded. He then recounted the unsuccessful television address he made concerning the integration at the University of Mississippi. "That did not seem to do much good," he said, "but this doesn't mean we should not keep on trying."

## The Television Manifesto

A young woman named Autherine Lucy hoped to be the first black person to study at the University of Alabama. When she arrived for her first day of classes in 1956, a mob of a thousand students was marching through the Tuscaloosa campus to the home of the university president shouting "Keep 'Bama white!"

Frightened by the stones being hurled at the car in which she rode and the ferocity of the rioting mob, Lucy left the university with a state police escort and gave up. President Eisenhower offered no encouragement to her. He wanted to avoid interference, and so he remained a bystander to the disgrace.

In the spring of 1963, when Vivian Malone and James Hood made plans to enroll at the same university, there was still hatred in Tuscaloosa, but there was a far different mood in the White House. The Kennedy administration, through the Justice Department, took command of protecting the rights of the two black students.

On June 11, Alabama's governor, George Wallace, kept his campaign promise to oppose any federal school-integration order. When Nicholas Katzenbach of the Justice Department arrived on the campus in mid-morning to oversee the entry of Malone and Hood, Wallace was waiting with a five-page proclamation to "denounce and forbid" the action by the "Central Government." CBS and NBC had hoped to broadcast the confrontation on live television, but Wallace prohibited that arrangement. Within hours, though, CBS was able to get the first picture report on the air.

Like Barnett in Mississippi, Wallace, too, faced a prison term if he remained in contempt of the orders of a federal judge. Later Wallace would claim, however, his show of defiance in the schoolhouse door was needed to appease Klansmen who would have stormed the campus if no symbolic protest was offered.

When the governor refused to step aside and allow the registration of the students to take place, the President ordered the Alabama National Guard be called into federal service. Four-and-a-half hours later, Wallace was asked by a brigadier general to "please stand aside so that the order of the court may be accomplished." With a final statement of protest, Wallace complied. Shortly afterward the students entered the administration building and were registered without incident.

It was a Kennedy administration victory. In the hours between his federalizing the Alabama National Guard and Wallace's ultimate capitulation, the President made a decision. He was going to do something that civil rights leaders had wanted him to do for a long time.

Almost a year earlier, in July 1962, during the midst of the ultimately unsuccessful civil rights demonstrations in Albany, Georgia, Kennedy was asked by a group of a hundred black ministers to address the civil rights crisis on national television. They wanted a second Emancipation Proclamation. But Kennedy was not ready. He was committed to civil rights, but not yet fervent.

About three weeks before the integration of the University of Alabama, on May 24, Robert Kennedy had a painful meeting at the Kennedy family apartment in New York with a group of prominent black Americans. Among those gathered were psychologist Kenneth Clark, entertainers Harry Belafonte and Lena Horne, writers James Baldwin and Lorraine Hansberry, Director of the Chicago Urban League Edwin Berry, and Martin Luther King's primary attorney Clarence Jones.

The meeting, which the Attorney General expected would be an upbeat and congratulatory review of Kennedy administration progress, was instead an angry and emotional session. Robert Kennedy was shocked at the depth of the bitterness to which he was subjected. The President and the federal government were berated.

Robert Kennedy was hurt and frustrated by the lack of understanding exhibited about the practical matters of governance. Few suggestions were made for actual actions the President could take. Although King's attorney did have a specific recommendation. Jones told the Attorney General that the President should make a series of televised speeches regarding racial discrimination. He also believed that John Kennedy should personally escort the black students who were to be enrolling at the University of Alabama onto the campus. The Attorney General dismissed the latter half of Jones's suggestion as ludicrous and unworthy of consideration.

Some of those who witnessed the brutality of the verbal attack on the Kennedys that day, have, in retrospect, found it extraordinary that Robert Kennedy did not turn his back on the civil rights movement. He recovered his composure, and with a deeper understanding of the bubbling anger in black Americans, continued to fight for what he knew was right. He conveyed his belief to the President that the time for a television address on civil rights was fast approaching.

On Sunday, June 9, 1963, a TV interview with Martin Luther King was aired on WPIX in New York City on David Susskind's syndicated talk show *OPEN END*. During the two-hour discussion, King was severely critical of the Kennedy administration's commitment to civil rights. While Eisenhower's approach to civil rights was "miserable," King said, Kennedy's was "inadequate." He called on the President to revive fireside chats and explain civil rights to the nation on television. He asked the President to speak not in purely political terms, but in moral terms.

So harsh were King's remarks on the television program that the *OPEN END* interview was reported on the front page of *The New York Times* and the *New York Herald Tribune* the next day. Other newspapers throughout the country also carried stories quoting King's dialogue with Susskind.

The following afternoon, with the success of the federal government at the University of Alabama likely, the President made an uncharacteristically sudden decision to go on television. At 6 P.M. the White House asked the television networks for a fifteen-minute block of time beginning at 8 P.M. Ted Sorensen finished working on the speech just a few minutes before the President took to the air. There was not time to compose a peroration; Kennedy would have to conclude his talk extemporaneously.

John Kennedy took twelve minutes to say what black Americans had been waiting three years to hear from this President. Civil rights was a moral issue:

> The heart of the question is whether all Americans are to be afforded equal rights and equal opportunities. . . . One hundred years of delay have passed since President Lincoln freed the slaves, yet their heirs, their grandsons, are not fully free. . . . We preach freedom around the world, and we mean it. And we cherish our freedom here at home. But are we to say to the world—and much more importantly to each other—that this is the land of the free, except for the Negroes? . . . Now the time has come for this nation to fulfill its promise. . . . It is time to act in the Congress, in your state and local legislative body, and, above all, in our daily lives.

After watching the television speech in Atlanta, Martin Luther King promptly wrote to President Kennedy. His note, not carefully proofread, said: "It was one of the most eloquent(,) profound and unequiv(oc)al pleas for Justice and Freedom of all men ever made by any President. You spoke passionately to the moral issues involved in the integration struggle." Later, King told reporters the speech was a masterpiece.

Informed observers noted a difference in the President's style. Tom Wicker wrote in *The New York Times*, "Mr. Kennedy's address was one of the most emotional yet delivered by a President who has often been criticized as too 'cool' and intellectual." Scholars have since placed the speech in its historical context. "No other Chief Executive had ever talked that way about human rights in America," wrote historian Herbert Parmet. Professor Carl Brauer believes of the television manifesto, which introduced Kennedy's plans to send new civil rights legislation to Congress: "It marked the beginning of what can truly be called the Second Reconstruction, a coherent effort by all three branches of government to secure blacks their full rights."

For civil rights activists, however, there was little time to bask in the afterglow of Kennedy's eloquent words. Just hours after the TV address, Medgar Evers, the NAACP field secretary in Jackson, Mississippi, was murdered by a gunshot in front of his home.

Less than a month before, while Evers was leading a campaign to desegregate Jackson's local businesses and public facilities, the mayor of the city went on television to ask Jackson's citizens not to cooperate with the NAACP efforts.

The following week, through the intervention of the FCC, Evers was permitted to make a televised response to the mayor. It was a personal and impassioned address. Evers spoke of his childhood in Mississippi and his service to his country in World War II. "Tonight the Negro knows from his radio and television," Evers said, "about the free nation in Africa and knows that a Congo native can be a locomotive engineer, but in Jackson he cannot even drive a garbage truck. . . . We believe there are white Mississippians who want to go forward on the race question. Their religion tells them there is something wrong with the old system. Their sense of justice and fair play sends them the same message."

Several days later, the Evers home was the target of a Molotov cocktail, and then, on the night of Kennedy's television speech, Evers was stalked and assassinated with his wife and children just yards away. Even though the President had thrown the full weight of his office behind the struggle for racial equality, the obstacles to be overcome were still tremendous.

Public opinion polling after Kennedy's civil rights address revealed, not surprisingly, a high disapproval rating among southern whites. A letter written by one such viewer to the local television station reflects some of the festering sentiment. On the evening of June 11, the author of the missive "was ready to watch a show I find extremely entertaining; The Outer Limits." "Rather than this show," the viewer continued, "I was greeted by the unmitigated garbage put out by the dictatorial Kennedy machine with regard to the so called 'civil rights' nonsense at the University of Alabama. . . . There is enough trash in this world to make me sick without watching the Kennedy Gestapo on television."

But television viewers who felt the same way as D. T. Kauer of Route 1 in Aiken, South Carolina, were in for a long summer and fall in 1963. Regular programming *would* be interrupted.

## The March on Washington:
## Determination Made Visible to the World

The week following his television address on civil rights, President Kennedy presented to Congress an omnibus bill called the Civil Rights Act of 1963. "I ask you to look into your hearts," he told the legislators, "not in search of charity, for the Negro neither wants or needs condescension—but for one plain, proud and priceless quality that unites all as Americans: a sense of justice."

On June 22, Kennedy met at the White House with top civil rights leaders to discuss the legislation, which, among its provisions, would give all Americans the right to be served in facilities open to the public; provide funding for more jobs, education, and training; monitor discriminatory employment practices; authorize federal intercession in lawsuits to end school segregation; and provide greater protection of the right to vote.

At this meeting Kennedy and the black leaders discussed plans for a massive demonstration to be held in the Capital in late August. When Kennedy earlier learned of the proposed march, his feelings were strongly negative. He was interested, he said, in "success in Congress, not just a big show." He feared possible violence might undermine the entire cause of civil rights.

But President Kennedy did not express outright opposition to the planned demonstration while meeting with the civil rights leaders. He did, however, tell the assembled group that he believed the legislation had a better chance of passing if black supporters appeared nonthreatening. He believed the demonstration could be counterproductive if it were construed as an attempt to intimidate Congress. "Some of these people are just looking for an excuse to oppose us," Kennedy said, "I don't want to give them the chance to say, 'Yes, I'm for the bill—but not at the point of a gun.' " The timing, he felt, was bad. To which Martin Luther King responded: "Frankly, I have never engaged in any direct action movement which did not seem ill timed."

When it became clear to the President he could not prevail upon the leadership of the civil rights movement to cancel the plans for a March on Washington, he became an ally. The Kennedy administration and the Democratic National Committee helped facilitate the physical and safety requirements of the huge undertaking.

At his televised press conference of July 17, Kennedy was asked if the March on Washington might be a handicap to civil rights progress. "No," the Chief Executive replied. It would be, he said, "a peaceful assembly calling for a redress of grievances. . . . they are going to the Washington Monument, they are going to express their strong views, I think that's in the great tradition. . . . arrangements have been made to make this responsible and peaceful. This is not a march on the capital." Although the President said "I look forward to being here," he presumably meant in Washington, D.C.—not as an active participant in the March.

During the planning stages of the March at the end of 1962, the intention of the demonstration—to be sponsored by a coalition of civil rights groups—was to demand jobs for black Americans and a higher minimum wage. It was called the March on Washington for Jobs and Freedom. But as the plans progressed in the summer of 1963, the focus shifted to support for the passage of Kennedy's civil rights legislation. "Pass the Bill" became the theme of the March.

At first, the networks planned individual coverage of the event. But, in mid-August, when the scope of the demonstration was realized, they agreed to pool coverage at the main sites. ABC would cover the Washington Monument with seven cameras. NBC was in charge of the White House and following the movement of the mass of people. The tools for this task included a camera on a cherry picker at the Federal Reserve building and a mobile unit to travel with the flow of the marchers. CBS had an eight-camera setup at the Lincoln Memorial. Each network also had its own exclusive cameras at various positions.

By the morning of Wednesday, August 28, the March organizers, the local police, and the federal government had taken all precautions to quickly subdue any occurrences of violence. In addition to large forces of police, national guardsmen, and civilian march marshals, four thousand Army and Marine troops were on call. Bars and liquor stores in Washington, D.C., were closed for the day and federal employees were encouraged to take the day off.

At dawn, a thousand people were already gathered at the base of the Washington Monument. By 10:30, over 50,000 participants had arrived in the capital via freedom buses and freedom trains. By early afternoon, a quarter of a million people—60,000 of them white—had congregated to demonstrate their resolve and bear witness before their countrymen and the world.

At 8:30 A.M. the *Today* show began the television coverage with a thirty-minute report by Martin Agronsky. Five-minute special reports were then inserted in NBC programming at 9:30 and 10:30. Half-hour reports were broadcast by the network at 11:30 and 2 P.M. And a two-hour NBC special recapping the March on Washington was aired at 4:30 in the afternoon.

ABC, too, hopped in and out of its regular schedule throughout the day, beginning with a fifteen-minute report at 9:30 in the morning followed by numerous two-minute and five-minute updates. ABC broadcast half-hour news specials at noon, 2:00, and 4:30 P.M.

At one point during ABC's return to entertainment programming, Dick Clark's *American Bandstand* was broadcast. It was noticed by one television reviewer that the dance party was "integrated by a single male participant among the youths bobbing away to hit disks." A check with the network disabused the reporter of the notion that the presence of the young black man was "a salute to the big event of the day." Dick Clark, ABC advised, "has been entertaining a few Negroes on shows of late."

CBS was the only network to carry continuous live coverage of the March on Washington from 1:30 to 4:30 P.M. It was a wise decision since the network commanded the largest share of the afternoon audience on a day in which actual TV viewership increased dramatically. In a seventeen-county area in New York, for instance, 46 percent more homes were tuned in to television on August 28 than were tuned in on the previous Wednesday.

Two transmissions of the March on Washington were sent to Europe via *Telstar* communications satellite and carried live by six countries. Most of the communist nations accepted and taped coverage of the event. And TV film crews from Japan, France, and West Germany also covered the demonstration in Washington.

Senator Strom Thurmond of South Carolina voiced strong objection to the *Telstar* transmissions. He believed the pictures would mislead European viewers into thinking that "Negroes in the U.S. have no freedom." But the Europeans were keenly interested. *The New York Times* reported that the coverage of the March, which contrasted to violent civil rights footage from the South, "rivaled that given to astronaut launchings."

"Will there be violence?" correspondent Roger Mudd asked, knowing there were provocateurs on the outskirts of the demonstration. But the marchers, CBS viewers were told, were "conscious of the fact the eyes of the world are on them."

President Kennedy watched much of the proceedings on television and, according to his closest aide, Ted Sorensen, he "marveled, as the world marveled, at the spirit and self-discipline of the largest public demonstration ever held in Washington." After the March, Kennedy met at the White House with the ten principal leaders of the event. With "relief written all over his face," he greeted the group by saying "I have a dream." When he realized the men had not eaten all afternoon, the President had a light meal— sandwiches, iced tea, and cherry cobbler—prepared for his exhausted, but elated guests.

"The cause of 20 million Negroes has been advanced," Kennedy stated after his meeting with the civil rights leaders, "by the program conducted so appropriately before the Nation's shrine to the Great Emancipator, but even more significant is the contribution to all mankind."

Each network produced an evening special. CBS ran an hour summation at 7:30 on *CBS Reports*. ABC offered a late-night wrap-up with Edward P. Morgan. But the most ambitious program was NBC's recap of the day's events from 11:15 to midnight. It was a superbly edited program that presented the March as a sacrament of democracy. Highlights of the speeches and musical performances by Mahalia Jackson, Peter, Paul and Mary, Josh White, Odetta, Joan Baez, and Bob Dylan were interposed with awesomely beautiful shots of the crowd around the reflecting pool and the Lincoln Memorial taken from atop the Washington Monument.

Broadcasting earned a gold star of public service by day's end. "I wish to thank them," Senator Hubert Humphrey said, "generously thank them for what they did today."

As the summer of 1963 waned, the networks tried to go beyond the visual drama of the civil rights movement in their coverage and examine the causes of tension and grievances of black Americans. In the weeks surrounding the March on Washington, for example, ABC presented a five-part documentary series called *Crucial Summer*. The most formidable documentary effort, though, was the program NBC aired on September 2, 1963.

*The American Revolution of '63*, broadcast from 7:30 to 10:30 P.M. without outside sponsorship, was hosted by Frank McGee and produced by Shad Northshield and Chet Hagan. The telecast was historic, Jack Gould noted in *The New York Times*, because "never before has so much valuable prime time been accorded to a single domestic issue in one uninterrupted stretch.''

The network was not pristinely altruistic in its presentation of the documentary, however. September 2—Labor Day 1963—was also the day CBS introduced the first thirty-minute network newscast. NBC hoped to steal some of the promotional thunder from its competitor by airing *The American Revolution of '63*—a program sure to generate newspaper copy—on the same day.

When Senator Strom Thurmond learned of NBC's plans for the extensive television examination of the civil rights movement, he said, "I would be amazed and pleased, in view of the networks' past performance on this issue, if this program showed objectivity and fairness in its presentation."

McGee's stirring introduction to the broadcast left little doubt, however, that segregationists would not regard *The American Revolution of '63* as an unbiased presentation of facts:

> There comes a time, there even comes a moment in the affairs of men when they sense that their lives are being altered forever, that an old order is dying and a new one is being born. That moment comes sooner for some. And for others it comes later. For some the moment arrives when a deed of new dimensions sets the hour apart. For others, when familiar words are spoken more sharply. Later, but still suddenly it seems, men are saying things and doing things that they've never said or done before. And then we know we are experiencing a revolution.

> But we cannot say, though historians will try, when it began. We know that autumn does not begin with the turning of the leaves, but earlier—on some forgotten afternoon when a shadow passed over the fields and it was no longer summer. So, did this American Revolution of '63 begin this year in Birmingham or in 1955 in Montgomery? Or did it begin in 1954 with a Supreme Court decision? Or in 1863 with a Presidential proclamation? Some of its roots reach back to 1776 to an independence declaration—even back to the year 52 when the Apostle Paul preaching in Athens said "God hath made of one blood all nations of men for to dwell on all the face of the earth."

The program presented profiles of American cities, in alphabetical order, that had critical relationships to the civil rights movement. Much of the network's news footage was incorporated with new material. And, for the first time, a black network correspondent, Robert Teague, covered the civil rights beat. Reporting from a picket line at a construction site in Elizabeth, New Jersey, he explained to viewers "what it felt like to be a Negro in a race protest."

The governor of Mississippi, Ross Barnett, found the whole enterprise offensive. Offered the opportunity to voice his belief during the actual broadcast, Barnett lambasted the medium: "Fellow Americans you are witnessing one more chapter in what has been termed the 'Television Revolution.' Information media, including the TV networks have publicized and dramatized the race issue far beyond its relative importance in today's world. The three-hour special program and the degree of coverage accorded to the August 28 March on Washington underlined the fact that the American public is being propagandized by overemphasis. . . . the real issue in America today is centralization of power in Washington and not the race issue."

Kennedy's popularity with black Americans soared in the weeks after the March on Washington as he pushed his civil rights legislation with earnest conviction. There was little doubt that in 1964 he would simply sweep the black vote. At his televised press conference of September 12, a reporter prefaced his question about the 1964 campaign by saying, "Mr. President, a Negro leader who helped organize the March on Washington says he feels you are greater than Abe Lincoln in the area of civil rights."

As they watched the March on Washington, millions of hopeful television viewers believed that it was possible for the nonviolent civil rights movement, in partnership with John Kennedy, to rectify the misdeeds of American society and allow the United States to get on with the cause of promoting freedom around the world. But on September 15, the news out of Birmingham, Alabama, extinguished those hopes.

A dynamite explosion at the Sixteenth Street Baptist Church killed four fourteen-year-old girls attending a Bible school class. And, on the same day in Birmingham, a young black man riding a bicycle was attacked and murdered by a group of white thugs. Even those devoted to the principles of Jesus Christ and Gandhi asked themselves if there was room left in the souls of young black Americans to suppress violence. Or, if the words of a kid on a Harlem street corner were prophetic: "There's gonna have to be a bustin' loose."

During the Kennedy years, network television news coverage of the civil rights movement inspired in some viewers the most noble of human instincts and in others the same programming incited the most abhorrent reactions.

Martin Luther King remembered that President Kennedy once told him, "It often helps me to be pushed." And he was pushed during his time in office, pushed by men and women who were putting their lives on the line for principle. "When he saw the power of the movement," King said, "he didn't stand there arguing about it. He had the vision and the wisdom to see the problem in all its dimensions and the courage to do something about it. He grew until the day of his assassination."

While John Kennedy was pushed by the force of events and the passion of his brother to champion the cause of black citizens, the American public was pushed by the force of television to acknowledge the civil rights movement as a struggle of consequence to the very nature of the republic.

# CHAPTER 5

# Hungering for Heroes

## THE SPACE PROGRAM

An aluminum alloy sphere about the size of a beach ball sent a shiver through the American psyche. When it became the first object hurled into earth orbit, all three networks dashed special reports into production—news programs explaining to the American people that the Space Race had commenced.

With the successful launch of *Sputnik*, the Soviets had taken the lead, but the United States was supposed to have been first. In 1955 the government announced an American satellite would be in orbit by early 1958. On October 4, 1957, though, the Reds pulled the rug out from under American assumptions of superiority.

Two months later, when the United States attempted to launch its first satellite, American television screens transmitted a horrible sight. The Vanguard rocket that was going to even the score barely ascended the launch platform when an explosion occurred and the rocket collapsed—almost in slow motion it seemed, prolonging the consternation of TV witnesses.

Americans were unaccustomed to playing technological catch-up ball, but television helped define the stakes of the game. Special programs like *Satellites, Schools and Survival*, which both NBC and CBS broadcast in the spring of 1958, contributed to the national mood of emergency and determination.

The Democrats, under the guidance of Senate Majority Leader Lyndon Johnson, seized space as a partisan political issue. The Republican administration was accused of being too conservative and budget minded, of failing to apprehend the irreparable consequences of falling behind the Soviet Union. Senator John Kennedy amplified his party's message when, early in

1959, he appeared on the CBS program *Can Democracy Meet the Space Age Challenge?*

In April 1960, in the middle of the presidential campaign primary season, a historic documentary was seen on more than a hundred local television stations across the country. *The Race for Space* was produced by a young documentarian named David Wolper. In 1958 an extraordinary collection of official Soviet footage documenting the USSR's space program was made available for sale. The three commercial networks needed time to consider the purchase. But, Wolper, after just one look, bought all 6,000 feet for the newly formed Wolper Productions.

He then convinced NASA to cooperate with his plan to produce a program about the space struggle between the United States and USSR. Wolper explained that his documentary would foster public appreciation of the agency's goals and projects. He was granted access to the NASA film archive.

Nine months later, when the film was completed and sponsorship secured, Wolper was unable to place the project on a network schedule. Each network adhered to an informal policy of not accepting public affairs programming produced out-of-house. Undeterred, Wolper devised an ad hoc network by convincing local stations to buy the documentary and to cancel network programming to air it. Those who did were rewarded for their independence. *Race for Space* captured a large audience, received glowing critical reviews, won a number of awards, and became the first TV program nominated for an Oscar.

The Republican candidate for president recognized that the American public longed for space victories. So, Richard Nixon departed from President Eisenhower's claim that the United States was more interested in scientific attainment than a race with the Soviets. In the campaign of 1960, both candidates promoted the space race and the need for the United States to be second to none on earth and in the heavens as well.

As president-elect, though, Kennedy was made more fully aware of the genuine superiority the Russians enjoyed in space and the direct blame he might be forced to bear for possible failures of the American program. Beginning with his inaugural address and throughout his first several weeks in office, Kennedy softened his stance on the space race. The importance of cooperative efforts with the Soviet Union highlighted his public remarks on space exploration.

But, on the evening of April 12, 1961, once again, all three networks were airing special telecasts devoted to a Russian space first. The successful launch into earth orbit and return of cosmonaut Yuri Gagarin was another startling blow to American self-esteem. The President, who had hoped to deflect some of the fallout from the inevitable discouragement Americans would feel, was now vulnerable to the same criticism Eisenhower experienced after *Sputnik*.

Within one week of Gagarin's flight, Kennedy had suffered his first major defeat as President. An invasion force of fourteen hundred anti-Castro Cuban exiles, which had been organized, trained, equipped, and transported by the CIA, met with disaster when it landed at the Cuban Bay of Pigs. The horrendous failure of the secret mission damaged American prestige even among allies. (Many men died and the President was haunted by the thought of more than a thousand being taken as prisoners. When Kennedy later learned that Castro would consider exchanging prisoners for farm equipment, food, and medical supplies, the President and the Attorney General secretly recruited Jack Paar to help in a Tractors for Freedom campaign. The TV talk-show host continued to solicit contributions for ransom on his late-night program despite charges that he was violating the Logan Act, which forbids interference with foreign policy.)

The CIA operation also brought to a head the issue of the right of a free press to know and disseminate information about the decisions of government. For President Kennedy, the launch of the first American into space had the potential to alleviate some of the destructive reverberations from the Bay of Pigs—but television would have to be on the team. The decision had already been made by NASA and the President to risk the hazards of live transmission and allow broadcast coverage of American space flights under government supervision. The networks marshalled all of their resources to telecast the suborbital flight of Alan Shepard on May 5, 1961.

Compared to the orbital Russian manshoot less than a month before, this accomplishment was thoroughly modest. But American television did not dwell on the fact it was a lesser feat. It was presented as the glorious beginning of the U.S. manned space flight program.

The networks pooled their coverage from Cape Canaveral. Images from all the live cameras at different sites were channeled into a newly built master-control room, which was housed in two 35-foot trailers. The live broadcast of Alan Shepard's mid-morning blast-off, wrote Jack Gould in *The New York Times*, "united a nation in holding its breath." Television viewers were able to watch the Navy commander being driven to the launching pad and hoisted up to the capsule. Viewers saw the rocket grow smaller and then finally leave the range of the camera. "The picture of the Redstone missile," Gould said, "first rising and then arcing with a bird's grace was unforgettable."

When the countdown started, a presidential meeting of the National Security Council moved from the Cabinet Room to the office of Kennedy's secretary, Evelyn Lincoln, to watch the progress of the mission. The President, spotting his wife as she passed by the doorway, rushed out and called, "Commander Shepard has been launched into space. Come in and watch this." So the first lady joined the group that included the Attorney General,

Secretary of State Dean Rusk, Ted Sorensen, Defense Secretary Robert McNamara, Assistant Secretary of Defense for International Security Affairs Paul Nitze, and General Maxwell Taylor.

As would become standard in the subsequent Mercury missions, Lt. Col. John A. Powers—Shorty Powers—was the voice of NASA. As spokesman for the agency, he provided a running commentary for broadcast coverage. Between blast-off and the recovery—almost an hour for the Shepard flight— the networks decided individually how to program their airtime.

A cadre of space correspondents emerged on the television networks. They each reported and interpreted the complexities of space exploration with their own stylistic imprint. Jules Bergman of ABC, who was awarded a science fellowship at Columbia in 1960 and was himself a pilot, was considered the most knowledgeable of the TV journalists on the new beat, but the roughest around the edges in terms of broadcast technique. "When you're on the air," he once said, "believe me, you're under more stress than the guy in the capsule. At least, I think I am."

For NBC, Peter Hackes and Roy Neal were the primary space team, both having liberal arts backgrounds. Neal had followed rocketry and aeronautics for NBC radio and television since the early 1950s. The CBS correspondents were Charles Von Fremd, a young man who studied international law in college and had covered the Pentagon, and Walter Cronkite, already a major on-air figure at the network. Cronkite had the least technical familiarity of the men on the TV space beat, but he exuded the most personal involvement with the story he was covering. It was not unusual for words like "Gosh!" and "Golly!" to earnestly punctuate his reports.

Ironically, Cronkite originally argued against the live televising of American space shots, "I felt a failure before the eyes of everybody would be such a blow to our space program that it wasn't worth it." But on the evening of Shepard's flight, Cronkite expressed a very different sentiment. As narrator of the CBS *Eyewitness to History* broadcast, "Our Man in Space," he confirmed that television was indeed on the Kennedy team. His closing remarks were made with sincere emotion:

> There is high drama in the risks a man is asked to take to ride a rocket into space. There is high drama, too, in the risks a free nation is asked to take to publicize that effort. Today America took the gamble and America won. A failure would have been a major Cold War defeat. A victory in the full glare of publicity was a free world victory. As Cold War victories are counted, America lost a propaganda battle when Russia's Yuri Gagarin was the first man to orbit the earth. But the battle is not the war and America came back strongly today. We still have a long way to go to match the Russians and to regain superiority in space, but this was a free world victory today in the way we did the job. We didn't lose any hero pilots in premature efforts as there are some suspicions the Russians did. And so public was our effort today that the world can have no doubts that

we did it. And the man who did it was Alan Shepard, Jr. History was made today and you were an eyewitness.

Americans were now spacefaring people. And on that evening, Friday, May 5, 1961, each network broadcast a celebratory special. The following Monday morning, the Washington arrival of Alan and Louise Shepard, a reception at the White House, and a press conference were all carried live by the television networks. After presenting Commander Shepard with the Distinguished Service Medal, the President decided the astronaut and his wife should join him at his next appointment—which was to deliver the keynote address to the National Association of Broadcasters convention. The President was taking advantage of the opportunity to trumpet a triumph of a free society and to avert criticisms of his recent covert actions.

With two extra passengers, it was a crowded ride from the White House to the Sheraton Park Hotel. The President and the Shepards sat in the back seat of the limousine, while Vice-President Johnson and Newton Minow sat on jump seats. Kennedy was in a jovial mood and teased the vice-president. "Lyndon," he said, "the vice-president of the United States is the chairman of the Space Council. Nobody knows it, but I want to tell you something, Lyndon. If that space flight had been a failure, everybody would have known it." Emboldened by the high spirits, Minow continued the jest, "Mr. President, if that flight had been a failure, the vice-president would have been the next astronaut." Though Johnson was not amused, the giddiness of the moment could not be deflated.

The broadcasters enthusiastically cheered when Commander Shepard— still wearing the gold medal hanging from a blue ribbon the President had pinned on him in the Rose Garden—was introduced. The broadcasters wanted to feel that they played an important part in the victory of American prestige. They wanted to be on the team. And as the convention delegates cheered, the President must have felt relief to know that as far as the space program was concerned, television and the government were indeed on the same side.

## The Lunar Challenge

Two days after Yuri Gagarin's flight, President Kennedy met with advisors to discuss the space race. Among those included in the group were the President's special assistant Ted Sorensen, science advisor Jerome Weisner, NASA Director James Webb, NASA Deputy Administrator Hugh Dryden, and Budget Director David Bell. *Life* magazine reporter Hugh Sidey, invited to attend the meeting, recalled Kennedy asking: "Is there any place we can catch them? What can we do? Can we go around the moon before them? Can we put a man on the moon before them?"

The President was told that a crash program similar to the Manhattan Project that developed the atomic bomb—an effort that might cost $40 billion—was the only hope of catching the Soviets. And still, it was only even odds.

Five days later, April 19, the very day President Kennedy learned of the catastrophe at the Bay of Pigs, he summoned Lyndon Johnson to his office and entrusted him with the job of finding a way to land an American on the moon. Empowered as chairman of the Space Council, Johnson accepted the challenge of manned lunar landing as a political, not technical one. Overcoming legislative obstacles, not soliciting the advice of the scientific community, was the way Johnson executed the task.

Lunar exploration was not an entirely alien subject to American television. Late in 1959, the CBS series *The Twentieth Century* carried a special report on the U.S. space program entitled "Reaching for the Moon." An updated version of the same program was aired in the spring of 1960, which featured Russian plans for moon flight. Two weeks later, an NBC program, *Report from Outer Space*, included NASA officials discussing American plans for lunar exploration. Yet, most citizens thought of the earth's only known natural satellite as a mystical, romantic, or totally unreachable orb. Ralph Kramden's recurring clenched-fist threat to his long-suffering wife on *The Honeymooners* was part of the American popular lexicon—"To the moon, Alice, you're goin' to the moon."

So, when President Kennedy announced on May 25, 1961, that it was now officially national policy to send an American to the moon and return him safely to earth before the decade was out, it was as unfathomable as it was exciting. His statement was made in a televised speech before Congress on urgent national needs. It signalled full speed ahead in the space program.

Many prominent members of the scientific community, including Dr. James Killian, Jr., the former president of MIT, expressed misgivings about the quest for a spectacular space first. They knew that unmanned probes could offer valuable scientific information at a fraction of the cost of manned missions. Symbolically, though, the dividends were not nearly as great.

NASA anticipated the opposition of those who would charge the space program with wastefulness. "The money expended," James Webb pointed out in his 1962 address to the National Association of Broadcasters, "will not be fired off into space. It will be spent in the Nation's factories, work-shops, and laboratories for salaries, materials, supplies and services."

The NASA director wanted broadcasters especially to be convinced of the altruistic underpinnings of landing an American on the moon. "Some historians and psychologists see activity in space as providing a constructive substitute for war," Webb told his audience. "If men must do battle, how much more worthy of civilized nations it is to seek to conquer the hostile environment of space and leave their neighbors in peace."

The space race, Americans were encouraged to believe, was part of a much bigger contest in which every citizen was a participant. In the early 1960s, physical fitness had less to do with what would eventually be called lifestyle, and more to do with patriotic duty.

In early June 1961, President Kennedy's youngest brother Ted Kennedy appeared on the popular daytime exercise program *The Bonnie Prudden Show* to deliver a message from the New Frontier: "We have to recognize in the United States that we are in competition with the Russians not only in space, science, and education—but in physical fitness as well. We see a very strenuous program with the young people in Russia and Eastern European countries. We see workers doing calisthenics, while here in the United States we are not undertaking such programs. Only in the last few days we have seen the first American spaceman soar into space. He was selected not only because of his knowledge in science, not only because of his knowledge as an astronaut—but because he was physically fit. What we must recognize in this country is that the vigor and vitality of our nation tomorrow will depend on the physical fitness of our nation today."

The menacing presence of the Soviet Union in space was a continuing undercurrent in television reporting on the American space effort. Programs produced outside of the network news divisions, though, such as David Wolper's 1961 syndicated *Project: Man In Space*, could exercise even more pronounced dramatic license in depicting Russian designs for domination.

With ominous opening music over a huge spinning apparatus, narrator Mike Wallace informs the audience: "What you are now witnessing is not a science fiction movie. This is a centrifuge machine located at a secret training base for Russian astronauts somewhere behind the Iron Curtain." Wallace proceeds to describe the surreptitiousness of the Soviet Union in space exploration and strongly implies that Russians put less value on human life than Americans—that perhaps the lives of many cosmonauts were lost in early Russian space experimentation.

The second half of the documentary, which was billed as "the complete story," features the American space program, which began, says Wallace, in January 1958. Curiously, no mention is made of the Vanguard rocket that failed in December 1957. The announcement of the seven astronauts selected for Project Mercury in April 1959 is presented as an open statement of America's respect for individual accomplishment and worth. Bright music accompanies a scene of the Mercury 7 astronauts happily experimenting with weightlessness. *Project: Man In Space* was a program without context. It was indeed black and white—they are bad, we are good. Over and out.

## Manshoot II: A Touch of TV Fraud

Since cameras and reporters were not allowed in the NASA control center during manned flight countdowns, and since the agency reserved the right to block television's presence during the flight if communication or tracking efforts might be impeded, the television networks were permitted to take rehearsal pictures of a simulated perfect flight. This way, correspondents could describe with some accuracy what the viewers could not witness.

On the day before the scheduled suborbital launch of Virgil Grissom, who was called Gus, NASA staged such a perfect flight and the networks were there to record it. The next day, July 19, 1961, Grissom was put into the capsule named *Liberty Bell 7* and the hatch was sealed. Four hours later, NASA was still waiting for cloud cover to clear. The networks intermittently returned to the live shot from the CBS pool camera of the sedentary spacecraft. Finally, the word came from NASA that the mission was being scrubbed.

On the morning of July 21, President Kennedy watched the rescheduled launch on television. The only live pictures available to TV cameras were the blast-off and some random shots of Cape Canaveral personnel and newsmen waiting for updated information on the flight's progress. In the effort to make the coverage more interesting to home viewers, CBS and NBC used the rehearsal-flight footage, which was shot on videotape, to supplement their reports. Unlike images recorded on film, these video pictures could not be differentiated from live coverage. Both networks had advised viewers through brief announcements that the prerecorded pictures were an "exact simulation." But still, many viewers were unaware of the discrepancy. When they realized they had been fooled, a controversy ensued.

Network news officials at both organizations were contrite—claiming no intention to mislead, but admitting a greater effort to identify the material as prerecorded should have been made. Critics were especially offended at the use of scenes that showed Alan Shepard in communication with astronaut Grissom, giving the impression it was an actual conversation.

Grissom's flight ended with tense moments for NASA. The escape hatch of the capsule that would ultimately be lost opened prematurely. As water poured in, the astronaut was forced to abandon the craft and keep himself afloat until he could be picked up by the rescue helicopter.

While the audience hoped to hear the news of Grissom's safe recovery, NBC showed prerecorded footage of a helicopter approaching the carrier, giving some viewers the impression the waiting was over. Minutes later, the network explained that what was seen was not the real event.

The issue of fakery brought back unpleasant memories of the quiz show scandals and the networks were eager to nip this new fuss in the bud. "We won't do it again, folks" was the headline *Broadcasting* magazine ran over the item that reported more care would be taken in the future to avoid confusion between live coverage and prerecorded material.

An American chimpanzee named Enos twice orbited the earth on November 29, 1961. NASA's experiment was launched while President Kennedy was conducting a televised press conference. The Chief Executive interrupted the proceedings when he received word that the simian dress rehearsal was underway. "The chimpanzee who is flying in space took off at 10:08," Kennedy announced. "He reports that everything is perfect and working well."

## Pulling Out All the Stops:
## The Astronomical Cost of Covering John Glenn

Other than the loss of the capsule, the success of Gus Grissom's flight— along with the safe return of Enos—reduced NASA's conviction that any more manned suborbital flights were necessary before an American could actually circle the earth in space. The fact that Russian cosmonaut Gherman Titov successfully completed a 17-orbit mission just sixteen days after the launch of Grissom's *Liberty Bell 7* added urgency to the goal.

The third manned flight in the Mercury program was going to be a triple orbital mission. The United States would still be second in the space race, but was moving into tagging distance.

Newton Minow and each of the FCC commissioners were among the government officials who received a telegram of invitation from Frank Stanton, the president of CBS, to view the final launch preparations from a specially equipped CBS monitoring center in Washington that would be linked to Cape Canaveral by closed circuit. Invited guests were told the center's multiple monitors would simultaneously show the three television networks as well as the pool coverage. Their presence, the invitation indicated, was welcome beginning at 4:30 A.M.

The networks, engaged in FCC program hearings at the time, wanted to bolster the image of commercial broadcasting in government circles. As flight preparations were being finalized at Cape Canaveral, FCC commissioners were being reminded that the profits of entertainment television allowed public service programming to take on contemporary challenges. The coverage of John Glenn's mission was being held up as a shining example of the responsibility to the American people the networks willingly assumed.

After ten flight postponements, which represented the loss of thousands of personnel hours for the networks and prevented the deployment of tons of equipment to other programming, February 20, 1962, was the day American television, in partnership with NASA, devoted itself totally to the modern national purpose.

The three networks signed on with their coverage at 6:30 in the morning. For the next eleven-and-a-half hours there was only the story of John Glenn on the air. The A.C. Nielsen Company estimated that, ultimately, 40 million households were tuned in to the coverage for an average of five hours and fifteen minutes, by far the largest audience ever assembled for daytime television. But millions of additional viewers were not watching on home receivers; they were gathered at school and work and in public places. It was a social ritual at once primordial and contemporary.

The normal routines of American life were suspended for the day. In stores and restaurants and hospitals and courtrooms and government offices, people were preoccupied with the TV screen. A total of more than 135 million American viewers followed some part of the event. In Catholic schools children clutched rosary beads during the countdown. In public schools noisier demonstrations accompanied the sound of lift-off.

In Grand Central Station an estimated 10,000 people stood statically in the central mezzanine riveted to an 11-by-14-foot TV screen, provided by CBS, that hung above the ticket windows. The silence that fell over the crowd in the thirty seconds before zero soon changed into a cheering roar. Tears were wiped from overflowing eyes and signs of the cross were made unselfconsciously.

Throughout the four hours and fifty-six minutes it took John Glenn to go three times around the world, TV viewers were kept abreast of the location of *Friendship 7* by pinpointed maps. They also heard recorded exchanges between the astronaut and ground stations in Africa, Australia, and Cape Canaveral, including the American hero's thank-you to the people of Perth, Australia, for turning on their lights to give him a beautiful view.

Simulations explaining flight logistics were labelled prominently—sometimes comically. "Who in his right mind could fail to recognize an animation?" asked one TV reporter in response to ABC's disclaimer caption attending animated segments.

As reentry time approached and the TV audience swelled to the largest of the day, the networks could already take pride in their virtuoso performance—but an enormous amount of coverage was still to come. After Glenn's recovery, there were interviews with his family, President Kennedy's call of congratulations, the NASA press conference at Cape Canaveral, and the comprehensive evening summaries to cap the dazzling day.

The next morning the networks continued to tell the story of the first American in orbit. The NBC *Today* show, for instance, provided the first look at films of Glenn taken in flight. The program also carried person-on-the-street reaction interviews, a report on the astronaut's physical condition, and interviews with NASA officials.

After only a two-day respite of normal programming schedules, the networks were back to live special-event coverage on Friday, February 23. John Glenn's triumphant return to Cape Canaveral to receive the Distinguished Service Medal from President Kennedy was a TV homecoming.

The astronaut had a gift for the Commander in Chief—a commemorative hard hat with the inscription "First U. S. Manned Orbital Flight, J. F. Kennedy, President USA." "This will make him an honorary member of the launch crew," Glenn said, and then started to put the hat on the head of the President who simply never tolerated souvenir hats. But a hero the magnitude of John Glenn could not be rebuffed. So, in an awkward instant, the President took the hat from the guest of honor, put it on and then took it off in the wink of an eye.

Television viewers were also able to mingle with the vice-president and the astronaut's family before the official ceremony began. "He's a television star, this fellow is," Lyndon Johnson said jocularly to Glenn's mother about her boy John, as cameras surrounded them.

Two weeks before the flight of *Friendship 7*, John Glenn visited President Kennedy in the White House. He remarked to the President that he was troubled by the great deal of personal publicity that astronauts received from the American media. In his case, even his wife's hairstyle was an issue. The President, who knew about such matters, expressed his belief that public interest about the personal lives of the astronauts had to be accommodated to a reasonable extent. Humanizing space travel, the President believed, was a good thing. John Kennedy understood that to the American public, Project Mercury was more about people than science.

Possibly reflecting on that conversation, the President said hyperbolically as he prepared to pin the medal on the astronaut: "The hazards of space flight only begin when the trip is over—and now that Col. Glenn has been launched into public orbit, we are proud of him, as we are all the other astronauts and those who are connected with this great effort."

After introducing John Glenn's wife and children on the dais, Kennedy pointed out the proud parents in the audience and added impishly, "We have Mr. and Mrs. Glenn, who launched Col. Glenn originally. . . . "

The networks then gave full coverage to the astronaut's first post-flight news conference, in which he displayed a gift for precise and heartfelt expression. Glenn discussed eating in outer space, speed sensations, and the brilliantly colored beauty of multiple sunsets as viewed from orbital flight.

Another break of two days allowed the networks to regroup their pooled resources to cover live John Glenn's trip to Washington on Monday, February 26. Rain made the task a little more troublesome for the technical crews, but it did not prevent a jubilant parade through the Capital.

Following the damp celebration, Col. Glenn appeared before a joint session of Congress, which included the Cabinet and the Supreme Court. Earlier in the day, when Glenn was leaving Palm Beach, Florida, with President Kennedy, Jacqueline Kennedy brought Caroline to meet the hero astronaut. Caroline curtsied politely, looked up at Glenn and asked, "Where's the monkey?" The child apparently had heard about the earlier unmanned mission. On the flight to Washington, Glenn asked the President if he would have any objection to his using the anecdote in that afternoon's speech. Kennedy, knowing the public relations value for both of them, laughed at his daughter's innocent faux pas and agreed Glenn should use it.

A hero's welcome ticker-tape parade in New York was scheduled for Thursday, March 1 and, again, the networks decided they had to be there. But this time, a competing story created an ironic juxtaposition. With most available remote equipment tied up on the parade route and at the Waldorf, the site of a luncheon celebration, a Boeing 707 jet crashed at Idlewild airport. Ninety-five passengers and crew members perished.

NBC diverted one of its non-pool cameras from Glenn coverage to the air tragedy. CBS threatened to pull one of its units from the Glenn parade route if NBC didn't make the crash footage available to them. NBC relented, making the pictures available to CBS and ABC as well. Testing the limits of cooperation, the networks were relieved when John Glenn's flight finally entered the annals of history.

Self-congratulation seemed to be perfectly appropriate. NBC took out a full-page ad in *Variety* with the headline "THE HEARTBEAT HEARD 'ROUND THE WORLD." The copy included this passage: "The National Broadcasting Company shares with the other networks its pride in broadcasting's finest achievement, and congratulates them on their contribution. We salute the 180 broadcast reporters and technicians who conducted the combined network pool coverage, as well as our own staff of 200 who were responsible for the special NBC coverage supplementing pool activities."

As the bills came in and the accounting took place, the trade press reported that with the John Glenn story television covered itself simultaneously in glory and red ink. Even though commercial breaks were included during lulls in network coverage, the advertising revenue didn't begin to meet expenses.

"How many John Glenns can television afford?" was the question being asked as the networks looked ahead to the next manned space flight, scheduled to take place in about eight weeks. Cost-cutting strategies and modified coverage plans were key agenda items in the network news bureau business meetings.

The adulation of John Glenn by the American people was in large measure fostered by television's unlimited attention to his heroic achievement. The networks were absolute team players. Eight days after his orbital flight, John Glenn appeared as a star witness at the Senate Subcommittee hearings in which NASA presented its 1963 budget request—which was double the 1962 budget. It was hard to deny that television was a major factor in enabling NASA and the Kennedy administration to garner the support needed to meet their goals in space.

## The Space Age Rage in Entertainment Television

During the Kennedy years, themes of outer space became commonplace in every type of television program. On variety shows, comedian Bill Dana was going gangbusters with his Jose Jimenez routine. It took an absurd situation to ridiculous heights—a Mexican elevator operator reluctantly thrust into the role of astronaut. "My name Jose Jimenez," the line that introduced each performance of the act, caught on as a catchphrase. Its exaggerated repetition was guaranteed to provoke hilarity among any group of Americans hip to the schtick—including the American astronauts who playfully indulged Alan Shepard in his fondness to mimic the gags he'd heard on TV.

Situation comedies were especially inclined to take up the out-of-this-world motif. Mr. Ed was not only a talking horse, but, in one episode, was selected to be the first equine astronaut. On *Leave It to Beaver*, in an episode called "Stocks and Bonds," Eddie Haskell gives some financial advice to the Cleaver boys. Avoid safe and traditional investments in favor of high technology companies, he tells them. When Beaver questions this wisdom, Eddie chastises him: "This is the Space Age, kid. Where have you been? This is the Space Age. You can get in on the ground floor—before they blast off." Buying into Eddie's logic, Wally later explains to his dad why Mayfield Electric and Light is a stock for squares, "I mean, after all, we're not going to the moon on electricity."

Dramatic series too tapped the public's fascination with the space program. In the spring of 1962, for instance, Perry Mason became involved in "The Case of the Angry Astronaut." Not only the career of Mason's client, but the whole moon project stalls with the murder of its chief officer. In a 1963 episode of *Dr. Kildare*, a patient at Blair General is the uncle of the next American astronaut to be launched into orbit. The young hero is adopted by the lonely patients on his uncle's ward. They all watch the coverage on the TV set in the hospital lounge and are held in anxious suspense as the astronaut experiences difficulty in repositioning the capsule for reentry into the earth's atmosphere. A daytime dramatic series, *The Clear Horizon*, appeared on CBS. The soap revolved around the personal and professional lives of a young Air Force wife and her husband, an officer involved in missile research at Cape Canaveral.

And, the animated series that has become symbolic of the space age, *The Jetsons*, first appeared in the fall of 1962. The day-to-day life of a typical family in the twenty-first century was a comic prophesy. The culmination of space exploration might result in humanity's total mastery of technology—but human foibles can never be conquered and human nature can never be changed.

## More Happy Endings

Deke Slayton was the next of the seven Mercury astronauts scheduled for space flight in the spring of 1962. But an erratic heartbeat grounded the disappointed Air Force major and Scott Carpenter got the nod.

As with John Glenn's mission, three earth orbits were planned. But unlike the smooth flight of *Friendship 7, Aurora 7* would encounter serious difficulties and television correspondents were forced to ponder how they might deliver unspeakably bad news.

The May 24 launch and first two orbits went off as scripted. A developing nonchalance about space travel among television viewers seemed to be an inevitable reaction to America's successes. But an incipient uneasiness was felt when a fuel shortage threatened cancellation of the third orbit. The OK was finally given for Carpenter to circle the earth once more. As he prepared for reentry, however, the capsule began tumbling. When communication between the astronaut and NASA was lost, for many viewers, the uneasiness became full-blown fear.

For almost an hour, the networks had no encouraging information to report and commentators were left by NASA to their own judgments on the situation. "I'm afraid," Walter Cronkite concluded on the air, "we may have lost an astronaut." Before word came that *Aurora 7* had overshot its splashdown target by 250 miles and that Carpenter had been located by a reconnaissance plane, NBC unwisely returned to regular network programming—and took the heat for the decision.

Since post-flight activities and the ceremonial celebrations honoring Carpenter were not covered live by the networks, the TV tab was not nearly as high as it was for John Glenn. Still, the trade press reported before all the accounting was completed, "The video webs may have dropped another $1,000,000 or so doing the coverage of the Scott Carpenter orbital flight." But prestige was what they bought along with "the good it might do on the Washington front by keeping some of the solons relatively happy."

Before the summer of 1962 ended, the Russians pulled another tremendous rabbit out of their space helmet. On August 11, the USSR launched *Vostok 3* and on the next day they launched *Vostok 4*. When the double mission ended on August 15, American newscasts were relaying flight statistics that dumbfounded viewers. One cosmonaut had logged 94 hours and 35 minutes in space and had orbited the earth 64 times. The other spent 70 hours in space and completed 48 orbits. The equipment and the men functioned flawlessly. Two days later the CBS series *Eyewitness to History* broadcast "The Falcon and the Eagle," the story of the Soviet heroes and of the profound human accomplishment. Tagging distance was slipping out of reach.

President Kennedy wanted to define ultimate victory in the space race in American terms: The first one with a man *on* the moon was to be the real winner. In this contest, America was still a contender. The President's September 1962 tour of four space installations was primarily devoted to the justification of billions of American dollars to be expended in the Lunar Challenge.

At Rice University in Houston, the President conceded to a stadium audience of 50,000 that NASA's $5 billion space budget was a "staggering sum." But he put the amount in perspective by noting it was somewhat less than Americans "pay for cigars and cigarettes every year."

By the time the fifth American in space, Wally Schirra, was launched on October 3, 1962, Americans were starting to feel less compelled by the very act of space travel and a touch complacent about the country's ability to return astronauts safely to earth.

Schirra's six orbits would keep him in space for more than nine hours, but to most citizens there was a routine feel about the flight. There was nothing routine, however, about the television image of the blast-off. For this mission the networks had access to a new photographic system. An electronic camera developed by the Bendix corporation was mated with a giant Air Force research telescope. Up until this process was available, television had only been able to follow space shots for the few seconds after the rocket lifted from the launching pad. The new Bendix camera was able to follow a rocket as it traveled across scores of miles. Viewers could actually spot the disengagement of *Sigma 7*.

A week before the launch, CBS had announced that it would cover the takeoff but not maintain continuous coverage. Rather, it would intermingle frequent progress reports with regular programming. Relieved of the pressure to compete with constant coverage, ABC too adopted this plan. NBC appreciated the relaxation of coverage because the network would look less delinquent for broadcasting, as planned, the first game of the 1962 World Series.

As it turned out, Schirra went into space on the same day the Dodgers met the Giants in a play-off game to break a tie in the National League pennant race. The textbook flight presented no complications to report. NBC superimposed flight updates across the bottom of the screen. The message that the astronaut had made a safe reentry was flashed while Maury Wills threatened to steal second base.

With 1962 drawing to a close, a graduate student at the University of Wisconsin at Madison was conducting a detailed survey of the Cape Canaveral press corps. The actual responses of the print, broadcast, and wire service correspondents—sealed in NASA Public Information Center files for more than twenty-five years—offer contemporaneous insight into the media coverage of the Mercury program.

A sense of pride in the openness of the American mission was apparent among the respondents. "The record shows," wrote one, "that by boldly opening its manned space flights to coverage, the United States has gained great respect around the world." Others commented: "A free society carries out its rituals in open." "Public policy is not served by secrecy and concealment." "The American way is to deal above the table."

Serious complaints about the way NASA handled the media did, nonetheless, surface. Primarily charges by print journalists of the agency's favoritism—in the person of Shorty Powers—toward television:

> This is show-biz to Shorty, I am convinced.
>
> Obviously he must hold court to the "big ones" of TV because of *their* power with Washington.
>
> I think most newsmen are agreed that Shorty shows preference for the television people.
>
> Certain TV people have been much more successful in getting what they want from him than other media people generally.
>
> Powers has favored the TV networks over the press.
>
> (There was) specific favoritism to old friends such as Roy Neal of NBC.
>
> He favored the television medium over the written word.
>
> (There were) an unusual number of "beats" scored by TV.
>
> At the Cape, TV types were permitted to use their own cars to come and go and were given information not given to other news types.
>
> Powers gravitates to a TV camera like a moth to a light bulb.

Despite the favored treatment television purportedly enjoyed, the networks protested vigorously in the spring of 1963 when NASA insisted that its own video unit would produce the pre-flight reports on the experiments Major L. Gordon Cooper would conduct during his 22-orbit, 34-hour flight. The network pool producer for the Cooper flight, Sid Darion of ABC, urged NASA to allow the networks to tape the experiments individually. But the agency insisted that either the NASA tapes were used or no coverage would be available at all.

The spat, though, did not seriously disrupt the team. The sentiment expressed in the broadcast procedures manual previously given to new reporters at Cape Canaveral was still operational: "From each of us who has worked here before—welcome and we hope you will join us in the pride we have always felt in being part of America's space effort."

On May 15, 1963, the journey of *Faith 7* received full television coverage before and during the launch and before and during splashdown. In the interim, numerous updates were broadcast and flash reports were superimposed over regular programming.

Broadcast history was made on the flight when the first live telecast of an astronaut in orbit was transmitted to home screens. Eleven times during the mission, grainy video images of astronaut Cooper, taken by a two-and-a-half pound slow-scan camera, were sent to earth.

Gordon Cooper's success in space brought the Mercury program to a close. Americans looked forward to the Gemini phase of U.S. space exploration, which would take the nation closer to the moon. On the last full day of his life, John Kennedy looked forward to the 1990s. He spoke in Houston, soon to be the home of a huge space center. For the sake of the next generation, he was determined "to make sure that in this great new sea—as on earth—the United States is second to none."

In the final hours of the New Frontier, outer space seemed to be an environment friendly to the American cause. To the scientific layperson, U.S. astronauts appeared to be protected by the virtue of their peaceful intentions. Television's six happy endings made the invulnerability of American heroes feel like an actual fact. No one wanted to believe that eventually, inevitably, victims would be claimed.

# CHAPTER 6

# Adventures in Reporting

## TELEVISION DOCUMENTARIES

When Edward R. Murrow delivered his signature sign off—"Good night . . . And good luck"—at the close of a *See It Now* documentary in the 1950s, attentive viewers knew what they were supposed to think. Their correspondent had taken them through a carefully constructed discussion of the issue at hand and led them to a summary conclusion. Encircled with the smoke from his omnipresent cigarette, Murrow was the voice of authority and *See It Now* was the model for serious television documentaries. The radio tradition, with the primacy of the written word, penetrated television documentaries throughout the 1950s.

While few in the broadcast industry questioned the patterns and limitations of American television documentaries, a *Life* magazine reporter and editor named Bob Drew gave deep thought to the subject while he spent a year at Harvard as a Nieman Fellow in the mid-1950s. It was the heavy use of narration in documentary films that troubled him. Drew wanted to lift the form above the realm of illustrated lecture.

Returning to his home base at Time-Life, Inc., after his time at Harvard, Drew experimented for a few years with motion-picture photojournalism and successfully captured highly visual subjects. His short film on NASA's tests on weightlessness, for instance, appeared on both *The Ed Sullivan Show* and the CBS news.

In early 1960, the Time-Life company offered to support Drew's efforts to develop more mobile, lightweight film equipment if he would work with the Time-owned television stations in cultivating their documentary offerings. With a pared-down TV news film camera patched to a one-quarter-inch sound tape recorder, Drew and his team were ready to try their hands at a new style of documentary filmmaking at precisely the same time John

Kennedy was ready to experiment himself with political communication in the new decade.

Time-Life had OK'd the idea of a film about the decision-making process in the Wisconsin presidential primary of 1960. At first, the senator from Massachusetts was skeptical when Drew and his associate, filmmaker Ricky Leacock, told him they wanted to record history in the making. The pair wanted Kennedy's permission to film in his hotel room while he listened to election returns.

Drew and Leacock flew to Detroit, where Kennedy was campaigning, but he couldn't talk to them there. So the two men boarded the candidate's private plane in hopes of having their discussion in the air. Kennedy never got around to it.

The next day the pair visited his home in Georgetown. "He had a cold," Leacock recalled, "that's what saved us." The candidate, in his pajamas and with his daughter running about, listened as Leacock said, "Look, I want to be with you alone. No interview, no questions, no lights, no tripods, no cables—just me and my camera want to be in your suite in Wisconsin when you listen to the election results." "That's a very personal situation," Kennedy replied, "you could make me look very silly." "Essentially, you have to trust me or you don't trust me," Leacock told the candidate. "That's it." Kennedy thought for a minute and said, "If you do not hear to the contrary, you can assume that you can do it."

Drew and Leacock didn't hear to the contrary—and they did it . . . along with Donn Pennebaker, Albert Maysles, and Terrence McCartney Filgate. The equipment they used was unique in early 1960. "Nobody else had it," Leacock said. "Everybody else was working with cameras stuck on tripods and all those goddam cables and things. We could go running and jumping and wiggling all over the place. . . . Nobody else could do this."

With *Primary* the Drew team introduced a style of unscripted documentary known as cinema verite to American television and gave viewers candid and intimate glimpses of their next president. Though *Primary* didn't air on network television, rather on just the four local stations owned by Time, Inc., it was a landmark piece of work not only for its innovation in technique, but perhaps more important, for its impact on John F. Kennedy's thinking about television.

After the election, Bob Drew visited the president-elect in Palm Beach, Florida, to show him *Primary*. Watching the film, Kennedy saw himself banter with kids and sign autographs for a crowd. The rigors of campaigning came back to him as *Primary* showed candidate Kennedy shaking hands with early shift workers at the factory gate. He witnessed the excited anticipation of a throng of people at Milwaukee's Serb Hall moments before he arrived. The president-elect observed the chemical reaction that took place in the room the instant he appeared. Women in babushkas swooned and, as he passed, everyone in proximity reached out for him. He saw his wife's delicate beauty fill the screen as she spoke briefly to the group. A close-up of Jacqueline Kennedy twisting her gloved fingers behind her back gently betrayed her discomfort. Kennedy studied the scene in the Wisconsin hotel room waiting for results. He observed himself under stress. He saw his characteristic nervous tapping and watched himself react as precinct reports came in.

Both John and Jacqueline Kennedy thought *Primary* was terrific. They were very impressed with the work of Bob Drew. Through the candid lens the president-elect realized, without vanity, how enormously attractive he was and how effectively moving images conveyed his rapport with the people.

The next night, the young filmmaker again visited the young chief executive-to-be. Drew showed Kennedy a film he had made on Latin America called *Yanki, No!* This program, which aired on ABC as part of the *Bell & Howell Close-Up!* series in early December 1960, was rife with haunting images. The abject poverty of the region was humanized through the stories of individual families. The lure of communism in offering to meet basic needs seemed reasonable in the context depicted in *Yanki, No!* Kennedy was distressed at the visual evidence of the overwhelming scope of the problem faced by the United States in dealing with Latin America. (It was also during this transition period in Palm Beach that the president-elect would be briefed by the CIA on the plans for its invasion of Cuba by Cuban exiles in an attempt to depose Castro.)

In *Primary* Kennedy saw himself as a leader with the innate ability to move people. The next night, in *Yanki, No!* he observed, at close range, the magnetism of Fidel Castro as he addressed a rally of one million people in Havana. It was a portentous juxtaposition.

Through the voice of a translator, the president-elect heard Castro say "before America and the world" that the dictator was "grateful for and accepts the help of Soviet rockets should Cuban territory be invaded by military forces from the United States." Unlike a written or oral report from an administrative aide, the film allowed Kennedy to see the enormity of the crowd and feel its passion for Castro. Kennedy could look into the eyes of his future nemesis and contemplate what kind of showdown might be looming.

After the viewing and discussion of *Yanki, No!*, Bob Drew and John Kennedy got to talking about Drew's innovations in documentary technique. Sync sound would facilitate a new form of history, the filmmaker told the president-elect. Kennedy agreed that the ability to record what happens as it happens could be a profound historical tool. "Think of what it would be like," Kennedy said, "if I could see what happened in the White House twenty-four hours before Roosevelt declared war on Japan." He was thinking of documentation different from official papers or posed photographs. Kennedy was imagining a film record that would provide the real looks on people's faces and their tone of voice.

Drew told the president-elect that he wanted to try to make such a document in the Kennedy White House. "I told him," Drew recalled of the meeting, "that when he moved into the White House that I'd like to move in with him, with two film teams. One with him on the business side and one with his wife on the home side." Drew remembered, "He liked the idea and called his wife over and sort of outlined the idea to her." Even though Jacqueline Kennedy appreciated the artistry of *Primary*, she wanted nothing to do with Drew's new idea. "Nobody is going to move into the White House with me," she told her husband. The filmmaker remembers the president-elect saying, to reassure his very private spouse, "Of course not, of course not. We're just thinking. . . . "

After his wife left the room, the president-elect said to the filmmaker, "Alright, let's try the office side. Not right away—but after I've been in office a few weeks why don't you come down and see if I can do it." Kennedy wasn't certain the experiment would work. "If I can actually lose consciousness of the camera and it doesn't intrude, we might be able to do something. If the camera is bothersome then we can't. But we could try it."

A short time after Drew's conversation with Kennedy in Palm Beach, ABC called Drew to a meeting with Bell & Howell, the sponsor of the *Bell & Howell Close-Up!* documentary series. Another producer, John Secondari, who headed the documentary unit at ABC, was also there. Drew was surprised and somewhat uncomfortable when he realized the meeting was a competition for a film assignment.

Secondari outlined his project, which Drew recalls had something to do with sewage treatment plants. "Bob, what have you got?" he was asked. "Well," said Drew, "I would like to make a film about the inauguration and I already have an arrangement to be with the Kennedys in the White House." Drew was given the assignment without delay.

Everyone wanted to get close to John Kennedy and each network wanted to provide that opportunity through documentary programming. After his happy experience with *Primary*, Kennedy was not nearly as reticent as might have been prudent for a new chief executive. George Herman of CBS recalled: "Very early on in the Kennedy administration I applied to Pierre Salinger for permission to have what we call a walking sound camera—two men, a sound man and a cameraman walking with equipment that they could walk around with in the President's office and make a sound film of him at work. . . . And Pierre Salinger, to my complete astonishment, after consulting with the President, came back and said, yes, this would be acceptable." CBS, as did Bob Drew, agreed to the condition that the White House would be allowed to review the program for sensitive security material.

On February 17, 1961, CBS aired an installment of the *Eyewitness to*

*History* series entitled "Kennedy Close-Up." Walter Cronkite's opening narration promised "a view of the President of the United States you have never seen before." In the next half-hour the audience saw footage and shot composition that was uncharacteristically rough for CBS News.

Kennedy was seen waiting for a call from Adlai Stevenson on the crisis in the Congo, visiting with the governor of West Virginia, and in a session with government agency chiefs and White House staff to discuss budget issues. In closing, Cronkite reminded his audience it was a privileged view: "Our eyewitness cameras were on the scene moving about the room for these informal views—the first time television has ever been permitted in the office of the president during the actual conduct of official business. . . . A president at work, viewed for the first time tonight in close-up. And you were there, an eyewitness to history."

Later in the month NBC aired the first of a series called *JFK Reports*. The producer, Shad Northshield recalled, "The idea was that in the New Deal days, Roosevelt made some enormous changes in the first forty days. So, this seemed to be a good idea. In the first forty days of the Kennedy administration, he did absolutely nothing. But, because of my extensive show business experience, I was able to do a one-hour show. . . . It was a puff. It had nothing to say except that this beautiful young man was president."

"JFK Report No. 1" was not an attempt at cinema verite, but rather a traditional documentary report with an emphasis on the President's life and career. It featured the striking still photography of Jacques Lowe which gave an intimate aura. The President liked the show very much and Northshield recalled: "I was summoned to the White House to discuss documentaries. After that meeting, forty-five minutes or so with him, he said, 'Why don't you have an interview with me next time?' "

Several weeks later, "JFK Report No. 2," which was a far more hard-hitting piece of journalism, did include the suggested interview with President Kennedy. In the Cabinet Room correspondent Ray Scherer discussed the duties of the members of the White House staff with the President. At the conclusion of the talk the reporter said, "We think you're very gracious for making yourself so available. If it isn't entirely irrelevant, may I ask you this—Why did you make yourself so available to us?"

The President—who had given thought to how television documentaries could be used to educate citizens and generate more effective government—replied: "The presidency is an office, which in a sense, is shared in by all the people. So, I would say the more we can communicate successfully beyond the White House and the more we can take back, the more effective this office will be administered—so that everybody has a piece of the White House. Everybody's lives and security are affected by the judgments which are made, inevitably, here. And I think everybody ought to know about it as much as possible."

In late March 1961, ABC's *Bell & Howell Close-Up!* presented the film Bob Drew and John Kennedy first discussed in Palm Beach. It was called "Adventures in Reporting: Adventures on the New Frontier." The voice-over introduction, written by Drew, promised, as did the earlier CBS program, that the viewer would get closer to the Chief Executive than ever imagined: "Now you will begin to move with the President—seeing and hearing for yourself, in a new kind of report—not a filmed version of summary and opinion you can find in print, but rather a personal adventure with the President as he confronts great problems of the U.S. and the world."

"Adventures on the New Frontier" was a more intimate document than CBS's "Kennedy Close-Up." Both, however, were criticized for being surface presentations meant to satisfy curiosity about the man, rather than being firsthand lessons in government. A columnist for *The New Republic* inaccurately predicted, "I think the networks may yet turn the glamorous JFK into the nation's number one bore."

In "Adventures on the New Frontier" viewers catch glimpses of the President in a workaday routine, sometimes chewing the arm of his eyeglasses or pacing in thought. Speaking into the Dictaphone he says, "Ah . . . This is a memorandum to David Bell, Bureau of the Budget. . . . " Most of the audience is, of course, less interested in the subject of the memo than in seeing the milieu in which the Chief Executive operates.

Later in the film the President's sisters interrupt their brother at work at his desk to ask if he would autograph some photos. Quickly accommodating the request, Kennedy says, "Well, listen, have a good trip," as the women take their leave. In a meeting on the economy, the President and Walter Heller share a belly laugh over an inside joke. The audience never learns the source of the amusement, but the fun of the moment is, nevertheless, delightful. Several minutes of footage from *Primary* were also woven into "Adventures on the New Frontier," thereby exposing a much larger audience to the first cinema verite images of John Kennedy.

Before "Adventures on the New Frontier" aired on ABC, Bob Drew took the film to the White House to show the President. If Kennedy had said something in the program that he felt compromised the presidency or would undermine a negotiation, he could ask that it be deleted from the sound track. This was the exchange for being allowed to shoot in the Oval Office. Drew recalls setting the film up in Pierre Salinger's office late one evening: "We sat down and looked at it," and when it was over Kennedy "stood up, smiled, and walked out." The filmmaker had the impression the President was pleased with what he had seen. No deletions were requested.

"Adventures on the New Frontier," though, was not a film that satisfied Bob Drew's desire to develop a new form of history. He knew that to create a revelatory moving image document, he would have to have access to the President during a time of crisis—when the Chief Executive's back was to the wall and he was making decisions under pressure. There would be no shortage of such times in the Kennedy White House, but in the heat of various crises the President did not accede to Drew's requests for entry to the Oval Office.

Finally, though, a situation emerged in the spring of 1963 that would allow the group known as Drew Associates to create a television documentary that captured the most humane and moral qualities of the New Frontier, and would become a permanent reference point in the legacy of the Kennedy administration.

## The Documentary Age

During the 1961–62 television season, the three networks broadcast a combined 254 hours of documentary programming. This remains the peak of documentary presentation for the entire history of American television.

Of course, many factors contributed to the great number of documentaries aired in the Kennedy years. The quiz show and payola scandals that rocked the broadcast industry as the 1950s came to a close led to more public service programming by the networks in an attempt to mollify the civic, religious, and educational constituencies offended by the fraud. This circumstance, combined with the more vigorous look of the FCC after Chairman John Doerfer's resignation in the spring of 1960, created the incentive for the networks to remain committed to documentary series already on the air and to plan for new projects.

But, still, the possibility of the FCC truly adopting punitive regulations seemed relatively remote until the appointment of Newton Minow. It was a new ball game then; the unwritten rules seemed to change. Who knew what his intentions actually were?

After the Vast Wasteland speech, the amount of documentary programming that erupted on American television was phenomenal. Following a stern word from the chairman about affiliate stations not clearing their networks' public affairs efforts, many local stations quickly changed their ways. For instance, the increase in clearances for *CBS Reports* jumped from 115 to 140 stations. And, in addition to increasing the clearance of network documentaries, there was a surge in the production of local documentary programming.

Independent documentary filmmakers and production companies found themselves in great demand. David Wolper, a young man whose Wolper Productions experienced a growth spurt in 1961, explained his good fortune: "Maybe we should thank Newton Minow for a fine publicity job on our behalf."

At the networks, the ranks of documentary and public affairs units swelled. Producer Shad Northshield recalled: "When I came to work at NBC News, which was early in 1961, I was the fourth producer in the News Division.

There was Reuven (Frank), Lou Hazam, and Chet Hagan, and I was the kid. By the end of that year there were twenty-eight. It had increased more than seven-fold."

Coincident with Minow's documentary push was a trend toward greater advertiser support of non-entertainment programming. In 1961 NBC enjoyed the patronage of a dozen advertisers for public affairs programming, compared to three such sponsors in 1960.

Documentary producer Lou Hazam contemplated the climate for documentaries in the early 1960s in the pages of *Television Quarterly*. In addition to "a friendly Mr. Minow," Hazam identified "intelligent sponsors" as a major component in the formula for success: "Who would have believed only a few years ago that we would ever be given $100,000 to produce a television documentary? . . . Not so long ago, even a prayer couldn't unearth a sponsor for a TV documentary."

The variety of nonfiction programming broadcast in the early 1960s was as impressive as its quantity. Naturally, not all documentaries were investigations of contemporary issues. A number of compilation documentary series used archival sources and newsreel footage to provide weekly history lessons to American viewers. *The Twentieth Century*, hosted by Walter Cronkite on CBS, for example, was the paragon of the genre. Events and personalities that shaped the modern world were explored in finely crafted thirty-minute programs with original musical scores. On ABC, *Winston Churchill—The Valiant Years*, a series based on the statesman's memoirs, chronicled the years leading into and during World War II.

The broad patterns of American art and culture were considered in series such as *Accent* on CBS. The first broadcast in February 1961, entitled "Robert Frost: An American Poet," included a four-minute appearance by President Kennedy in which he discussed the invigorating role of the artist in American life. Three weeks later, Jacqueline Kennedy appeared briefly on an *Accent* program which was a tribute to the National Gallery of Art on the occasion of its twentieth anniversary.

Biographical documentaries were the theme of the NBC series *The World of . . .* , which ran from October 1961 through April 1963. "The World of Jacqueline Kennedy" installment featured interviews with Leonard Bernstein, Oleg Cassini, and Eleanor Roosevelt. The CBS series *Portrait* consisted of informal visits with people of various walks of life to discuss their experiences and personal philosophies. The first guest highlighted on the series was Pierre Salinger.

Another style of documentary series was the commentary show built around a single personality. *David Brinkley's Journal*, for instance, was produced for NBC by Ted Yates and Stuart Schulberg. The second program in the series entitled "Maybe Crime Does Pay," broadcast in October 1961, featured a discussion with Attorney General Robert Kennedy on legal loopholes that make crime profitable. Brinkley pointed out that some notorious criminals "are not in jail, they're here," as the picture showed lavish mansions in Grosse Pointe, Michigan. He provided the residents' names and indicated their specialties, whether narcotics or counterfeiting.

Bob Rogers was a young associate on the series at the time. He recalled that the President's brother "encouraged us—and that's an understatement—to undertake programs revealing the evils, as he saw it, of certain portions of the Labor Movement. One of the results was an hour special, which was quite good, called 'Inside Jimmy Hoffa.' " The program Robert Kennedy lobbied for aired on *David Brinkley's Journal* on April 1, 1963.

Another notable nonfiction series in this form was ABC's *Howard K. Smith—News and Comment.* In October 1961, Smith resigned his post as a Washington correspondent with CBS News in a dispute over the fine line between editorial comment and analysis. Newton Minow, who was supportive of the outspoken newsman, received a note of thanks from Smith a few weeks after his departure from CBS. "Don't let up on the bastards," Smith wrote to the aggressive chairman, referring to the television networks. "They nearly monopolize the common people's culture and they are not doing a good job of it."

Smith's new series on ABC was meant to be provocative and often stirred controversy. And none was more resounding than after the November 1962 broadcast of "The Political Obituary of Richard M. Nixon." Following Nixon's defeat in the 1962 gubernatorial race in California, the program attempted to assess the career and future of the politician. One of those interviewed was Alger Hiss, a former State Department official who was linked with communist espionage in a case developed by Nixon for a Congressional investigation. Hiss was ultimately convicted of perjury before the House Committee. His remarks in the program called Nixon's sincerity and objectivity into question.

Many viewers found Smith's invitation to Alger Hiss to serve as a character witness for Nixon to be reprehensible. But, the FCC, urged to take action against ABC, supported the privilege of documentarians to exercise editorial judgment—as the agency had on other occasions. Minow's response stated, "The right and duty of broadcasters to present all sides of controversial issues freely and courageously must be kept secure."

Each week *Eyewitness to History* on CBS devoted thirty minutes to a single subject of immediate news value, such as "Jackie's Journey to India," which detailed the goodwill tour of the first lady. This series, though—which exploited the most advanced video technology available—was more in the mode of breaking news or the instant special, rather than reflective documentary. And, for each of the three summers of the New Frontier, the ABC News department presented the best of local nonfiction television produced by ABC affiliates in the series *Focus on America*.

But, in addition to all these programs, each network maintained a *prestige* documentary series as well. *CBS Reports* filled the void left by the cancellation of *See It Now*. Executive Producer Fred Friendly guided the eclectic succession of programs. Some, like the November 1961 "Biography of a Bookie Joint," which followed an actual police raid in Boston and resulted in the firing of the police commissioner and several officers, generated complaints of bias to the FCC. All the programs were marked by a boldness of theme and tone. "The Fat American," "The Silent Spring of Rachel Carson," in which the author-scientist discussed the dangers of chemical pesticides, and "The Great American Funeral" were among the shows that examined newly emerging social concerns.

The *NBC White Paper* series, which began in November 1960, was intended to emulate *CBS Reports*. Executive Producer Irving Gitlin and producer Al Wasserman, who had worked on both *The Twentieth Century* and *CBS Reports*, were the creative team behind the series. Courageous programs such as "Angola: Journey to a War," in which cameras snuck past border guards, and muckraking programs such as "The Battle of Newburgh," in which a controversial welfare program was exposed, won the *NBC White Paper* series high acclaim.

Shortly after Newton Minow announced his departure from the FCC, Irving Gitlin wrote to thank the chairman for his influence on the broadcasting industry: "Just let me say, as a program producer, that your support and pressure have been tangible assets in the pursuit of my work. . . . Yours has been a most noteworthy contribution."

*Bell & Howell Close-up!* was a series that created a flap at ABC shortly after its debut in the fall of 1960. Since ABC did not have nearly the same degree of resources as the other two networks to produce documentary programming, the work of outsiders such as Drew Associates was considered for broadcast with less soul-searching than might take place at CBS or NBC.

ABC's vice-president of News and Public Affairs, John Daly—who apparently had no qualms moonlighting as a game show host and advertising spokesman—questioned the integrity of the network's decision to air *Yanki, No!* as part of the *Bell & Howell Close-up!* series. He complained that no one in the ABC News Department had "seen a foot of that Cuban film." Unhappy with ABC on other accounts, Daly made a splashy break from the network over the *Yanki, No!* decision. The series continued, however, to be an innovative force in shaping the modern documentary aesthetic. "More and more we must let the camera tell the story," said Jim Hagerty, John Daly's successor as ABC's vice-president of News and Public Affairs.

In addition to the array of nonfiction series on American television, documentary specials aired during the Kennedy years with great frequency. The networks routinely preempted their regular entertainment schedules. Well over two hundred such programs were telecast. Most were prompted by current news events such as space launches, civil rights demonstrations, deaths of major figures, natural disasters, and presidential travels. Some, however, were not time-bound programming and were presented as special-event television.

Notable among these special presentations was a 1962 NBC documentary, *The Tunnel*. The ninety-minute program, produced by Reuven Frank, who was co-writer with reporter Piers Anderton, documented the secret excavation under the Berlin Wall by a group of engineering students, which allowed the escape from East Berlin of fifty-nine refugees. The documentary, which Reuven Frank defined as "an adventure of the human spirit," was the first news broadcast ever to be awarded the Emmy as Program of the Year.

Yet, the special event documentary that received the most attention of any in the Kennedy years was a walk through a newly remodelled house.

### A Tour of the White House with Mrs. John F. Kennedy— Or, "The Jackie Show"

When Jacqueline Kennedy was taken on an inspection tour of the White House by Mamie Eisenhower in December 1960, the young wife of the president-elect reportedly thought the mansion "looked like a hotel that had been decorated by a wholesale furniture store during a January clearance." As first lady, Jacqueline Kennedy planned to make the White House a living symbol reflecting the presidency of the United States.

After convincing her reluctant husband of the worthiness of the project, she undertook to restore the White House with competent determination. A Fine Arts Committee was appointed to guide the work. A curator was hired. And the first lady herself took charge of an expedition through fifty-four rooms in the White House and sixteen baths in search of forsaken historical treasures.

The aristocratic Jacqueline Kennedy was doing what she truly loved to do. As the one-year, $2 million project was drawing to a close, she was justifiably proud of what she had accomplished.

"I can't remember whose specific idea the broadcast was," wrote Charles Collingwood, who was the first lady's escort on the TV tour. "But whosever inspiration it was, it was immediately seized upon by everyone at CBS." In *The Powers That Be*, author David Halberstam writes that the President himself suggested the idea and "easily talked CBS into doing a show with Jackie at the White House."

The producer of the *Tour*, distinguished CBS documentarian Perry Wolff, remembered that NBC, too, was interested in producing such a program and was offering to shoot it in color—something CBS was not yet equipped to do. But the program idea was presented to the first lady by Blair Clark, the vice-president of CBS News whose friendship with the President went back to their Harvard days when Clark was chairman of the *Crimson*.

During the six months of pre-production planning for the program, Perry Wolff and director Franklin Schaffner had, according to Wolff, "almost no face-to-face contact with the President or Mrs. Kennedy." Four drafts of the program were prepared by Wolff. They were extensive outlines written in consultation with the Restoration Project staff. It was understood, however, that Jacqueline Kennedy would put the information into her own words.

The Kennedys spent the weekend before the January 15, 1962, taping at Glen Ora, the family retreat in Virginia, during which time nine tons of lights, cameras, and cables were moved into the executive mansion and put into place by fifty-four technicians. Great pains were taken not to involve the star in the tedious logistical tasks of television production. The initial blocking for the various segments was worked out with the help of a model approximately the first lady's size and coiffed in a "Jackie hairdo."

Program material not involving Jacqueline Kennedy and cutaway shots were videotaped in advance. The principal taping began around 11:00 A.M. that Monday and finished a little after 7:00 in the evening. "She was nervous," producer Wolff recalled about the long production day. "It was exhausting. She drank a couple of scotches and was smoking Marlboros."

Jacqueline Kennedy had been fitted with a battery-operated wireless microphone. The first lady's young press secretary, Pamela Turnure, was shown how to adjust the mike and battery pack, which were hidden under her boss's suit jacket. If a problem were to arise, Charles Collingwood explained at the time, "We couldn't have a technician fiddling with the first lady's person."

President Kennedy's first press conference of 1962 was being held on the same afternoon. Among the issues on which he fielded questions were segregation in federally assisted housing, the Berlin Wall, nuclear testing, Cuba, and the prospects for war in Southeast Asia. The burden of the presidency weighed heavily on him that day.

Kennedy agreed to make an appearance on the television tour and taping was scheduled to take place immediately after the press conference. At about 4:30 he caught up with his wife and the CBS production team. During the brief delay needed to position lights and cameras in the Treaty Room, the President reviewed the gist of his remarks. But, when the taping began, the President was still in the press conference mode and his answers to Collingwood's questions were, producer Wolff recalled, "sharp and pointed."

After all the taping had been completed and after dinner, John and Jacqueline Kennedy viewed the unedited tapes in the White House theater. "They asked me to join them," Collingwood remembered, "but I thought my presence might inhibit their discussion of how things had gone, so I begged off."

Perry Wolff did go to the screening, however. "I sat right behind the two of them," he said. "He was very proud of her. They were very cuddly." Despite the strains the Kennedy marriage was purportedly suffering under, Wolff had no doubt "they cared deeply about each other." "I know," he said remembering the scene, "because I observed it."

The President was not happy with the tone of his delivery. He felt it needed to be softer. He turned and asked the producer, "Is it possible for me to redo it?" The cameras, Wolff remembered with a laugh, were scheduled to be in another city the next day "to shoot the Pillsbury Bake-Off." But the request from the President was "unrefusable." CBS would, of course, allow the President to re-record his segment in the morning.

Jacqueline Kennedy could not be there the next day, so Irja Wolff, wife of the producer, sat next to Charles Collingwood in order for the President to make proper eye contact. The assignment, Wolff remembered, did unnerve her slightly.

With warm sincerity the President commented on the importance of preserving the history of the White House, especially for children. "I have always felt that American history is sometimes a dull subject. There's so much emphasis on dates." The President could not know how quaint and telling his next statement would soon become: "But I think if they can come here and see—alive—this building and in a sense touch the people who have been here, then they'll go home more interested and I think that they'll become better Americans and some of them may someday live here themselves which I think would be good." And then with a chuckle he added the afterthought, "even the girls." John Kennedy would not live to know the monumental impact of the Women's Movement on American life.

Public anticipation about the TV event was great. It was not the story of the President's house that compelled viewers, of course. It was the possibility his regally inward wife would reveal something more about herself during the rare sixty minutes in which she willingly took her place on America's center stage. The cover of *TV Guide* the week of the broadcast featured a close-up shot of Jacqueline Kennedy with slightly tousled hair and direct gaze. The casually posed photo suggested the TV tour would be a more candid affair, however, than it turned out to be.

*A Tour of the White House with Mrs. John F. Kennedy* was telecast, without commercial interruption, simultaneously on CBS and NBC at 10:00 P.M. on Wednesday, February 14. The following Sunday it aired on ABC at 6:30 P.M. Though the program was completely produced by CBS News, the other networks contributed to the production cost for the privilege of broadcasting the tape. This highly irregular arrangement also satisfied the White House tradition of not giving exclusive access to any one news organization.

On the evening of Valentine's Day, the President and Jacqueline Kennedy had dinner at the White House with Benjamin Bradlee, Washington editor of *Newsweek*, and his wife Tony Bradlee. The other two guests were Max Freedman, American correspondent of the *Manchester Guardian*, and Josephine Fell, a society hostess from New York. After dinner, the group retired to the small sitting room next to the Lincoln Room. In his memoirs *Conversations with Kennedy*, Bradlee recalled: "There had been a lot of talk at dinner about how good CBS was, what a good director they had in Frank Schaffner, but ironically the President's set wouldn't bring in the CBS channel, and we watched the show on NBC, and we watched it in virtual silence."

About 46 million other people, three out of every four Americans watching TV at that time, were also tuned to "The Jackie Show." Not only was this an enormous share of the audience, but Jacqueline Kennedy's appearance actually increased the number of homes using television. Nielsen data revealed that at least four million more homes were tuned in to television that Wednesday night than the preceding Wednesday. And what all these viewers saw was an inhibited first lady and a somewhat fawning network correspondent tiptoe through a panoply of treasurable historical artifacts. It was the antithesis of cinema verite.

The intriguing substance of the White House tour and the antique still-picture vignettes that provided the thematic continuity were bogged down by the weight of the event itself. Jacqueline Kennedy's three strands of pearls, the simple cut of her neckline, and her low-heeled shoes were vivid long after the beautiful paintings by great American artists faded from viewers' memories.

The awkwardness of the first lady was palpable to any objective observer. The 1962 audience overlooked the program's shortcomings, however. Most viewers were just as smitten as the *Chicago Daily News* critic who wrote hyperbolically, "Here was an example of television at its best."

Ben Bradlee remembered, "As soon as the broadcast was over the telephone started ringing." One call was from the President's sister, Eunice Shriver. After speaking with her brother, she asked for her sister-in-law. "But Jackie shook her head," the evening's guest remembered, "and the President said she had gone off to bed—in tears."

The morning after the broadcast, the *New York Herald Tribune* suggested in a front page story that the first lady was amenable to participating in the television program because of an understanding that the three networks would contribute handsomely to the Fine Arts Committee Fund. The President was reportedly angered by the story. The monetary incentive theory was denied by Pierre Salinger and CBS chairman William Paley who called the charge "sheer nonsense." The head of ABC News, Jim Hagerty, however, said that he understood a donation to the Fine Arts Committee was "expected to be included in the bill for the show," and he protested the arrangement saying, "under no conditions will ABC make a donation to a government."

Also the day after the broadcast, Newton Minow received a highly unusual personal call from President Kennedy. "I want to know what the rating was on that program. Can you find out?" the President asked the FCC chairman. Minow dutifully called Frank Stanton, the president of CBS, and asked uncomfortably for the ratings on *A Tour of the White House with Mrs. John F. Kennedy*. "Who wants to know?" Stanton wondered, "the ratings aren't in yet—it was only yesterday." "Let's not get into that," Minow said, "when will you get it?" Stanton promised to get the information to Minow as soon as it was available, a few days at least. When the numbers arrived, the chairman forwarded the favorable figures to the Oval Office and made a follow-up call to the President. "It's on the way over there," he said, "you'll be interested to know it's higher than your press conference."

The tour of the White House was an international event as well. A brief introduction to the program was recorded by the first lady in French and Spanish for foreign distribution. In the early summer of 1962, again at the request of the President, Newton Minow compiled a list of the countries that had purchased and broadcast Jacqueline Kennedy's tour. They included the United Kingdom, Australia, Japan, Ireland, the Philippines, Switzerland, Sweden, Puerto Rico, Finland, Denmark, Belgium, and Italy. Thirty-four other countries, including Communist China, Czechoslovakia, and Poland, requested permission from the USIA to service a print of the documentary.

The international reviews were as glowing as those domestic. *The London Times* playfully suggested that the American first lady's charm was a new "diplomatic weapon." "For the British viewer," the *London Times* reported, "the program had its embarrassments because of the occasional references to the burning of the White House in 1814. Mrs. Kennedy is, however, obviously incapable of bearing grudges."

Not everyone was enchanted with the first lady's performance, though. The July 1962 issue of *Esquire* carried a Norman Mailer piece entitled "An Evening with Jackie Kennedy." He was not afflicted with the generous blind spots of most other critics. Rather, the Mailer essay displayed a savage insight that Jacqueline Kennedy would find hard to forgive.

"Do you remember the girl with the magnificent sweater who used to give the weather reports on television in a swarmy singsong tone?" Mailer asked his readers in describing the first lady's "public voice." He had heard better voices "selling gadgets to the grim" in Macy's at Christmastime than the "manufactured voice Jackie Kennedy chose to arrive at." She walked through the tour, according to Mailer, "like a starlet who is utterly without talent."

"Mrs. Kennedy moved," he wrote, "like a wooden horse." The program "gave us precisely no sense of the past," Mailer felt, but "it inflicted the past upon us, pummeled us with it, depressed us with facts." With para-doxical compassion, the author concluded that Jacqueline Kennedy was a "royal phony." "She was trying, I suppose to be a proper First Lady and it was her mistake."

Those who have assessed the tenures of American first ladies have con-cluded the contributions made by Jacqueline Kennedy were indeed signif-icant. While the restored White House stands as an enduring legacy to the people of the United States, the program that officially presented it to the public, *A Tour of the White House with Mrs. John F. Kennedy*, remains a monochrome memento of the New Frontier . . . a national souvenir, evoc-ative and bittersweet.

At the end of 1963, television's Documentary Age began its path toward extinction. Several nonfiction series were cancelled and the number of special documentary broadcasts declined after the presidency of John Kennedy. In discussing the history of television documentaries, newsman Robert MacNeil observed, "The period of comparative excellence reached its peak in 1963, after which the networks appeared to have exhausted their reserves of moral courage." And, of course, under the Johnson administration, the networks felt far less regulatory pressure to prove their public service obligations were being met. The times simply changed.

But, during the Kennedy years, television documentarians experienced an exhilaration they probably knew could not last forever. "It was a different time," Burton Benjamin recalled. "No one ever came to me and talked about ratings and numbers. I wasn't even aware for awhile that they did that. I was left alone. During the Kennedy administration there were a lot of very good stories out there." And Shad Northshield reflected: "There was a lot of time available for us. . . . You know we have our credit cards and press cards and bosses who say 'Go do it!' And at that time there was a hell of a lot more of that."

During the New Frontier, television documentaries were pushed to the limits of their potential—and, in the process, Americans were offered priv-ileged views of their leaders, their country, and their world never before possible.

## An Unprecedented Television Documentary—
### *Crisis: Behind a Presidential Commitment*

In May 1963, Greg Shuker, a former *Life* magazine reporter, was on a research trip for Drew Associates. He was looking for documentary stories with a beginning, a middle, and an unknown outcome. The ideal was to get as close to drama as possible without putting actors in front of the camera.

Shuker happened to be a guest at a barbecue along with the deputy director of the USIA, Don Wilson—who, because of director Edward R. Murrow's illness, was actually in charge of the agency—and the director of its motion picture division, filmmaker George Stevens, Jr. Wilson, who had been a *Life* bureau chief in Washington, was a member of the White House crisis committee, Ex Comm. He had been intimately involved in the President's decision-making process regarding the integration crisis at the University of Mississippi in September 1962, and the Cuban Missile Crisis in October 1962. Wilson and Stevens began discussing how valuable it would be to have film documentation of how those two incidents were handled. They both agreed, in front of Greg Shuker, that Drew Associates would be the logical organization to produce such a record the next time a crisis arose.

A short time later, Shuker read a brief article buried in the newspaper about the upcoming integration of the University of Alabama and George Wallace's stated opposition to it. Shuker recognized the elements of a good documentary story in the Drew tradition. He got in touch with Don Wilson and asked him to push the idea with the administration. Wilson told Shuker: "I can set it up for you to meet Bob Kennedy because he's going to handle the integration thing with his deputy Katzenbach. If you can sell it to him, you can sell it to the President because he already knows you guys."

Shuker recalls: "I went to Washington and met with Bob Kennedy and he was a little suspicious. But he thought it sounded like an interesting idea. He still wasn't sure. I got the impression—and I'll never know—that the President said 'It's up to you Bob, it's your show.' . . . I went back to New York and a couple of days later I got a call from Bob Kennedy's press aide Ed Guthman saying, 'The Attorney General would like to see the documentary about that lawyer you guys did in Chicago. We understand it's terrific.' "

Robert Kennedy's aide was referring to the Drew Associates film entitled *The Chair*, which documented the 1962 struggle of a young Chicago lawyer to save his client, Paul Crump, from the electric chair. It was a well-known case that pitted the prosecuting attorney Jim Thompson—who would later become governor of Illinois—against the charismatic defense attorney Don Moore and, in a surprise development, the famed New York attorney Louis Nizer. The documentary, which would become part of the syndicated *Living Camera* series, had not yet been broadcast, but had been submitted to the Cannes Film Festival.

Shuker flew back to Washington and met in a USIA screening room with Robert Kennedy, his aide Ed Guthman, Don Wilson, and George Stevens, Jr. Shuker remembered: "When it was over Bob Kennedy was grinning all over and said, 'Gee, I really like that guy,' meaning Don Moore—a young, aggressive lawyer. And he obviously totally identified with him." (Don Moore would, before long, be hired to work for the Justice Department.)

Robert Kennedy asked Shuker about the print of the film, "Can I keep this?" "You can borrow it," the filmmaker said. "I'll get it back to you," the Attorney General promised, and Greg Shuker went back to New York.

The next day Robert Kennedy called Shuker and said, "Come on down, we'll talk about it." The night before, the Attorney General had taken *The Chair* to the White House and it was shown as the evening movie for the President.

Right after Memorial Day, about ten days before the scheduled integration at the University of Alabama, Greg Shuker and Robert Kennedy met to discuss the logistics of the filming. At this point Drew Associates did not yet have a solid commitment from any network to air the documentary. It was a film being made on speculation.

The members of Drew Associates voted to begin shooting the film without outside financial support, even if it meant investing their own rent money. When ABC learned, however, the group was determined to make the documentary, the network agreed to finance just the shooting. A decision would be made later, after the event transpired, about whether to invest in developing and syncing the film.

The story was to be one of decision making in the Justice Department. Shuker remembers: "We had an agreement right up front, but not in writing, that this film would start and end at the Justice Department. And if the story ended up in the White House, so be it, but we weren't going to arrange anything in the White House per se. The President liked that—it was no 'Day in the Life.' "

Soon after the informal arrangement with the Kennedys had been agreed upon, Bob Drew—who had long been lobbying through Pierre Salinger to gain access to the White House during a crisis situation—received a call from Salinger. "Would you give some footage to Wolper?" the press secretary asked, referring to documentarian David Wolper who was producing *The Making of the President, 1960* at the time. Drew was not inclined to share his material, but, in an attempt to grease the wheels of access, he took the opportunity to negotiate. "Look," Drew said to Salinger, "we're shooting something on Bobby. . . . This is the crisis. This is it. If you can make sure we're included in the White House, I'd be glad to give the footage to Wolper." Drew was amazed to hear Salinger say "OK, it's set." He remembered: "I was surprised to hear that Salinger thought he had the authority to say 'Yes.' Heretofore he had always gone to the President."

Another member of the Drew Associates, Jim Lipscomb, was charged with soliciting the cooperation of Governor George Wallace of Alabama, which would be crucial in documenting the confrontation. Governor Wallace's PR assistant Bill Jones promised he would get Lipscomb in to see the governor, but after sitting outside his office for three days, Lipscomb was about ready to quit.

In a final attempt, he slipped a note to Wallace via his secretary saying a film was going to be made about the event at hand and that the Kennedys had agreed to be recorded. "If you want your side of the story told, you ought to talk to me," Lipscomb advised the governor. The filmmaker was let into the office and Wallace agreed to participate. The governor did not want to be upstaged by the Kennedys and he could use the opportunity to convince his own constituency of the depth of his commitment to segregation. The right of preview afforded the Kennedys was not asked for by Governor Wallace and was not offered by Drew Associates.

With the help of Jack Greenberg of the NAACP Legal Defense Fund and John Doar of the Justice Department, Greg Shuker worked with the black students, Vivian Malone and James Hood, who would be at the center of the confrontation between the federal government and the state of Alabama. Shuker secured their assent for the project.

The plot of the story and the cast of characters were set. The outcome, of course, was unknown. Would Governor Wallace be arrested? Would troops be deployed? Would the students be peacefully registered?

On June 10 and 11, 1963, Drew Associates was ready to cover the action. Robert Drew remained in New York to receive film and begin editing as it arrived. Producer Greg Shuker and Donn Pennebaker were filming the events in Washington. Jim Lipscomb and Mort Lund were with Governor Wallace in Alabama. Ricky Leacock and Patricia Powell, also in Alabama, were assigned to Nicholas Katzenbach, Robert Kennedy's deputy. And Hope Ryden and Abbot Mills, who had already been filming the students, continued their work with them as they prepared for the ordeal ahead.

A new twist entered the drama when President Kennedy, who had been contemplating a television address to the nation on civil rights, had to decide whether or not to deliver it on the night of the Alabama encounter. It was a delicate question of timing and his closest associates were not in agreement on the course of action he should take.

The opening scenes of the documentary show the Robert Kennedy household at full tilt around the breakfast table. The Attorney General begins the momentous day surrounded by youthful exuberance. Kids and animals seem to have the run of the place. In contrast, the governor's mansion in Montgomery is a sedate domicile. His daughter is attended to by a black nanny.

Wallace directs the camera to view the portraits of Southern Civil War heroes displayed in his home. He admires the sentiment attributed to one of the military men: "I'd rather live a short life of standing for principle than live a long life of compromise." Wallace says point blank to the film team, "Of course that may not mean much to you folks." Moments such as these contribute to the power of *Crisis: Behind a Presidential Commitment* in portraying the ideological misalignment between the North and the South. To Wallace, only those imbued with true Southern heritage could grasp the redemptive power derived from a noble defeat.

In Washington, Robert Kennedy sent Nick Katzenbach off to Alabama. Then the Attorney General went to the White House to participate in a strategy session—including a discussion regarding the television speech on civil rights. So, as agreed, Greg Shuker and Donn Pennebaker went to the White House too. But their presence was kept low key. "I was very aware," Shuker said, "that as we went in and out of the White House, we went in and out through the back."

Ted Sorensen, Kennedy's special counsel and closest aide, recalled walking into the Oval Office and being surprised to see a man with a camera. He looked to the President as if to ask "What's going on?" The President put up his hand in a reassuring gesture as if to say, "It's OK. They're alright."

The meeting proceeded without accommodation to the filmmakers. Shuker recalled it was not a situation in which he could say, "Hold on while I get this stuff ready." There were "no arrangements, no presetting of anything, no lighting. If we weren't ready it would have gone right by."

In Alabama, Ricky Leacock was filming Nicholas Katzenbach as he consulted over the phone with Robert Kennedy about strategy. Out of the blue, the deputy attorney general said, raising the pitch of his voice, "Hi, Kerry, how are you, dear?" and then chatted playfully for a moment, presumably with a child on the other end of the line. It was not until footage from both ends were viewed in New York that anyone realized the entire conversation between Katzenbach and three-year-old Kerry Kennedy had been preserved. It was a scene of tremendous warmth and charm—an inspiring instance of cinema verite.

Throughout the crisis, producer Greg Shuker was with Robert Kennedy. While at the Justice Department, he was in charge of sound recording. As he witnessed the Attorney General's phone conversations with Katzenbach, the young filmmaker reached an epiphany: "Bob Kennedy hits the button and says something like, 'You know, Nick, I think your attitude with Wallace....' Then he pauses and says, 'Well, he's really a second-rate character to you. He's wasting your time. He's wasting the students' time. And, let's not make a big deal about it. I don't want to put the students through that indignity. I don't want the man to stand there and say things to them.' And then he says, 'Well, no, I wouldn't pick the governor up.' Suddenly, you see this tough kind of Jesuit brain—it's tough, it's compassionate. 'Don't let him say anything to the students. They've had a hard enough life being black.' It's all there in that one scene at the Justice Department. To me, that was the best of the one thousand days. To me, with a kind of romantic streak, that's the best of the Kennedy presidency right there—pragmatic and compassionate. That was the moment I knew, not only that I liked this man, but also, that no matter what happened, we really had something."

The portrait of Vivian Malone and James Hood that *Crisis* revealed was entirely different from what was delivered in standard news footage. Black citizens shown in the news coverage of civil rights demonstrations were men and women who had already fortified themselves for confrontation. In this documentary, the two students were seen in the process of finding their personal strength. They wonder about the details of their safekeeping, they discuss their ambitions, they exchange nervous but determined laughter. Vivian Malone and James Hood are thoroughly appealing young people—and it becomes difficult for viewers not to feel a vested interest in their futures.

When George Wallace actually fulfilled his promise to stand in the schoolhouse door, he was confronted by Nicholas Katzenbach. Jim Lipscomb was trying to find a way to record the face-off. In the crush of reporters and guards it was difficult for the filmmaker to secure a good vantage point. But the building had bars in front of the windows and finally Lipscomb worked out a solution. "I stood on the low sill of the window and I took my belt and I tied my leg to the bars so I could hang there. . . . That's the only way I could get the shot of Katzenbach and Wallace facing each other."

On that evening, when President Kennedy was preparing to deliver the television address on civil rights, Robert Kennedy intimated to Shuker and Pennebaker that he did not want the filmmakers to go home with him and shoot any more footage at Hickory Hill. "You guys should go to the White House," the Attorney General advised. "We took the hint," said Shuker. Robert Kennedy provided a car and a driver and the two men went to the White House and "hung out in the back" even though they had purposely decided not to shoot the President presenting the speech. That footage would be taken from other sources.

As Shuker and Pennebaker stood in the covered walkway behind the White House, a pregnant Jacqueline Kennedy stopped and chatted with them. "I don't remember you from *Primary*," she said to Shuker who had not yet joined the Drew team when that film was shot. But she did remember Donn Pennebaker and she certainly remembered the innovative film.

The presence of Shuker and Pennebaker in the White House during the integration crisis was not reported in daily press coverage of the President's activities. It was not until over a month later that the filming of the documentary became a news item. On July 25, 1963, the front page of *The New York Times* carried a report of the Kennedy-Drew collaboration. The article mentioned that the Attorney General would screen the finished film.

Two days after the straight news item, the *Times* carried a surprisingly sharp editorial condemning the admission of cameras into the Kennedys' offices during the decision-making process. Whether *The New York Times* was smarting at having been passed over in gaining privileged access, or whether it was taking a sincere editorial position, is open to debate. "To eavesdrop on executive decisions of serious Government matters while they are in progress is highly inappropriate," the commentary concluded. "The White House isn't Macy's window."

After *Crisis: Behind a Presidential Commitment* was shot, and ABC realized a dramatic confrontation had been captured, the network put up the money to develop and sync the film. The president of ABC-TV, Tom Moore, later viewed approximately two hours of selected footage. He was tremendously impressed. There was no question that ABC would fund the remainder of the project to its completion.

Moore knew it was a scoop on the other networks. While CBS and NBC were in the heat of battle, ABC had the freedom to experiment. And the other networks regarded it with some envy. Burton Benjamin, executive producer of *The Twentieth Century* on CBS, reflected on the cinema verite documentaries of Drew Associates: "It was obvious to me that they could get closer to the essence of the truth through this technique than you could get through the conventional technique. It just seemed to be a breakthrough."

In August, *Show*, a monthly magazine about television, movies, and theater, was preparing to run a preview picture story about the documentary in its next issue. Greg Shuker assembled a layout of stills taken from the footage of *Crisis*, which synopsized the story. As a courtesy, he called on Robert Kennedy to show him the photos. "He really had a problem looking at himself with the dog in the office and his daughter," Shuker recollected. "He wasn't sure if that was dignified. He was confused. He just didn't know for sure. I was saying, 'Oh it makes you look human. It's a great moment.' And he said, 'I think you better take these ones over to the White House.' "

So, Greg Shuker and the editor of *Show* magazine visited President Kennedy in the White House on a hot and quiet Saturday afternoon. Smoking a cigar, the President looked through the layouts and chuckled. Teasing Shuker he asked, "Where's the one of you and me and your microphone?" The President then took the layouts and left the room for about ten minutes. "We'll never know where he went with them," said Shuker. "He may have gone to see Mrs. Kennedy. He may have gone to call his brother. I don't know. But he came back in the room, dropped them on the table and said 'Terrific'—quite sincerely."

The article in the September issue of *Show* was entitled "A New Kind of Television Goes Backstage with History." Though the final version of *Crisis* was not yet completed, the publication recognized the breakthrough of Drew Associates. They were able to "accustom the principals to the presence of their minimal equipment," and to achieve "an intimacy and lack of self-consciousness almost impossible to the mastodon lumberings of ordinary documentary-making."

Also in the late summer, Robert Kennedy and Ed Guthman were shown a rough cut of *Crisis* in the New York office of Bob Drew. The Attorney General, pleased with the work, arranged a second screening for his Justice Department staff and family at his Washington office. When the lights came up, there was murmuring among some aides about the candid discussion of pending civil rights legislation that had taken place in the Oval Office. It was decided the film should be taken to the White House for the President's review.

Shortly after, Greg Shuker and Bob Drew met with Nicholas Katzenbach, who asked that they omit some of the direct remarks that might offend Congressional sensitivity. The compromise the men reached was that the images would stay intact, but a voice-over narration explaining the crux of the discussion would replace comments such as one referring to "nut cutting on the Hill."

Before its ultimate October 21, 1963, airdate on ABC, the documentary, without the minor sound alterations yet made, was shown at Lincoln Center in a double feature with *The Chair* as part of the first New York Film Festival. In the *New York Herald Tribune*, columnist John Horn previewed the film for television viewers and attempted to rebut criticism of the project: "The warm breath of human life is felt in every scene of this absorbing document. . . . evidently the documentarians became an unobtrusive part of the scenery. Not less but more such television journalism should be produced and telecast."

But, when the program aired, controversy continued to swirl around it. In *The New York Times* Jack Gould questioned the sincerity of the key players in participating in such "an incredible bit of play-acting." And, New York's educational TV station, Channel 13, ran a half-hour panel discussion titled "Crisis: Presidency by Television," which explored the validity of the documentary.

On the 23rd of October another critical editorial appeared in *The New York Times*. Headlined "Government on Camera," the piece called *Crisis* an improper way to enlist sympathy for the civil rights movement. The *New York Herald Tribune* also editorialized against the program, referring to it as satisfying entertainment, but noting "the President has no business in show business."

And Jack Gould vented his displeasure yet again in an October 27 piece in the Sunday *Times*. He especially faulted Robert Kennedy for "demeaning government through a careless flirtation with the entertainment business."

Pierre Salinger recalls the President "was quite upset about it" after *Crisis: Behind a Presidential Commitment* aired. "He thought he'd gone too far. . . . He said he had forgot the cameras were there. He was not sure that the image he gave was the right image."

How much of President Kennedy's discomfort with the documentary stemmed from the highly charged criticism rather than his own aesthetic assessment, Salinger could not say. But it was clear to the press secretary that this was the last time such a project would be sanctioned. Then, re-membering the program aired just a month before Dallas, he added, "We wouldn't have a chance to do it again."

So, *Crisis: Behind a Presidential Commitment* remains a solitary historical artifact. As a television documentary and as a chronicle of the executive branch of government, it is a peerless document. "I felt privileged to be able to be a part of that group who was going to record a presidential confrontation in a manner that had never before been done and I don't think has ever been done since," Jim Lipscomb reflected. "Very seldom is it that a politician has absolutely nothing to hide in a confrontation. Always there are some things they don't want you to know. In this case Robert and John Kennedy had nothing to hide and they had a story to tell and they chose us as the instrument for the story to be told. We may have told it a little more intimately than they'd ever imagined."

During the last months of the Kennedy years, a rare set of circumstances allowed for the creation of this extraordinary television documentary. It was a narrow space of time in which the filmmakers of Drew Associates had achieved a confidence with equipment and technique and the Kennedy brothers, having been through many crises, also felt confident enough to open their doors to television viewers. Never again would a chief executive and high officers of government be so unstudied before searching cameras. It was the period immediately before television's relationship with government burst forth as a burning academic and social issue.

John Kennedy experimented with television documentaries in a transitory era. The American public had not yet cultivated an automatic suspicion of their president's motives in media appearances. Yet, by the end of Kennedy's life, elite opinion makers had become more familiar with the nature of film and television production, and were beginning to think more critically about the medium.

None of Kennedy's successors would take the risk that genuine cinema verite inevitably posed. They were not honestly intrigued by adventures in reporting. John Kennedy was the first and last American president to seriously ponder the ways in which television documentaries could enrich the public understanding of the democratic process as well as leave a historical record of enduring value.

JFK accepts the nomination of his party. (© 1984 The Estate of Garry Winogrand; Courtesy Fraenkel Gallery, San Francisco and the Estate of Garry Winogrand)

*Top*: An American family watches the first of the Great Debates. (Courtesy Bettman News Photos). *Bottom*: The most privileged position in the inaugural press box is reserved for television. Walter Cronkite is in the window directly above the President. (Courtesy John F. Kennedy Library)

Newton Minow being prepared for an interview with Walter Cronkite on *The Twentieth Century*. (From the Terrence O'Flaherty Collection of the UCLA Theater Arts Library)

The FCC in November 1962—(from left) Frederick W. Ford, Robert E. Lee, Rosel H. Hyde, Chairman Newton N. Minow, Robert T. Bartley, T. A. M. Craven, and E. William Henry. (Courtesy *Broadcasting* magazine)

"It could be either a new western or a report from Newton Minow."

*"I'll bet Newton Minow isn't watching that junk!"*

Minow is a popular subject for cartoonists. Not before or since has an FCC chairman been a household name. (Reprinted by permission of Bill Mauldin and Wil-Jo Assoc. Courtesy Bil Keane. Courtesy Dana Fradon.)

LeRoy Collins, former Democratic governor of Florida, is chosen NAB president in 1961. (Courtesy *Broadcasting* magazine)

George Maharis and Martin Milner portray destinationless highway traveling partners on *Route 66*. (From the Terrence O'Flaherty Collection of the UCLA Theater Arts Library)

*Top*: Officers Toody and Muldoon are bungling partners on *Car 54, Where Are You?* (From the Terrence O'Flaherty Collection of the UCLA Theater Arts Library). *Lower left*: The Prestons, the father-and-son legal team from *The Defenders*. (From the Terrence O'Flaherty Collection of the UCLA Theater Arts Library) *Lower right*: Rob and Laura Petrie are a stylish and fun-loving couple who capture the spark of the early 1960s. (From the Terrence O'Flaherty Collection of the UCLA Theater Arts Library).

June 11, 1963—President Kennedy delivers his television manifesto on civil rights. Within weeks, scripts about black Americans are written for dramatic TV series. (Courtesy John F. Kennedy Library)

A sign protesting "TV's Vast Wasteland for Negroes" is carried in the March on Washington. (Courtesy *Ebony/Jet* magazine)

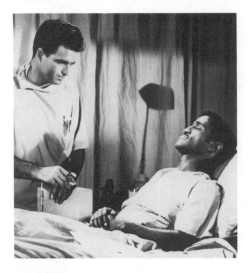

A scene from "Allie" on *Ben Casey*. (From the Terrence O'Flaherty Collection of the UCLA Theater Arts Library)

Brash and prolific producer David Susskind took programming risks during the Kennedy years. (Courtesy *Broadcasting* magazine)

Diana Sands and James Earl Jones in "Who Do You Kill?" (Courtesy Wisconsin Center for Film and Theater Research)

"No Hiding Place" from *East Side/West Side*. (Courtesy Wisconsin Center for Film and Theater Research)

Teacher and principal confer in *Mr. Novak*. (Courtesy Wisconsin Center for Film and Theater Research)

*Telstar* relays a portion of this press conference to viewers across the Atlantic. (Courtesy John F. Kennedy Library)

Sander Vanocur, George Herman, and Bill Lawrence engage in *A Conversation with the President*. (Courtesy John F. Kennedy Library)

Chet Huntley and David Brinkley anchoring the 1960 Democratic Convention. (Courtesy *Broadcasting* magazine)

President Kennedy is interviewed for the *CBS Evening News with Walter Cronkite* on the program's first thirty-minute edition. (Courtesy John F. Kennedy Library)

The President and Jacqueline Kennedy watch the progress of America's first manned space flight. (Courtesy John F. Kennedy Library)

JFK, LBJ, Alan and Louise Shepard appear before the NAB convention. (Courtesy John F. Kennedy Library)

To promote its public service coverage of John Glenn's flight, CBS installs a huge TV screen above the ticket counter in Grand Central Station. (Wide World Photos)

Robert Drew, holding the microphone, follows Kennedy during the filming of *Primary*. (Courtesy Drew Associates)

A contemplative moment from *Adventures on the New Frontier*. (Courtesy Drew Associates)

The first lady and Charles Collingwood during the taping of *A Tour of the White House with Mrs. John F. Kennedy*. (CBS Photo)

An Oval Office meeting concerning the integration of the University of Alabama is captured in *Crisis: Behind a Presidential Commitment*. (Courtesy Drew Associates)

A revealing close-up from *Crisis*. (Courtesy Drew Associates)

The Attorney General and Ethel Kennedy greet trick-or-treaters on the kids' show *1, 2, 3—Go!* (Courtesy of the National Broadcasting Company, Inc.)

*Top left*: Supreme Court Justice William O. Douglas guests on *Reading Room*. (From the Terrence O'Flaherty Collection of the UCLA Theater Arts Library) *Top right*: *Exploring* host Dr. Albert Hibbs. (Courtesy Wisconsin Center for Film and Theater Research) *Bottom*: A sketch called "When Mommy and Daddy Were Young" from *DISCOVERY '62*. (Courtesy Jules Power)

The *DISCOVERY* video truck being lowered to the deck of the *Constellation* to show life aboard a modern aircraft carrier. (Courtesy Jules Power/ABC)

From a commercial for Wisk liquid detergent—the first integrated network television advertisement. (Courtesy Lever Brothers)

A full-page newspaper ad for all-channel TV sets. (*Washington Sunday Star*)

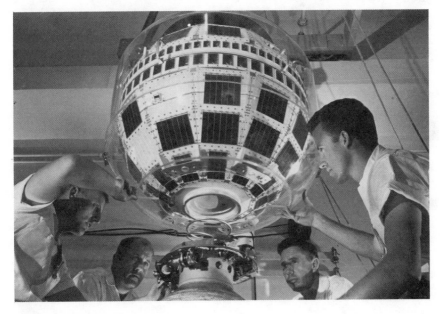

Technicians mating the *Telstar* satellite to a Delta rocket for launch into earth orbit. (Courtesy AT&T Archives)

A television camera follows the President's casket. (Courtesy John F. Kennedy Library)

The cortege passes the East steps of the Capitol, under which the control room for the broadcast pool is located. (Courtesy John F. Kennedy Library)

# CHAPTER 7

# A Peace Offering

## PROGRAMMING FOR CHILDREN

Strong bodies and strong minds would be needed to beat the Russians, American children of the Cold War were told—inoculating them with the fear that the Soviets were raising a generation better trained to cope with the modern world. Kids in the Soviet Union got plenty of fresh air and exercise, parents and teachers said. They went to school on Saturdays without complaint. And they didn't watch television when they were supposed to be doing their homework.

The introduction of every mass medium of popular culture raised questions about its effects on children. In their time, dime novels and pulp magazines were criticized for eroding traditional values and debasing artistic taste. The sensory impact of radio and motion pictures caused even greater concern in the 1930s and 1940s.

The swift penetration of television into American family life and the socialization process of American children provoked predictable alarm. Television was far more accessible than the movies and it relied more heavily on violent themes than radio dramas. The rising juvenile crime rate in the years just after the emergence of television seemed to justify the fears that impressionable youngsters could suffer detrimental consequences as a result of heavy TV viewing.

In 1954—the same year the frozen TV dinner first appeared in American supermarkets—the government became involved in the controversy. Senator Estes Kefauver, who had attained national prominence four years earlier when he chaired nationally televised hearings into organized crime, led a Senate inquiry into juvenile delinquency. Television violence was a prime suspect in the problem.

By the mid-1950s, television was dominating the waking hours of American children, but academic research on the issue was still scarce. Abundant market research, however, was indicating that television commercials could affect consumer behavior. The broadcast industry was proud of its record in this regard. Advertisements in trade journals boasted of TV's selling power. The effect of entertainment programming on behavior was a different matter, though. The industry did not accept responsibility.

The television violence children were being exposed to was found primarily in programming designed for adult viewing. Children's programs were not considered to be contributors to the problem. In fact, genial children's programming such as *Kukla, Fran and Ollie, Winky Dink and You*, and *Mr. I. Magination*, was relatively abundant in the early and mid-1950s. At this time the function of network programming was not only to deliver audiences to advertisers, but also, perhaps more important, to encourage the sale of TV receivers to the public.

Since families with children in the household were more likely to purchase television sets, they were targeted for incentive. According to economist William Melody, "Specialized children's programming of high quality was viewed as a valuable stimulus to the purchase of television sets." As the number of television households increased, the need to make special programming efforts in behalf of children dwindled. By the late 1950s, the purpose of children's programming shifted from convincing parents a TV set was a worthwhile investment to selling products for advertisers.

The first landmark work of academic research in this country on the relationship between children and television was published only a month before the Vast Wasteland speech. Based on the findings of several important studies, *Television in the Lives of Our Children*, by Wilbur Schramm, Jack Lyle, and Edwin Parker, was positive in tone about the potential that television held for beneficial effects. But, the underlying theme of the book was one of urgency about the status quo. An FCC interoffice memorandum reveals the tome was not ignored. On April 24, 1961, Dr. Hyman Goldin of Newton Minow's research staff, sent the new chairman the following memo:

1. I think this book "Television in the Lives of Our Children" is one of the best on the literature.
2. May I suggest a quick reading of pp. 169-188 (Chapter 9). I think there is *red meat here for your NAB speech*.
3. How about calling on the industry in your NAB speech to make available funds (with no strings attached) necessary and adequate for long-range and continuing work in this field (see pp. 186-188).

The suggestion in point number three of Dr. Goldin's memo was not acted upon, although the responsibility of the industry to children was a major theme in Minow's Vast Wasteland speech. The chairman told the broadcasters:

If parents, teachers and ministers conducted their responsibilities by following the ratings, children would have a steady diet of ice cream, school holidays and no Sunday school. What about your responsibilities? Is there no room on television to teach, to inform, to uplift, to stretch, to enlarge the capacities of your children? Is there no room for programs deepening their understanding of children in other lands? Is there no room for a children's news show explaining something about the world to them at their level of understanding? Is there no room for reading the great literature of the past, teaching them the great traditions of freedom? There are some fine children's shows, but they are drowned out in massive doses of cartoons, violence and more violence. Must these be your trademarks? Search your consciences and see if you cannot offer more to your young beneficiaries whose future you guide so many hours each and every day.

Minow's chiding hit a sensitive nerve. Politically it would be counter-productive for an industry licensed to operate in the public interest to argue the First Amendment offered protection from the duty to serve children. Concessions were made quickly and, on the surface, willingly. The chairman's suggestions for appropriate topics for children's programs were taken quite literally. For instance, within seventy-two hours of Minow's NAB speech, a spokesman for Taft Broadcasting announced, "In response to Chairman Minow's challenge to our creativity . . . we will increase the significance of TV programs for children in the area of news and special events."

The networks too responded to "Minow's irritation" with plans for a "rash of ambitious children's programs." Less than two weeks after the Vast Wasteland speech, NBC announced a Saturday afternoon program with the working title *Student News Report*, later to be called *UPDATE*. The concept of the program, hosted by NBC News correspondent Bob Abernethy, was described in the network press release of May 26, 1961, in this way: "To bring world affairs into sharp, understandable focus for the nation's 20–25 million students of pre-college age (without talking down to them)." A personal friend of Minow's at NBC sent the chairman a copy of the press release. The memo attached read, "Dear Newt, Here's one *specific* result of your needles."

ABC came up with a similar program for the approaching fall season. *American Newstand* was a ten-minute newscast for youngsters. It was broadcast as the final segment on *American Bandstand*, which aired each weekday afternoon from 4:00 to 5:00 P.M.

Dr. Gerald Lesser, of the Harvard Center for Research in Children's Television and the Children's Television Workshop, recalled that his introduction to work in children's television came when he was hired as a child development consultant to NBC shortly after Minow "uttered his now legendary accusation." Said Lesser, "Each network responded quickly by developing plans for a high quality children's series that would proclaim the network's commitment to public service."

In May 1961, Jack Kuney was a producer with the News and Public Affairs department at CBS. During the mid-1950s he had spent eighteen months as an associate producer of an educational children's show on CBS called *Let's Take A Trip*. It was produced by Irving Gitlin. Kuney recalled that one day out of the blue he received a phone call from his former boss. Gitlin had since moved to NBC and he wanted to find out if Kuney was interested in producing a prime-time children's show.

"During Gitlin's call," Kuney remembered, "he had asked me if I had read Minow's speech to the NAB, and when I replied that I had not, he said that he would send me a copy. We were now living in Greenwich Village and the speech was at my front door within the hour."

The portion of the Vast Wasteland text referring to children and television was highlighted on the copy Kuney received from Gitlin with a black line down the side of the page. Kuney recalled, "There was a small note scribbled on the end of the speech. It indicated that Gitlin had hopes that we could be on the air by the beginning of the Fall season. Within a week, I was in an office at 30 Rockefeller Plaza."

As the show was being planned, Kuney said, "Our objective was to teach, to inform—it was a direct response to the Minow speech. Irv Gitlin had his edict from NBC brass, 'Let's do something with children's programming.' "

As the spring of 1961 turned into summer, the heat on the TV industry to improve children's programming was rising. Television was coming under a double-barrelled attack that June. While Minow kept up the pressure, Senator Thomas Dodd opened what would become almost three years of Congressional hearings on juvenile delinquency, with an emphasis on the examination of television violence on American youth.

The Kefauver hearings had done nothing to stem the tide of TV violence. Dodd compared a typical week of 1954 TV programming to a typical week in 1961: "During the so-called prime viewing hours, when millions of children and teenagers watch TV, shows of this type (depicting crime and violence) increased from 16.6 percent of total programming to 50.6 percent in a given week."

Minow—the father of three young girls—was invited to appear before the Dodd subcommittee. "I have recently called much of television programming a Vast Wasteland," he said in his statement of June 19. "Nowhere is that waste more critical than in the programming aimed at children."

Two days later, Robert Kennedy, the featured speaker at an American Jewish Committee fund-raising dinner, recognized the importance of Minow's position on the medium's responsibility to children. "One of your citizens is doing a splendid job for the children of our community," the Attorney General said. "I was brought up with the idea that three things shape children growing up—family, church and school. There is no question now that there are four things and the fourth is television." "My children," Kennedy continued, "know all the advertising slogans, westerns, gangsters, and I would hope that they will know more when they grow up. I am counting on Newt Minow. He cannot do it by himself as far as education is concerned, but what they are going to be like twenty years from now depends a great deal on him and his success."

ABC, the network with the prime-time schedule most heavily weighted with the violence of action-adventure, introduced the most ambitious plan for a children's series. In early August 1961, Minow received a letter from Jules Power, executive producer of ABC's new project for children, who, for eight years had served as the producer of the classic kids' show *Watch Mr. Wizard*. "Although you have by now had many indications of how effective your brief tenure in office has been," Power told the chairman, "I thought you might be pleased to know of another project which I feel resulted in great measure from your forthright stirring of the industry's conscience."

The producer informed Minow that ABC's new show would be called *DISCOVERY* and would air every weekday from 5:00 to 5:30 P.M. beginning October 2, 1961. "It's the most extensive effort any of the networks have announced to date," Power continued, "and while many of the program executives insist they've been 'thinking of doing it for a long time,' your name nevertheless comes up so frequently at each meeting that you're beginning to sound like the co-producer."

"Even more important," Power wrote in closing, "I detect an increasing recognition at both the network and agency level that your position on program content makes excellent sense, and that the sooner the industry does something about it, the better off both it and the viewing public will be."

By the time the vacationing Minow read Power's letter, however, less than two weeks later, *DISCOVERY* had already been tossed out of the 1961–62 lineup because of insufficient affiliate clearance. "Dear Jules," Minow wrote back in a missive labelled PERSONAL, "I have just returned to the office and found your letter. I have since learned that *DISCOVERY* is not going to be on the air in October, which, of course, is a great disappointment. Some time when you are down this way I would like to have a talk with you to learn a little more about the reasons why shows like *DISCOVERY* do not achieve affiliate clearance."

*Broadcasting* reported, "*Discovery*, ABC-TV's answer to FCC Chairman Newton Minow's demands for better children's programming, has turned out to be a mirage." The network offered the program to stations in 152 markets. Seventy-six stations cleared the prestige kids' show and seventy-six did not. More important, however, of the stations that refused the show, the great majority were among the top 100 U.S. television markets. According to ABC calculations, this meant that more than half of American TV households were unable to tune in to *DISCOVERY*. Under these conditions, the program was a most inefficient advertising vehicle and attracting sponsors was difficult.

ABC-TV president Oliver Treyz made an unsuccessful personal closed-circuit plea to the affiliates to "pick up the show in view of the prevailing winds in Washington." But *DISCOVERY*'s daily afternoon time slot was a major stumbling block in gaining clearance. Local stations preferred to air their own inexpensive programming during the time period and keep all the advertising revenue instead of sharing it with the network.

To explain the problem of affiliate clearance to his *Saturday Review* readers, critic Robert Lewis Shayon put words into the mouth of a typical affiliate program director being asked to schedule an edifying kids' show. "Count me out," he would be likely to say. "The show will be a bomb. And even if I carried it, I wouldn't put it in a good time period, I'd produce my own local show and make more money on it because it wouldn't be educational."

ABC estimated it would suffer a half-million dollar loss on *DISCOVERY* for the six-month period from autumn 1961 through spring 1962. With increasing network expenditures in news and public affairs programming, it was decided that *DISCOVERY* would be, according to the network president, "too great an additional financial burden to undertake."

As the first summer of his tenure on the FCC was drawing to a close, Minow received a personal letter from a family friend. She praised his fight to improve the quality of television programming, but sincerely expressed doubt that any significant changes could be made because of the low level to which public taste had slipped. Minow wrote back, "I agree—the real hope is with the children and that's what I've decided to concentrate on."

### Newton Minow and Robert Kennedy Collaborate for Kids

The second major speech of Minow's chairmanship came on September 22, 1961. The subject of the address—which was regarded as a follow-up to the Vast Wasteland speech—was exclusively children's programming. The Radio and Television Executives Society was meeting in New York City and Minow spoke to an audience of more than a thousand at the Roosevelt Hotel. "Some friends suggested in view of my last speech to some broadcasters that I might need a body guard as I approached all of you. I tried to get Eliot Ness, but he was unavailable—he didn't want to be identified with any more violence," Minow joked before getting down to his serious remarks.

The chairman characterized the nature of most children's programs then on the air as "timewaster shows, dull, gray, insipid, like dishwater, just as tasteless, just as nourishing." Minow outlined the case history of *DISCOVERY*'s demise and his disappointment was clear: "It is not my purpose to argue that this particular program should be on the air . . . but assuming with me for a minute that *DISCOVERY* did have all the values suggested, then where does the responsibility rest for killing a children's program with so much hope and promise? Is it enough to shrug and say, 'Too bad' . . . there is something fundamentally wrong with a system in which the potential of reaching the homes of 14 million children is not enough to go ahead."

Minow then offered a suggestion for improvement—a blueprint of sorts, a share-the-risk scheme. He urged the three networks to rotate a regularly scheduled afternoon educational show for children, with each web airing the program twice a week. *Television Magazine* referred to the idea as Minow's "plan to save U.S. children from TV."

Dividing the competitive disadvantages three ways seemed logical and fair, but the antitrust implications were worrisome. Minow assured the networks that he had discussed the matter with Attorney General Robert Kennedy, at that point the father of seven children. "He authorized me to tell you today that the Justice Department will give prompt and sympathetic consideration to any plan you may devise involving a combined effort to improve children's programs."

Robert Kennedy's involvement in the plan was more than secondary, however. As it was reported in the trade press: "There is solid reason to believe that Kennedy, in fact, actually got the ball rolling on the proposal, and perhaps even conceived it. It was the young Attorney General who last summer set up a closed-door luncheon confab with CBS Board Chairman William Paley, prexy Frank Stanton, NAB President LeRoy Collins and Minow to hash over what should be done about TV fare for youngsters."

Twenty-five years later Minow recalled about that meeting: "I was invited to lunch over at the Attorney General's office. And we had a talk about children's television. I remember that very, very well. And I know that Frank (Stanton), who later became a very close friend and for whom I have the utmost respect, resented the fact that the government was getting into this business." But the determined Robert Kennedy, Minow remembered, was "very interested in doing something about children's programming."

Three days after Minow presented the tripartite plan to the television industry, a member of the House of Representatives submitted for publication in the *Congressional Record* three newspaper articles detailing the proposed arrangement. In introducing his request, Congressman Harris B. McDowell said, "Mr. Speaker, children have been the forgotten citizens of our country when it comes to television programs. Now Newton N. Minow, FCC Chairman, and Attorney General Robert F. Kennedy have come forward with a brilliant solution to the establishment of programs which will challenge and enrich the lives and minds of all children."

Minow, apparently delighted with the Congressman's assessment of the scheme, sent a copy of the remarks from the *Congressional Record* to the Attorney General. Attached was a memo with just the phrase, "*NOTE*: 'A brilliant solution.' "

The same day that Minow delivered his children's programming speech, the producer of the aborted *DISCOVERY* series wrote to the chairman. "It was, as I expected," said Jules Power, "a great speech, destined to set off a whole new cycle of anguish and protestations, to be followed, in turn, by the inevitable soul-searching, and finally further awareness that your position is fundamentally correct."

The industry reaction to Minow's address to the Radio and Television Executives Society was amazingly quick. According to *Variety*, "The ink was hardly dry on the big play Minow got in the dailies when everybody and his brother had a children's show to offer the networks." Independent producers and packagers, the article said, seemed to be "laying [*sic*] in readiness to pounce." New programs appeared and old shows were being reactivated as "just the thing Minow's talking about."

Within four hours of the luncheon speech, the three networks agreed to sit down and discuss the rotating series idea. NBC was the first network to respond publicly. A press release was issued quoting president Robert Kintner: "We will give immediate and affirmative study to Chairman Minow's proposals within our own organization . . . to consider ways and means of carrying forward the objectives outlined."

Minow's children's programming speech didn't make the same kind of headlines as the Vast Wasteland speech in the non-trade press. There was no element of surprise since Minow's position on programming had become common knowledge and no catchy phrase was coined. But, to those involved in the production of kids' shows, or hoping to be, the September 22 speech was bigger news than the first.

Letters and telegrams began to arrive in Minow's office asking him to view programs or read script ideas for children's series and offer his imprimatur. Minow was understandably reluctant to add fuel to the fire of his critics, who charged he was trying to mold TV programming to suit his own tastes. The chairman became increasingly careful to avoid the appearance of endorsing programs or series ideas.

One producer of a show already on the air, called *On Your Mark*, wrote with a highly improper, but typical request. After providing a description of the series, he queried: "May I, in conclusion, ask if it would be feasible and appropriate for the Chairman of the FCC to comment on such a program for the record. It seems to me that this type of programming can benefit by such official encouragement."

The request was routed to Minow's assistant, Tedson Meyers, for reply. Meyers brought the letter to Minow's attention and attached a memo indicating that he had already informed the correspondent his wish could not be fulfilled. "But he insists upon trying," wrote Meyers in his memo to the chairman. Minow's response was boldly handwritten on the bottom of the same memo—"*Ted*—Answer is NO."

In early October, the top brass of all three networks met to discuss the Minow-RFK rotating children's hour. But no agreement could be reached.

Each network had already invested some time and effort in the area of children's programming and did not wish to share resources—or glory.

ABC was the first network to break away from the idea. President Oliver Treyz issued the following statement: "ABC-TV is convinced that the networks must assume direct responsibility in this vital programming area and retain direct supervision and control of production. The cost for each network will be greater, but the result is certain to be better and more diversified programs, with consequent greater stimulation of American youth." In other words, what Treyz was saying was, all that work on *DISCOVERY* shouldn't go down the drain. The program would be resurrected for the 1962 TV season.

Reflecting on the three-network plan many years later, Minow felt, "I made one big mistake." ABC's Treyz had called the chairman before making the break official. Treyz said, as Minow recalled, "We would like to do our own program every day. Are you going to be upset if we don't go along as part of the NBC-CBS three-way package?"

"I made a mistake there," said Minow remembering the conversation with the ABC-TV president, "because what I responded was to say, 'Look, it's your business, the government's not going to interfere. You do what you think is best.' So, that's what I said. ABC then promptly went its own way. I should have simply said, 'I've got to think about that.' I should have let them stew in it for a couple of weeks. Then I think they would have gone along."

The series for which NBC had recruited Jack Kuney immediately after the Vast Wasteland speech made its debut on October 8, 1961. *1,2,3—Go!* starred an engaging ten-year-old named Richard Thomas, who, in the next decade would become well known for his portrayal of John-Boy in the successful dramatic series *The Waltons*. The youngster's co-host was NBC personality Jack Lescoulie.

The magazine format of the show, designed for elementary school children, had the two of them travelling around the country learning about American life and society. "We decided to get into a series of adult adventures from a child's point of view," producer Kuney said. "On the first show we had Richard walking in the Cascade Mountains out in Washington with Justice William O. Douglas. And Douglas was telling him about the glory of outdoors and the glory of mountains and how it is important to save these things for posterity. It was a big ecological pitch way before it became a major issue."

Jack Kuney recalls with special fondness, though, the *1,2,3—Go!* episode that aired the last week of October. "We had taken Richard down to McLean, Virginia," he said, "to the home of Robert Kennedy." Thomas was filmed trick-or-treating with the Kennedy children. Filming began early in the afternoon and the Attorney General was not scheduled to be home to record his part in the program until later. But, when Ethel Kennedy saw the children in their costumes, she called her husband and told him he should come home early to see the wonderful sight. Kuney recalled, "In the space of twenty minutes he was there. He came home and he followed the kids around. He was delighted. What I saw that day was real. He was a compassionate, loving, indulgent father."

The producer remembered, "We rang doorbells in a few neighboring houses in McLean, finally ending up at the big Kennedy house—it was a lovely sequence." Kuney described the Attorney General's performance: "Unbelievably charming, Bobby opened the door himself, feigning surprise at the masked kids who were trick-or-treating, then inviting them in to tell them about some children in the world who wouldn't be able to celebrate Halloween because they were hungry. He finished with a plea for the United Nations Children Emergency Fund, UNICEF. It made a great Halloween show."

Unfortunately for the cast and crew of *1,2,3—Go!*, most young children watching TV at seven o'clock on Sunday evenings, however, preferred the adventures of a talking horse. *Mr. Ed* on CBS, with consistent Nielsen shares above 30, was devastating competition. But NBC stuck it out for thirteen weeks. And then, *1,2,3—Go!* was gone.

The ripples of Minow's influence on children's television were reaching local stations as well in the fall of 1961. Many stations made modest attempts to improve their in-house children's programming. But the format of local kids' shows generally remained the same. An in-studio host in the guise of a sea captain or fire chief or cowboy or clown or circus ringmaster or practitioner of some other exotic profession introduced large quantities of animated filler or short films, such as *Our Gang* comedies or a *Three Stooges* feature. It was a solidly entrenched, inexpensive formula.

In the early 1960s a package of sixty-five old cartoons could be purchased from a film distributor at a flat price as low as $250, which allowed for unlimited broadcasts. Many of these cartoons, however, were originally made for adult theater audiences in the 1930s. They were filled with sadism and offensive stereotypes. For example, black African savages pot-roasting white missionaries was a common cartoon formula. The penny-pinching stereotype of Jews was reinforced in cartoons such as the one in which a golfer shouted "Fore!" and a long-bearded rabbi shouts back "$3.98."

The producers of syndicated material for kids' programming responded to the regulatory climate and the apparent need for infusing educational elements into their product, which was sold to local stations. King Features Syndicate, for instance, supplier of the popular Popeye cartoons, decided in the fall of 1961 that it would be good business to make the Sailor Man public relations conscious. Many public service subjects were introduced in

220 newly produced cartoons. Olive Oyl, Brutus, Wimpy, Swee'Pea, and Popeye illustrated good dental care, fire safety, forest conservation, and the importance of safe driving habits. Of course, the vast majority of the cartoons and short films used by local stations were not designed with educational themes.

The attempts to improve local children's programming were highly publicized by the National Association of Broadcasters and the Television Information Office with the publication of a book entitled, *For the Young Viewer: Television Programming for Children ... At the Local Level*. The three authors of the manual, specialists in the field of child development, offered constructive program ideas based on children's needs and abilities of comprehension. The publication won a Peabody award and was sent to libraries across the country as a gift of the Television Information Office.

The objectivity of the document was marred, however, by the inclusion of listings of local children's shows which were described, on the basis of information provided by the broadcasters themselves, in unrealistically flattering ways. The function of *For the Young Viewer* was really more public relations than an agenda for improvement and change. The burden of making genuine progress in the field of children's television rested with the networks.

## Kids' TV '62: A Spurt of the Smarts

Along with ABC's break from the rotating children's series in the fall of 1961 came the announcement of a new programming unit within the network. Jules Power wrote to Chairman Minow and reported that after Minow's speech of September 22, "ABC approached me with an offer to become Director of Children's Programming." With Power's acceptance, ABC became the first network to maintain a Children's Programming Department. At CBS and NBC, children's shows were still produced by the Public Affairs Department. Power expressed delight with the challenge and hoped his department's efforts would "foreshadow a new era in children's television."

The FCC's threatened plans to pursue more direct regulation over the networks were greatly feared. Economist William Melody pointed out that such regulations would "surely interfere with the financial boom the industry was then enjoying." So, Melody wrote, during this period of mounting tension, network children's series served as "a peace offering" to the New Frontier.

In the fall of 1962, a new *quality* kids' show would debut on each network. These programs appeared, in the words of Jack Gould, "to deflect the chill critical winds of Washington." Although the networks preferred that the public did not perceive their efforts in children's programming to be the result of government pressure, the link was hard to miss. In the spring of 1962, NBC president Robert Kintner, testifying before the Senate Subcommittee investigating TV violence and juvenile delinquency, decided to announce his network would have a new educational offering for kids—a show called *Exploring*.

At the time of Kintner's gesture of appeasement, the program was little more than a title and a few ideas contributed by Craig Fisher, a young producer working on the *Today* show. After the announcement, Fisher was told to "develop his '*Exploring*' idea in a hurry."

NBC, beginning in 1960, and throughout the Kennedy years, aired a much-loved children's program on Saturday mornings. *The Shari Lewis Show* featured a petite and enormously talented ventriloquist-singer-dancer and her coterie of quirky animal friends, who were expressively manipulated hand puppets. But, since the program was not explicitly educational, the network felt it would be prudent to expand its schedule for kids to include Minow-style programming.

*Exploring* was an ambitious project. The weekly one-hour program was hosted by Dr. Albert Hibbs, a thirty-seven-year-old physicist with the Jet Propulsion Laboratory of the California Institute of Technology. The program was most at home with segments involving science and math, but often Hibbs and his supporting cast—Albert the chipmunk, Calvin the crow, Sir Geoffrey the giraffe, and Magnolia the ostrich, brought to life by puppeteers Paul and Mary Ritts—tackled more humanistic subjects. Well-known performers such as Celeste Holm and Peter Ustinov would narrate films for the series. Elementary schools could receive *Exploring* teacher guides from NBC that previewed upcoming shows and suggested student projects that dovetailed with the TV curriculum.

The CBS offering in the fall of 1962 was *Reading Room*, presented for thirty minutes each Saturday. Unfortunately, it was scheduled at noon, the same hour *Exploring* went on the air. The rotating kid series proposed by Newton Minow and Robert Kennedy was meant to avoid just this kind of scheduling conflict.

*Reading Room* was a studio-based production for eight- to twelve-year-olds. Host Ned Hoopes discussed a book-of-the-week with a panel of kids and a guest authority. Compared to the elaborate production efforts of the other two networks, *Reading Room* seemed to be a cursory undertaking. Perhaps the network felt less compunction about children's programming because it continued to air the *Captain Kangaroo* show every morning, as it had since 1955.

As a daily afterschool program, *DISCOVERY*, now called *DISCOVERY '62*, received the most attention. The show, designed for seven- to twelve-year-olds, was hosted from New York's Ritz Theater by the wholesome, young adult team of Frank Buxton and Virginia Gibson. The two also had a sidekick, a melancholy looking bloodhound named Corpuscle. Viewers were guided through segments on a broad range of topics such as "A Trip to the Moon," "The Voyage of Christopher Columbus," and "A Day in the

Life of a Zoo Doctor," and then were returned to home base at the Ritz. In search of new ideas on how to improve the program's educational effectiveness, the producers solicited the input of the academic community through the award of research grants.

In late September Jules Power wrote to Minow: "*DISCOVERY '62* finally goes on the air Monday, October 1, and this is simply a personal note of gratitude for the support and encouragement of this past year and a half. I have grave doubts that we could have made it without you."

ABC vice-president Armand Grant sent Minow a detailed progress report on *DISCOVERY '62* two weeks after its premiere. Grant informed the chairman that the network was collaborating with the American Library Association to compile supplemental reading lists for young viewers. "In addition," Grant wrote, "we have worked out an arrangement with *Scholastic Magazine*." Each issue of the publication would contain material related to *DISCOVERY* programs. Minow was also told that Jules Power had embarked on a speaking tour of PTA meetings to discuss the show with educators and parents and to solicit program ideas.

The ABC vice-president also gave the FCC chairman the facts and figures regarding affiliate acceptance of the show. "Our people were successful, having a year's time in which to work, to improve the *DISCOVERY '62* clearance picture markedly." Although thirty markets still did not clear the series, 92 percent of U.S. households were included in its new coverage pattern.

*DISCOVERY '62* was met with a mixed critical reaction from professional TV observers. Most of the complaints, however, dealt with the hard-pitch commercials inserted into the program, not the show itself. The well-intentioned content of the series received widespread plaudits.

Shortly after the 1962 season got underway, the TV editor of the *Atlanta Journal & Constitution* wrote a column reminding his readers that "Newton Minow raked the television industry over the coals for not putting greater emphasis on children's programming." The columnist then went on to praise *DISCOVERY* as an important contribution to American children. The implication was that Minow was responsible for its being on the air. A few days later the chairman wrote to the critic: "I have just seen your column about children's television. I am very grateful for your informing the public about these improved efforts."

While parents, teachers, and newspaper critics applauded the networks' 1962 offerings for kids, advertisers were not fans of the Minow-inspired shows. Ad agencies were not supportive of efforts to improve children's programming by infusing it with language arts, music appreciation, mathematics, social studies, and science. Attracting commercial sponsorship became a major obstacle. "Run-of-the-mill cartoon and comedy shows have a greater chance of survival than the so-called 'quality' ones," *Sponsor* magazine reported.

The networks complained about the lack of advertiser support and a resentment began to develop in the advertising community. One ad agency executive said candidly, "Too much is being done to appease Washington, not enough to strengthen the over-all advertiser picture."

In the early 1960s, most national sponsors were more interested in family shows than programs appealing just to children. Although it would change very soon, the overriding philosophy in 1962 was still, "We don't sell to kids. Purchases are made by adults."

If the audience for educational kids' shows had been larger, advertisers might have been willing to experiment. "Much thought has been given to the possibility of using children's programs to sell products children do not use," *Television Age* indicated, "but which they in turn might 'sell' to their parents." However, the size of the audiences never grew to a point that would make large-scale investment in "second-hand" advertising worthwhile.

"The only hope for these intellectually based programs for children," one TV industry insider noted, "would appear to be the concern of some advertisers that they do, after all, have a responsibility beyond the mass movement of their own merchandise." The advertising industry never accepted such responsibility. Unregulated by the federal government, advertisers did not need to make a peace offering to the New Frontier. Goodwill was not what mattered on their bottom line.

As the season progressed, *DISCOVERY '62* ran up against a stonewall of advertiser resistance. "Were it less altruistic in its aims," said a representative of ABC's sales department, "it would be much easier to sell." The national sales manager at ABC-TV, Edward Bleier explained, "We know *DISCOVERY's* a new program and we admit it has some problems (regarding commercial reach). But there's no interest—even when we ask somebody to *make us an offer*. We're willing to give the program to clients at a cost-per-thousand comparable to almost anything else they can buy. There are no takers."

As the 1962–63 season came to a close, the idea of educational kids' series on commercial television was in trouble. The networks could not, or would not, keep them on their schedules without secure sponsorship. And that was just not in the cards.

The creative staffs of these new kids' shows believed, given time, the series could have become efficient advertising vehicles. "All of us have put in a year of work on the programs now," one producer said, "and we've learned a lot about improving the shows to make them better. It would be a crime to let that knowledge and effort go to waste."

A representative of a major toy company took issue with such an idealistic view: "Last year Newton Minow took one broad look at children's television and was appalled—not only at the sameness in entertainment but at the complete lack of any real instructive material for millions of children who watch an average of 5 hours per day. In a speech he asked that each network devote at least a half-hour per week to good, educational programming for children. All complied almost instantly. . . . Wonderful! Except that no one's watching, except possibly Mr. Minow and his family. The advertisers who thought it was a good idea to participate in educational tv may start looking elsewhere. And who can blame them?"

Optimistic observers hoped the 1962–63 season was a modest beginning in a trend toward improved children's programming. It turned out to be the peak in network commitment, which soon declined. Although *Exploring* survived and lasted three more seasons, *DISCOVERY* was relegated to a Sunday afternoon slot, and *Reading Room* was cancelled.

Lasting improvement in children's programming would have required the establishment of "noneconomic criteria as a permanent part of the decision-making process," wrote economist William Melody. The threat of government regulation provided only temporary incentive to change normal operating procedures in regard to children's programs. Later in the decade, public television, not commercial, would begin to master the combination of education and entertainment in the programs of the Children's Television Workshop.

For a short time, though, during the Kennedy years, there was real hope that commercial television could become an ally in the education of American school children—that the medium could stimulate curiosity about an increasingly technical world, generate enthusiasm for culture and the arts, and foster pride in a heritage of freedom.

It was a quixotic notion, as so many on the New Frontier were. But maybe, just maybe, watching American television could help build strong bodies and strong minds.

On the eve of his departure from the Commission in May 1963, Minow was interviewed about the accomplishments of his term. NBC's David Brinkley asked, "When you came into office, one point you made frequently was that there wasn't enough programming for children. How do you feel about it now, two years later?" Minow responded:

> I still feel that way. Some people make the argument that television is bad for children . . . I don't think that's necessarily the case. . . . The really gory, bloody stuff where you get the idea that every problem is solved with a kick in the belly or a smack in the head—some of that is harmful, but my main point was different. That is, the time is wasted.
>
> One broadcaster sent me a book one day which was a study . . . and the conclusion was that with children who watch television and children who don't watch television, at the age of about twelve there's not really any difference. . . . And the broadcaster said, "Well, you see, it hasn't affected them at all." I said, "My God, I can't think of a worse indictment of television than that; that this great gift

should have no effect upon a child's mind or a child's heart after years and hours and hours of watching it."

Looking back on his FCC tenure after more than two decades, Minow admitted, "I think if I had to do it over again, I would have zeroed in on one thing. I would have concentrated on children's television. That is where you could have gotten the most public support. And I would let them argue that I was being a censor. It would have been easier to face it on children's television. If I had to do it over again, that's where I would have drawn the battle."

# CHAPTER 8

# Consuming in the National Interest

## TELEVISION ADVERTISING

"Use it up. Wear it out. Make it do or do without." The old Yankee slogan extolling the virtue of frugality was a familiar refrain during World War II, years of shortages and rationing. In the prosperous postwar period, when sacrifice was no longer required, the wisdom of the rhyme eroded. Throughout the 1950s, with the population and the formation of new households exploding, a commodity culture was solidifying and the effectiveness of television advertising was dramatically established.

Any sponsor's decision to invest in national TV promotion invariably resulted in sharp sales increases. Planned obsolescence, impulse buying, and elaborate packaging were entrenched concepts in the marketplace before the 1950s ended.

By the beginning of the new decade, the old motto had virtually no application to the mainstream of life in the United States. In just fifteen years the sentiment had become archaic. Consumer indulgence, not restraint, was encouraged. A dynamic economy demanded the responsibility of uninhibited purchasing.

For the Kennedy administration, during this period when the economies of all industrialized nations were rapidly expanding, material growth was a critical factor in the maintenance of America's dominant position in the world. "In short," President Kennedy explained, "our primary challenge is not how to divide the economic pie, but how to enlarge it."

To those involved in American manufacturing and advertising, their mission assumed a higher plane. While pursuing their business ambitions, they were also supporting the goals of the country. An editorial in the advertising trade press succinctly summarized the scope of the relationship between economic expansion and the public interest on the New Frontier: "Most everyone by now knows that consumers should be spending much more than they are on consumer goods—so that we could eliminate unemployment, make plants work up to capacity, prevent our government from operating at a deficit, and enable our private economy to support the space-defense burden." Not only prosperity, but survival seemed to depend on developing all sources of productivity.

The networks clearly had as much of a vested interest in economic expansion as did manufacturers and advertisers. The enormity of the potential for profit by encouraging growth did not escape the consideration of those in broadcast corporate offices. For instance, a farfetched proposal presented in October 1961 to NBC chairman Robert Sarnoff by Harry Bannister, vice-president in charge of station relations, reveals that network people were thinking in extremes about the American consumer:

> I don't want to be a nuisance, but I want to urge you to give further consideration to the idea of bomb-shelter construction as an issue you should advocate. . . .
>
> What I am thinking about is for NBC to announce a program with the aim of educating our people so that ultimately every American home will have its own protection against atomic attack. . . .
>
> I would think the RCA people would be interested in this, because such a construction program would certainly open up enormous uses of electrical equipment such as air conditioning, washing machines, television, radio, phonographs, not to mention power supply, etc. . . .
>
> Not unimportantly, this might make us an awful lot of friends in Congress and the Government as a demonstration of the great public service that a network can perform. At the same time, this could open vast avenues of expenditure for television advertising.

The falling cost of energy combined with the postwar flowering of technology created in American industry a tremendous productive capacity. But the demand for the output—the urge to buy—needed to be aroused. And no more potent method of stimulating wants and creating needs, of turning luxuries into necessities, existed than television advertising.

Success stories abounded. After switching the bulk of its advertising dollars from magazines to television, the Sunbeam Corporation experienced such a buying rush that it was forced to use planes and helicopters to speed distribution of its products. A Valentine's Day TV ad campaign for CandyGrams resulted in the company running out of the special delivery confections in ten cities. Bic ballpoint pens, introduced in the United States in 1960, quickly became hot sellers. "Television has done everything for us," said the account executive for Waterman-Bic in 1962, as he announced the company would more than double its TV advertising budget for 1963. Bic's TV spots featured the product mounted in an electric drill. After the pen was forced through a piece of wallboard, the audience saw for itself that "Bic will write the first time every time."

The most critical priority in the early years of "The Selling Sixties" was the development and promotion of entirely new markets. An avalanche of new products, especially food, drugs, and cosmetics, was introduced in the marketplace primarily through television. Shelf space in cornucopian supermarkets became prized real estate. New flavors, new colors, new sizes, and new ideas in consuming greeted the housewife weekly.

In one year the Colgate-Palmolive Company added thirty new brands to its product line, including Baggies Plastic Bags, Action Bleach in dissolvable packets, Cold Power cold water detergent, Away Air Deodorant, and Soaky Fun Bath—a liquid bath soap for children packaged in plastic bottles in the shapes of popular cartoon characters.

"Consider the humble potato, that used to sell by the bag," said the president of Young & Rubicam as he discussed the changing marketplace of the early 1960s. "Today you buy it as a potato puff, a potato pancake, potato au gratin, instant mashed, French fried, flaked, frozen and heaven knows what else."

During the Kennedy years, the American populace was growing younger each day. The average bride was twenty years old and television advertisers were anxious to convince her to take the acquisitive road to domestic happiness. The bulk of entertainment programming, especially situation comedies, bolstered the message of the commercials by portraying ideal middle-class American families surrounded by an abundance of possessions. Much of prime-time television offered the spectacle of consumption.

The teenage population was, as one adman noted, "bursting its denim britches." Naturally, manufacturers were eager to sate immediate youthful cravings as well as cultivate loyalty for future consumption. The under-twenty-five generation, less discriminating about purchases than their elders, and with more discretionary income, was the most desirable target for television advertising. As demographics became an imperative consideration in marketing strategy, young consumers became the first group to be distinguished as a "market segment."

In the 1950s, motivational research—probing the mind of the American shopper—became a fashionable endeavor in the advertising world. Though most everyone agreed there were simply too many imponderables for advertising ever to become an exact science, research in marketing effectiveness continued to be a top industry priority.

In 1962, the president of the Advertising Council urged putting academic social scientists to work at reducing some of advertising's unknowns. Like so many others, he felt a standard of living that was envied around the world could be an important Cold War weapon. "The country's universities are think factories," the top adman said. With the United States "engaged in a fateful battle of brains with the communist world," he asked, "why should these think factories not now be working on the problems of advertising?"

Among the most nagging questions were: Is a hard-sell commercial effective for one audience and not another? Is it possible to determine what kind of advertising influences different groups of consumers? Does an advertisement sometimes increase sales while tearing down corporate image? What happens when viewers like the product but dislike the advertising?

Most of the products competing against each other on television were only marginally different. All shampoos, toothpastes, aspirins, soft drinks, gasolines, chewing gums, nasal sprays, and the like were similarly satisfactory. So, as Professor George Gerbner noted, "A small army of specialized talent must convince us, therefore, that one brand of ordinary peas is like no other brand of ordinary peas."

Consequently, rather than stress product claims and price, most advertising strove to associate corporate image and brand name with psychic satisfaction. Through television advertising consumers were given the assurance, one social observer pointed out, that with the proper purchases they could be "lovable, kissable, respectable, honorable, clean, odorfree, immune to insecurity and, in general, not missing any pleasure which others may be enjoying."

By 1960, a formidable amount of creative, performance, and technical talent had been enticed into the making of TV commercials. Television advertising was ensconced in American popular culture. A film festival to celebrate high production and entertainment values in commercials—the Clio Awards—started in 1960. Admen and adwomen longed to have their work joyously saluted as a commercial classic, to create the spot viewers looked forward to seeing.

But research was showing that enjoyment and aesthetic appeal often had little to do with success in pushing products. In 1961, David Ogilvy, of Ogilvy, Benson & Mather, Inc., addressing two hundred of the country's top-level industrialists, offered some advice on advertising: "Let me warn you of one trap. Don't demand that your agency pursue *originality* for the sake of originality. There is a school of advertising which substitutes originality and cuteness for serious salesmanship. These monkeys give each other awards. They enthrone the highbrow copywriter and the avant-garde art director. They are totally ignorant of advertising research. They don't know what they are doing."

A trend toward naturalism in TV commercials did become apparent mid-way through the New Frontier. For instance, a spot for Oxydol detergent featured two plain-looking women in ordinary houseclothes discussing the product. It was, according to a competing executive, "unsophisticated and undramatic, but very effective."

The intention of such homely vignettes was to make it seem as if the viewer were eavesdropping. In an ad for Ajax All Purpose Liquid Cleaner—which would move past Mr. Clean into first place—a neighborly housewife is shown straightening her sweater before speaking in order to build realism and empathy. For many products, ordinary looking people radiated a truthfulness more beautiful models did not. While cosmetic and cigarette sponsors still wanted glamour on the TV screen, in the early 1960s commercial casting directors broadened their view of the exemplary American face.

During a typical week in the Kennedy years, more than two hundred companies advertised well over five hundred different products on network television. None represented as enormous an investment to the American consumer as the automobile. And perhaps, along with the television set itself, no other product represented such revolutionary changes in life in the United States. By the early 1960s, corner grocery stores, neighborhood diners, hotels, and downtown shopping districts had already been feeling the hard push of supermarkets, drive-in restaurants, motels, and shopping centers.

At the outset of the sixties, it was estimated that the auto industry, intrinsically bound to the national economy, needed to sell between six and seven million cars per year to function profitably and efficiently. Fast replacement sales rather than product durability was Detroit's priority.

Following the lead of the packaged goods industries, American auto manufacturers greatly multiplied their offerings. An abundance of new models in various sizes and prices appeared. In 1963, 408 new models—twenty more than in 1962—were introduced having no significant engineering changes.

Each fall the new television season coincided with new model introductions in the auto industry. During the fifties, the Growth Decade for both autos and television, car makers sponsored many lavish TV specials and the weekly programs of their star sales people such as Pat Boone, Dinah Shore, and Lawrence Welk.

In the early sixties, the advertising strategy underwent a change as the high cost of sole sponsorship continued to climb. Like soap and food manufacturers, the auto companies wanted to spread their message in varied time slots and to varied audiences. Action-adventure programming, for instance, appealed to younger audiences—presumably the viewers most interested in Detroit's new lower-priced compact cars. Daytime TV, too, offered a new breed of potential customers—housewives who might convince their husbands of the necessity of becoming a two-car family. At the same time, the petroleum industry was spending the lion's share of its advertising dollars on television to promote increased passenger car driving and gasoline consumption.

In the economic boon years of the early 1960s, television advertising blessed consumer extravagance. Air pollution, fuel shortages, toxic waste, and a landfill crisis were in the offing, but during this heady time Americans were invited to drive and shop with abandon—habits that would be hard to break.


## Kindling the Cigarette Controversy

Maybe people looked askance when nice girls lit up. But for the most part, smoking was an innocent pleasure as the GIs returned from overseas. Cigarette companies, with swollen advertising budgets, wasted no time in using the new medium of television to reach so many millions of potential customers. The sponsorship of top-rated programs such as the *Camel News Caravan* maintained tobacco's secure footing in American life.

At the dawn of the 1960s, smoking was a widely sown national habit and cigarette advertising was an institution on American television. Lucky Strike reminded viewers, "You can smoke on the job." The jingle claimed, "Never was a man who could forget the taste of a genuine cigarette. Get the honest taste a man can like—the honest taste of a Lucky Strike."

Even the characters in family programs, heroes and fathers, would be shown enjoying a smoke now and then. After one of Aunt Bee's legendary Sunday dinners, for instance, Sheriff Andy Taylor of Mayberry—the kindest and wisest of men—might sit on the front porch and relax with a cigarette.

Few smokers harbored serious fears over health hazards, but the weight of evidence was growing heavier. In late October 1961, after a two-year review of the scientific literature, the Royal College of Physicians in Great Britain reported unequivocally, "Cigarette smoking is a cause of lung cancer." The high probability of a relationship between smoking and heart disease was also acknowledged. Tobacco companies in Great Britain responded to the indictment by voluntarily eliminating cigarette commercials before 9:00 P.M. And, the Independent Television Authority began a move to prohibit cigarette advertisements that made special appeals to young people.

In the United States, cigarette smoking was also assumed by the Public Health Service to be the principal reason for the rising death rate from lung cancer. But an absolute connection would not be the official government verdict until the January 1964 release of the study by the Surgeon General's Advisory Committee on the effects of cigarette smoking. While the American jury was still out in the case against tobacco, the cigarette, advertising, and broadcast industries felt no compunction to restrict in any way commercials encouraging the smoking habit.

So, in November 1962, when the president of the NAB *urged his own membership* to adopt restraints on cigarette advertising, it was an astonishing turn of events. Speaking at a regional NAB meeting in Portland, Oregon, LeRoy Collins asserted that the number of teenage smokers in the United

States was increasing because of advertising geared to youngsters. "Certainly the moral responsibility rests first on the tobacco manufacturer," he said. "Certainly it also rests on the advertising agencies. Certainly it also rests on the outstanding sports figures who permit their hero status to be prostituted." (At the time of Collins's speech, one of the most widely aired cigarette spots featured a youthful sports idol, Green Bay Packers star halfback Paul Hornung. A critic in sympathy with Governor Collins noted that Hornung "lights up a Marlboro on tv almost every hour on the hour all through the long fall weekends.")

"But where others have persistently failed to subordinate their profit motives to the higher purpose of the general good health of our young people," Collins continued, "then I think the broadcaster should make corrective moves on his own. This we could do under code amendments, and I feel we should proceed to do so, not because we are required to, but because a sense of moral responsibility demands it."

With cigarette advertising on television amounting to more than $104 million annually, the altruism of LeRoy Collins was not appreciated by the beneficiaries of the nicotine habit. Broadcasters were resentful that Collins made his utterances without clearance from the NAB board, and, in fact, in defiance of the influential board members whose opinions he had solicited. His condemnation of early evening cigarette ads that focused on the teenage market and contained allusions to athletic prowess, popularity, and sexual glamour, was a statement of personal belief.

The networks disassociated themselves from what was being called the "Ban the Butts" speech. ABC and NBC issued pronouncements of disagreement. CBS—which two months earlier had alienated the tobacco industry with a *CBS Reports* documentary on teenage smoking—offered a public "no comment" and asserted it was a matter for the NAB Code Authority to decide. The network did reassure its tobacco clients, however, that CBS did not share the conviction of LeRoy Collins.

The Tobacco Institute accused the NAB president of applying a "layman's judgment of finality" to complex and debatable questions of medical science. Leaders of the advertising industry declared that a limitation on the advertising of a perfectly legal product would establish a dangerous precedent. Fairfax Cone of the Foote, Cone & Belding agency suggested that if Governor Collins was successful in his crusade, "there is no reason why someone else should not undertake to restrict some other advertising for almost any quixotic reason."

Cigarette manufacturers, sensing the possibility of a public relations crisis if parents, educators, and the health care community rallied behind Collins, did make some scheduling adjustments. In 1962, close to 60 percent of all cigarette commercials on American television appeared before 9:00 P.M. But, after Collins had his say, the appeal of earlier evening time slots diminished.

The R.J. Reynolds Company, for instance, cancelled its sponsorship of *Hootenanny*, an ABC folk music show that aired Saturdays from 8:30 to 9:00 P.M. Because the program was recorded at college campuses across the country and was designed to appeal to a young audience, this also made it an unattractive buy in light of the new consciousness raised by LeRoy Collins.

Writing to NBC president Robert Kintner, Democratic Senator Maurine Neuberger of Oregon expressed her distaste with the spineless position of all three networks: "Governor Collins has challenged you to react in the best traditions of industrial self-regulation. He has given you the opportunity to convince a disturbed and skeptical public of your good faith and responsibility. He did not, after all, recommend the total abolition of cigarette advertising, but asked only that you eliminate the calculated seduction of children to the smoking habit. Should you fail to act, it is inevitable that the need for regulation will eventually find its expression in a Congressional mandate."

Sending Newton Minow a carbon copy of her correspondence to Kintner, Senator Neuberger jotted a quick note in the bottom margin: "Dear Newt, These bungle heads should develop *good* public opinion by a little self-inspection. Collins is *too* good for them!"

LeRoy Collins's contract with the NAB was scheduled to expire at the end of 1963. In January of that year, the NAB board, meeting in Phoenix, Arizona, was to determine whether or not the trade association would offer its president a contract renewal. To any outside observer, the prospects looked grim. His iconoclastic style of advocacy was bitterly rejected by a good many NAB members. The trade press speculated Collins might not be long for the radio-TV world.

Yet the board voted unanimously to grant the NAB president a new three-year contract. The deal provided an immediate salary increase to $75,000, a $12,500 living allowance, the payment of travel, entertainment and other expenses incurred while performing the functions of office, and the use of a Cadillac.

While it might have been galling to beleaguered broadcasters, it was a shrewd move by the NAB board—an act of self-defense. LeRoy Collins—who had given the Kennedy campaign select treatment in 1960 while he was chairman of the Democratic National Convention—owned the respect and gratitude of the President. If Collins were given his walking papers by the NAB, he would most likely land a high position in the Kennedy administration, perhaps Secretary of Commerce. *Variety* reported the networks were "sorry that the industry ever got mixed up with Collins in the first place," but realized it was easier to live with him than "have him wind up where his views about cigarette ads and everything else imaginable might well be far more consequential." (A year-and-a-half later, however, Collins would again wind up in government service as a federal conciliator in civil rights disputes for the Johnson administration.)

At the same gathering in Phoenix where the contract of LeRoy Collins was extended, the TV Code Review Board of the NAB did approve "continued study of the relationship between cigarette advertising and minors." But, it decided that no industry position would be taken on the matter until the outcome of the Surgeon General's report was announced.

During the last year of the Kennedy administration, LeRoy Collins could not persuade his membership to take the high road with regard to cigarette advertising. The broadcast industry displayed a stubborn shortsightedness. Early in 1964, the fact that cigarette smoking curtailed the lives of a great many Americans was no longer arguable by men and women of clear and open minds. The publication of "Smoking and Health," the 387-page report of the Surgeon General's Advisory Committee set in motion a series of events that would ultimately lead to the elimination of all cigarette advertising on American airwaves. But it was during the Kennedy years that American television was first forced to grapple with its accountability in the major public health crisis caused by tobacco.

## Dismantling the Color Line

The affability of Art Linkletter made him an ideal commercial spokesman and television personality. As host of the daily afternoon show on CBS, *Art Linkletter's House Party*, he popularized the phrase "Kids Say the Darndest Things." Each program included a segment with Linkletter interviewing a panel of children who would invariably give comical answers to probing questions. They were always rewarded with the prize of a doll or wagon or a game or some other desirable toy. But one day in 1960, as a novelty, the panel consisted of black children. And instead of a toy, each little boy was given a regulation outdoor shoeshine kit and told to "go out and earn some money."

It was an astonishing lack of sensitivity, an unawareness that the wishes of black children were no different from the wishes of white children. As the new decade commenced, however, inattention to the material aspirations of black Americans permeated national television programming and advertising.

By any business standards the neglect was irrational. The number of black Americans—approaching 20 million—exceeded the entire population of Canada, and was growing 57 percent faster than the white population in the United States. It was a market estimated to have an annual purchasing power of $20 billion—and black incomes were rising. Black consumers were spending more on food, autos, and clothing than whites with equal incomes. And, they were more likely than white shoppers to purchase brand-name products. This difference in consumer behavior, some analysts speculated, was related to denied social equality. Black Americans were unable, for the most part, to purchase dream homes, take luxury vacations, or be entertained in exclusive surroundings; therefore, daily amenities took on greater significance.

Segregated advertising aimed at the black market jumped sharply in magazines and radio stations geared toward black audiences in the early 1960s. In print ads, some sponsors ran double campaigns, posing white models in ads for the general media and minority models in ads for black media. But television advertising was not as easily pinpointed. Except for a rare few local shows, TV programs were not created exclusively for black audiences.

In Philadelphia in the summer of 1961, the *Del Shields Show Case*, a panel-talk show sponsored by C. Schmidt & Sons, the largest brewery in Pennsylvania, was created to promote Schmidt's beer in the black community. The campaign was saluted by the *Public Relations Journal* as an example of effective minority targeting. The live commercials using black talent were labelled a first. "In them," the journal noted with enthusiastic surprise, "a Negro actually handled the product. In this case, it was a food product, which added to the effect on the Negro viewing audience." Given this prevailing disposition, the earliest integration of national television advertising was not the result of a natural social evolution, but rather the activism of the Congress of Racial Equality.

In the spring of 1963, a report based on a five-month study by the New York State Commission for Human Rights blamed advertising agencies for the racial biases in television commercials. Agencies clung to the fear of southern reprisals against sponsors' products by retailers and consumers opposed to integration. So, the strategy of a CORE-sponsored "television image campaign," which began in June, was not to pressure ad agencies to cast black talent in commercials, but rather to deal directly with the advertisers themselves.

Clarence Funnye, an architect with the U.S. Corps of Engineers and the New York area director of CORE, decided to negotiate first with the Big Three soap companies. "Wouldn't it be nice," said Funnye, "if now and then on television a little Negro girl came running in shouting, 'Look Ma, no cavities'? That's all we want, just ordinary things. We're not asking for anything revolutionary." If television's top advertisers set a trend, Funnye and his group knew, smaller companies would not block their efforts.

Lever Brothers was the first company CORE contacted. Running third in the soap derby behind Colgate-Palmolive and Procter & Gamble, it was the most vulnerable. CORE also considered the "flashy New York headquarters" of Lever Brothers an "eminently picketable building" sure to garner media attention.

The company did not respond affirmatively to Funnye's initial request for a meeting. CORE then threatened Lever Brothers with a boycott of its products by black customers—or, as CORE preferred to call it, "a selective buying campaign." The company then answered Funnye with a letter claiming that 33 of 1200 Lever Brothers employees were Negroes and that, in fact, several years earlier, a Negro woman had won a national contest sponsored by a Lever product.

The plans for the product boycott proceeded with the help of the NAACP, the Urban League, and various civic, religious, and labor groups. In the face of survey figures, Lever Brothers decided it would not be wise to hold out. The Center for Research and Marketing, an independent organization, estimated that "89 percent of the Negro population would adhere to a product boycott, 33 percent would urge their friends to join, and 11 percent would never buy the product again." In a negotiating session with CORE's national leader, James Farmer, the company conceded to the group's demands.

Lever Brothers officially urged the advertising agencies for all its products to come up with suggestions for more effective and natural use of minorities in the company's advertising. As a show of good faith, the company rushed into production a commercial for Wisk liquid detergent that included a black child as a Little Leaguer tagging a white boy sliding into third base.

The black boy appears on screen for no more than five seconds. The mother of the white boy whose pants were dirtied in the play is then seen at her washing machine touting the cleaning power of the product—"Wisk puts its strength where the dirt is." The ad ran for the first time on August 14, 1963, on the CBS daytime game show *Password*. Another integrated spot for Lever Brothers All detergent soon followed. This commercial featured Art Linkletter interviewing a black housewife about her laundry problems.

Feeling empowered in the summer of 1963, CORE successfully sought agreements for integrated television advertising from Colgate-Palmolive and Procter & Gamble. In the months to follow, Kellogg, National Biscuit, Beech-Nut Lifesavers, and Bristol Meyers were among the advertisers to consent to CORE's requests. The bandwagon effect Funnye hoped for was in evidence as the year drew to a close. As many as twenty companies not yet directly pressured by CORE committed themselves to use black talent in their advertising.

While the CORE campaign was in full swing in New York, on the West Coast the NAACP also took up the cause of integrating advertising. In early August, James Tolbert, the president of the Hollywood-Beverly Hills branch of the NAACP, speaking before an invited audience of 125 broadcast and advertising agency executives, equated fairness with good business: "We Negroes watch *Bonanza* and buy Chevrolets. We watch *Disney* on RCA sets. Jack Benny entertains us and we buy General Foods products. Our babies eat Gerber baby foods and we photograph them with Polaroid cameras. . . . We buy all the advertised products, the same as you do."

Just four days later, S. I. Hayakawa, the well-known semanticist and professor of English at San Francisco State College, linked the rising tide of discontent—what he called the growing "revolutionary fervor"—among young black Americans, with the fact that American culture "is not willing to live up to its advertising." Television commercials, Hayakawa believed, conveyed a false impression of consumer equality. "Here is an advertisement telling you to order this new sparkling soft drink with the thrilling new flavor," he explained. "It doesn't tell you that if you are Negro you will have to drink it standing on the sidewalk outside the cafe." When confronted with the reality of the American caste system young black citizens felt betrayed. "It is deeply significant," said Hayakawa, who would later become a U.S. Senator from California, "that so many young people are at the heart of current racial demonstrations. Teenagers by the hundred have been hustled off to jail by the Southern police—and they are singing and cheering as they go!"

In retrospect, Hayakawa's remarks can be interpreted as a foreshadowing of racial violence later in the decade. Devastating urban riots in the mid- and late-1960s would leave deep scars in the American spirit. But, during the Kennedy years, the promise of constructive change was still bright. The possibility of popular culture leading the way to a truly integrated society was a reasonable and widely shared expectation.

## The Trophy of Public Opinion

In 1959, American television viewers and consumers had every reason to believe that Rapid Shave shaving cream possessed such superior emollient qualities that it would allow anyone with the desire to shave sandpaper to do so—in one clean stroke. A TV ad for the Colgate-Palmolive product produced by the Ted Bates agency showed the task being executed without difficulty. But it was a spurious demonstration. Sand-coated Plexiglas was substituted for real sandpaper. The Federal Trade Commission, with an increasing interest in TV trickery, objected to the misleading commercial and the spot was withdrawn from broadcast.

Advertising entered the new decade with the specter of a crusade against deceptive TV ads sparking the public. Other factors carried the potential for alienating consumers as well. The audio level of television commercials, for instance, was often considerably and irritatingly higher than the volume of the main program. And the rise in multi-sponsorship, product diversification, piggybacked spots, and an increase in on-air network promotions resulted in advertising clutter. The growing number of exhortations and imperative commands pitched at viewers at each program break could lead to the feeling of overcommercialization.

As the Kennedy administration was getting settled in Washington, the American Association of Advertising Agencies was concerned about public image—particularly with regard to television advertising. Research surveys conducted for the organization showed there was not a preponderance of ill will toward advertising on the part of the general public, but a critical attitude was widespread among men and women who were in positions to mold public opinion. While the economic role of advertising was understood and appreciated among opinion leaders, research revealed their "deep-seated, emotional distrust of the ethics, believability and taste of advertising."

The theme of the AAAA's annual meeting in the spring of 1961 was Growth Through Advertising. The most important business item on the agenda was a public relations program designed to improve opinion-leaders' regard for advertising. "Missionary work" was deemed particularly important among "some of the high-ranking members of the Kennedy administration who have been outspokenly anti-advertising."

Philip Elman, however, a Kennedy-appointed FTC commissioner, was not among the converted. On January 3, 1962, the Federal Trade Commission, in a unanimous decision, ruled that deception could not be used in demonstrating the qualities of a product offered for sale on television. Elman wrote the opinion for the Commission: "The limitations of the medium may present a challenge to the creative ingenuity of copywriters; but surely they do not constitute lawful justification for resort to falsehoods and deception of the public. . . . Stripped of polite verbiage the argument boils down to this: where truth and salesmanship collide, the former must give way to the latter."

The Federal Communications Commission, preoccupied with programming and technological concerns, paid little formal attention to broadcast advertising until the spring of 1963. In what industry loyalists believed was Newton Minow's "last official poke" at broadcasting, the outgoing chairman proposed a rule-making procedure to put a ceiling on the amount of time that radio and television stations could devote to advertising.

What Minow had in mind was adopting the commercial time limits specified in the NAB radio and television codes of self-regulation: for television, four minutes of commercials were allowed within any half-hour period in prime time, and six minutes per half-hour in non-prime time periods. The FCC passed the proposal by the narrow margin of four votes to three.

The NAB, unhappy with being put in the awkward position of arguing against its own standard as a yardstick of reasonable commercialization, asked for a four-month postponement of any formal action on the matter. While E. William Henry was breaking in as FCC chairman following Minow's May 1963 resignation, the overcommercialization issue seemed to be a dead one. For months, the new FCC chairman was quiet on the subject. But, in his maiden address to the industry, just as Minow had done two-and-a-half years earlier, Henry aggravated the broadcast powers that be with a threat of harnessing their strength.

Speaking before a gathering of more than one thousand members of the International Radio and Television Society at the Waldorf-Astoria on September 24, Henry addressed the "inundation of commercialization" and "electronic huckstering" in American broadcasting. His remarks rejuvenated the FCC rule making on advertising time standards.

Criticizing teaser openings of news programs, Henry indulged in a couple of gags that his audience found less than amusing. "Good evening ladies and gentlemen. The President has just asked Congress to declare war. We'll be back with that story after a word from our sponsor." Getting no laughs, Henry continued, "And so, ladies and gentlemen, it looks like the end of civilization as we know it. And now here's David Krank for the Ajax Oil Company."

"That was a first-class speech you delivered," Henry's predecessor Newton Minow wrote to him a few days later. "Keep it up and keep the backbone firm, despite what I know will be a barrage from the industry. You scored with the public—especially on the Huntley-Brinkley show, and after all that's what really counts. . . . "

But, echoing the sentiment of the business community, one advertising trade editorialist asked his readers, "Is it beyond consideration to suggest that Henry might fulfill his job responsibilities better, in a larger sense, if he thundered on behalf of MORE commercial time on television for the purpose of persuading more people to buy more goods?"

Opponents of the FCC plan had two options. They could wait for the Commission to put the rules into effect and contest them in court. Or, more effectively, they could push for legislation that would forbid the FCC to dictate standards with respect to the length and frequency of advertisements. In August 1963, Texas Congressman Walter Rogers had introduced just such a bill—H.R. 8316 would deliver advertising from the FCC's jurisdiction. Immediately following Chairman Henry's speech in New York on overcommercialization, Rogers announced his subcommittee would hold hearings in early November on the FCC's proposed rule making.

The first day was for the Commission to defend itself. Testifying before the Rogers subcommittee, Henry explained that the amount of commercial time making up each broadcast day was steadily increasing. Though the problem was most acute in radio, Henry predicted: "If the government does not clarify its policy against overcommercialization, the radio of today may be the television of tomorrow."

"I would stress that I fully recognize the contribution of radio and television advertising in our gross national product," Chairman Henry said in closing. "On the other hand, it is clear that the framers of the Communications Act sought to preserve the broadcasting spectrum primarily as a medium of communication, rather than advertising."

In the following two days, thirty-six representatives of the broadcast industry argued that Congress never intended the FCC to oversee broadcast advertising, and that if the Commission were allowed to impose time and length restrictions, smaller broadcast stations might go out of business. Congressman Rogers pointed out "repeatedly in an angry drawl" that the FCC was trying to usurp the power of Congress. To no one's surprise, the subcommittee approved the Rogers bill and, in the last days of the Kennedy administration, it was headed for the floor of the full House.

As November 1963 was drawing to a close, E. William Henry was preparing for the FCC's own hearings on the overcommercialization rule making, scheduled for early December. But the success of the regulatory enterprise looked bleak. No ground swell of public support for the FCC's position materialized. It was still an elite, rather than grass roots concern.

The chairman received a letter of support, for instance, from an associate professor at the University of Pennsylvania's Annenberg School of Communications. The professor wrote of watching the "Who Do You Kill?" episode on *East Side/West Side*. "The first segment ended with a Negro mother being informed that her child has just died, the victim of rat bites in a tenement," he said. "Then to the station identification switchover— and, count them, *eight* spot announcements, the second of which concerned the use of Saniflush to keep toilet bowls 'hospital clean.' "

But Chairman Henry's academic correspondent sensed the fruitlessness of his complaint. "I suppose nothing can be done about this. The Congressmen who have broadcasting interests or who fear broadcasters, will speak up, bleating about freedom. And we will get the usual pious statements and semi-profundities from network spokesmen."

The fact was that at the close of the Kennedy years, Congress was in no mood to see a limit imposed on broadcast commercials. While only about twenty-five federal legislators had direct financial connections to the broadcast industry, many were sympathetic beneficiaries of free exposure. Each week hundreds of public service interview programs with office holders appeared on local radio and TV stations across the country. Such programs were not mandatory. They were aired at the discretion of station management. And 1964 was an election year.

But, above all, the abuses and excesses of advertising just never captured the public attention as a meaningful issue for the well-being of the country. Survey research showed a growing appreciation of commercials on the part of the American public as 1963 faded into history. Studies indicated that consumers believed television commercials gave them "new ideas on how to live more exciting, richer lives."

Instead of resentment, Americans accepted broadcast advertising as an integral part of daily life. The average consumer did not consider advertising to be inherently vulgar. Its purpose seemed clear and respectable. Advertising made entertainment and informational programming possible by the flip of a switch. And, while enlarging consumption habits, it was thought of as an essential component in a thriving society—a spark plug in the economic machine.

During the Kennedy years, when men and women in the advertising industry asked themselves what they could do for their country, the answer was unmistakably, "Promote national growth and full employment by encouraging American consumers to live the good life—without apology or regret."

# CHAPTER 9

# A New Network Serving All the People

## EDUCATIONAL TELEVISION AND THE ALL-CHANNEL RECEIVER BILL

As a female FCC commissioner in the late 1940s and early 1950s, Freida Hennock was a conspicuous enough Washington anomaly. But the politically ambitious Truman appointee also had brassy manners and a proclivity for publicity. Though these qualities irritated her male colleagues, Hennock put them to use for a good cause.

From 1948 to 1952, the FCC allocated no new television licenses. While this freeze was imposed, the Commission was attempting to construct an equitable and workable table of assignments for the mushrooming medium. Channels would be reserved in both bands of the electromagnetic spectrum— VHF, very high frequency; and UHF, ultrahigh frequency.

When the first version of the table of television assignments was presented by the Commission in 1949, not one channel on either band had been reserved for noncommercial purposes. Freida Hennock was the only FCC commissioner to raise a loud and clear objection. Her grandstanding on the issue and rallying of educators were not considered to be businesslike or ladylike by those who hated to see potentially profitable TV licenses sheltered by the government. But, had Freida Hennock not been hell-bent on preserving some channel allocations for educational television, the commercialism of American broadcasting would have simply suffocated any hopes of establishing a system of public television.

When in 1952 the freeze on channel allocations was lifted, 242 channels— the large majority in the UHF band—had been reserved for educational television stations. In announcing the plan, the FCC also warned commercial licensees that their duty to carry programs meeting the educational needs and interests of their communities was not relieved by the new noncommercial provisions.

The first ETV station signed on the air in 1953. KUHT, in Texas, was licensed to the University of Houston. Throughout the remainder of the decade, new stations sprung up, some licensed to communities, some to local or state school boards, and others, like KUHT, to universities. By the beginning of 1960, there were forty-four ETV stations in operation and they were beginning to feel like a force of some consequence.

Candidate John Kennedy decided it would be wise to acknowledge educational broadcasters as they met for their 1960 convention. He sent a message of encouragement:

> American progress and even our national survival is directly dependent on what we as a nation do now about the shameful weaknesses and deficiencies of our educational system. . . . Television, a device which has the potential to teach more things to more people in less time than anything yet devised, seems a providential instrument to come to education's aid.

The principal supplier of programming for educational television stations was the National Educational Television and Radio Center in New York, known most commonly as NET. (In 1962, the organization dropped its activities in radio and became simply National Educational Television.) Each week NET provided affiliate stations with ten hours of programming. Some of it was produced by NET, some of it by ETV stations contracted by NET, and some programs were procured from outside sources, such as the BBC or American syndicators.

NET was referred to as the Fourth Network. But educational stations subscribing to NET's service were not physically connected by AT&T long lines the way the commercial networks were. The ETV network was not a true web; it was not a network of live transmission. Films and kinescopes were manually packaged and mailed to member stations. A complex scheduling system, called bicycling, was devised in which stations sent programs on to other stations after broadcast.

A typical ETV station was on the air for eight hours a day Monday through Friday. The morning was devoted to elementary school classroom instruction and the early afternoons were for high school students. Television courses in math, science, history, and foreign languages were produced by the station to harmonize with the lesson plans of local teachers.

After school was the time for children's programming. In 1960, following a year of research and testing, NET introduced a show for seven- to twelve-year-olds called *What's New*. Each program in the daily half-hour consisted of three individual segments on topics such as baseball or space science or animals. There was no host, but rather the segments were held together by bits of animation and music.

In the late afternoon, ETV stations might air a locally produced lecture on something like home safety or home economics. And following the dinner hour came adult NET programming. Roughly speaking, it fell into the categories of humanities and the fine arts, behavioral sciences and public affairs, and natural science.

Educational television grew at a steady pace during the 1950s and programming improved with the passage of time. But in 1960, ETV, along with the rest of American society, literally bubbled with possibility. New ideas and big ideas seemed to be floating in the air.

For instance, in the fall of 1960, NET joined with four other broadcast organizations in the major English-speaking nations of the world to produce a series of hour-long television documentaries. The Intertel project was the first organized cultural exchange through global television. Along with the Westinghouse Broadcasting Company of the United States, the Australian Broadcasting Commission, the Canadian Broadcasting Corporation, and Associated Rediffusion Ltd. of Great Britain, NET produced programs on international themes that were seen bi-monthly on American ETV stations, as well as the five commercial stations owned by Westinghouse. The TV critic for the *New York Herald Tribune* wrote of the Intertel worldwide program exchange, "It augurs perhaps an awakening on the part of broadcasters that television can be an effective weapon for peace and not merely a profit-making device."

In October 1960, many viewers who had never paid much attention to NET's programming might have read about an extraordinary scoop. David Susskind's talk show *OPEN END*, which was produced by his own company and which experimented with undetermined program lengths, had been purchased by NET for distribution to ETV stations. When Susskind learned that Nikita Khrushchev was coming to New York to attend the General Assembly of the United Nations, he requested and was granted a television interview with the Soviet Premier. Their ninety-minute discussion was followed by a panel of journalists and academics offering analysis of the exchange.

In response to criticism for distributing the program and giving Khrushchev airtime for propaganda purposes, John White, the president of NET said: "A fundamental assumption of education in a free society is that it is safe to trust people with information; that they are capable of making distinctions between self-serving propaganda and truth; that they are not so gullible as some of their so-called protectors fear; and that, since there is no safety in trying to suppress opposing points of view, our best hope is full exposure and debate."

As 1960 came to a close, and the number of ETV stations had grown to fifty-one, the Ford Foundation, which had been generous in providing funding for educational television, offered an attractive incentive to get more ETV stations on the air. The Foundation would equip any ETV station signing on before the end of 1962 with a free Ampex videotape recorder and a year's supply of magnetic tape. To have the large expense of this essential piece of studio hardware covered provided momentum for many wavering ETV licensees to make the ultimate commitment to join the movement. Later, the offer was extended to September 1963.

Educational broadcasters knew they had a strong advocate in the Kennedy administration's FCC chairman even before he was sworn into office. In their hometown of Chicago, Newton and Jo Minow had been supporters of educational station WTTW, Channel 11. In his first weeks at the Commission, Minow became deeply involved in the effort by a group of influential New Yorkers to purchase a VHF commercial station and convert it to a noncommercial educational enterprise. That New York, Los Angeles, and Washington, D.C., lacked ETV stations was distressing to the new FCC chairman.

When he delivered the Vast Wasteland speech in May 1961, and explained the fundamental principles that would be his guide in office, Minow left no room for interpretation of his motives: "If there were a limited number of printing presses in this country, you may be sure that a fair proportion of them would be put to educational use. Educational television has an enormous contribution to make to the future, and I intend to give it a hand along the way. If there is not a nationwide educational television system in this country, it will not be the fault of the FCC."

On July 25, 1961, President Kennedy made a television address to the country regarding the Soviet Union's attempts to seal off East Berlin and the possible Russian effort to choke off NATO air and road access to West Berlin. A military response to the crisis seemed probable. The President's speech was sobering. "We do not want to fight—but we have fought before," he said. Kennedy proposed an overall expansion in American military preparedness, including a 217,000-man increase in the armed forces.

The following day, NET's president John White wrote to the Chief Executive and offered to put the capabilities of the educational television network at the disposal of the New Frontier: "As the nation makes plans for its defense . . . the facilities of the educational television stations are an important national asset, ready to play an appropriate role in conveying information to youngsters in school and to adults at home, as well as for the training of specific civilian groups."

Though a direct military confrontation did not happen, White wanted President Kennedy to know NET was there for him: "Should the turn of events bring us to the point where a declaration of national emergency is deemed necessary, I assure you, Mr. President, that the National Educational Television and Radio Center . . . stands prepared to render any help which you deem appropriate and necessary."

In October 1961, when Minow gave the keynote address to the annual meeting of the National Association of Educational Broadcasters, he reminded his audience that communist countries were developing educational television programming with alacrity. Soviet children, for instance, had been learning English through televised lessons since 1959. And with the aid of technicians and equipment from Russia, Red China, and East Germany, even the tiny country of Albania was airing three and one-half hours of educational television each day.

Minow's NAEB address was a pledge of government support as well as a critique of some of the amateurish and dull programming that was broadcast in the name of education. Television, said Minow, "demands a large slice of showmanship. I'm afraid that many educators consider 'showmanship' a dirty word. Many educators brush off showmanship as arty and gimmicky, and they are leery of it. But tawdry theatrics are a world away from true showmanship. . . . Great teachers have always been exciting and challenging. Great teachers use showmanship every day."

But the chairman understood as well as his audience that professionalism was almost wholly dependent on funding. Minow noted that "$8.5 million a year is now being spent on programming by all the educational television stations. The three commercial television networks spend more than $8.5 million on programming in *one week*." "It is shocking," Minow said, "that we in America—the richest country in the world—have been spending our time, not in debating how we should expand educational television—but whether it should be expanded at all."

The FCC chairman assured the educational broadcasters that on the New Frontier the debate was over: "President Kennedy and this administration strongly support a nationwide educational television system. . . . There must be an aggressive and militant campaign to put educational television on its feet financially—and every other way."

The first step was the passage of a bill sponsored by Warren Magnuson, the Democratic senator from Washington, which would provide seed money—up to one million dollars for any one state which matched that amount—to put new ETV stations on the air. Minow told the membership of the NAEB it was up to them to mobilize support for the legislation.

Aside from securing cold cash, the biggest problem facing ETV was the inability of millions of potential viewers to tune in UHF channels on their home receivers. Educational broadcasters on UHF stations, Minow said, "often play to an empty house."

With most available VHF channels already in use, ETV's future depended on the utilization of UHF stations. Minow told his listeners, "The Federal Communications Commission has proposed legislation which would require that television sets manufactured for shipment in interstate commerce be capable of receiving all channels." This meant the twelve channels on the VHF band, as well as the seventy UHF frequencies. "Why should any television set manufactured in this country leave the factory incapable of receiving seven-eighths of the channels available for broadcasting in America?"

The all-channel legislation had already been introduced in the House by Congressman Oren Harris and in the Senate by Warren Magnuson. Again, Minow asked for a serious lobbying effort from those engaged in educational television.

The chairman also announced that the FCC was establishing a new office, the Division of Research and Education. Its function would be to aid educational television stations by conducting research, the kind of market research that commercial stations relied on and ETV stations could not afford. The new office, providing assistance akin to that offered by the NAB for commercial stations, would compile information on trends, supply special help with license application and renewal forms, and in general serve as a clearinghouse for ETV and a liaison with other government agencies.

As the first year of the Kennedy administration passed, educational broadcasters felt a reassuring touch from the helping hand of government. They were being told that they deserved respect and support. They felt elevated. They were serving their country in an entirely new way—educational broadcasters were patriots in the television age.

## 1962: ETV's Year of Arrival

NET's prestigious public affairs series was the discussion program *Prospects for Mankind*, produced by WGBH in Boston and hosted by Eleanor Roosevelt. Days after Minow made his October 1961 address to the NAEB, Mrs. Roosevelt wrote to express her approval, "I am glad that you have taken active leadership in helping to further the power and effectiveness of the educational stations as an important national service." The former first lady told the young chairman that she hoped to devote a future program to "the implications of television as an educating force on a national and international scale."

In early spring of 1962, Minow joined Eleanor Roosevelt and a panel that included television critic Marya Mannes, NBC News producer Irving Gitlin, and NET president John White. "What we're trying to do in government," Minow said on the show, "is to provide more opportunity, to provide more stations, to provide more choices." It was the hope of the Kennedy administration, Minow declared, that educational television would become truly a great Fourth Network.

By the time the interview program was distributed to ETV stations, President Kennedy had signed into law the Educational Television Facilities Act. On May 1, 1962, the federal government promised to invest $32 million over the next five years, to be administered by the Department of Health, Education, and Welfare, into the building of new ETV stations.

The President likened the legislation to the Morrill Land Grant College Act of one hundred years earlier: "The Morrill Act reduced old barriers to education and afforded new opportunities for learning. This act gives equal promise of bringing greater opportunities for personal and cultural growth to every American."

The first time Minow presided over a meeting of the FCC, many months before, one of the items on the agenda was whether or not the Commission, as a body, would take a stand in favor of the Educational Television Facilities Act. Legislation to aid ETV had been pending in Congress for seven years, but the Commission had never officially gone to bat for it.

The majority of the staff and commissioners felt the FCC should remain neutral on the matter. It was a legislative not a regulatory issue, they argued. But Minow said, "No. I think our job here, under the law, is to advance the public interest, and I think the FCC should say that." Years later Minow recalled of his dissenting statement: "That was sort of a signal to the view I held that our job there was to be more than a referee. It was to be an advocate and do what we could to advance educational television."

With the infusion of government money in facilities, NET continued to build support for programming. In 1962 the Ford Foundation awarded the organization an interim grant of well over four million dollars while undertaking a comprehensive study of the potentialities of a national ETV system.

The same infatuation the commercial networks, and mass media in general, were experiencing with John Kennedy in 1962 was also surfacing at NET. One of the Kennedy-inspired offerings was made available to member stations in June. *Youth Physical Fitness: A Report to the Nation* was hosted by the film actor and dancer, Gene Kelly. The purpose of the program was to explain and interpret the recommendations of the President's Council on Youth Fitness. Kennedy himself appeared on the show, and explained, "A country is as strong as its citizens, and I think mental and physical health, mental and physical vigor, go hand in hand."

The President also was featured in the first program of a series called *White House Seminar*, which was produced by NET in cooperation with Washington D.C.'s brand new ETV station, WETA. Each program was an introduction to a different branch of the federal government and various agencies presented by men at the top levels of government, including Justice William O.Douglas, Edward R. Murrow, Robert Kennedy, and Newton Minow.

## The All-Channel Receiver Bill

At the outset of the 1960s, approximately six million television sets, with a life expectancy of ten years, were being sold annually—and only about seven percent were equipped to receive UHF television signals. Throughout the 1950s, UHF television did not prove to be economically feasible and the FCC explored ways to resuscitate it.

Commissioner Robert Lee believed the best way to ensure that the vast potential of UHF would not go to waste was to create a situation in which UHF did not have to compete with technically superior VHF channels in the same community. Lee's idea, called deintermixture, made established VHF broadcasters shake in their boots. They feared a massive uprooting of their profitable stations. The government, broadcasters had no doubt, would strangle them in good intentions and red tape.

"What this country needs is more television, not less," Newton Minow proclaimed in his January 1962 address to the National Press Club. The chairman explained to his audience that an all-channel receiver bill, which would empower the FCC to require newly manufactured television sets to be capable of tuning in 82 channels, was the "painless way" to save the life of UHF. The painful way, the broadcast industry knew, was deintermixture—a shift to all-UHF in some markets. Minow seemed to be offering a trade-off. The networks and the NAB recognized that it was in their best interest to support such legislation.

The original proposal by the FCC for an all-channel receiver bill, made in July 1961, would also allow the Commission to proceed with deintermixture in eight geographic areas if deemed necessary. Members of Congress were powerfully pressured by the broadcast lobby to provide a statutory moratorium on deintermixture. Minow's public statements in January, however, alleviated some of the anxiety.

But when Minow appeared before the Senate committee conducting hearings on the all-channel legislation in February, just weeks following his remarks to the Press Club, he resisted any curtailment of FCC authority in what seemed to be a reneging of the earlier understanding that UHF-capable receivers would negate the need for deintermixture. The chairman still wanted all the marbles. He wanted 82-channel sets and he wanted the Commission to retain the right to invoke deintermixture.

Minow argued that the fears of broadcasters were unfounded. "If it was our purpose to shift TV to UHF we wouldn't need this bill," he contended. "We could do it this afternoon." Senator John Pastore, chairman of the communications subcommittee, took umbrage at the young bureaucrat's self-assured attitude. "Perhaps you could order the shift this afternoon," Pastore said in a power play. "But what do you think the Senate would do tomorrow?"

It soon became clear there would be no all-channel bill without an end to the threat of deintermixture. Congress essentially made a deal with the FCC—drop deintermixture and you'll get the legislation you want on receivers. Once the FCC relented, the bill faced few obstacles.

It was, most connected with it could see, a piece of legislation that met commercial as well as educational needs. As Minow explained: "We are convinced that getting UHF sets in the hands of the public will provide the basic prerequisite for opening up this service. . . . If this proposal is enacted, there will be available, within four to six years, a large enough percentage of all-channel sets in use to mark a beginning of the end of the television allocations problem. . . . Meanwhile, our population expands; new families are formed; per capita income trends upward; leisure time becomes increasingly available; and new products and new companies seek advertising outlets."

The loss of freedom to consumers in being forced to pay the estimated twenty-five-dollar increase in the price of the average television set—whether or not they were in markets with UHF stations on the air—was the primary argument against the All-Channel Receiver Bill. But it seemed a comparatively small sacrifice for the ultimate good that would accrue. Minow suggested the government might drop the excise tax on all-channel television sets to offset the price increase.

Traditionally, the power of government over products sold to the consumer had always been limited to matters of public health and safety. Here, however, a law would be applied to a retail item on the basis of a social, cultural, and economic need. And, although the American Civil Liberties Union reported that it found no constitutional defects in the bill, this was the basis of the major opposition it encountered from the Electronics Industries Association, a Washington trade group that represented most of the manufacturers of television receivers.

The Admiral Company went on record as being strongly opposed to the legislation, claiming the language of the bill was so all-inclusive that it appeared "to be an attempt at complete Federal regulation of the television receiver manufacturing industry." The executive vice-president of Motorola echoed the belief, "I regard this bill as a direct challenge to the American free enterprise system by placing in the hands of a government agency the authority to dictate to private manufacturers the kind of products they can build."

Minow was surprised that the electronics industry regarded the legislation as an infringement, rather than an opportunity. In terms of manufacturing, design, and retailing, Minow said, "Here was a whole new world for them to get into." But, nonetheless, the chairman understood politics. "I learned early on in Washington," he recalled, "that if a major industry was unified in its position on legislation, it was very tough to defeat that industry's position. But if the industry was divided, and had different opinions, it would work. So I tried to find a couple of manufacturers—and succeeded here in Chicago. I talked to the people at Zenith, and they saw the future and they supported the bill. After they did, a couple of others did, too."

The President signed the All-Channel Receiver Bill on July 10, 1962, which conferred the authority on the FCC to rule that all television sets manufactured in the United States and shipped in interstate commerce be all-channel receivers as of April 30, 1964. For practical purposes, however, supportive manufacturers began implementing changes without delay. If it were not for the foresight and determination of the Kennedy administration, American broadcasting might have been permanently wedded to an inadequate, noncompetitive twelve-channel system.

In retrospect, Minow regretted that the FCC's rule making on the specifications of the UHF tuner in the all-channel set were not stronger. A much tougher standard, he felt, should have been prescribed so that UHF channels were not just available, but as easy to tune in as VHF channels. But, despite this shortcoming, the All-Channel Receiver Bill drastically altered the television marketplace in the years following its passage in much the way the FCC had hoped. As one broadcast historian who closely studied the law has noted, "It had favorable results beyond all expectations."

As American families began replacing their first generation television sets and began more frequently to purchase a portable model as a second set, ETV viewership rose in conjunction. NET could not have hoped for a more effective coupling of legislation than the Educational Television Facilities Act and the All-Channel Receiver Bill. ETV was now undoubtedly on the map.

### The Fight for a Flagship Station

Although NET was headquartered in New York City, there was no educational television station in that community—which was not only a major population center, but a major programming resource as well. When the commercial station WNTA, Channel 13, owned by National Telefilm Associates, went up for sale in early 1961, Frank Stanton took John White under his wing. The president of CBS advised the president of NET how to go about getting a broker and an estimate of the station's fair market value. Although acquiring the station for ETV was, according to White, "a sheer dream at that point."

Learning the station had a $4 million price tag, White decided to go visiting. His first call was to George Stoddard, a member of the NET board and the vice-chancellor of New York University. "George, who do I have to see to start working on a station for this town?" White asked. "You've got to go to see Arthur Houghton," the NET president was told. "He heads Steuben Glass, he's very active at the Lincoln Center, he's also at the Metropolitan. He's interested in things culturally. I think there's where you start."

Houghton was happy to see Jack White and wanted to be counted in. "You've got to go see John Rockefeller," he told the NET president. And then Houghton arranged an appointment with Rockefeller for White.

Rockefeller said, "I'm with you. . . . We're going to make this thing work."

Together White and Rockefeller went to see Henry Heald, president of the Ford Foundation. "What's this station going to cost?" he asked the men. "Well," said White, "our broker estimates $4 million."

"All right, John," Heald said to Rockefeller, "the Ford Foundation will put up two million if you will go out and raise the other two." "You're on, Henry," Rockefeller replied.

White's next stop was to see Devereux Josephs, the former chairman of the board of the New York Life Insurance Company. He too wanted to help. Josephs made a date to see Howard Shepard, the soon-to-be retired chairman of the First National City Bank. Shepard agreed to lead the effort to purchase the station.

Not long after, Newton Minow read in his morning paper about the group of prominent citizens hoping to acquire Channel 13 for ETV. The chairman called a staff meeting to brainstorm. "How can we help them achieve that? We've got to get an educational station in New York," he told his colleagues. Minow was advised by those who had been in the regulatory business a lot longer, "There really isn't any way you can help. . . . The owners can sell it to whomever they please."

While the additional $2 million was being raised, other potential buyers, including David Susskind, were driving up the price. Minow told the Commission staff, "We have the right to approve the transfer, and we have the right to disapprove it." "But," the neophyte bureaucrat was told, "you can't arbitrarily disapprove it."

Before long Minow received a call from the owner of WNTA, the station for sale. "Is it true that you're opposed to the sale of this station to a commercial buyer?" he asked the chairman. "Yes, sir, it's true," Minow replied without the benefit of law to back him up. "It will be approved over my dead body. As far as I'm concerned, we're going to get a noncommercial station in there, one way or another. I don't know how yet, but I'm going to be very straight with you—I'm going to oppose any transfer to another commercial licensee. Nothing against *you*—I'm just telling you, this is what is going to be."

Minow truly believed that the FCC had made a mistake in its table of allocations in not designating one of the VHF channels in New York for education in the first place. He planned to initiate a rule-making proceeding to change the table of allocations, allowing the Commission to reassign a VHF signal to ETV. But the other commissioners didn't like the precedent that might be set by the bold idea.

Minow asked Commissioner Rosel Hyde, who had formerly served as FCC chairman, for advice. Hyde suggested Minow initiate an inquiry instead of a rule making. An inquiry was a less formal procedure and it would send out the same message. Minow recalled, "I didn't even know the difference between an inquiry and a rule making; it made no difference to me. I said, 'Fine.' " All the commissioners agreed to the plan.

The commercial buyers could see their efforts to operate the station would be impeded at every turn, but by now the price had gone above $6 million. The $2 million needed to match the Ford Foundation money, and somewhat more, had already been secured through quarter-million-dollar contributions from ABC, CBS, NBC, Metromedia, and the *New York Daily News*. But now the fund-raisers had to scramble to find the difference.

The two independent television stations in New York had something to gain by having their competition go noncommercial. So they contributed to the cause. And ultimately, the Ford Foundation again came to the rescue so the purchase could be made in the name of ETMA—Educational Television for the Metropolitan Area.

A glitch developed, though, when the paperwork on the transfer went to the FCC. The station actually was a VHF assigned to New Jersey—the only VHF station then allocated to New Jersey. And the governor of the state was threatening to bollix the whole deal. He felt it was his duty to keep the license assigned to his state.

Through the persuasion of Newton Minow—which, to some, was of questionable appropriateness—Eleanor Roosevelt, and *Saturday Review* editor Norman Cousins, New Jersey Governor Robert Meyner compromised. He would back off if the new station maintained one studio in Newark and the station be identified occasionally on the air as a New York-Newark station.

Reflecting on Newton Minow's involvement in securing a flagship station for the NET network, Dr. Hyman Goldin, who was the director of the FCC's research staff during Minow's tenure, recalled: "He was a believer in individual intervention. And he was also a believer in public opinion. He worked outside the system as much as he worked in the system. He was much more interested in the outside than in the internal workings of the FCC."

The call letters of Channel 13 were changed to WNDT, which stood for New Dimensions in Television. (Later, in 1970, when the station merged with NET, the call letters were changed to WNET.) In August 1962, as plans were being made for the station's September sign-on, Edward R. Murrow sent a confidential memorandum to the Ford Foundation outlining his ideas on the future of educational television in the United States. "No effort should be made to create a news organization designed to compete in terms of speed with the existing (network news) services," Murrow wrote. "The (ETV) network should become the mature, discerning gadfly to all mass media in this country.... With a little courage and lots of judgment this network could become the conscience of communications in this country. ... This fourth network could become what is the missing conscience of journalism."

The legendary CBS newsman also added his belief that a new name for the system was needed: "Anything that is tagged educational in this country is handicapped at the outset. The American people don't really believe in

education. (We had to pass laws to force parents to send their children to school.)"

Channel 13's changeover to a noncommercial TV station had a rocky start. Even before the premiere broadcast, WNDT ran into union problems. AFTRA, the American Federation of Television and Radio Artists, prevented musical comedy star Zero Mostel from taping a half-hour performance that was to be aired as part of the debut festivities. The union was in a dispute with WNDT over the status of the teachers, university professors, government officials, and other nonprofessional performers who would appear in educational programs. The labor group wanted them to receive the same residual payments given to professional performers. WNDT adamantly refused to consider every single person who appeared on camera as a performance professional deserving of union benefits.

The week before the station's sign-on, John White issued a strong statement addressing the controversy: "It is exceedingly unfortunate that AFTRA has seen fit to interfere with the successful opening of educational station WNDT. After the long, hard labor by so many citizens to obtain this channel, and at a time when non-commercial broadcasting begins its important educational and cultural service to the people of the metropolitan area, this effort to prevent its availability to schools, as well as children and adults at home, is unforgivable."

On Sunday, September 16, 1962, the day of WNDT's first broadcast, an AFTRA picket line assembled. Minow recalled: "Ed Murrow and I went to the dedication of the station together. . . . Ed Murrow had never crossed a picket line in his life. Neither had I. We wondered about it, but we both decided to go anyway."

At 8:00 P.M. after a specially commissioned piece of animation in honor of Channel 13 was run, the master of ceremonies for the evening's three-hour inaugural program said, in a way reminiscent of his introductions on CBS programs, "Good evening. The name of this station is Channel 13, WNDT. My name is Edward R. Murrow."

Clips of NET programs that the station's viewers could look forward to were shown. And Murrow informed the audience that Channel 13 would rebroadcast President Kennedy's press conferences in their entirety on the evenings of the days they took place.

Later in the program FCC chairman Minow saluted "the many men and women, civic organizations, charitable foundations, the New York commercial television stations, and business concerns that have created WNDT." With supreme understatement he then added, "We at the Federal Communications Commission take pride in having played a modest part in its achievement."

Included in the three-hour broadcast was an eighty-three minute documentary produced by the BBC, called *Television and the World*. The decision to air the program required some of the "conscience-of-communication" spirit that Murrow wrote of to the Ford Foundation the month before. The documentary was an indictment of American commercial television and the way in which it sent its violent programming to countries around the world.

The next issue of *Variety* carried the headline "WEBS STEAM AT WNDT PREEM." The networks, especially CBS, which had donated not only money but equipment and studio space to WNDT, had been boosters of the new educational station. They felt betrayed by the acidulous portrait of the American television networks. The webs, *Variety* reported, were "fighting mad over the manner in which the station made its public debut. In fact, they're so mad that it could cost WNDT a lot of future financial support."

But the storm passed. Hurt feelings mended, the union negotiated, and WNDT became a jewel in New York's crown. "What'll it be," a man said to his wife in a popular New York cartoon panel of the time, "Channel 13, or shall we just wallow in the wasteland?" WNDT was much more than a community resource, however. It was the needed flagship station that strengthened the NET network for the coming decade of growth and accomplishment.

## The High Price of Programming

The headline "Educational TV Goes Commercial," in the June 1963 *Sponsor* magazine, was the kind of thing that made ETV purists cringe. But corporate support of programming was a noncommercial TV fact of life. The business readership of *Sponsor* was informed that the "low-pressure sell" via ETV underwriting had become a "corporate blue-chip video trend."

While NET enjoyed the philanthropy of public-spirited businesses, ethical questions could not be avoided altogether. Many thoughtful viewers, not just cynics, wondered about the relationship between the corporate underwriter and the content of the program. Some examples of corporate underwriting that prompted such thoughts include the National Association of Manufacturers sponsorship of a ten-part series called *The American Business System*; the IBM sponsored *Computers and the Mind of Man*; the six-program series entitled *The Family Doctor*, funded by Mead Johnson Laboratories; the American Medical Association's contribution to *You and Your Doctor*; and American Cyanamid's funding of *Science Central*.

Even though NET's vice-president for development insisted, "We are not bent into giving a point of view of the underwriter," some critics regarded the underwriters' power over the selection of topics as editorial interference enough.

In late 1961, the Boeing Company pitched the idea of a public affairs program to NET on the theme "Jet Age President," in which viewers would travel on Air Force One. A Boeing representative wrote to NET president John White: "I conceive the program as a one-hour film not only documenting the President's trip (whether it be to Moscow or South America) but providing the history of Presidential trips of state. There would be some emphasis on the intricate care taken to assure the President a reliable air trip. But the primary emphasis is on the President as he functions in this day of rapid transportation. . . . We would like to direct the film shooting and have a hand in writing and editing."

NET's Director of Programming, Bob Hudson, recognized the Boeing project would set a bad precedent and dissuaded the NET development staff from encouraging it. But, even when the intentions of a corporate underwriter seemed beyond reproach, a controversy could develop.

The Humble Oil and Refining Company was the underwriter for the most popular of NET's cultural series in the early 1960s. The rights to broadcast the fifteen-part BBC Shakespearean series, *An Age of Kings*, was acquired by Humble Oil for $100,000. An additional $150,000 was spent on promoting the series with booklets outlining the episodes, library and school posters, and newspaper advertising. The commercial connotations of the prominent newspaper displays led the Educational-Commercial Broadcaster Committee to propose that a set of guidelines on "commercialism in ETV" be drafted.

In the fall of 1963, after NET received another major programming grant of $6 million from the Ford Foundation and decided to drop the production of exclusively instructional programs in favor of "high-quality informational and cultural shows," *Broadcasting* magazine editorialized against the move toward more popular offerings:

> There will always be the danger that the noncommercial service will be given unfair advantages in its competition with commercial TV. . . . It is a short step from a simple credit line to a short advertising message, and once that step is taken the noncommercial stations will be competing with commercial stations for advertising support. . . . We have no doubt that an NET, if it succeeds in producing attractive programs and clearing them on noncommercial stations throughout the country, will have little trouble raising money from businesses if those businesses and perhaps their products are mentioned on the air.

The commercialism of ETV was not as galloping as *Broadcasting* suggested, but it was a creeping condition that required vigilance and would continue to generate heated debate for years and decades to come. While NET worried about the propriety of securing big money, the local ETV stations concerned themselves with the modest contributions of their everyday viewers.

Station KQED in San Francisco had come up with a fund-raising gimmick that was catching on with other stations—the annual auction. For five days out of the year, ETV viewers were treated to what *TV Guide* called "one long, hollering, hustling commercial."

The 1963 KQED auction was a grand success, netting $120,000, which was 20 percent of the station's annual budget. For months before the event, six hundred volunteers set out to wheedle businesses and individuals into donating items to be auctioned. Between segments of special entertainment, such as a belly dancer called Siva and a stripper named Tempest Storm, celebrity auctioneers ran the bidding on items like a banana cake baked by Bernice Brown, wife of Pat Brown, the governor of California, and an engraving of the White House signed by Jacqueline Kennedy. A pair of lavender sheets slept in by movie star Kim Novak, and guaranteed unlaundered, were bought by a necktie maker in the hopes of parlaying the investment.

Actress Shirley Temple managed to get a fifty-dollar bid on a five-foot boa constrictor. Comedienne Phyllis Diller auctioned a necklace worn by Elizabeth Taylor in the film *Cleopatra*. "Ooh, I think it's still warm," Diller cracked about the medallion which had rested so elegantly on Taylor's cleavage. But black comedian Dick Gregory gave the 1963 audience a little something to think about. "A hundred years ago," he said, "*I* would have been for sale."

## NET and the Race Revolution

During the summer and fall of 1963, though NET could not cover breaking news as the commercial networks did, it did not ignore the pounding urgency of the civil rights movement. ETV could offer a resource that was extremely scarce among the commercial networks—the time to consider varying points of view in genuine depth.

The first program in an impressive series of civil rights examinations was called *The Negro and the American Promise*. It was distributed to ETV stations the third week in June, although the interviews it contained with Malcolm X, Martin Luther King, and James Baldwin were recorded the first week in June—before President Kennedy's TV address on civil rights. NET issued a memo to the local stations advising them to inform their audiences of that fact in order to be "scrupulously fair," since some of the criticism of the President voiced in the program was based on his unwillingness to make such a public stand.

For some southern ETV stations, the network's decision to devote so much attention to civil rights created discomfort. Channel 8 in New Orleans, for instance, decided it could not run *The Negro and the American Promise*. A sheepish memo from the station manager sent to NET about the decision said: "This production is A–1 quality and, as far as I'm concerned, of award winning stature. I regret, therefore, that I could not include it in our schedule."

The station manager informed the network that an "inter-faith council" had viewed the program. One of the citizens, described in the correspondence as "a Negro who is a member of the Catholic Council on Human Relations, about 25 years old, thoughtful, studious," felt the program should be shown. The young black man believed it "covered so well the different shades of opinion in the Negro community."

But the majority decision of the inter-faith council was that airing the program would not be in the community's best interest. "The number of adherents to the Malcolm X approach in New Orleans is an unknown factor," the memo stated. The station manager went on to say he feared that to publicize the provocative beliefs of Malcolm X would not help his community. NET was informed that every program on civil rights it sent in the future would undergo the same review process.

The Director of Programming for the educational network wrote back to say, "The risk in exposing a community—any community—to the personality and ideas of Malcolm X certainly cannot be discounted; however, the democratic premise is that it is safer to expose people to look at a perplexing and complicated phenomenon like this so that the community can deal with it rather than let it take them by surprise."

Other civil rights programs included *For Freedom Now*, a discussion of the strategy and leadership of various black organizations. Psychologist Kenneth Clark moderated the exchange among Roy Wilkins of the NAACP, James Farmer of CORE, Whitney Young of the National Urban League, James Forman of SNCC, and Martin Luther King representing the Southern Christian Leadership Conference.

*We Shall Overcome* and *Non-Violence in Mississippi* were two programs depicting training in nonviolent tactics for voter registration volunteers and techniques of self-protection for civil rights demonstrators. Programs attempting to put regional influences into perspective were *The Southern Conservative, The Southern Liberal, Profile of the Southern Moderate,* and *The Northern White*.

*James Baldwin in San Francisco* presented the author in conversation with blacks about their lives in that city. And *Confronted*, shot by cinema verite filmmakers Albert and David Maysles, chronicled the tensions in five U.S. cities when whites with deep-seated prejudices were forced to contend with blacks demanding their rights. For instance, a barber in a fashionable shop on Chicago's Loop who recently had refused to cut the hair of trumpeter Dizzy Gillespie, explained why he'd rather quit the business than be forced by public accommodations laws to cut a black man's hair.

## Minow's Farewell Idea

As Newton Minow prepared to take his leave from government service in late May 1963, he appeared on *David Brinkley's Journal* to review the state of American broadcasting. "Mr. Minow," the NBC newsman asked, "what do you hope will happen in the way of programming on educational television?" The chairman had quite a specific vision:

> I think educational television should take one subject and devote itself to it and make or break its reputation on it. I have the idea that educational television should do *the* great course in American history . . . in an organized, coherent way, but in an exciting way. I would hope it could be done under the auspices of perhaps the American Society of Historians or some respectable academic group—and then run on all the educational stations, as many as five times a week, for maybe an hour, so the public would have five cracks at it. If they wanted to watch the *Untouchables* one night they wouldn't have to miss the Civil War. . . .
>
> I have another idea to get the thing started. There have been few times in American history where you have four living presidents. . . . I would like to suggest that the first lecture consist of President Hoover, President Truman, President Eisenhower, President Kennedy—four presidents spanning four decades of American life, who would spend an hour with the American public telling them why Americans must understand American history.

After the interview with Brinkley was taped, Minow wrote to Arthur Schlesinger, Jr., to ask him to encourage the President's participation: "With your sense of history, Arthur, think what it would mean 25 or 50 years from now to have an hour on tape with four living Presidents!"

In October 1963, with eighty-three ETV stations on the air, private citizen Minow was elected to the NET board of directors. He was anxious to see his idea implemented. Time might be running out. President Hoover was ailing. And who could say how long Truman and Eisenhower would be alive?

For American educational television, the Kennedy years were the most exhilarating of times. Exceptional achievements were made in children's, documentary, and public affairs programming by decade's end. The seeds of innovation and independence in public television—the very qualities which would so threaten President Richard Nixon in the early 1970s—were planted with hope and determination during the New Frontier.

# CHAPTER 10

# A One-World View

## SATELLITE COMMUNICATION

When the East Coast and the West Coast of the United States were linked by coaxial cable and microwave relay in 1951, when the Atlantic and the Pacific were seen simultaneously, the miracle and wonder of television seemed almost complete to the viewer at home. But those with a farther vision regarded the accomplishment not as a culmination, but merely an introduction to the television age.

Transmitting live moving pictures across the continent was soon commonplace, but sending live images across 3,000 miles of ocean was impossible in the 1950s. In 1959, the BBC introduced a system called Cable Film, which transmitted moving pictures through transatlantic phone cable at about 1/100th of their natural speed. So, a picture that occupied one minute of screen time would take slightly more than an hour to reach its destination across the ocean. The system was first used to relay pictures of President Eisenhower and the Queen of England at the opening of the St. Lawrence Seaway back to Great Britain. Since it took nine or ten hours to transport footage by jet plane, Cable Film speeded the process of international newsgathering considerably. As the 1960s began, however, live transoceanic images were still locked in the realm of theory. But advances in rocketry promised the transformation into reality might be just around the corner.

In January 1961, as the United States embarked on the New Frontier, the FCC issued an authorization to AT&T to conduct an experimental program involving communication satellites. "Shortly after I arrived at the FCC," Minow recalled, "in fact within a matter of a few days, I was convinced that the most important communications issue in the next few years would be communications by space satellite."

The President, too, immediately made communication satellites an item of high priority on his agenda. In his first State of the Union message the month he took office, Kennedy invited all nations to join with the United States in considering the peaceful uses of communication satellites. On May 25, 1961, the day Kennedy made the Lunar Challenge in his address before Congress, he also asked for an additional $50 million to accelerate the use of space satellites for worldwide communication. And in June 1961, the President requested that the Space Council make the necessary studies and recommendations needed to bring communication satellites "into optimum use at the earliest practicable time."

In his September address before the United Nations, Kennedy again raised the critical importance of satellite communication in carrying out the charter mission of the United Nations. Before the world community, the United States was promising to champion "a global system of communication satellites linking the whole world in telegraph, telephone, radio, and television."

By spring of 1962, the public was beginning to anticipate the marvels that were about to unfold in the sky. On the series *The Twentieth Century*, Walter Cronkite presented a program entitled "The Satellite That Talks." "Before too long," Cronkite told viewers as they watched a man-made star being assembled, "these satellites, shrinking time and space, will bring London, Rome, Tokyo immediately into your living room. . . . promising to expand man's contacts with his fellow man as radically as the invention of printing."

FCC chairman Newton Minow, a guest on the program, was asked by Cronkite, who had a perceptive understanding of American interests, about the 1964 summer Olympic games in Japan. "Do you think that there's any hope that with these communication satellites, people in the United States might see direct broadcasts of these events?" "Well, Walter, it's too early to tell," Minow responded. "I would think that it'd be a great dream and a great inauguration of satellite communication. We'll know more when we start sending up several of the experimental communication satellites."

The CBS newsman also queried Minow about the heavenly exportation of American entertainment television: "When we get these communication satellites in use, are we going to ship overseas the same sort of programming that we have on television in this country today?" "Well, I hope not, Walter," the chairman said. "At least, not most of it. It would be—it seems to me—a terrible waste to use this great miracle to send over a lot of bad impressions of the United States. If we fill it with private eyes and westerns . . . I think it would be a travesty. . . . If we don't use this communication device for achieving a greater understanding between us and the rest of the world, we're just throwing away the greatest opportunity ever given us."

## The Thrall of *Telstar*

The AT&T experiment the FCC had OK'd in January 1961 was ready to be tested in the summer of 1962. On the tenth of July, at 4:30 A.M., a Delta rocket blasted off from Cape Canaveral transporting a 170-pound ball of cargo. AT&T had spent in the vicinity of $50 million developing and designing *Telstar*, which was built by the Bell Telephone Laboratories in Hillside, New Jersey. For a fee of $2.7 million, NASA was launching the communications satellite into an egg-shaped orbit ranging from 600 to 3,500 miles above the surface of the earth.

For many weeks before the launch, the three American networks, along with the USIA, NASA, AT&T, and the European Broadcasting Union, engaged in negotiations concerning a debut international broadcast. The networks took the position that they would participate only if they, not the government, controlled the program content, and that was the agreed-upon arrangement.

The formal inaugural broadcast was scheduled for two weeks after the successful boost of *Telstar* into orbit. In the meanwhile, AT&T would conduct some strictly experimental transmissions—at least that was the understanding of the networks. But, as the day of the launch approached, AT&T decided it should present a program to mark the historic occasion and to take full advantage of the opportunity for publicity. The networks were not pleased. Such a pre-inaugural broadcast would steal some of the thunder from the extravaganza they were planning for later in the month—and the fact AT&T was producing the "newscast" was ethically troublesome.

CBS had independently prepared a news extra on *Telstar* for the evening of July 10, and chose not to carry AT&T's thirty-minute program, which included Newton Minow and other members of the FCC, Vice-President Johnson, and Frederick Kappel, the chairman of AT&T. Richard Salant explained, "It was the view of CBS News that it was not desirable or appropriate for it to cover such a historic event without exercising its own editorial judgment concerning the components of the broadcast. . . . Particularly because there are competing satellite systems and because there is a current legislative controversy over ownership."

ABC and NBC, without their own news specials in the works, were caught in the awkward position of looking unprepared for a major newsbreak. They carried the AT&T- supplied program in its virtual entirety.

Fifteen hours after the satellite was positioned in space, *Telstar* was ready to initiate a new era in modern communication. The first transmission was a domestic exchange between a ground station in Andover, Maine, and one in Holmdel, New Jersey. The AT&T program began with taped footage of a waving American flag and the national anthem, followed by simple interviews.

In summarizing the day's events, ABC's Jules Bergman pointed out to viewers that it was just 118 years earlier that Samuel Morse tapped out the words "What Hath God Wrought?" to demonstrate his invention, the telegraph. "God hath wrought much this day," Bergman concluded about July 10, 1962.

The following evening all three networks interrupted regular programming to broadcast an eight-minute *Telstar* transmission from France, which included night scenes of Paris, the French Telecommunications minister, and the performer who symbolized Parisian romance and charm to Americans, Yves Montand.

The day before the official premiere broadcast of intercontinental television, Newton Minow was the guest on *Meet the Press*. Asked for his prediction on how long it would be before satellite communication became a staple of American broadcasting, the chairman took the opportunity to plug the foresightedness of President Kennedy's pending satellite bill, which would create a private, profit-making corporation with publicly held stock to own and operate the space communication system of the United States, under FCC controls. "As always in this country," Minow said, "technology is ahead of public policy. This time we want to keep our national legislative policy abreast of science."

On Monday, July 23, 1962, on *Telstar's* 123rd orbit, when the satellite was high over the Atlantic ocean, it would be in line of sight with both the United States and Europe for twenty-two minutes. And during that time, Walter Cronkite, Chet Huntley, and Howard K. Smith were going to show 100 million Eurovision viewers, along with Americans at home, the distinctive splendor of the United States.

Moments before the broadcast Walter Cronkite was giving last-minute instructions to coordinate the international relay: "Eurovision, we are now putting up our Statue of Liberty in New York harbor on the left side of our monitor.... Please put up your Eiffel Tower in Paris next to it. When you have both the Statue of Liberty and the Eiffel Tower on your line monitor, that will mean that the circuit is closed and this electronic bridge across the Atlantic is open. We will go on your signal." The newsman then heard: "This is Brussels ... stand by ... stand by ... stand by.... Go, America, go.... Go, America, go...."

"Good evening, Europe," Cronkite began over a live picture of New York. "This is the North American continent live via AT&T *Telstar* ... July 23, 1962, 3 p.m. Eastern Daylight Time. On the East, the New York skyline on the Atlantic Ocean. That's the Brooklyn Bridge—"

The picture then changed to the Golden Gate Bridge and Cronkite continued: "On the West, 3,000 miles away—San Francisco. Twelve noon at the Golden Gate Bridge, high above the entrance of San Francisco Harbor.... The same sun which has just set over the Mediterranean and the English Channel has reached its zenith here."

Next, over a panoramic view of a natural wonder, Cronkite said: "On the North—one of the longest unguarded borders on this planet. . . . This is Niagara Falls, part of the Canadian–U.S. frontier that extends from New Brunswick to British Columbia on the Pacific." After a pause to hear the roaring sound of the water, the tour continued.

"On the South, the Rio Grande River . . . for 1,000 miles the only border between Mexico and the United States. Here the cities of Juarez, Mexico, and El Paso, Texas, touch. . . . "

With Washington, D.C., on the screen, Cronkite noted: "The plain facts of electronic life are that Washington and the Kremlin are now no farther apart than the speed of light, at least technically."

Taking over the reins, Chet Huntley transported viewers to the State Department auditorium, where a presidential news conference was in progress. In his opening remarks, Kennedy had told the assembled correspondents: "I understand that part of today's press conference is being relayed by *Telstar* communications satellite to TV users across the Atlantic, and this is another indication of the extraordinary world in which we live."

The President's podium was equipped with a small red tally light which told him when he was on transatlantic television. He was only on the air about four-and-a-half minutes. But it was long enough for Europeans to hear the Chief Executive express regret that the Russians were conducting nuclear testing and to hear his claim the United States would not devalue the dollar—which was good news for holders of foreign currency.

After the quick introduction to the give-and-take between an American president and the press, viewers continued on to Cape Canaveral to meet John Glenn, an American hero instantly recognizable around the world, and Wally Schirra the next astronaut scheduled for space flight.

"If the international competition for outer space will be part of *Telstar*'s orbital beat," Huntley remarked, "so, too, will an older, simpler contest— the sporting event. . . . " At that moment, the public-address announcer at Wrigley Field, where Chicago's Cubs were hosting the Philadelphia Phillies, told the crowd in the stadium: "Ladies and gentlemen, we have just been informed that this baseball game is being seen in Europe right now over the *Telstar* satellite! Let's give all the baseball fans in Europe a big hello from Chicago!" The crowd let loose with a monumental roar.

The program then quickly hopscotched from an expressway in Detroit to a view of Quebec and then to Stratford, Ontario, where the audience caught a glimpse of Christopher Plummer in rehearsal for *Macbeth*. A montage of scenes from the Seattle World's Fair was followed by a spectacular view of Mount Rushmore accompanied by the three hundred voices of the Mormon Tabernacle Choir singing "A Mighty Fortress Is Our God."

One hundred years ago, Huntley noted, President Lincoln said, "The dogmas of the quiet past are inadequate to the stormy present. . . . As our case is new so we must think anew and act anew." It was said about a divided country, Huntley observed, "but today it has equal meaning to a divided planet."

Bringing the program to a close, Howard K. Smith took viewers to the prayer chapel, or what some preferred to call the meditation room, of the United Nations. "As we contemplate how we are going to use our inheritance in space, it is perhaps proper that a moment of silence be transmitted from this room of quiet to our satellite and back to another side of earth. . . . For ten seconds now our transmitters will be silent in many languages."

After the credits were announced, Walter Cronkite informed viewers, "In approximately two hours and forty-five minutes from now, Europe to America will be beamed to us via *Telstar*." And when the satellite came around for its 124th orbit, another video scrapbook was presented. While the American production was the work of three networks and the cooperation of the Canadian Broadcasting Company, the European transmission was a more complicated piece of committee work. The thirteen nations in the European Broadcasting Union combined forces for the telecast.

Fifty-three cameras presented picture-postcard scenes—from reindeer feeding on the Arctic Circle to fishermen in Sicily; from the Sistine Chapel in Rome to dancing horses in Vienna. The sound of opera and the sight of famed paintings gave a sense of the greatness of European artistic tradition. The European transmission concluded, however, with technical difficulties, ending abruptly after sixteen minutes. As one critic wrote of the broadcast, "It was beheaded, perhaps fittingly, at the Tower of London when Telstar moved over the horizon."

The public was captivated by the possibilities held by *Telstar*. "The first formal transmissions, both ways, were almost unbearably exciting," Gilbert Seldes wrote in *TV Guide*. "Telstar makes you want to call back all the big words you have ever used, so that now 'magnificent' and 'epoch-making' and all the rest could be fresh-minted for the event."

AT&T received and declined numerous requests to allow *Telstar* to be used for commercial promotions. AT&T itself, however, was enjoying tremendous public goodwill without exerting much time or energy to the cause. People were simply fascinated in reading and hearing about the satellite.

In October 1962, in London, a musical group called the Tornadoes recorded a synthesized, futuristic-sounding instrumental song called "Telstar." Metallically melodious, yet hardly a dance tune, the ethereal recording topped the pop charts in both the United Kingdom and the United States.

The networks soon began to incorporate satellite feeds into news broadcasts. The convening of a Vatican Council in Rome in fall 1962, for instance, which would ultimately change the daily lives of millions of American Roman Catholics, was a highly visual story of ancient customs that modern technology brought directly to home screens.

In May 1963, *Telstar II* was launched and on July 10, to celebrate the first anniversary of satellite communication, CBS introduced a new series of occasional documentaries called *CBS Town Meeting of the World*. Major political figures from various points on the globe would engage in live satellite-connected discussions.

A little more than two weeks later, July 26, a new generation of communications satellite was propelled into orbit. *Syncom*, the first successful synchronous satellite, owned by the Hughes Aircraft Company, was positioned over the mid-Atlantic. Unlike *Telstar*, which only offered short windows of opportunity for transmission as it came into view of designated ground stations, a synchronous satellite was always capable of relaying messages in its footprint of coverage.

*Syncom*, also known as a stationary or hovering satellite, was fixed 22,300 miles above the earth, which meant that one orbit took exactly 24 hours. As the artificial star moved with the planet, it seemed to hang motionless, parked in space. Just three synchronous satellites, properly placed, could provide constantly available TV coverage to virtually every part of the globe. In the Kennedy years, television wonders never ceased.

## Laying the Groundwork for Blue Skies

While the actual accomplishment of space communication absorbed scientists, the more mundane questions of ownership and regulation of satellites challenged bureaucrats and politicians. Arrangements between government and private industry needed to be sorted out in order for research and development to continue.

In the effort to create a single American system to participate in a global satellite network, three options were considered: an enterprise owned and operated by the government, similar to the Tennessee Valley Authority; a closed consortium of common carriers with an interest in space communication, such as AT&T, RCA, General Telephone, and Western Union; or a privately owned corporation with publicly held stock.

In the spring of 1961, after soliciting the views of various communication companies on how to organize space communication, the FCC came out in favor of the closed consortium. Minow recalled that much of the debate focused on "whether or not the general public should have a chance to buy stock, or whether it should be limited to existing communications carriers." "I was of the latter school," Minow said. "I felt that the communication carriers should participate and that the general public could, if it wanted, buy stock in any of the existing or future communication carriers."

But soon, Minow remembered, "the President personally entered the picture and made a basic judgment." In his July 1961 policy statement on communications satellites, Kennedy made it clear he did not want to consolidate communication power in too few hands. He wanted to assure maximum competition and full compliance with antitrust legislation.

With Kennedy's wishes known, the FCC, Minow recalled, "worked with the Department of Justice, and eventually the President presented a bill. This was not greeted with great enthusiasm by my colleagues who had their own ideas about how to proceed, and this raised an interesting question for a chairman who was the only Kennedy appointee on the Commission."

In proposing his Communications Satellite Bill in February 1962, the President explained: "Throughout our history this country's national communications systems have been privately owned and operated, subject to governmental regulation of rates and service. In the case of the communications satellite operation, our studies have convinced us that . . . national objectives . . . can best be achieved in the framework of a privately owned corporation, properly chartered by the Congress. The attached bill authorizes the establishment of such a corporation, financed through the sale of public stock."

Minow remembered modestly: "I tried to follow a path that was as close to the President's view as possible, which meant that I had to make some concessions to my colleagues' judgment, but I was able to at least succeed in not sending up a bill of our own and allowing us instead to give our comments on the President's bill."

But the chairman was a persuasive lobbyist for the President on the FCC. The month following the proposal of the bill, Minow appeared before a Congressional committee to give testimony. His statement of the Commission's support for Kennedy's bill was a surprising about-face.

Minow was asked by Congressman William Springer of Illinois, "Mr. Chairman, this statement which you have made today, does this represent the composite thinking of the seven members of your Commission?" "Yes, it does, sir," Minow responded. "This is official?" Springer wondered. "Yes, sir," said Minow. "And unanimous?" "Yes, sir."

With the FCC now in Kennedy's camp, any hope for a closed consortium faded. But there were many who supported the notion of a government-owned satellite system. Congressman William Fitts Ryan, a New York Democrat, expressed their beliefs when he argued, "In view of the billions taxpayers have spent in developing space technology, creation by the government of a private owned system would be the greatest giveaway of the nuclear age."

Stumping for the Kennedy bill, Minow responded to the giveaway charge this way: "The issue is not markedly different from that involving the development of jet aircraft or radar or fertilizer as a result of government research. The government could have taken over the commercial operation of all research discoveries made partly possible with public funds. It could, for example have assumed the production of jet aircraft on the ground that it had contributed so largely to its development. But it did not do so—nor

were there any contentions that it should. For such production has traditionally been by private enterprise in this country. That is equally true in
the case of the communications industry."

When the plan for a privately owned satellite corporation passed in the
House, *I.F. Stone's Weekly* editorialized, "This bill, if it now passes the
Senate will be the first Big Steal in Outer Space. . . . there is a myth that
A.T.& T. embodies the virtues of free enterprise."

Supporters of a governmentally owned system worried about the possibility of AT&T sabotaging progress in satellite communication to protect
its enormous holdings in existing technology, specifically undersea cables.
Senator Russell Long of Louisiana, an opponent of the Kennedy bill, pointed
out that in the attempt to protect investments in obsolete equipment, such
innovations as one-piece telephones, modern switching devices, and the dial
phone were not placed on the market until years after they had been
developed.

The timing of the *Telstar* launch could not have been more fortuitous for
AT&T. Just as the Senate prepared to debate the Administration's bill—
and as a group of dissident senators demanding government ownership, led
by Estes Kefauver, began a filibuster to block the plan for a private corporation—American viewers were awed by the *Telstar* spectacular. It was,
wrote one social critic, "a brilliant bit of lobbying." Public support for
congressional action on the satellite bill added to its bipartisan appeal.

On August 31, 1962, President Kennedy signed the Communications Satellite Bill into law. The Act established a private corporation, the Communications Satellite Corporation—COMSAT, to build and operate a
commercial satellite system in conjunction with foreign governments and
foreign communication entities. Half the voting stock would be owned by
communications common carriers, the other half was to be owned by inves-
tors from the general public.

The Satellite Act also charged NASA to cooperate with COMSAT in a
program of research and development and to provide launching and tracking
services on a reimbursable basis. The FCC was vested with regulatory powers, including the regulation of rates, construction programs, and technical
specifications. The FCC was also to oversee a policy of non-discriminatory
access to the satellite system.

"History will record that the Russians were the first to send a man into
space," Minow told the International Radio and Television Society in October 1962, "but history will also record that this year the United States
achieved something more enduring. We were the first to launch an idea into
space—and ideas outlive men. The idea is to use international communication for peace. The idea is to build, not a wall sealing in ignorance and
prejudice, but a window opening toward truth and freedom."

In January 1963, Minow delivered a progress report to the Senate Commerce Committee summarizing development in the space communication

program since the enactment of the bill five months earlier: "There is still much work to be done before we are ready with a reliable operational system. . . . In recent weeks, technical experts of the Commission have been represented on government teams which have been sent to South America, Mexico, and Western Europe for the purpose of exchanging views with other nations. . . . Our government in recent months has endeavored to inform many foreign administrations of the policies and purpose of the Satellite Act."

At a Rose Garden ceremony in April 1963, President Kennedy, empowered by Congress, proclaimed Sir Winston Churchill an honorary citizen of the United States. The rite was instantly televised throughout Europe via the *Relay* satellite. The aging leader watched the program at his London home—touched by the tribute and amazed at the sight.

In the last months of his life, John Kennedy began to display an evolving view of America's place in the world. At American University, on June 10, 1963, he spoke with the wisdom of an elder statesman who had been tempered by trial and adversity. Kennedy bravely expressed his true fear of the fallibility of human judgment in the nuclear age. It was time, the President declared, "to reexamine our attitude toward the Cold War. . . . We are not here distributing blame or pointing the finger of judgment. We must deal with the world as it is, and not as it might have been had the history of the last eighteen years been different."

The future lay on a spectrum between annihilation and communication. And with the expanding possibilities for human communication came expanding visions of human kinship. "Enmities between nations, as between individuals, do not last forever," Kennedy said. "And if we cannot now end our differences, at least we can help make the world safe for diversity. For in the final analysis, our most basic common link is that we all inhabit this planet, we all breathe the same air. We all cherish our children's future. And we are all mortal."

Before decade's end, the chant "The Whole World Is Watching" would connote the divisiveness of a brutal war. But, on November 20, 1963, in one of his last official acts, President Kennedy issued a declaration from the White House inviting all nations, small as well as large, to join with the United States in a global system of satellite communication. It was a peaceful horizon that stretched ahead in the final hours of the New Frontier.

# EPILOGUE

# Ineffable Sadness, Indelible Images

President Kennedy was thinking about television and the 1964 campaign. He'd seen an ad for Volkswagen that said "Think Small" and the whimsy impressed him. The advertising agency responsible, Doyle Dane Bernbach, had a reputation for creating dramatic impact. The President instructed his brother-in-law, Stephen Smith, to talk to them about taking over the Democratic Party account.

He was also thinking about TV debates in those last weeks. In 1960, after the election results were final, Robert Kennedy said categorically that as an incumbent, President Kennedy would not debate his opponent in 1964. But the President said he would be willing. And now, after three years more experience with the medium, a confident John Kennedy was still in favor of televised debates. He was planning on four telecasts. Just prior to Dallas, however, media advisor J. Leonard Reinsch was trying to discourage the President from appearing in an unnecessarily risky forum. "I got him talked down to two debates," Reinsch recalled, "and I hoped to eliminate those two by the time I got around to the campaign." But the President was convinced Barry Goldwater was going to be the Republican candidate. And the two men, who personally enjoyed each other, had already worked out a deal between themselves that they would debate.

Another thing on the President's mind was his image. Looking like a statesman rather than a politician was going to be even more critical in 1964. So, two days before he left on his blatantly political trip to Texas, President Kennedy decided to forgo some dubious television exposure. The Poultry and Egg National Board, which represented the nation's turkey raisers, had come to the Rose Garden to present a Thanksgiving bird to the White House. A reporter who was there recalled the President being "so acutely embarrassed by the tawdry commercialism of the occasion that he delivered only the minimum courtesies and refused to be photographed with the turkey."

The President delivered his last formal speech at the Houston Coliseum on the evening of Thursday, November 21. Station KTRK in Houston had arranged to broadcast the event. And because it did, one of the most charming examples of John Kennedy's finesse as a public speaker has been preserved. Telling the audience about Houston's vast new space center, the President made a minor misstatement. It would soon fire, he said, "the largest payroll . . . payload . . . into space." To the delight of the audience, he then added with a knowing grin, "It will be the biggest payroll, too."

On Friday morning in Fort Worth, the Chamber of Commerce sponsored a breakfast for the President and the first lady. Presented with a wide-brimmed hat as a souvenir of Texas, the President laughed in appreciation, but had no intention of putting it on. Lunch was to be in Dallas. Originally, the President was scheduled to speak at the Women's Building at Fair Park. But, in order to accommodate television equipment, the event was moved to the more spacious Trade Mart.

The visit to Texas was being covered by a pool of local stations. Rather than dispatch a full complement of technical personnel for the presidential trip, the TV networks would rely primarily on the footage shot by their affiliates for the evening news.

The late arrival of Air Force One at Love Field was broadcast live by WFAA-TV, the ABC affiliate in Dallas. For almost ten minutes the President and Jacqueline Kennedy walked along the fence that separated them from a crowd of thousands. They touched extended hands and greeted their well-wishers with "hellos" and "how-are-yous?"

The station signed off the coverage about ten minutes after the motorcade got underway. The WFAA mobile cruiser was assigned to stay at the airport to cover the Kennedy departure later in the afternoon. No live coverage along the parade route was planned. The next remote was to be produced by KRLD-TV, the CBS affiliate, at the Trade Mart luncheon. But before that broadcast would air, the New Frontier came to an end in an abrupt, hideous instant.

Just minutes later, network newsrooms in New York were jolted into action as the first UPI bulletin came over the wire—THREE SHOTS WERE FIRED AT PRESIDENT KENNEDY'S MOTORCADE TODAY IN DALLAS—and reflex prevailed over numb shock. Within a half-hour of the President's limousine passing the School Book Depository, ABC, CBS, and NBC had suspended all regular programming. Without preparation or precedent, the most massive broadcast coverage of any event in history was underway.

Early information was confusing. Fact and rumor were hard to separate as reports came streaming in. The President is still alive, viewers were told, but in very critical condition with blood transfusions being given. In Washington, David Brinkley called the White House to find out whether anyone there had any late information. "No," replied a tearful member of the White House staff, "we were watching you to see if you had any."

Setting up phone lines between the local stations in Dallas and the networks was a critical priority. Finally, pictures started to come in. A live feed from the Trade Mart presented the inescapable reality. The camera lingered on the empty lectern from which the President was to speak, then panned across milling guests, uneaten food, and finally revealed a waiter drying his eye with a napkin.

Had anyone stopped and considered the logistical enormity of what needed to be done, it would have been deemed utterly impossible. Instead, reporting assignments were given, planes were chartered, engineering schematics were drawn. Producers culled through endless amounts of film and tape footage in network archives to assemble material for retrospective special reports.

At the FCC, members of the staff of Chairman E. William Henry began gravitating toward his office. They sat and watched the television in horrified silence. The official announcement of President Kennedy's death came about one hour after the first bulletin, and with it came a new responsibility for television. The medium was now a principal determinant in how well the American democracy would maintain its course.

Lyndon Johnson understood this instinctively. Without assurance of an orderly transition of government, domestic panic could spread. Foreign governments, too, needed to see and hear the new President in command. The importance of a documenting photograph was clear to most in the cramped stateroom of Air Force One as the vice-president prepared to take the oath of office. But Johnson also wanted the sound of the ceremony preserved. When he realized that no audio recording equipment had been brought on the plane, Johnson ordered, "Use the Dictograph on the desk." Though faint and scratchy, the recording was made available to each broadcast network.

The new President decided he wanted to address the American people as soon as he stepped off Air Force One. With less than two hours notice, a crew of TV and telephone technicians set to work. The necessary wiring was completed just two minutes before the jet stopped on the runway. "There was no time for testing," one of the men recalled, "We just turned on the switches, aimed the transmitter toward Washington and prayed."

Jacqueline Kennedy, too, had a dark awareness of the power visual imagery would wield in the hours and days to come. Urged to change her bloodstained suit and stockings, she refused. She wanted the waiting television cameras to convey the horror of what happened in Dallas. And viewers did shudder at the sight of the President's spattered blood when his widow emerged from the aircraft. On the flight from Dallas, she decided to use President Lincoln's burial as a model for her husband's. The first martyred president of the television age, Jacqueline Kennedy resolved, would have a state funeral of grandeur and poignant symbolism.

Shortly after the official word of President Kennedy's death was aired, CBS broadcast its intention to carry no commercial announcements and no entertainment programming until after the funeral. By Friday evening, NBC and ABC had reached the same decision.

As more network newspeople and technicians began arriving at the local stations in Dallas, the burden of filling network airtime between news developments was addressed quickly. Memorial concerts, church services, and panel discussions began to appear on the air Friday night.

But the audience's need to stay in contact with events was strong. Great numbers of viewers switched channels in search of news whenever filler programming appeared, even though no new information was available. The repetition of what was known was preferable to being disconnected from the story. There was vague comfort in having familiar faces review the monumental day. As one viewer wrote to NBC's Chet Huntley, it was like "old friends we are accustomed to, telling us about the tragedy until we could absorb it."

While television viewers saw the suspected assassin for the first time from the chaos of the Dallas police station, the networks were trying to locate footage of the crime. No TV or professional film cameras had recorded the fateful moment. But a spectator taking eight-millimeter home movies of the motorcade heard a gunshot, and then, through his viewfinder, he saw the President slump. Realizing JFK had been wounded, Abraham Zapruder kept his Bell & Howell focused on the limousine until it entered the underpass.

The next morning, negotiations with various news organizations for the rights to Zapruder's seven seconds of celluloid had begun. Representing CBS, Dan Rather was allowed to see the film one time, without taking notes, before making a bid. After viewing the awful scene, Rather hurried back to the CBS affiliate station and described on the air what he had witnessed. By the time the newsman returned to discuss dollar figures, *Life* magazine had closed a deal with Zapruder.

ABC and NBC executives decided against trying to obtain the footage when they realized how graphic the content was. After viewing the film, and seeing the spray of the President's brain, a newsman from the ABC affiliate advised the network: "I recommend that you don't even bid on it. It's too dramatic; I don't think it is the thing for home television." His network colleague agreed: "It's the greatest news film I've ever seen, but I think it would be in bad taste to show it." CBS, though, continued to pursue the possibility of renting the film for one broadcast—but *Life* would not allow it. What surely would have been the most difficult editorial judgment call in the history of television journalism became academic.

When news of the assassination reached the offices of Drew Associates, Greg Shuker recalls everyone asking, "What do we do?" Acting independently, not on a network assignment, Shuker remembers, "We all got on the first Eastern shuttle the next Saturday morning and went down to Washington, D.C. It's like the juggler story at Christmas, you give what you can offer. We'll shoot something and it'll be our tribute."

On Saturday, the President's body rested on a catafalque in the East Room of the White House. Throughout the rainy day television cameras covered with plastic shields followed the steps of notable mourners as they arrived at the mansion to pay their respects. Luminaries such as Presidents Eisenhower and Truman, Chief Justice Earl Warren, the Russian ambassador, governors, senators, members of Congress, and representatives of the armed forces made the sad trek to view the coffin.

Though the housekeeping concerns of most Americans had been completely put aside, in the Oval Office President Kennedy's personal effects were being packed and removed—file cabinets, a globe, model ships, and paintings of naval battles were loaded on a dolly. The sight of his rocking chairs being unceremoniously carted away for storage through a side door was not meant for television. But the cruel image did not escape the camera's eye.

Dallas remained the center of news activity as the networks supplied curious viewers with a growing body of information on Lee Harvey Oswald and the progress of the investigation. News teams were relentless in their pursuit of details and the policy of the local police was complete cooperation with the press. Some critics have speculated the active assistance the Dallas police and prosecutors lent to the media that weekend had less to do with protecting the public's right to know than with their own desires to appear on television.

The corridor outside the homicide office on the third floor of the police and court building, where Oswald was being interrogated, was quickly overrun by newsgatherers. More than a hundred bodies stationed themselves in a hallway that was only about seven feet wide and 140 feet long.

The presence of the group referred to as "television people" contributed most to the resulting congestion and chaos. A Secret Service agent who was present at some of the questioning of the prisoner recalled: "You would have to elbow your way through, and step over tripods and cables and wires. . . . They had cables run through one of the deputy chief's offices, right through the windows from the street up side the building, across the floor, out to the boxes where they could get power—they had wires running out of that, had the wires taped down to keep people from actually falling or stumbling. . . . It was just almost indescribable."

Oswald was led through this mass of humanity and equipment sixteen times. Each time he was escorted from the jail elevator to the interrogation room—a distance of about twenty feet—cameras whirred, microphones were thrust in his face, and questions, many presuming his guilt, were shouted out.

The frantic pace of news coverage at police headquarters was described as "every man for himself." Though some cooperative arrangements among reporters arose spontaneously, a formal equipment pool, which might have reduced the congestion considerably, was not established.

The due process of law withered under television lights. As one attorney studying the case noted, "The police department policy toward the press was not only open-door, it was open-mouth." Broadcast interviews with the Police Chief, the Homicide Captain, the District Attorney, and the police press relations officer were filled with misinformation and opinion. Television viewers not only heard the suspect proclaim his innocence, but heard police Captain Will Fritz declare that the case was "cinched" and Prosecutor Henry Wade's claim, "We have sufficient evidence to convict him."

Saturday was also the day television brought the American public world reaction to their President's assassination. As the news of the murder circled the globe, network news bureaus in foreign capitals immediately arranged interviews with world leaders. In Moscow, Khrushchev appeared at the U.S. embassy to convey condolences. At the Vatican, Pope Paul spoke in broken English of his sorrow. From London, the Prime Minister of England, Sir Alec Douglas-Home, expressed his grief elegantly. But, perhaps, the images Americans found most consoling were of the great crowds of ordinary people gathered in the streets of cities throughout the world.

Behind the scenes, the networks spent Saturday planning the pool coverage of the President's funeral. By the flip of a coin on Friday night, CBS News producer Art Kane had won the job of taking charge of the broadcast arrangements from the capital.

It was initially assumed that after a brief period of lying in state in Washington, John Kennedy would be buried in Boston. But at a 2 A.M. meeting on Saturday, called to discuss television coverage plans, Pierre Salinger alerted the networks that arrangements were not final and that they should be prepared for a funeral of grand scope in Washington. Just three months earlier, Art Kane had supervised the three-network coverage of the March on Washington, but this time he was undertaking a monumental task on much shorter notice.

Following the meeting with Salinger, Kane presided over a caucus of pool engineers and technicians at the House press gallery in the Capitol building. Possible routes the funeral cortege might take were discussed with District of Columbia officials. The White House architect informed the group of suitable locations for TV cameras at the mansion. In the early hours of Saturday morning, scaffolding was ordered built and each network's territory was assigned along the route. For an inaugural parade, the networks allowed three months to prepare such a setup.

It wasn't until three o'clock Saturday afternoon that Arlington National Cemetery was officially announced as the burial site. At 7 P.M. the producer again met with Salinger. Kane was given information on Sunday's move of the President's body from the White House to the Capitol rotunda and details on the Monday funeral. From 8 P.M. to midnight, the producer and the other members of the pool crew reviewed what was known and organized the logistics of the coverage.

Kane then headed to St. Matthew's Cathedral with Norman Gorin, his CBS colleague who was the network pool director in Washington. After getting acquainted with the church where the funeral Mass would be celebrated on Monday, the two made their way to the Capitol, where, throughout the night, a tremendous lash-up of broadcast equipment was taking place.

The center of pool operations was the control room under the East steps, an area normally used for the storage of cement. But it became a thirty-by-ten-foot electronic bunker from which forty-one cameras would be coordinated, allowing each television viewer a privileged position from which to join the national rituals of mourning.

Throughout the weekend, many of broadcasting's standard operating procedures were overlooked. Technical unions, for instance, normally inflexible about divisions of labor, paid no attention when camera operators handled sound equipment or directors made their own adjustments. And, just for the asking, network feeds were made available without charge to educational and independent local stations.

Sunday was to be a day devoted to solemnity. But before the ceremonial transfer of the President's coffin from the White House to the Capitol rotunda even began, another act of violence jolted a traumatized nation. In Dallas, too, a transfer was scheduled to take place.

All three networks were planning live coverage of the move of Lee Harvey Oswald from the city jail to the county jail in the late morning. CBS and NBC had their cameras ready in the basement-garage of the city jail. ABC had a reporter and an affiliate station film camera there, but its remote unit was at the county jail for the broadcast of Oswald's arrival.

Just two minutes before the prisoner appeared, NBC switched to a remote pick up from Hyannis Port. In Dallas, producer-director Fred Rheinstein was on the phone to the network-operations control room. "Give it to me now," Rheinstein told Chet Hagan, NBC's on-the-air producer. Accommodating his colleague's instinct, Hagan abruptly cut away from Hyannis Port and connected Dallas to the network in an instant. The elevator door opened and Oswald, with a detective on each side, stepped out and began his walk past reporters and police toward an unmarked squad car. Within seconds a man emerged from the lower right-hand corner of the TV screen, charged toward the prisoner and shot him. Oswald, his face contorted in pain, buckled over and fell to the pavement.

Incredulous television viewers heard NBC correspondent Tom Pettit exclaim, "He's been shot! He's been shot! Lee Oswald has been shot! There is absolute panic. Pandemonium has broken out."

CBS switched to the live picture in Dallas two seconds after the shooting, as policemen were struggling with the gunman. Within one minute, the CBS network was able to air a videotape replay of the actual shooting sequence. Later the network would show the footage in slow motion. The technology that so elevated the experience of watching sports on television was automatically thrust into a new context. Instead of the impressive form of an athlete in competition, an actual murder was captured and elongated in what was described as a "grotesque ballet."

Amid the tumult, a stretcher was brought in and the victim was lifted into an ambulance. ABC, without video footage, cut to its remote unit at the county jail and aired the reactions of people in the street to the news of the attack on Oswald.

At the same time, in Washington, the parade was forming for the march to the Capitol. The networks had to cut away from the confusion in Dallas as the ritual was about to begin—a ritual that was at once narcotizing and moving, and would produce indelible television imagery.

When Jacqueline Kennedy appeared at the north portico of the White House with her fatherless children each holding a hand, hearts ached. As she watched, dry-eyed and erect, the military pallbearers place the casket on the caisson, viewers marvelled at her strength.

Extreme long shots of the cortege provided a spectacular view of the Capitol dome and the size of the crowds lining the street. When commentators interrupted the ominous sound of muted drums and the clicking of horses hooves, they did so briefly and softly. Though the weight of their burden was tremendous, the young men carrying the coffin ascended the thirty-six steps of the Capitol without faltering.

Inside the magnificent rotunda the body of John Kennedy was placed on the very catafalque that held Abraham Lincoln. Three brief eulogies were delivered. Then Jacqueline Kennedy took Caroline's hand and the two walked to the catafalque and knelt together at the casket for a wrenching moment. The widow kissed the flag draped over the coffin. And the child, wanting to do the right thing, put her gloved hand under the cloth and gently touched the box that held her father.

With the formal ceremony ended, the networks announced the death of Oswald and news crews began a probe into the background of his murderer. Within hours, interviews with people who knew nightclub owner Jack Ruby were on the air.

Late Sunday afternoon, as Rose Kennedy, mother of the late President, his sister Eunice Shriver, and his brother Edward left Hyannis Port for

Washington, television covered their departure. At Dulles airport remote broadcasts showed the arrival of heads of state. And, as evening fell, the line of mourners waiting to file past the casket of John Kennedy was miles long.

Art Kane met with White House representatives at 8 P.M. on Sunday to get approval on camera positions for the next day's events. J. Leonard Reinsch was coordinating the church and cemetery coverage for the Kennedy family and he made certain that a full-face close-up of a family member would not appear on television screens. Camera placements allowed only for side and back views. Without question, the networks respected the minimal request for privacy.

A brutal, revue-style satire of the news called *That Was the Week That Was*, or *TW3* for short, was a popular Saturday night television series on the BBC in 1963. In a bold stroke of entertainment experimentation, NBC presented a pilot of an American version of *TW3* on November 10, 1963. It was not as cutting as the British original. Topical political humor with genuine barbs directed at government leaders, was not yet typical American TV fare. But the favorable audience reaction led NBC to immediately schedule *TW3* as a regular weekly series beginning in January 1964.

On this weekend, though, the irreverent British cast prepared, literally overnight, a tribute to President Kennedy that touched viewers deeply. The program aired in Great Britain on Saturday, November 23. A tape of the show was flown to the United States and broadcast by NBC on Sunday night.

The host of the series, David Frost, articulated the feeling of emptiness viewers shared: "It was the least likely thing to happen in the whole world. If anyone else had died—Sir Winston Churchill, de Gaulle, Khrushchev—it would have been something that somehow we could have understood and perhaps even accepted. But that Kennedy should go, well, we just didn't believe in assassination anymore, not in the civilized world anyway."

Another young man in the troupe recalled: "When Kennedy was picked to be the Democratic candidate for the Presidency in 1960, the general opinion was that Kennedy was too perfect, too good to be true, a sort of public relations officer's ideal American: the film-star image, the beautiful wife, the great speeches with easy quotations from Burke and Shakespeare, the ice-cold efficiency, respect for facts." But once he was in office, another in the cast stated, he was the first Western politician in thirty years "to make politics a respectable profession. . . . He was simply and superlatively a man of his age."

A young woman sang a dirge with painfully moving lyrics: "The heart of the world weighs heavy with the helplessness of tears for the man cut down in a Texas town in the summer of his years." Dame Sybil Thorndike, one of Britain's most famous actresses, recited a poem "to Jackie": "What can we say to you, we who all pray with you, widow and mother?" When the broadcast ended, more than a thousand phone calls flooded the NBC switch-board from appreciative viewers and eventually thousands of requests for excerpts from the *That Was the Week That Was* tribute reached the network.

NBC did not sign off the air on Sunday night. Instead, it stayed with the endless procession of people filing past the bier, mourners who stood in the cold for six, maybe eight hours before they reached the rotunda. All night, faces of every kind were seen as they gazed at the coffin. NBC News vice-president Julian Goodman explained, "We covered President Kennedy all through his career. We felt we should stay there as long as he did."

Through the night Art Kane coped with problems as they arose. A con-tractor had to be hired to rebuild the camera platforms in the church because they were too wide to satisfy the District of Columbia fire department. And word came that the TV cameramen who would be recording the funeral Mass in St. Matthew's were required to wear formal mourning suits. So, the owner of a clothing rental business was awakened and persuaded to open his store early the next morning to outfit thirteen technicians.

A meeting of pool crews to coordinate information on Monday's events lasted until 2 A.M. Kane and director Norman Gorin then went to the church to check on details. At 4 A.M. they returned to their hotel to eat and shower and by 5:30 A.M. were back in the control room.

By nine o'clock on Monday morning an estimated four hundred thousand people had passed through the rotunda. Finally, the bronze doors were shut as final preparations could no longer wait. Soon the family would be leaving the White House to escort the coffin from the Capitol.

Each network carried the pool pictures, but would occasionally cut to one of several of their own network cameras that were in search of compelling shots. Throughout the funeral, the commentary that came from the indi-vidual networks was kept to a minimum. In a few instances, when it was deemed in a network control room that the commentator's remarks would disrupt the poignancy of the scene, the audio was simply not relayed.

After recording the full military funeral procession leaving the Capitol, it was necessary for some camera crews to tear down their units and leapfrog ahead to make new connections to cover the march further down the route.

From the Capitol, the cortege slowly proceeded to the White House. As it neared the mansion, the bands played Chopin's haunting "Funeral March." Abandoning limousines, Jacqueline Kennedy and her two brothers-in-law led a contingent of family, friends, and dignitaries walking behind the caisson from the White House to St. Matthew's Cathedral. This group of more than two hundred mourners, representing ninety-two nations, in-cluded reigning monarchs and heads of governments. In ad-lib formation the imposing assemblage surged from the White House gates to join the funeral parade.

In front of the cathedral, Cardinal Cushing of Boston, in tall mitre and black vestments, received the body. As the pallbearers brought the coffin into the church and the camera following them panned across the pews, some viewers might have recognized Newton Minow in the crowd. Also among those present at the requiem Mass were several men whose prominence was amplified by television in the Kennedy years—Richard Nixon, John Glenn, George Wallace, and Martin Luther King, Jr.

After the ceremony, as the casket was being placed back on the caisson for the trip to Arlington cemetery, Jacqueline Kennedy leaned over to whisper something to her fidgeting son. He handed his mother a pamphlet he was holding and then took a step forward. Straight and stiff he raised his arm to his forehead in a perfect salute to his father. That this very day was John F. Kennedy, Jr.'s third birthday heightened the pathos of the image that would become a permanent part of the iconographic heritage of the United States.

With the funeral Mass concluded and the procession to Arlington about to begin, television viewership attained its highest level in the history of the medium—93 percent of American sets were tuned in to the coverage.

Eighteen months after the first *Telstar* broadcasts christened the age of international television, viewers in twenty-five countries saw portions of President Kennedy's funeral rites as they occurred. The telecast was fed by NBC via the *Relay* communications satellite. In the network's New York studio, eight European reporters narrated the picture transmission in their own languages. And, for the first time, satellite relays reached beyond the Iron Curtain. As Americans watched an unruly and riderless black horse— the symbol of a fallen leader—follow the flag-draped coffin of their President, the same picture, at the same moment, was being seen in the halls of the Kremlin.

On its journey the cortege passed the shrine of another assassinated president. The Lincoln Memorial provided a dramatic backdrop as the procession started to cross the bridge to Arlington. During the funeral, all commercial air traffic at National Airport had been halted. In a rare interjection by a TV commentator, Bill Leonard of CBS noted, "Even the heavens are silent."

Upon entering the cemetery, the coffin was slowly carried to the graveside to the lamenting sound of bagpipes. As it reached the site, fifty fighter planes—one representing each state—zoomed overhead in formation, followed by Air Force One.

Supplying the coverage for the pool, seven NBC cameras maintained an unobtrusive distance of 250 feet from the grave. One camera fitted with an eighty-inch telephoto lens—which was supposed to be put into use for the first time at the 1964 political conventions—provided selected close-ups of ceremony details.

As the nation watched, prayers were intoned, a twenty-one-gun salute was fired, and the bugler playing taps hit a trembling note. The American flag was folded with perfect precision by the young men who had carried the body of John Kennedy, the strain of their assignment never showing.

Holding the keepsake of her husband's service to his country, the widow lit the eternal flame that had been constructed at her request.

The ceremony now over, the family left the cemetery. But pool cameras continued to photograph the scene at the graveside through the lowering of the coffin. Anxious to seal the vault and fill the grave without public witness, the superintendent of Arlington cemetery ordered the electrical power cut.

Throughout the evening television continued to broadcast replays of the events that had riveted American viewers. Interpretation, special reports, and dedicational programs, such as a rebroadcast of *That Was the Week That Was*, filled the hours of Monday night.

When the networks signed off the air, the hundreds of men and women who had performed beyond the limits of human endurance could finally stop to reflect on their part in American history. The medium had served a vital mission during a time of crisis. But, it also shared responsibility with the press for the debacle of the coverage surrounding Lee Harvey Oswald.

On Tuesday, November 26 at 7 A.M., commercials and entertainment shows returned to American television screens. But it wasn't immediately programming-as-usual. Special reports continued. And the networks carefully reviewed their offerings to eliminate material and references that would be in poor taste in the wake of the tragedy.

For instance, *The Joey Bishop Show* taped on November 15, featured Vaughan Meader as a guest star. The plot revolved around Mr. Meader's impression of President Kennedy. The tape was erased. The producers of *The Patty Duke Show* deleted a scene in which she was to receive a medal from a man seated in a rocking chair, presumably President Kennedy. And, the Sunday after the funeral, Ed Sullivan decided his program should have a sober tone and a production without comedy was assembled.

NBC postponed the broadcast of a *White Paper* documentary called "Cuba: Bay of Pigs," and substituted a show called "The Best on Record." Originally scheduled for air on November 24, this program presented the recording industry's annual Grammy Awards. But even part of the replacement show had to be cut because it included a segment with Vaughan Meader.

NBC also dropped plans for a December rebroadcast of *A Tour of the White House with Mrs. John F. Kennedy*. And now, there could be no second three-network rocking chair interview with the President, as had been scheduled for taping and broadcast during the coming holiday season.

Particular efforts were made to screen network series for programs with murderous themes. A *Route 66* episode scheduled that week, for example, unfortunately titled "I'm Here to Kill a King," was replaced with a more innocuous story. A substitute was found for an episode of *Channing* that dealt with a student's attempt to murder a university professor. NBC withdrew a drama about an armed revolt against the president of an Arab country on the *Espionage* series. And the title of a *Defenders* episode, "The Gentle Assassin," was changed to "Climate of Evil."

Network executives were sensitive to the kind of criticism levelled by Harriet Van Horne in the *New York World-Telegram* on November 26. If, as one scholarly panelist on a TV roundtable discussion suggested, all Americans shared culpability for the President's murder, "then surely," she wrote, "a heavy sense of guilt should rest with the gentlemen who determine what's seen on your TV screen. . . . In its own defense, television may proclaim that it is doing its duty by bringing us the news every day. I submit that this is not enough. . . . If TV would like to establish a fitting memorial to President Kennedy, let it be a series of public affairs programs that will improve the decidedly shabby moral fabric of our society today."

In *The New York Times* Jack Gould too wrote harshly of television shows rooted in violence and "the constant and unremitting use of the gun to resolve dramatic situations." Although recognizing that violence is a legitimate dramatic tool, he urged that men of goodwill in broadcasting ask themselves how many and how often violent acts are really needed in programming.

But the Van Horne and Gould denunciations nevertheless were embedded in overall appreciation for television. Disparagement was an uncommon reaction. In the days following television's coverage of President Kennedy's assassination and funeral, the medium became the object of prodigious thanks and congratulations from the public, the press, and government officials. As *Television Magazine* noted, "Years of critical whining seemed to vanish into a sea of praise." In a very distinct way, the medium's extraordinary performance during those tragic four days marked the end of a period of intense scrutiny for television.

Great volumes of emotional letters from viewers, such as these to Chet Huntley and David Brinkley, came to all network news commentators:

> God bless you and fellow workers on all the networks, you deserve a mourning nation's heartfelt "thank you." I hope that those critics, so quick to find fault, are as quick to recognize monumental reporting of this tragic event.

> We all felt our world had toppled. But you two who have become such a great part of our daily lives, gave me a great feeling of stability.

> As today is Monday, and the funeral is over, we watched TV continuously from early morning seeing the hundred thousands of people the world over who came to pay tribute. It made me feel good to know they thought so much of Mr. Kennedy and what he stood for.

> Although the nation and the world is poorer in the loss of our president; you have made us all aware of the deeper, truer strength of America and our heritage of purpose. Television has truly proved its maturity in this tragic time.

My husband and I who are 76 and 77 years old ate our quickly gathered meals in front of the T.V. and listened day and night. As the night wore on we suffered with you as we watched your faces grow tired and more tired.

I wish to thank all the engineers and newsmen on the street and behind the scene who so heroically and unselfishly had to suffer through pain and grief in delivering to our nation the news that could not possibly have been worse.

I will always remember the sad procession from the White House on Sunday. Not one announcer broke the spell of sorrow and sadness. The muffled beat of the drums, the sound of marching feet, and the tear-stained faces of thousands on the streets told the story far better than words. Millions of us with tears in our eyes watched this sad event in our homes.

Television critics in every city wrote in superlatives about how the medium heroically rose to the tragic occasion and how it provided public service of the highest order. Even though, at times, NBC drew more viewers than the other two networks combined, little of the post-coverage commentary singled out one network as having done the best job. Rather, it was the entire industry, the *medium*, that was embraced. A headline read, "In Time of Crisis Wasteland Bloomed."

The message from the halls of Congress was that TV bashing was no longer a fashionable activity. Congressman Claude Pepper proposed a formal resolution expressing deep thanks for the great patriotic service rendered by the television and radio networks and independent stations.

The Chairman of the House Commerce Committee, Oren Harris, said, "I certainly feel that the performance of the industry during the last few days, in the minds of the American people, tends to offset much of the criticism which has been levied." And Illinois Congressman Roman Pucinski told his colleagues, "Before we again attack TV and radio as a 'wasteland,' let us ponder its impressive contribution to help democracy."

Even television's most outspoken detractors offered kudos. Senator William Proxmire of Wisconsin said, "Not only was the coverage dignified and in immaculate taste, it was remarkably competent and soared with imaginative, if tragic beauty." Tennessee's Senator Albert Gore remarked, "Heretofore I have been a harsh critic of the programming and commercialism of television and radio. The action of the industry in the last few days is one which I admire and appreciate very deeply."

The television industry's combined financial loss from the preempting of commercials and the harnessing of vast technical resources by the networks and local stations was ultimately estimated to be $40 million. NBC and CBS each suffered approximately $4 million in losses, ABC somewhat less. Such a sacrifice was only possible, the industry liked to have pointed out, because of the revenues generated from programming that was characterized by critics as a "wasteland."

E. William Henry's controversial proposal to limit commercial time on television, unpopular in Congress before the assassination, was now truly bound for extinction. The full House debate on the Rogers bill prohibiting any such FCC action was scheduled for early 1964. Congressman Kenneth Roberts stated: "We have been very vividly shown the value of the broadcasting media during the past sorrowful days. This has been accomplished through the desire of media to provide a public service at considerable operating expense—not to mention the loss of revenues from prohibiting commercials." Roberts urged his colleagues to support the bill that would suppress the FCC and its desire to limit the number of broadcast commercials: "Remember the commendable way in which this great medium conducted itself during the events of the past few days."

A quarter-page newspaper advertisement taken out in the *Washington Star* on November 26 by the general manager of radio station WQMR, bluntly expressed a prevailing sentiment among broadcasters: "The voluntary suspension of commercial operations by most radio and television stations for three and a half days, coupled with tremendous news and human interest coverage provided to the American people, should show FCC Commissioner Henry that Broadcasting can and does serve America without Government intervention."

In a gesture of public service, instead of demanding credit from broadcasters for commercials that didn't air, about 50 percent of advertisers agreed to the delayed broadcast of their spots. The trade press advised against blatant commercial overloading during the Christmas season, however. It was feared that some of the goodwill broadcasters earned might be "squandered by a careless lapse into overcommercialization."

Seizing the moment of television's elevation in public esteem, the NAB prepared and sent a mock-up of a full-page newspaper advertisement to its membership two days after President Kennedy's funeral. Containing quotations of praise from national public figures, it was suggested that stations insert the comments of local and regional leaders and use the advertisement in their own communities.

Under President Johnson, a new tone in broadcast regulation was quickly established and the crusading spirit of New Frontier reform dissipated. On the evening of December 3, Johnson met at the White House with the chairmen of all the regulatory agencies. In essence, what he told the group, which included FCC chairman Henry, was that the federal government should stimulate not harass business. Regulators should be more concerned, the President said, with "new areas of cooperation" than "new areas of control."

Johnson told the agency chiefs their challenge was to "reexamine and to reassess and to reevaluate the regulatory role." Later in the week *Broad-casting* magazine editorialized: "The regulatory pattern isn't likely to change overnight. But it has already slowed down because the control-everything zealots are not so cocksure."

E. William Henry, a liberal New Frontier activist, who enjoyed the support of the White House, suddenly found himself serving a president who was a broadcast industry insider. Johnson wanted the FCC to run a cautious and restrained operation. Henry's best lobbyist in the Oval Office, Attorney General Robert Kennedy, no longer had special influence with the Chief Executive. Henry was left, as one observer aptly noted, "out in left field without his sunglasses."

The Kennedy years, now bookended with TV milestones, were over. As 1963 drew to a close, color television sets were selling almost as quickly as the picture tubes could be manufactured. On New Year's Day 1964, for the first time, all three networks were simultaneously broadcasting in color. The live telecasts of the Rose Parade from Pasadena on NBC and CBS and the Mummers Parade from Philadelphia on ABC symbolized, however unintentionally, the beginning of a new era for television.

For American schoolkids it was a glum winter. The blanket of security that was assumed to be their birthright had become disheveled. Abruptly forced to realize mortality, they recognized the vulnerability of all that seemed certain. There were effusive reminders of President Kennedy's vitality and promise, from special edition magazines to memorial trinkets. Everywhere was evidence of a society bereft.

In early February 1964, the appearance of a singing group on a television show began a phenomenon that assuaged the vacancy of spirit felt by young Americans. The Beatles on *The Ed Sullivan Show* marked the beginning of a major shift in popular culture. It was the event that truly struck the line of demarcation between the Kennedy years and the remainder of the decade.

In the weeks after Dallas, Jacqueline Kennedy was deluged with more than 800,000 messages of sympathy and grief. On January 14, 1964, she chose to express her thanks in a television message to those who wrote to her of their love for the late President. The three networks recorded her statement at the Justice Department office of the Attorney General.

Fifty days earlier Jacqueline Kennedy did what needed to be done with breathtaking composure and television conveyed her stoicism. This task was minute in comparison—just thirteen sentences were to be spoken to the camera. Though no less valiant in her performance, this time television conveyed her frailty.

With Robert Kennedy and Senator Edward Kennedy sitting nearby, the widowed first lady spoke softly and haltingly, at moments, holding back tears. "Whenever I can bear to, I read them," she said of the letters filling countless mail sacks in the Executive Office Building. "All his bright light gone from the world. All of you who have written to me know how much we all loved him and that he returned that love in full measure."

Of the various memorial shows the networks aired in the months following the assassination, *John F. Kennedy, May 29, 1964,* presented by CBS on the day the President would have been 47 years old, was an especially intriguing television event. The thirty-minute live program, which included three separate satellite feeds from Europe, was broadcast internationally via *Telstar II*. It was a technological feat impossible at the outset of the Kennedy years.

The CBS team that worked on the TV tour of the White House—producer Perry Wolff, director Franklin Schaffner, and correspondent Charles Collingwood—were brought together again for this telecast. From Hyannis Port, Jacqueline and Robert Kennedy shared reminiscences on camera. The widow chose as the theme of the program her late husband's belief: "One man can make a difference and every man should try."

Also appearing, to remember President Kennedy, were Prime Minister Harold Macmillan speaking from Great Britain; from West Berlin, Mayor Willy Brandt; and from Ireland, Prime Minister Sean LeMass, joined by Senator Edward Kennedy who was visiting Ireland.

The family would have preferred that John Kennedy's birthday would become the occasion on which Americans paused to remember their 35th President. But, in large part because of television's immense impression on the national consciousness in November 1963, the date of his death rather than the date of his birth would be the time for retrospection—much of it sustained by television's own anniversary tradition of evoking the New Frontier.

The Kennedy years were the most profoundly historical juncture in the development of American television. The flux of technology, government regulation, and public opinion—combined with electrified social and political dynamics—emerged as a confluence of factors that put the medium in a spotlight that has never been brighter or more searching. It was a coincidental alignment that widened TV's view.

Television as a bond of American common culture reached its acme of cohesion during the early 1960s. The news, entertainment programs, and commercials of three networks permeated public perceptions and defined the popular American identity. Of all the shared experiences, the nearness to John Kennedy television provided to American citizens was the most encompassing. His campaign for the presidency, his administration, and his death constitute a discrete chapter in broadcast history—one in which the medium and American life had been transformed.

# Notes on Sources

The explanatory power of narrative history is attractive to authors whose purpose is to convey the context of crucial events in one era to readers whose contemporary world has been influenced by those events. And, when the period is as inherently dramatic as the Kennedy years, the urge to storytell is strong and logical.

The foundation of narrative social history is the historical-critical methodology, scholarship based on primary source documentation. In addition to textual materials, the particular nature of television research requires involvement with documents that move and speak—the ribbon-like media of audiotape, videotape, and film.

The story of any major event in American history since mid-century would be incomplete without considering its television component. Television programs must be considered legitimate historical artifacts. But the need to collect, preserve, and catalogue television programming for the benefit of the historical record was not always a clear vision. Television broadcasts were largely regarded as ephemeral. Even recorded programs, though, were often disposed of by the networks and stations in a cavalier fashion when storage space was in short supply.

In fairness to the broadcast industry, however, providing a historical sanctuary for the tremendous amount of material transmitted over American airwaves is not its mission. Universities, mandated government agencies, private foundations, and private collectors have fortunately taken some leadership in rescuing an enormous part of the American story in the electronic age.

The men and women whose professional lives are dedicated to the protection of our video heritage deserve the gratitude of current and future historians of the latter half of the twentieth century. To reconstruct the American experience since the end of World War II is simply impossible without reviewing the television chronicle.

The moving image research for this book was conducted at The UCLA Film and Television Archives, The Wisconsin Center for Film and Theater Research, The Museum of Broadcasting, and the Audiovisual Archive of the John F. Kennedy Library.

Drawing conclusions based on film and video artifacts, just as with written records, is always a more accurate scholarly enterprise when the genesis of the document in question is understood. Therefore, paper records are as critical in the execution of television history as are the actual programs. The examination of the files of government officials, broadcast and advertising industry executives, program producers, scriptwriters, and performers reveal much information about the reasons certain television programming was created and broadcast, and the public reactions provoked.

Textual documents—such as personal and business correspondence, inter-office memoranda, scripts marked with deletions and additions, casting lists, production notes and contingency plans, drafts of speeches and speeches ultimately delivered, personal clipping files, appointment books, invitations accepted and invitations declined, invoices and receipts—can offer illumination that adds texture and veracity to television research.

The manuscript archive at The Mass Communications History Center of the State Historical Society of Wisconsin houses a phenomenal number of collections that were pertinent to the research for this study. The History Center is the primary repository in the country for textual records that document the evolution of American broadcasting. The files of written records tended by the John F. Kennedy Library were also invaluable.

Another necessary component of primary source, historical-critical research is oral history. It has become an increasingly important way to document contemporary events that have no written record—particularly in the television industry and the realm of politics where much decision making is conveyed verbally, mostly through telephone communication. Though not a flawless investigative tool, when properly and carefully conducted, the oral history can elicit telling details that add color and substance to the permanent record.

Some of the oral histories examined for this book were previously conducted by others and are part of collections with their own focus and purpose. For instance, the oral history collection at the John F. Kennedy Library contains approximately twelve hundred formal recollections of the Kennedy administration, of which seven hundred transcripts are now open to researchers. Obviously delving into the President's use of and relationship with television was not the primary concern of the questioners assigned to the JFK oral history project. Therefore, supplemental interviews were conducted for this book with key figures in the Kennedy administration.

For someone researching the New Frontier in the 1980s, a unique situation existed. Many of the men serving the President were so young at the time, that almost three decades later they remain professionally active and lucid in their recollections—yet possess the benefit of a lengthened perspective. This useful circumstance is rarely true in presidential scholarship.

Also in regard to oral history, a dialogue needed to be cultivated with those in business and creative decision-making positions within the broadcast industry. While some media professionals resisted an over-intellectualization of their fit in American history, others readily acknowledged their work was intended to endure. This author, however, is grateful that regardless of their viewpoints, the media professionals contacted were all cooperative and patient in discussing American television in the Kennedy years.

Of all the secondary sources consulted, the most useful were industry trade journals. *Advertising Age*, *Broadcasting*, *Sponsor*, *Television Age*, *Television Magazine*, and *Variety* covered industry-government relations in this period in great depth. Trade journals served as a forum for broadcasters and the advertising industry, revealing bitterness at criticism, pride in accomplishments, and strategies for continued growth. The Broadcast Pioneers Library and the National Association of Broadcasters Library were especially gracious in accommodating requests for access to these journals.

Periodicals that were not officially trade journals, but were clearly affiliated with the television industry, such as *Television Quarterly* and *TV Guide*, also provided a rich source of information on the controversies of the era. The National Association of Educational Broadcasters *NAEB Journal* was particularly helpful in issues pertaining to educational television.

The general biographical literature on President Kennedy is, of course, abundant and includes the memoirs of his closest associates as well as his support staff. Occasionally these recollections provide a glimmer of insight into the Chief Executive's involvement with the medium.

Another category of literature is presidential scholarship, which always simmers with controversy—and the historical evaluations of the New Frontier are wide ranging. Issues of presidential communication, news management, and image tending are often woven through this body of work relative to John Kennedy.

The scope of writings on the history of American broadcasting ranges from nostalgic accounts to comprehensive studies. Institutional biographies of networks, stations, or network divisions provide a useful information base, as do the numerous memoirs of news correspondents and television personalities. Perhaps the most valuable books in this division, though, are the many compendia that provide listings of individual programs, with descriptive information, airdates, and production credits.

Finally, as with every aspect of life, in archival research you often find things you weren't even looking for. An ecumenical approach toward historical documents invites good luck. This book benefited from several such strokes of serendipity.

Naturally, a work of narrative social history, a cultural exploration, requires at times that the author exercise the interpretive impulse we all share. Just as the desire to quantify is a human propensity, so is the desire to express our understanding of the themes and symbols of our environment.

It is the humanistic instinct that drives us to analyze our own mythologies and pay credence to intuitive knowledge. Of course, one person's intuitive knowing might be another's inferential leap. Some of the characteristics, context, and meaning of the New Frontier permeating *The Expanding Vista: American Television in the Kennedy Years* are colored by this author's own Catholic, ethnic childhood during that time. This is offered not as apology, but as explanation. Each of us has the prerogative to see the world through our own glasses. In the end, I want to believe that readers who share the vision of this study will do so because of the weight of primary evidence, not the inevitable flickers of a personal ideology.

The following legend lists abbreviations that appear throughout the remainder of this bibliographic essay:

*Ad Age—Advertising Age*
*BRD—Broadcasting Magazine*
JFKL—John F. Kennedy Library
*JOB—Journal of Broadcasting*
*LAT—Los Angeles Times*
MOB—Museum of Broadcasting
*NYT—The New York Times*
SHSW—State Historical Society of Wisconsin

*TV Age—Television Age*
*TV Mag—Television Magazine*
*TVQ—Television Quarterly*
UCLA—UCLA Film and Television Archive
*VAR—Variety*
*WSJ—Wall Street Journal*

All quotations from President Kennedy's news conferences are documented in the transcripts published in *Kennedy and the Press: The News Conferences*, edited and annotated by Harold W. Chase and Allen H. Lerman (NY: Thomas Y. Crowell, 1965).

## Notes to Prologue

Many thoughts presented in these pages were prompted by secondary sources covering television, presidential politics, and American history in the early 1960s. Included among such background books are: *Presidential Leadership of Public Opinion*, by Elmer E. Cornwell, Jr. (Bloomington, IN: Indiana University Press, 1965); *The Unraveling of America: A History of Liberalism in the 1960s*, Allen J. Matusow (NY: Harper & Row Publishers, 1984); *John F. Kennedy, President*, Hugh Sidey (NY: Atheneum, 1963); *The Making of the President 1960*, Theodore H. White (NY: Atheneum, 1962); and *Johnny, We Hardly Knew Ye, Memories of John Fitzgerald Kennedy*, Kenneth P. O'Donnell and David F. Powers with Joe McCarthy (NY: Pocket Books, 1970).

Historical information on the 1956 campaign is discussed in the paper "TV and the 1956 Presidential Campaign: Insights into the Evolution of Political Television," by Craig M. Allen, presented to the History Division, Association for Education in Journalism and Mass Communication Convention, August 1987. Additional background on Stevenson and Kennedy is available in *Candidates 1960*, edited by Eric Sevareid (NY: Basic Books, 1959).

Additional treatments focused specifically on political communication are provided in *The Image Candidates: American Politics in the Age of Television*, by Gene Wyckoff (NY: Macmillan Company, 1968); "Presidential Power: The Influence of Broadcasting," Samuel L. Becker, *Quarterly Journal of Speech*, February 1961; and "Has Television Reshaped Politics?" Angus Campbell, *Columbia Journalism Review*, vol. I, no. 3, Fall 1962.

An analysis of Richard Nixon's use of television is well presented by David Culbert in "Television's Nixon: The Politician and His Image," *American History/American Television*, edited by John E. O'Connor (NY: Ungar Publishing Company, 1983).

The crucial evidence revealing both the emergence and the incremental coalescence of the Kennedy-television alliance is contained in moving image documents. Among the many hours of programming viewed are the following pre-presidential appearances, which were screened at the Audiovisual Archive of the JFKL: *Meet the Press*, NBC, December 2, 1951, discussion of the 1952 campaign; *Keep Posted*, on the DuMont Television Network, October 7, 1952, Q & A with Senator Henry Cabot Lodge and Congressman Kennedy on the theme "who will do more for the country . . . Eisenhower or Stevenson?; *Person to Person*, CBS, October 30, 1953, interview with Senator and Jacqueline Kennedy by Edward R. Murrow; *Face the Nation*, CBS, July 1, 1956, discussion about whether Kennedy wants to be the vice-presidential candidate, Kennedy is coy and evasive regarding McCarthy's censure; CBS News footage of the 1956 Democratic National Convention, including Kennedy's delivery of "The Pursuit of Happiness" speech; CBS News coverage of the 1956 Democratic National Convention, August 16, 1956, which includes Kennedy's nominating speech for Stevenson; *Outlook*, NBC, August 16, 1956; *Look Here*, NBC, November 25, 1957; *Face the Nation*, CBS, February 22, 1959, Kennedy questioned about his pretense of non-candidacy; *Small World*, CBS, October 18, 1959; *Meet the Press*, NBC, January 3, 1960, Kennedy announces candidacy; *Face the Nation*, CBS, April 3, 1960, pre-Wisconsin broadcast, Kennedy shows controlled anger over the charge by Humphrey's campaign that the Kennedys exploited the religion issue; *The Jack Paar Show*, NBC, June 16, 1960; CBS News, July 15, 1960, Kennedy's acceptance speech at the Democratic National Convention; *Presidential Countdown: Mr. Kennedy, A Profile*, CBS, September 19, 1960, interview with Walter Cronkite; *Eyewitness to History*, "The Campaign," CBS, October 14, 1960; *CBS Election Night Coverage*, November 8, 1960; coverage of the Inaugural Parade, NBC, January 20, 1961; and network inaugural coverage.

The process of integrating the evidence extracted from program viewings with the information contained in the plethora of literature on John Kennedy was enhanced through firsthand accounts by key figures in the Kennedy campaign. The author conducted interviews with Dave Powers, February 17, 1987; J. Leonard Reinsch, July 1, 1987; and Pierre Salinger, October 16, 1988. *In Search of History*, by Theodore H. White (NY: Harper & Row, Publishers, 1978), covers the West Virginia primary and Kennedy's TV appearance addressing his Catholicism, which were also described in the interview with Dave Powers.

Donald C. Lord in *John F. Kennedy: The Politics of Confrontation and Conciliation* (Woodbury, NY: Barron's, 1977) cites Kennedy's belief in the value of nonpolitical talk to the unconvinced.

The most helpful sources detailing the advances in television technology and new traditions in reporting employed in the coverage of the 1960 political conventions include: "TV Is '60 Political Arena," William R. McAndrew, *VAR*, July 29, 1959; "Here We Go Again, Boys," *Sponsor*, January 23, 1960 on the networks' anticipation of convention coverage; *1960 Convention Handbook*, compiled and edited by NBC News (Davis Publishing); several articles—including a report on the dissatisfaction of print journalists at the Democratic National Convention—in the July 13, 1960, issue of *VAR*; and "TV's New Convention Look," Jack Gould, *NYT*, July 17, 1960. "Politics in the Air—and Little Else: Networks Go All Out as Conventions Preempt Prime Programming Hours," by Murray Jillson, *NYT*, July 10, 1960, also addresses the technical sophistication of convention coverage.

The origin of the tone set by the Kennedy administration with regard to the public interest in television is documented in "The Rights of Man," the 1960 Democratic Party Platform. The search for national purpose is further discussed by Arthur Schlesinger, Jr., in "The New Mood in Politics," *Esquire*, January 1960, and Robert D. Sweeney, in "National Purpose: A Program to Combat Society's 'Critical Weakness,' " in *Public Relations Journal*, July 1962.

The trade press and newspapers of the period provided prodigious accounts of television's relationship to the 1960 campaign, the candidates, the Great Debates, and the election. The following selected sources were particularly helpful: the *Variety* issue of September 14, 1960, which reported on Kennedy's voice coaching and use of Mobile Video Tapes; "Kennedy Rehearsed Long for TV Debates," Associated Press story in the *Columbus Post Dispatch*, April 29, 1963; "Kennedy Won 'Great Debates' Survey of 22 Surveys Finds," *NYT*, September 3, 1961; " 'Great Debate' Rightly Named: Nixon, Kennedy Set a Precedent That Will Be Hard to Abandon," *BRD*, October 3, 1960; "The Architect of a Triumph on Television, Broadcaster Reinsch Planned Kennedy's Use of TV," *BRD*, November 14, 1960; and "Television: The Vigil on the Screen," *Time*, November 16, 1960, which reported on the election coverage.

Other references provided more thorough discussions on aspects of television that relate to presidential politics. Those supporting the ideas in this chapter include: "Superman Comes to the Supermarket," Norman Mailer, *Esquire*, November 1960, which explores Kennedy's personal style; and "Reactions to John F. Kennedy's Delivery Skills During the 1960 Campaign," by James G. Powell, *Western Speech*, Winter 1968. The role of Kennedy's media advisor, J. Leonard Reinsch, was discussed during the author's interview of July 1, 1987, and documented in the transcript of the J. Leonard Reinsch oral history at the JFKL.

An analysis of political advertising can be found in "Political Programs on National Television Networks: 1960–1964," Lawrence W. Lichty, Joseph M. Ripley, and Harrison B. Summers, *JOB*, vol. 9, no. 3, 1965, which covers the Democrats' five-minute spots versus the Republicans' use of commercial time. *The Spot: The Rise of Political Advertising on Television*, by Edwin Diamond and Stephen Bates (Cambridge: The MIT Press, 1984), also deals with the Kennedy and Nixon ads.

Three comprehensive foundation reports provided critical information on the campaign and debates: "The 1960 Campaign and Television," Freedom of Information Center Publication no. 66, October 1961, the School of Journalism, University of Missouri, Columbia, Missouri; "The Great Debates," Freedom of Information Center Publication no. 67, November 1961, the School of Journalism, University of Missouri, Columbia, Missouri, from which figures on the Gallup polls before the first debate are cited; and "The Great Debates," Center for the Study of Democratic Institutions, Fund for the Republic, Inc., 1962. *The Great Debates: Background— Perspectives—Effects*, Sidney Kraus, editor (Glouchester, MA: Peter Smith, 1968), remains a definitive source.

Robert Kennedy's remark to Richard Nixon before the first of the Great Debates is relayed in *The Unfinished Odyssey of Robert Kennedy*, by David Halberstam (NY: Bantam Books, 1967). Russell Baker's reflections on the Great Debates, as well as a fascinating discussion of John Kennedy's relationship with the press, are found in the reporter's memoir *The Good Times*, (NY: William Morrow and Company, Inc., 1989), in the chapter titled "Player." And the discussion centered around the fifth debate, including Kennedy's public challenges to Nixon, is derived from the Democratic National Committee Press Releases which are filed in the pre-presidential papers (JFKL).

An account of the incident involving Associated Press's reliance on NBC News for election returns appears in *Broadcasting and the News*, by Robert E. Kintner (Harper & Row, Publishers, 1965).

*The Kennedy Promise: The Politics of Expectation*, by Henry Fairlie (Garden City, NY: Doubleday, 1972), and "Report on Coverage of Inauguration," in Jack Gould's

"TV Notebook" column, *NYT*, January 29, 1961, were among the materials reviewed pertaining to the inaugural festivities.

## Notes to Chapter 1

The philosophy of the FCC commissioners before the term of Newton Minow is characterized in "The Impact of FRC and FCC Commissioners' Backgrounds on the Regulation of Broadcasting," by Lawrence W. Lichty, *JOB*, VI, no. 2, 1962. *A Thousand Days*, by Arthur Schlesinger, Jr. (Boston: Houghton-Mifflin, 1965), also provides a sense of the strengthened regulatory spirit of the Kennedy administration. The Democratic attitude regarding the lax state of broadcast regulation is expressed in "The Rights of Man," the 1960 Democratic Platform as adopted by the Democratic National Convention, July 12, 1960.

Newton Minow's reflections on his tenure as FCC chairman were documented in an interview with the author, March 6, 1986, at Minow's Chicago law office. The resulting article, "The Vast Wasteland: Newton Minow Looks Back," was published in *TVQ*, Vol. XXII, no. 3, 1986. Also, "The New Frontier and the Vast Wasteland," by M.A. Watson, appears in the anthology *John F. Kennedy: The Promise Revisited*, edited by Paul Harper and Joann P. Krieg (Westport, CT: Greenwood Press, 1988).

Newton Minow's value as a liaison between Adlai Stevenson and the Kennedy administration was discussed with Arthur Schlesinger, Jr., at his New York office, April 28, 1989. "Trouble Ahead," *TV Age*, May 1, 1961, and the *San Francisco Examiner* column by Dwight Newton, January 20, 1961, also provided information on the impact of Minow's appointment in the broadcast industry.

Background on John Doerfer's resignation is provided in *Tube of Plenty* by Erik Barnouw (NY: Oxford University Press, 1975). Specifics of his departure were reported in "Social Note from Florida," *BRD*, March 7, 1960; and "Doerfer Out, Ford In, Seat Open," *BRD*, March 14, 1960.

President Kennedy's appointment book lists the chronology of Alan Shepard's visit to the White House and the National Association of Broadcasters on May 8, 1961.

An evaluation of Minow's delivery of the Vast Wasteland speech is presented in "The TV Wasteland: A Rhetorical Analysis," by Paul H. Boase, *The Ohio Speech Journal*, vol. 4, 1966. Contemporaneous news accounts of the speech were abundant in the trade press, notably *Broadcasting* magazine and *Variety*, as well as newsweeklies. Details of immediate reactions appear in "Black Tuesday at the NAB Convention," *BRD*, May 15, 1961; and the May 22, 1961, issue of *Newsweek*.

The story of the genesis of the "Vast Wasteland" speech stemmed from the author's March 6 interview with Minow, as well as these documents: letters from John Bartlow Martin to N.N. Minow dated March 20 and April 8, 1961—contained in Minow's papers (SHSW)—which reveal Martin's suggestions on what tone to assume and the value in threatening network licensing; "I Meant Every Word," an exclusive interview with Newton Minow, *TV Mag*, July 1961; "The Bloodshot Eye," by Roy B. Huggins, *TVQ*, vol. I, no. 3, 1962; "Needed: More Light Than Heat," *BRD*, May 15, 1961.

It should be noted that Edward R. Murrow addressed the Radio and Television News Directors Association Convention in Chicago, October 15, 1958, and challenged the broadcast industry to assume higher standards in a speech similar in tone and substance to the Vast Wasteland speech. And, according to *Variety*, David Susskind, in April 1960, referred to the state of the industry as a "vast desert of TV Drivel."

Personal reactions to the May 1961 event were extracted from the following: the President's response was revealed by Newton Minow on "Washington Conversation," a CBS TV broadcast, May 14, 1961; and Joseph Kennedy's remarks are from Schlesinger's *A Thousand Days* and the author's interview with Minow. The following correspondence is preserved in Newton Minow's papers (SHSW): Eunice Shriver's telegram, May 11; Arthur Schlesinger, Jr.'s letter, May 11; Clarence Dill's letter, May 12; Edward R. Murrow's letter May 12. LeRoy Collins's comments were reported in "What Collins Thought of Minow Speech," *BRD*, May 15, 1961. Collins's position with regard to the FCC's concern with programming was cited from "Television and 'The Public Interest,' " *Newsweek*, September 11, 1961, and his recollections on the period are recorded in his oral history transcript at the John F. Kennedy Library.

The controversy over the degree to which the government should control the television industry spawned a vigorous debate in the trade press, which was reported in the months following the May 1961 speech: "Focus on News," *TV Mag*, June 1961; "Needed: More Light Than Heat," *BRD*, May 15, 1961; "The New Critics," *TV Age*, August 6, 1962; "Behind the Lifted Eyebrow," *TV Age*, April 2, 1962; "TV Viewers Dig Newton's Law," by Jay Lewis, *VAR*, October 25, 1961; "Formula for Success: Rap TV," George Rosen, *VAR*, August 30, 1961; "The Critical Week," *BRD*, May 22, 1961; "Wasteland Revisited," Fairfax M. Cone, *TVQ*, Summer 1963; "Who Knows Programming?," *TV Age*, December 25, 1961; "TVB, TIO, Justify Themselves," *BRD*, May 15, 1961; "How About Giving TV a Chance?," *BRD*, May 29, 1961; "Playback," Lee R. Rich, *TV Mag*, February 1962; and "A Minority View of the Majority Will," *TV Mag*, June 1961.

The conflict between constitutional free speech versus legal protection of the public's airwaves was addressed in "Pierson Attacks Minow as 'Cultural Czar,' " *VAR*, August 9, 1961; "Shakespeare vs. Minow: 'Gotta Talk Up'—and He Does," *VAR*, October 11, 1961; "Hayes Blasts TV's Cultural Tyranny," *VAR*, February 14, 1962; "TV's Image Shines Untarnished," *BRD*, February 12, 1962; and "Lassoed by Roper," *BRD*, February 12, 1962. The Stanton and Sarnoff remarks were covered in the trade press. Arthur Schlesinger's corresponding interpretation is recorded in a memo to Minow dated December 15, 1961, and filed with Minow's other records (SHSW), as is Minow's letter to Pierre Salinger dated February 1, 1962, regarding the controversy. Jimmy Durante's quip was reported in *TV Guide*.

Many press reports covered the chairman's celebrity status and his Peabody award: "Question Peabody Award to Minow," *VAR*, March 28, 1962; "Minow Promises Creative Hotfoot for TV," *BRD*, April 23, 1962; "Time to Bury the Peabody," *BRD*, April 23, 1962; "Broadcasting: New Way of Life," *VAR*, August 1961; "Television and the 'Public Interest,' " *Newsweek*, September 11, 1961; and "Getting to Know You Themes B'Casters Vox Pop on Minow," *VAR*, April 3, 1963.

*The 1962 Emmy Awards Show* was viewed at UCLA.

## Notes to Chapter 2

The dissertation *A History of Anthology Television Drama Through 1958*, by William K. Hawes, Jr. (The University of Michigan, 1960), is a rich record of the medium's early era. Paddy Chayefsky's thoughts about the genre were included with a collection of his scripts in *Television Plays* (NY: Simon & Schuster, 1955).

Aspects of the metamorphosis of prime-time television from the fifties to the sixties were synthesized from sources that include: "The Season," *Time*, March 31, 1961, on the poor quality of the 1960 offerings; John Frankenheimer's comments are quoted in "Television USA: Wasteland or Wonderland?" by John Bartlow Martin, *The Saturday Evening Post*, October 21, 1961; the grim prospect for new writers is reflected in "Disillusion Between the Lines," in *TV Mag*, June 1961; "The Quality of American Life," by August Heckscher, September 13, 1960, is contained in the NET Records (SHSW); and the papers of Rod Serling, also housed at the Wisconsin repository, include "Special Report of the Craft-Forum Committee, Writers Guild of America West, Television Branch," by Gene Rodenberry, February 21, 1961.

The networks' efforts to salvage their programming schedules immediately following the Vast Wasteland speech were analyzed by the trade press in the following articles of the day: "Fresh Troops into the Beach," *TV Mag*, June 1961; "Focus on News," *TV Mag*, March 1961; "Big Image Scrimmage," by George Rosen, *VAR*, May 24, 1961; "Networks Hack Away at Violence," *VAR*, July 12, 1961; "Fall Programming," *Telefilm*, Fall 1961; "Let's You and Him Fight—Off Screen," *BRD*, August 28, 1961; "ATV-ITV applies 'Minow Touch' to Program Plotting," *VAR*, May 24, 1961; and "Vidfilms 'Forgive Us Our Trespasses' as It Shapes Patterns for the Fall," *VAR*, August 2, 1961.

The proceedings of the Dodd hearings are documented in " 'Main Event' This Week as D.C.'s TV Probers Go on Location (N.Y.)," *VAR*, June 14, 1961; and "TV Curtain Up, Hopes Down," *VAR*, September 6, 1961, which contains Frank Shakespeare's remarks. "Creators Turn on the Created," *BRD*, June 26, 1960; and the FCC Memorandum by Ashbrook P. Bryant, Chief, Office of Network Study, June 21, 1961—catalogued in Newton Minow's FCC Hearings papers in Wisconsin— contain information on the FCC inquiry of June 1961. Minow's papers also contain the Mikva letter of July 5, the July 11 Minow response, the October 3 Kibbee telegram, and Meyers's letter of October 3. The *Broadcasting* editorial ran July 3, 1961, and "The Blessings To Be Had from a Little Peace and Quiet," the *TV Mag* comment, also appeared in July 1961. "New TV Season: Help," by George Rosen, *VAR*, October 4, 1961, reviewed the creative climate of the time.

Ernest Kinoy's comments on *The Defenders* are quoted in "Great Shows: The Defenders," by Melissa Moore Wilson, *Emmy*, Spring 1980. The series is characterized by John Bartlow Martin in "Battle of the BIG THREE," *The Saturday Evening Post*, October 28, 1961. "The TV Hits of '61-'62," *VAR*, February 7, 1962, addresses Minow's influence in curtailing the action-adventure genre.

Background on situation comedies, including *I Love Lucy*, is provided in *Watching TV: Four Decades of American Television*, by Harry Castleman and Walter J. Podrazik (NY: McGraw-Hill, 1982). "The American Made-For-TV Movie," an essay by Gary Edgerton, profiles the emergence of this form of programming. It is included in *TV Genres: A Handbook and Reference Guide*, edited by Brian G. Rose (Westport, CT: Greenwood Press, 1985).

The introduction of slow-motion video playback capabilities was covered in "Slow Count," *TV Age*, November 27, 1961. Information on the audience and advertising for sports programming in the early 1960s was found in "Sponsored Sports: A Giant TV Industry," *Sponsor*, May 6, 1963. The article "Sports Telecasting," by Gary

Edgerton and David Ostroff, in *TV Genres*, was a helpful resource, in addition to "Big Numbers Game," *Newsweek*, December 30, 1963; "The 28-Million-Dollar Deal," *Sports Illustrated*, February 3, 1964; and *Inside ABC*, by Sterling Quinlan (NY: Hastings House, 1979).

Movie directors' objections to advertisements mutilating films shown on TV are quoted from the letter of G. Sidney to N. Minow, February 2, 1962, filed in E. William Henry's papers (SHSW).

*Bus Stop* producer Robert Blees is quoted in "What's Different About the New Hollywood Produced-on-Film Network Programs?" in *Telefilm*, Fall 1961. *Watching TV*, by Castleman and Podrazik, and "The Bloodshot Eye," by Roy B. Huggins, *TVQ*, August 1962, address the program "A Lion Walks Among Us."

The furor over what the broadcast industry perceived as government efforts to influence program content stimulated spirited commentary in the early 1960s. Senator Dodd's indictment at the January 1962 hearings was gleaned from a press release labelled "Senate Subcommittee to Investigate Juvenile Delinquency," dated January 23, 1962. Other material is cited from various trade press reports. The inside controversies related to *Route 66* and *Bus Stop* were covered in "The Hearings That Changed . . . Television," in *Telefilm*, Fall 1962. The *TV Age* comment is from a "Letter from the Publisher," February 5, 1962.

On the emergence of network self-censorship, the following sources were pertinent: "Anatomy of the Unmentionable," *TV Age*, March 19, 1962, which covers the post-FCC hearing era; "The Bloodshot Eye," *TVQ*, by Roy B. Huggins, August 1962, addresses the industry's decline in spirit; producer Leonard Freeman is quoted in "No TV Violence on 'Untouchables' Without Motivation, New Edict," by Dave Kaufman, *Daily VAR*, July 26, 1962; material on NBC's practices is from "NBC Programmers Get 'Guidelines' on Do's and Don'ts for '62-'63 Sked," *VAR*, April 18, 1962; Mark Goodson's "Minow paragraph" is defined in "Playback," *TV Mag*, July 1962; a perspective on the industry's lack of new ideas is documented in "Is Network Creativity Sterile?" by Hal Humphrey, *Telefilm*, Fall 1962; Frank Stanton's remarks were made May 3, 1962, to the Eighth General Conference of CBS Television Network Affiliates; "The Ominous Quiet on the Potomac . . . " Dave Kaufman, *VAR*, January 9, 1963, lays blame for the insipid nature of the drama of the day; and the industry's assessment of Minow's bearing on prime time is reported in "Agency Vox Pops Producers on Minow Influence on Programs; FCC Chieftain Comes Out Ahead," Bill Greeley, *VAR*, March 27, 1963.

Information on the Kennedy references in entertainment programming came from a combination of personal viewings and descriptions found in the trade and popular press. Jacqueline Kennedy's reaction to Vaughan Meader's Kennedy parody was described in *My Life with Jacqueline Kennedy*, by Mary Barelli Gallagher (NY: Paperback Library, 1969). The President's comical press conference response regarding Vaughan Meader is in *Kennedy and the Press: The News Conferences*, edited and annotated by Harold W. Chase and Allen H. Lerman (NY: Thomas Y. Crowell, 1965). Vaughan Meader's first television appearance on *Talent Scouts* was viewed at UCLA.

Included in the background sources pertaining to blacks on prime-time entertainment are J. Fred MacDonald's *Blacks and White TV: Afro-Americans in Television Since 1948* (Chicago: Nelson-Hall, 1983); "Negro Participation in Television," by Jack Gould, *NYT*, June 23, 1963; the column by Jonathan Miller in *The New Yorker*,

November 16, 1963; and the publication *Reruns: The Magazine of Television History*, which was helpful in identifying specific program synopses.

The files of E. Jack Neuman, producer of *Mr. Novak*, are housed at the State Historical Society of Wisconsin. They contain the newspaper clipping, sent anonymously, that reported on the Ku Klux Klan rally and other personal correspondence referred to in the text.

David Susskind's comments on the series *East Side/West Side* were documented during a personal interview with Lawrence W. Lichty in April 1967. Letters pertaining to the series and the two shows examined are contained in the Susskind papers (SHSW), as is the transcript of Jacob Javits's statement of November 1963.

Industry speculation regarding the post-Minow FCC is from "Oh Henry (That Ain't Candy)," Mike Mosettis, *VAR*, May 22, 1963; and "Cautious Crusader," *TV Age*, April 1, 1963. Lyndon Johnson's stance on regulation was covered in the trade press of the time and is discussed in *Tube of Plenty*, Erik Barnouw (NY: Oxford University Press, 1975).

Scripts for "A Single Isolated Incident," "No Hiding Place," and several other New Frontier character dramas were reviewed at the State Historical Society of Wisconsin, where the files of a significant number of scriptwriters and producers of the era are preserved. Among them are Ernest Kinoy, E. Jack Neuman, Arnold Perl, Reginald Rose, Adrian Spies, and David Victor.

*The Lieutenant* episode "To Set It Right" was screened at UCLA. *The Dick Van Dyke Show* episode "That's My Boy" was made available to the author courtesy of the program's director, John Rich. "The Non-Violent" and several episodes of *The Defenders* were viewed at The Center for Film and Theater Research at the University of Wisconsin-Madison. "Who Do You Kill?" is in the audiovisual library at the University of Michigan. Many other programs considered for this chapter, such as *Car 54, Where Are You?* and *Leave It to Beaver*, continue to be aired in syndication.

## Notes to Chapter 3

"The Quiz-Show Scandal," by Walter Karp, in *American Heritage,* May/June 1989, offers a thorough account of this pivotal episode in television history.

Historical background pertaining to the relationship of television and the chief executive is contained in these sources: *Use of Radio and Television by Presidents of the United States,* Glen D. Phillips (Doctoral Dissertation, the University of Michigan, 1968); *Political Television*, Bernard Rubin (Belmont, CA: Wadsworth Publishing Company, Inc., 1967); and "Mass Communications and Their Obligations to Society," by Edward P. Morgan, address at the Golden Anniversary Celebration of the Marquette University College of Journalism, 1963.

Sources providing background specifically on the live Kennedy press conferences include: *Kennedy and the Press: The News Conferences,* edited and annotated by Harold W. Chase and Allen H. Lerman, with an introduction by Pierre Salinger (NY: Thomas Y. Crowell Company, 1965); "Live from Washington: The Telecasting of President Kennedy's News Conferences," by Harry Sharp, Jr., *JOB*, Winter 1968–69; "The President and TV," *TV Mag*, May 1961; *Presidential Leadership of Public Opinion*, Elmer E. Cornwell, Jr. (Bloomington, IN: Indiana University Press, 1965); and "Mr. Kennedy's Calculated Risk," *Saturday Review*, February 11, 1962.

Senator Kennedy's remarks to the Radio-Television News Directors Association are preserved on audiotape in the radio collection of the MOB.

Pierre Salinger's involvement with live press conferences was considered in many periodicals of the time. His meeting with the American Society of Newspaper Editors was reported in "Salinger v. The Press," *Time*, April 28, 1961; and "Plucky," *Newsweek*, May 1, 1961.

Reporters' recollections and comments are cited from the following sources: Robert Pierpoint's view of Kennedy's psychological advantage is from notes collected in his personal papers (SHSW) on the preparation of his book *At the White House: Assignment to Six Presidents* (NY: Putnam, 1981); George Herman and Peter Lisagor's reflections are documented in the transcript of the Press Panel Interview, which is part of the JFKL Oral History collection; Hugh Sidey's comment appears in his book *John F. Kennedy, President* (NY: Atheneum, 1964); the Ben Bradlee quote is from Ralph G. Martin's *A Hero for Our Time* (NY: Ballantine Books, 1983).

Information on press conference ratings comes from *The People Machine: The Influence of Television on American Politics*, by Robert MacNeil (NY: Harper & Row, Publishers, 1968). The flood of telegrams and letters to the White House is mentioned in "New Tool for Politics," by Rowland Evans, Jr., collected in *The Eighth Art* (NY: Holt, Rinehart, and Winston, Inc., 1962). The letter to David Brinkley is filed with his papers (SHSW).

Evidence of JFK's keenness and curiosity with regard to both his television image and the process of television production was found in the following: "JFK: A Rhetorical Legacy Reassessed," by Gary C. Woodward, presented at the annual meeting of the Speech Communication Association in Chicago, Illinois, November 14, 1986; "What You Didn't See—How Three Presidents Came to Grips with Television in the White House," by Ray Scherer, *TV Guide*, January 13, 1962; and *Franklin J. Shaffner*, by Erwin Kim (Metuchen, NJ: Scarecrow Press, Inc., 1985), which discusses the filmmaker's professional relationship with John Kennedy.

Kennedy's steel crisis rhetoric is considered in *The Effete Conspiracy and Other Crimes by The Press*, by Ben H. Bagdikian (NY: Harper & Row, 1972).

A thorough and enlightening study that chronicles the Cuban Missile Crisis, with a critical focus on the print news media, is provided in "The Uneasy Allies: The Press and the Government During the Cuban Missile Crisis," by William LeoGrande, Occasional Paper no. 3, published by the Center for War, Peace, and the News Media, New York University, 1987. "John F. Kennedy and the World," by Thomas G. Paterson, presented at the "John F. Kennedy: Person, Policies, Presidency" Conference, University of Wisconsin-LaCrosse, October 18, 1986, offers a provocatively harsh critique of Kennedy's performance in foreign policy.

Other sources providing background include: *Thirteen Days: A Memoir of the Cuban Missile Crisis*, by Robert Kennedy (NY: Signet Books, 1969); and *John F. Kennedy, President*, by Hugh Sidey, which carries a description of President Kennedy's public activities during the crisis.

A copy of the broadcast of President Kennedy's national television address, October 22, 1962—including the regular-program interruption announcement—was reviewed at the MOB.

Selected contemporaneous reports specifically related to media performance include: "Broadcasters Near War Footing," *BRD*, October 29, 1962, which addressed television coverage; "Classic Conflict: The President & the Press," *Time*, December 14, 1962, containing information on press performance; and "TV-Radio: Week to Remember—Medium Alerted to Cuban Crisis," *VAR*, October 31, 1962, which described the nature of network coverage and news bulletins.

Accounts of John Scali's involvement as an intermediary between the U.S. and Soviet governments were found in "Cuban Crisis: How Close We Were to War," by Roger Hilsman, *Look,* August 25, 1964; "Man in the Middle," *Newsweek*, August 17, 1964; and "ABC Newsman's Role in Cuban Missile Crisis," *BRD*, August 10, 1964. A description of Mal Goode's on-air duties during the Cuban Missile Crisis appears in *BRD,* November 3, 1986.

References to President Kennedy's graciousness in the aftermath of the crisis and the Democrats' off-year victory are cited in "John F. Kennedy as Cold War Rhetor: The Cuban Missile Crisis of 1962," by Denise M. Bostdorff, Purdue University, delivered at a meeting of the Speech Communication Association, November 1987. *America Inside Out: At Home & Abroad from Roosevelt to Reagan*, by David Schoenbrun (NY: McGraw-Hill, 1984), includes a description of Salinger's call urging Marvin Kalb not to refer to a Soviet defeat. And *Decade of Disillusionment: The Kennedy-Johnson Years*, by Jim F. Heath (Bloomington, IN: Indiana University Press, 1975), also reports on the President's objection to "crowing."

A copy of the letter from Theodore S. Repplier, President Advertising Council, Inc., to President John F. Kennedy, dated December 4, 1962, which details the public service announcement campaign to promote greater voter participation, is filed in Minow's papers (SHSW).

Details on network arrangements for the broadcast *A Conversation with the President* are contained in "JFK's 3-Web 'Rocking Chair Chat' TV Journalism's Loftiest Hour, But Stirs Industry Bickering," *VAR*, December 19, 1962. Manuscript notes filed in Pierpoint's papers (SHSW) for his book *At the White House* address the Kennedy administration's deference to the networks. "NBC's Mr. K and JFK: Pals," *VAR*, December 26, 1962, announced NBC's decision to air the program in prime time.

George Herman and Mary McGrory's recollections are part of the Press Panel transcript that is included in the JFKL Oral History collection. *Political Television*, by Rubin, cites the controversy between CBS and Pierre Salinger over the editing arrangement. The program *A Conversation with the President* was viewed at the Audiovisual Archive of the JFKL.

The following articles of the day relate to the favorable climate that contributed to TV news growth in the Kennedy years: NBC's challenge to CBS's dominance and ABC's push in news programming were reported in "TV News Gets into the Money," *Business Week*, June 9, 1962; "News: Fad or Way of Life," by Art Woodstone, *VAR*, November 1, 1961, and "All That News & No Dolls: TV Minowized, Deglamorized," by George Rosen, *VAR*, June 6, 1962, discussed the increase in news programming and its relationship to Newton Minow; and "Crisis, Conflict and Change in TV News," Thomas B. Morgan, *Look*, November 7, 1961, examined quiz shows, Minow, and competition as catalysts in the news explosion. "2 TV Networks Vie in Newscasts," *NYT*, January 31, 1963 was also helpful.

A report on the growing popularity of TV newsmen with the American public appears in "The Crisis Boys in Television," by George Rosen, *VAR*, July 11, 1962. "Bulls Are Loose in Rockefeller Plaza," *BRD*, December 10, 1962, reviews the

NBC network's commitment to news programming. Profiles of Chet Huntley and David Brinkley were published in "First Team," *Newsweek*, March 13, 1961.

Two retrospective pieces provided historical accounts of NBC in the early 1960s. "Nobody Does It Better," *BRD*, November 10, 1986, offers a profile of David Brinkley. Diane Mermigas's overview "NBC at 60: Enthusiasm for News Generates List of 'Firsts,' " *Electronic Media*, June 9, 1986, includes Kintner's "CBS plus 30" dictum.

"The Secret Life of Walter (Mitty) Cronkite," by Lewis H. Lapham, *Saturday Evening Post*, March 16, 1963, profiles the CBS anchorman. "CBS and NBC: Walter vs. Chet and Dave," *Newsweek*, September 23, 1963, contains a discussion of the competition between CBS and NBC over thirty-minute newscasts.

*The Powers That Be*, by David Halberstam (NY: Alfred Knopf, 1979), includes a description of Kennedy's newswatching habits. *The Kennedys: An American Drama*, Peter Collier and David Horowitz (NY: Summit Books, 1984), contains Chet Huntley's remark concerning the President's father.

An oral history with Leslie Midgley, executive producer of *Eyewitness to History*, was conducted by Richard C. Bartone in May and June 1988. The transcript of this valuable exchange included a discussion of how this series was an important precursor to the thirty-minute version of the CBS evening news. The Bartone collection of oral histories will, in 1993, become part of Columbia University's Oral History Research Library.

The premiere of the thirty-minute version of the *CBS Evening News with Walter Cronkite*, which aired September 2, 1963, was viewed at the Audiovisual Archive of the JFKL.

## Notes to Chapter 4

Indispensable sources on the civil rights movement during the Kennedy years include: *John F. Kennedy and the Second Reconstruction*, by Carl M. Brauer (NY: Columbia University Press, 1977); *Parting the Waters: America in the King Years 1954–1963*, by Taylor Branch (NY: Simon and Schuster, 1988); *Robert Kennedy in His Own Words: The Unpublished Recollections of the Kennedy Years*, edited by Edwin O. Guthman and Jeffrey Shulman (NY: Bantam Books, 1988); *Eyes on the Prize: America's Civil Rights Years, 1954–1965*, a companion volume to the PBS television series, Juan Williams (NY: Viking Penguin, Inc., 1987); *Portrait of a Decade: The Second American Revolution*, by Anthony Lewis and *The New York Times* (NY: Bantam Books, 1964); and *Decade of Disillusionment: The Kennedy-Johnson Years*, Jim F. Heath (Bloomington: Indiana University Press, 1975).

A descriptive analysis of civil rights activities in the Kennedy years is presented as an important part of the narrative in *The Making of the President 1964*, by Theodore H. White (NY: Atheneum, 1965). Also a vital source was "Civil Rights and the Kennedy Administration: The Evolution from Passive Observation to Public Advocacy," Steven R. Goldzwig and George N. Dionisopoulos, paper presented to the Task Force on Presidential Communication, Speech Communication Association, Boston, November 1987.

The following chapters in *Fire in the Streets: America in the 1960s*, by Milton Viorst (NY: Simon and Schuster, 1979), provided helpful background: "John Lewis: Sitting

In, 1960," "James Farmer: Freedom Riding, 1961," and "Bayard Rustin: Marching to Washington, 1963." Also consulted was *Let the Trumpet Sound: The Life of Martin Luther King*, by Stephen B. Oates (NY: Harper & Row, 1982).

Essential to the development of this chapter was *Race and the News Media*, edited by Paul L. Fisher and Ralph L. Lowenstein (NY: Frederick A. Praeger, Publishers, 1967), especially the sagacious essay "Television: The Chosen Instrument of the Revolution," by William B. Monroe, Jr.

Information on early television coverage of the civil rights movement and President Eisenhower's actions at Little Rock was found in "Decentralizing Central High: It Was TV's First Jab at the Nation's Conscience," by Marshall Frady, *Panorama*, November 1980. Also consulted were "The Unsung Heroes of TV News," by Reese Schonfeld, *Channels*, March/April 1983; and "Covering Racial Tensions: Has TV Learned Anything from the 1960s," by Edward Tivnan, *Panorama*, February 1981.

Background information on black voters and Kennedy's 1960 margin of victory is provided in *The Americans: The Democratic Experience*, Daniel J. Boorstin (NY: Random House, Inc., 1973). Specific accounts and analyses of the civil rights factor in the Kennedy campaign are found in various sources. Among those used directly were *The Unraveling of America, A History of Liberalism in the 1960s*, Allen J. Matusow (NY: Harper & Row, Publishers, 1984); and *In Search of History*, by Theodore H. White (NY: Harper & Row, Publishers, 1978).

Information on television ownership by black Americans was derived from "TV and the Negro Revolt," S.I. Hayakawa, in *TVQ*, vol. III, no. 3, Summer 1964.

A copy of "The Children Were Watching" was acquired from Direct Cinema Limited, Los Angeles. The letter referring to the program was published in *TV Guide* in the March 11, 1961, issue.

The discussion of the likelihood of President Kennedy's slow pace on civil rights, between Ray Scherer and Sander Vanocur, was part of "JFK Report No. 1," broadcast on NBC on February 28, 1961. It was viewed at the JFKL.

John Lewis discussed his experiences in *From Camelot to Kent State*, by Joan Morrison and Robert K. Morrison (NY: Times Books, 1987).

The *NYT* review of "Walk in My Shoes" appeared in Jack Gould's column, "TV: Struggles of Negroes," September 20, 1961.

Dan Rather's account of covering the integration of the University of Mississippi and the events in Birmingham, Alabama, for CBS news is found in *The Camera Never Blinks: Adventures of a TV Journalist*, by Dan Rather with Mickey Herskowitz (NY: Ballantine Books, 1977).

Contemporaneous news accounts consulted on Ole Miss include: "The States: The Edge of Violence," *Time*, October 5, 1962; "The States: Through the Heavens Fall," *Time*, October 12, 1962; and "Kennedy's Strategy: Capital Impressed by the President In His Handling of Mississippi Test," by James Reston, *NYT*, October 2, 1962.

The events at the University of Mississippi were also covered in the trade press, notably in "Ole Miss Coverage Courageous, Complete," *BRD*, October 18, 1962; and "Riots, Rockets and Baseball," *VAR*, October 3, 1962.

The chapter "The Pursuit of Justice: Ross Barnett and George Wallace," in *Robert Kennedy and His Times*, by Arthur Schlesinger, Jr. (Boston: Houghton-Mifflin, Co., 1978), provides a personal and knowing review of President Kennedy's relationship to the civil rights movement.

President Kennedy's address to the nation during the violence at Oxford, Mississippi, was viewed at JFKL.

Information pertaining to the controversial sketch by the Premise Players on the *Today* show was found in the papers of E. William Henry (SHSW). Included in the file are a report from *VAR*, "The TV Promise in 'Premise': NBC Reaction to Mississippi Squawk Heartens Producer of Topical Review," February 27, 1963; and the letter from Thomas E. Ervin to Ben F. Waple, acting secretary of the FCC, February 19, 1963, which included a script of the sketch in question.

The CBS program *Dinner with the President* was viewed at the MOB.

A report on the hiring of black newscasters is found in "Negroes Seek More On-Camera Jobs in TV," by Richard F. Shepard, *NYT*, August 14, 1963. The letters P. Jay Sidney sent to David Susskind and President Kennedy are in the Susskind papers (SHSW). The networks' non-discrimination policies were reported in "NBC-ABC Also Takes Up Cudgels on Behalf of Negro Artist in TV," *VAR*, June 6, 1962. The hearings presided over by Adam Clayton Powell, Jr., were covered in the trade press, including "TV Networks Deny Negro Bias," *BRD*, November 5, 1962. The NAACP demands were itemized in "Next NAACP Stop: New York," *BRD*, July 29, 1963.

A discussion of the symbolic importance of the television news coverage of the civil rights movement, particularly Birmingham, is incorporated in *The Unfinished Journey: America Since World War II*, by William H. Chafe (NY: Oxford University Press, 1986). Also, the images of terror in Birmingham were considered in *America Inside Out: At Home & Abroad from Roosevelt to Reagan*, by David Schoenbrun (NY: McGraw-Hill, 1984); and White's *In Search of History*.

George Wallace's justification for his performance on June 11, 1963, was explained in "Thanks to TV . . . He'll Always Be Remembered for Standing in the Schoolhouse Door," by Michael Lehy, *TV Guide*, April 4, 1987.

Contemporaneous news accounts of Wallace's stand include "The Long March," *Time*, June 21, 1963; "Alabama Admits Negro Students; Wallace Bows to Federal Force; Kennedy Sees 'Moral Crisis' in U.S." by Claude Sitton, *NYT*, June 12, 1963; and "JFK and the Bully Pulpit," *Newsweek*, June 24, 1963.

Robert Kennedy's difficult meeting with black luminaries has been recounted in various New Frontier histories and was widely covered in the press at the time. His own version of the confrontation is contained in *Robert Kennedy in His Own Words*.

Martin Luther King's remarks made on the David Susskind *OPEN END* show were reported in "Dr. King Denounces President on Rights," *NYT*, June 10, 1963. Also, a June 25, 1963, letter from David Susskind to Dr. King thanking him for his appearance and commenting on the widespread attention it received is in the Susskind papers (SHSW).

Events surrounding the murder of Medgar Evers are recounted in *Standing Fast, the Autobiography of Roy Wilkins*, by Roy Wilkins with Tom Mathews (NY: Penguin Books, 1984), which also describes John F. Kennedy's meeting with civil rights leaders after the March on Washington.

A copy of the D.T. Kauer letter is in E. William Henry's papers (SHSW). Martin Luther King's note to President Kennedy after the television manifesto is cited in *Parting the Waters*. Historian Herbert Parmet's assessment of the TV speech is found in *JFK: The Presidency of John F. Kennedy* (NY: The Dial Press, 1983).

Pertinent news accounts of the March on Washington include "200,000 March for Civil Rights in Orderly Washington Rally; President Sees Gains for Negro," E. W. Kenworthy, *NYT*, August 29, 1963; and "On the March," *Newsweek*, September 2, 1963.

Reports detailing television coverage of the March include "500 From Television, Radio to Cover Civil Rights March," *The Washington Post*, August 20, 1963; "March Provided Unequal TV Show," *The Washington Post*, August 29, 1963; "TV: Coverage of March," Val Adams, *NYT*, August 29, 1963; "Big March, Big Coverage," *BRD*, September 2, 1963; and "TV's 'Great Coverage of Great Event' Citation on D.C. March," by Bill Greeley, *VAR*, September 4, 1963. Also, NBC production notes outlining the logistics of the network's coverage are filed with Robert Asman's papers (SHSW). The CBS coverage of the event was viewed at the JFKL.

A brief discussion of *The American Revolution of '63* is incorporated in *Broadcasting and the News*, by Robert E. Kintner (NY: Harper & Row, 1965). A tape of *The American Revolution of '63* was made available through the courtesy of Shad Northshield.

Martin Luther King's reflections on President Kennedy cited in the conclusion of this chapter are in "Eight Views of JFK: The Competent American," by T George Harris, *Look* magazine, November 17, 1964.


## Notes to Chapter 5

A cultural consideration of America's space program is woven into the text of *The Americans: The Democratic Experience*, by Daniel J. Boorstin (NY: Random House, 1973). Other important sources of background were *The Right Stuff*, by Tom Wolfe (NY: Farrar, Straus & Giroux, 1979); *Mission to the Moon*, Erlend Kennan (William Morrow & Co., 1969); and *Pride and Power: The Rationale of the Space Program*, Vernon Van Dyke (Urbana: University of Illinois Press, 1964).

President Kennedy's personal interest in the space program is reflected in many biographical works, including *John F. Kennedy, President*, by Hugh Sidey (NY: Atheneum, 1964). The political context of the American space program during the Kennedy years is considered in " 'To Land a Man on the Moon and Return Him Safely to Earth': The Kennedy Challenge as Political Crisis Management," Jennifer L. Stone, University of Southern California, paper presented to the Task Force on Presidential Communication, Speech Communication Association, Boston, Massachusetts, 1987.

A review of the technological inferiority of the United States compared to the Soviet Union is provided in "From Russia's Sputnik I to America's Schirra, Five Years of the Space Age," *Newsweek*, October 8, 1962. Among the news accounts of the day that reported on the Vanguard rocket collapse, the following articles from the December 7, 1957, edition of *The New York Times* were consulted: "Excerpts from News Conference on Vanguard," "Capital Dismayed at Test's Failure," and "Vanguard Rocket Burns on Beach; Failure to Launch Test Satellite Assailed as Blow to U.S. Prestige."

The question of the wisdom of manned space flights vs. unmanned scientific probes was considered in *Decade of Disillusionment: The Kennedy-Johnson Years*, Jim F. Heath (Bloomington: Indiana University Press, 1975).

Public addresses presented by NASA officials offered helpful background on the history of the space program and, in some instances, its relationship to television. Among these public remarks reviewed were: a luncheon address by James E. Webb, at the National Association of Broadcasters Convention, April 4, 1962; a presentation to the tenth annual aviation day, Mason City, Iowa Chamber of Commerce, by Addison M. Rothrock, associate director of plans and program evaluation for NASA, July 14, 1962; "Progress of National Space Program," an address by Thomas F. Dixon, NASA deputy associate administrator, before the 44th Annual Convention of the American Legion, Wheeling, West Virginia, July 28, 1962. The texts of these speeches are preserved in the NASA Public Information Center Records (SHSW).

Information on the program *Race for Space* and how it was placed into station schedules is from "Shulton's 'Race': Network Reject to Run on 110 Stations," *BRD*, March 28, 1960; and "What 'Race for Space' Bumped, 105 TV Stations Moved Regular Shows to Take Shulton's One-Shot," *BRD*, May 9, 1960.

The emergence of television space correspondents is the subject of "The Interpreters and 'The Golden Throats,' " *Newsweek*, October 8, 1962, which provides information on the way in which the space beat was being covered on network television. "Television in Pursuit of Wonder," Jules Bergman, *TVQ*, vol. II, no. 2, Spring 1963, was also helpful.

The programs *Project: Man In Space*, produced by David Wolper, and the *Bonnie Prudden Show*, which included the comments of Edward Kennedy, were viewed at UCLA.

*Special Edition: A Guide to Network Television Documentary Series and Special News Reports, 1955–1979*, by Daniel Einstein (NJ: Scarecrow Press, 1987), was an absolutely critical source for information on broadcasts on the space program.

Thoughts on the flight of Alan Shepard were developed from the following: "Space Age Spectacular: TV Will Cover First U.S. Man-Shoot with All of Its Resources," *TV Guide*, April 29, 1961; "TV's Bangup Job on Shepard & Shot" *VAR*, May 10, 1961; "Kennedy's 'Freedom of B'casting' Speech, Shepard Appearance Spark NAB; Endorses 'Shoot' Coverage," *VAR*, May 10, 1961; and "Radio-TV: Well Done!: Live Account of Flight Into Space Gives Public Feeling of Active Participation," by Jack Gould, *NYT*, May 6, 1961. Minow, in his personal interview with the author, March 6, 1986, described the ride from the White House to the NAB convention. Alan Shepard's surprise appearance at the broadcasters' meeting was widely covered in the contemporary trade press.

The President's secretary, Evelyn Lincoln, recounts Kennedy's viewing of Alan Shepard's space flight in *My Twelve Years with John Kennedy* (NY: David McKay Company, Inc., 1965).

*Eyewitness to History*: "Our Man in Space," which examined the flight of Alan Shepard and was broadcast on May 5, 1961, was viewed at the JFKL. CBS News stock footage of President Kennedy introducing Alan and Louise Shepard to the NAB and the President's address on free communication was also viewed at the JFKL.

The involvement of Jack Paar in the Tractors for Freedom campaign is mentioned in the autobiographical *P.S. Jack Paar: An Entertainment* (Garden City, NY: Doubleday & Company, Inc., 1983), and in *The Tonight Show*, by Robert Metz (NY: Playboy Press, 1980).

Contemporaneous sources that reported on President Kennedy's "Lunar Challenge" include: "Kennedy Tells U.S. Aim to Be First in Space," Howard Simons, *The Washington Post*, September 12, 1962; "Race to the Moon," *Newsweek*, March 19, 1962; and "Kennedy Asserts Nation Must Lead in Probing Space," *NYT*, September 13, 1962.

Sources related to the television story on the flight of Gus Grissom include: "Capsule Lost, but Astronaut Swims to Safety: Two Networks Used Rehearsal Shots," *NYT*, July 22, 1961; "Kennedy Phones Salute to Pilot: Watches Astronaut on TV— Signs Space-Fund Bill," *NYT*, July 22, 1961; "Hokum & Deceit, A Few Moments of Real Drama: Grissom's Flight," *VAR*, July 26, 1961; and " 'We Won't Do It Again, Folks,' " *BRD*, July 31, 1961.

The development of the narrative pertaining to the John Glenn orbital flight stems from the following reports: "The High Price of History," *TV Mag*, April 1962; Glenn's meeting with the President, in which the astronaut objects to excessive personal publicity is reported in "Glenn Visits President, Asks Science Publicity," *The Washington Post*, February 6, 1962; the same meeting is also recounted in "Glenn Pays Visit to the President," *NYT*, February 6, 1962; the story of Caroline Kennedy asking the astronaut "where's the monkey" was relayed by Col. Glenn in his oral history recorded for the JFKL; "Video and Radio 'Go, All the Way' for Col. Glenn's Historic Orbiting," by Art Woodstone, *VAR*, February 21, 1962; "Miracle in Space: Intricate Global Network Established for Coverage of the Glenn Flight," *NYT*, February 25, 1962; "Networks Convey Drama of Glenn Feat: Give Dazzling Display of Modern Electronics," Jack Gould, *NYT*, February 21, 1962; "Networks' Space Shot Costs: $3 Million," *BRD*, February 26, 1962; "New York Pauses to 'Watch' Glenn: Millions Rivet Attention on Astronaut in Flight," by Nan Robertson, *NYT*, February 21, 1962; "John Glenn: One Machine that Worked Without Flaw," *Newsweek*, March 5, 1962; "Spaceman's Ordeal," *Newsweek*, February 5, 1962; "Pooling of Glenn Shot Convinces TV Webs They Can Live Together," *VAR*, February 28, 1962; and "TV Networks in Terrif Single-Day Coverage of Glenn & Air Disaster Even With Intramural Squabbling," *VAR*, March 7, 1962.

A symbolic analysis of the Glenn flight was proffered in "Images or Objectives?: John H. Glenn, Jr. and the American Space Program," James L. Kauffman, Indiana University, presented at the Speech Communication Association Annual Convention, Chicago, Illinois, November 1986.

Details of viewership statistics are listed in a press release from the broadcast division of the A. C. Nielsen company labeled "40 Million Homes Follow Telecast of First U.S. Orbital Flight."

Frank Stanton's telegram inviting the FCC commissioners to view the Glenn launch in the special CBS viewing suite in Washington is collected with Minow's papers (SHSW).

The CBS News Special Report *John Glenn's Homecoming*, broadcast on February 23, 1962, was viewed at the JFKL, as was footage of John Glenn's Washington parade of February 26, 1962.

Deke Slayton's bad luck was reported in "Slayton Grounded For Solo Flight by Heart Trouble," Associated Press news release, July 12, 1962.

For coverage of the difficulty encountered during Carpenter's flight, these sources provided information: " . . . Of Space, Money & Ratings," *VAR*, May 30, 1962; "Painful Gap: Hour of Uncertainty Was Bridged with Tact and Understanding," Jack Gould, *NYT*, May 25, 1962; "TV and Radio into Fluid Drive with Bangup Coverage of Orbiting Carpenter," Art Woodstone, *VAR*, May 30, 1962; and "Silence . . . Heartbeats . . . 'Wow!' " *Newsweek*, June 4, 1962.

Accounts of the scaled-down coverage of Schirra's flight include: "Video Coverage of Schirra Space Shot Blankets all the Highlights without Second-by-Second Network Attention," *VAR*, October 10, 1962; "An Astronaut's Day: Networks Cover Schirra's Odyssey—Details Superimposed on Ball Game," Jack Gould, *NYT*, October 4, 1962; and "Rhymes with Hurrah," *Newsweek*, October 15, 1962. The press release "Schirra Space Shot to Have New TV 'Look,' " October 1962, from the NASA Public Information Center Records (SHSW), was also consulted.

Some of the information contained in the narrative on the "Space Age Rage" in entertainment programming was gleaned from the network press releases filed in the Terrence O'Flaherty collection at the UCLA Theater Arts Library. The publication *Reruns, The Magazine of Television History*, was useful in pinpointing specific episodes. Alan Shepard's enjoyment of Bill Dana's Jose Jimenez character was noted in Tom Wolfe's *The Right Stuff*. Information and the script on the episode of *Dr. Kildare* were found in the papers of David Victor (SHSW). Some series such as *Mr. Ed*, *Leave It to Beaver*, and *The Jetsons* are, of course, still syndicated broadcast fare.

The TV story on Cooper was enlightened by "Space Flight: Coverage of Capsule Includes Slow Scan Films Taken by Cooper," Jack Gould, *NYT*, May 16, 1963; "Coop's Loops Get TV Whirl," *VAR*, May 22, 1963; "Space Coverage Bill: Over $2 Million," *BRD*, May 20, 1963; "Networks Blast Astronaut News Curb," *TV Guide*, June 1, 1963; "Family Following Flight By TV," *NYT*, May 16, 1963; and "With Faith 7: Networks' Coverage of Re-entry Unites World in Apprehension and Relief," by Jack Gould, *NYT*, May 17, 1963.

The television reporters' sense of participation in the U.S. space effort is revealed in "Operational Procedures MA 6, Radio-TV Pool." This publication, along with all the original data from the survey conducted by Major Minter L. Wilson, Jr., is preserved in the NASA Public Information Center Records (SHSW).

### Notes to Chapter 6

Books reviewed for general background on television documentaries include A. William Bluem's *Documentary in American Television* (NY: Hastings House Publishers, 1965), which remains a staple source for early history and analysis of the TV documentary. Erik Barnouw's *Tube of Plenty* (NY: Oxford University Press, 1975) includes brief accounts that are particular to the documentary, covering the rise of the documentary in the early 1960s, the Robert Drew projects on John Kennedy, and Kennedy's interest in the documentary. *Special: Fred Freed and the Television Documentary* (NY: Macmillan Publishing, 1973), by David G. Yellin, presents comments by the peers and co-workers of NBC producer Fred Freed that offer insight into the place of documentaries in the broadcast industry during the era being considered.

Articles in the trade press that provided information on the factors involved in the documentary surge in the early 1960s include, "Big Swing to Information Shows," *BRD*, September 12, 1960; "JFK Documentaries?" *BRD*, April 3, 1961; "An Exclusive *TV Mag* Interview with FCC Chairman Newton Minow," *TV Mag*, July 1961;

"You've Got to Be a Documentary Lover," *BRD*, November 27, 1961; "Will 1962 Be Documentary Year?" *BRD*, December 25, 1961; "Documentaries Grow in Stature," *BRD*, December 24, 1962; "The Great Events of an Uneasy Year," by Albert R. Kroeger, *TV Mag*, January 1963.

Two compendia that provide comprehensive information on documentary programs aired on American television, including production credits, airdates, subject matter, and capsule descriptions of series and specials, are *Special Edition: A Guide to Network Television Documentary Series and Special News Reports, 1955–1979*, by Daniel Einstein (NJ: Scarecrow Press, 1987) and *Factual Television in America: An Analysis of Network Television Documentary Programs, 1948–1975*, by Ray Carroll (Doctoral Dissertation, University of Wisconsin-Madison, 1978).

Scholarly discussions of cinema verite can be found in Robert C. Allen and Douglas Gomery, *Film History: Theory and Practice* (NY: Knopf, 1985), which includes a case study entitled "The Beginnings of American Cinema Verite," with a strong discussion of the technological context, as well as the aesthetic principles, of the technique. Also Stephen Mamber's *Cinema Verite in America: Studies in Uncontrolled Documentary* (Cambridge: MIT Press, 1974) covers the early work and history of the Drew Associates, as well as profiles of documentaries discussed in this work, notably *Crisis: Behind a Presidential Commitment*. An interview with Robert Drew is included in *New Challenges for Documentary*, Alan Rosenthal, ed. (Berkeley: University of California Press, 1988).

It should be noted, however, that much of the scholarship on the work of Drew Associates deals with its place in film history and its role in the development of film aesthetics, rather than its position in television history. More important, the history of Drew Associates is at the center of these inquiries, rather than President Kennedy's actual connections with the programs.

Contemporaneous reports that cover the work of Drew Associates and review individual programs include: "Television's School of Storm & Stress, Robert Drew's Documentaries Aim at Photographic Realism," *BRD*, March 6, 1961; "Day of the President," by Jack Gould, *NYT*, March 29, 1961; and "The Presidential Image," John Cogley, *New Republic*, April 10, 1961. Among the news articles that specifically address *Crisis: Behind a Presidential Commitment* are: "How Involved is White House in Wolper's 'Making of a President,' Drew's Kennedy-Wallace Program?," Art Woodstone, *VAR*, June 12, 1963; "TV Filmed Kennedys in Alabama Crisis," Val Adams, *NYT*, July 25, 1963; "Not Macy's Window," *NYT*, editorial, July 27, 1963; "TV: Too Many Cameras," Jack Gould, *NYT*, October 22, 1963; "Government on Camera," *NYT*, editorial, October 23, 1963; "Behind Closed Doors—Television Coverage of Matters Involving Executive Decision Can Tarnish National Dignity," Jack Gould, *NYT*, October 27, 1963; "Lights, Action, Camera—JFK," *U.S. News & World Report*, November 4, 1963; by John Horn in the *New York Herald Tribune*, "Preview: A TV Milestone," September 16, 1963, "TV Reviews: Documentaries Score," October 22, 1963, and "A Criticism of 'Crisis' Program's Critics," October 25, 1963; "No Business in Show Business," editorial, *New York Herald Tribune*, October 24, 1963; and "CRISIS: A New Kind of Television Goes Backstage with History," *Show* magazine, September 1963.

The narrative developed in this chapter regarding President Kennedy's involvement with documentaries, and particularly the work of Drew Associates, was enlightened by many printed sources on the subject, but is based primarily on personal interviews in conjunction with program viewings.

Background on the context of the emergence of cinema verite on American television, as well as the networks' experiences and relationships with the Kennedy administration in producing documentaries, was the subject of an academic conference held at the University of Michigan, October 24, 1987. The proceedings are summarized in the *Television Quarterly* article by this author entitled "The Golden Age of the American Television Documentary," vol. XXIII, no. 2, 1988.

The participants in the documentary conference included Burton Benjamin, who, during the Kennedy years, was executive producer of the CBS documentary series *The Twentieth Century*; Reuven Frank, who was a writer/producer for NBC News including documentaries and the *Huntley-Brinkley Report*; Richard Leacock, a member of the Drew Associates; Robert Northshield, NBC producer for documentaries as well as several installments of the series *JFK Reports*; and Robert Rogers, who was an associate on NBC's *David Brinkley's Journal*.

In addition to these personal accounts, interviews were conducted by the author with the following: Theodore Sorensen, a brief discussion regarding the presence of filmmakers in the Oval Office took place at LaCrosse, Wisconsin, at the "John F. Kennedy: Person, Policy, Presidency" conference on October 17, 1986; Pierre Salinger, personal interview conducted in Toronto, Canada, October 16, 1988; James Lipscomb, phone interviews conducted on November 1, 1988, and June 6, 1989; Greg Shuker, series of extensive interviews conducted at the University of Michigan during the week of January 30 through February 3, 1989; and Robert Drew, phone discussion, March 17, 1989. Also, comments by George Herman were taken from the Press Panel transcript that is part of the JFKL Oral History collection.

The following programs were among those viewed in researching this discussion: *Primary*; the *Bell & Howell Close-Up!* report "Yanki No!"; "The Chair," from the *Living Camera* series; and *Crisis: Behind a Presidential Commitment* were acquired through Direct Cinema Limited, Los Angeles, California. The *Bell & Howell Close-Up!* program "Adventures in Reporting: Adventures on the New Frontier"; the *Eyewitness to History* installment "Kennedy Close-Up"; and *JFK Reports*, "JFK Report Number 1" and "JFK Report Number 2," were viewed at the Audiovisual Archive of the JFKL.

A content analysis revealing the ballooning in hours of documentary programming on American television in the early 1960s can be found in Ray Carroll's *Factual Television in America: An Analysis of Network Television Documentary Programs, 1948–1975*.

Articles of the period that convey the climate for documentaries include: "It's Now Touchable," *VAR*, November 18, 1961, which includes information on the increase in affiliate clearances for *CBS Reports*; "Local Television: Good Getting Better," by Albert R. Kroeger, *TV Mag*, August 1962, reviews the surge in production of local documentary programming; "You've Got To Be a Documentary Lover," *BRD*, November 27, 1961, including comments by David Wolper on Newton Minow's influence; and "Documentaries and Dollars—'This Fair Conjunction,' " by Lou Hazam, *TVQ*, Winter 1963, which discusses the financial boon for producers in the early 1960s.

Descriptions of documentary series and content capsules were derived from Dan

Einstein's *Special Edition: A Guide to Network Television Documentary Series and Special News Reports, 1955–1979*. Bob Rogers's comment on "Inside Jimmy Hoffa" appears in the author's "The Golden Age of the American Television Documentary," *TVQ*, vol. XXIII, no. 2, 1988.

The Irving Gitlin letter to Newton Minow is filed with Minow's papers (SHSW), as is the Howard K. Smith letter to Minow. The controversy over Smith's program "The Political Obituary of Richard M. Nixon" is reported in "Smith-Hiss Aftermath . . . TV Must Fight All Censorship: Minow; Have Right to Guard Repute: Frawley," *Ad Age*, November 26, 1962; and "An Angry Outburst Rises Against ABC: Nixon Supporters, Anti-Communists Protest Hiss Interview," *BRD* November 19, 1962. The author viewed the program at the Mass Communication History Center (SHSW).

A version of the case study on *A Tour of the White House with Mrs. John F. Kennedy* appears in *Presidential Studies Quarterly*, by Mary Ann Watson, Winter 1988. Sources that give background information on Jacqueline Kennedy's tenure as first lady include: *Jacqueline Bouvier Kennedy Onassis*, by Stephen Birmingham (NY: Grosset & Dunlap, 1978); and *The Kennedys: Dynasty and Disaster 1848–1984*, John H. Davis (NY: McGraw-Hill Book Company, 1984). Jacqueline Kennedy's reaction to the condition of the Eisenhower White House was described in *Dateline: White House*, by Helen Thomas (NY: Macmillan Publishing Co., 1975).

Charles Collingwood's reflections are from personal correspondence sent to M. A. Watson, July 26, 1985. The author also conducted a telephone interview with producer Perry Wolff October 2, 1985. The description of President Kennedy's phone call to Minow is derived from an interview with the former FCC chairman March 6, 1986, in his Chicago office.

Other sources with information relating to the event include *The Powers That Be*, by David Halberstam (NY: Alfred A. Knopf, 1979), "The Presidency: Simply Everywhere," *Time*, February 23, 1962; *A Tour of the White House With Mrs. John F. Kennedy*, Perry Wolff (NY: Dell, 1962); *Conversations with Kennedy*, Benjamin C. Bradlee (NY: W.W. Norton & Co., 1975); "The White House: That TV Tour," *Newsweek*, February 26, 1962; *A Hero For Our Time*, Ralph G. Martin (NY: Fawcett Crest, 1983); "White House Tour a Memorable TV Event; Quid Pro Quo Sequel," *VAR*, February 21, 1962; "An Evening with Jackie Kennedy," Norman Mailer, *Esquire*, July 1962.

*A Tour of the White House with Mrs. John F. Kennedy* was reviewed at the Audiovisual Archive of the JFKL. It is also available for viewing at the MOB and at UCLA.

## Notes to Chapter 7

Books containing background information on children's television in the early 1960s include *Children's Television: The Economics of Exploitation*, by William Melody (New Haven: Yale University Press, 1973); and *Television in the Lives of Our Children*, Wilbur Schramm, Jack Lyle, and Edwin Parker (Stanford, CA: Stanford University Press, 1961).

*Children's Television: The First Thirty-Five Years, 1946–1981, Part I: Animated Cartoon Series* and *Part II: Live, Film, and Tape Series*, by George W. Woolery

(Metuchen, NJ: Scarecrow Press, 1985) are vital references for both historical background on various children's series and details of individual series and program broadcasts.

Of the many articles reviewed, the following also offer general information on the historical context of children's television in the early 1960s: "Everybody's Got a Kid Show," *VAR*, September 27, 1961; "Was There a Golden Age of Children's TV?" Jack Kuney, *TVQ*, vol. XXII, no. 3; "Into Their Minds: The Sell," *TV Age*, January 8, 1962; and "No Room for Quality?" *TV Age*, April 15, 1963.

Several facets of this history of children's television in the Kennedy years were constructed by combining evidence extracted from many individual pieces of personal correspondence sent to FCC chairman Newton Minow with accounts in other sources. Specific letters and memos referred to in this chapter include: H. Goldin's memo of April 24, 1961; S. Frankel's memo regarding *Student News Report* dated May 26, 1961; Jules Power's letter of August 2, 1961, and Minow's August 14 reply; Jules Power's letters of September 22 and November 20, 1961, and September 24, 1962; letters by Oliver Treyz dated October 10 and October 16, 1961; E. Nemkov's letter of October 2, 1961, and Minow's October 2 reply; letter by J. Perlis dated October 6, 1961, and attached to the memo of Tedson Meyers; A. Grant's letter of October 15, 1962; and Minow's November 6, 1962, letter to P. Jones.

The broadcast industry's knee-jerk response to Minow's Vast Wasteland directive to improve children's programming was reported in *Broadcasting*, May 15, 1961, which carried Taft Broadcasting's pronouncement that they would increase kids' programming; "Minow Magic," *Newsweek*, August 14, 1961; Kuney's *TVQ* article; and *Children and Television: Lessons from Sesame Street*, by Gerald Lesser (NY: Vintage Books, 1974).

Senator Thomas Dodd's assessment of increasing violence in children's television was reported in "More and More Violence on American TV," *U.S. News & World Report*, June 19, 1961.

Excerpts of the address by Attorney General Robert Kennedy before the American Jewish Committee Dinner, July 21, 1961, are filed in the Minow papers (SHSW).

Sources referring to ABC stations' lack of clearance for *DISCOVERY* include: the correspondence between Jules Power and Newton Minow and from Oliver Treyz to Minow; "ABC-TV Gives Up Its *Discovery*," *BRD*, August 14, 1961; "Secret to Power if ABC Still on *'DISCOVERY'* Kick," *VAR*, August 16, 1961, which reports on Treyz's unsuccessful plea; and "Growing Better Pains," by Robert Lewis Shayon, *Saturday Review*, September 1, 1962.

The Newton Minow–Robert Kennedy collaboration on the share-the-risk children's programming plan, including industry reaction, was the subject of "Networks Weigh Children's Hour," Val Adams, *NYT*, October 3, 1961; "Focus on News," *TV Mag*, November 1961; and "Everybody's Got a Kid Show," *VAR*, September 27, 1961, which explains RFK's involvement. Additional sources include the NBC press release dated September 22, 1961; Jules Power's September 22 letter to Minow; and ABC's statement by Oliver Treyz abandoning the plan, which is contained in an October 4, 1961 ABC press release. Minow also discussed this topic in an interview with the author on March 6, 1986, in his Chicago law office.

The story of the genesis of *1,2,3—Go!* was derived from "Was There A Golden Age of Children's TV?" by Jack Kuney, *TVQ*, vol. XXII, no. 3; as well as Woolery's *Children's Television: The First Thirty-Five Years*. The author also conducted a series of interviews with producer Kuney at the University of Michigan during the week of March 13–17, 1989, in which one of the details he reported was Ethel Kennedy's call to her husband.

A discussion of the state of local television, including the purchasing arrangement of old movie cartoons, appears in "We Can Have Better TV for Our Children!" by Bob Keeshan (Captain Kangaroo) with Ed Linn, *Good Housekeeping*, January 1963. The article "I'm Popeye, the PubService Man," *VAR*, November 22, 1961, reveals the King Features Syndicate plan to introduce public service cartoons.

The publication *For the Young Viewer: Television Programming for Children . . . At the Local Level*, issued by the Television Information Office of the NAB, was edited by Ralph Garry, F.B. Rainsberry, and Charles Winick (NY: McGraw-Hill, 1962).

The 1962 debuts of quality kids' shows were addressed in the following: "TV: Three New Formulas for Children's Programs," by Jack Gould, *NYT*, October 15, 1962; "*Discovery* Fills a TV Vacuum," in the "As I See It" column of Paul Jones, *Atlanta Journal & Constitution*, October 28, 1962; *Children's Television: The First Thirty-Five Years*, by George Woolery, which describes Kintner's announcement regarding *Exploring* before the Senate Subcommittee on violence; Jules Power's letter of September 24, 1962; and A. Grant's letter of October 15, 1962, which mentions the *DISCOVERY–Scholastic Magazine* connection.

The industry controversy over children's programming being used to sell products to young viewers was the subject of the following contemporaneous reports: "Tougher than It Seems—the TV Kid Show Problem," *Sponsor*, August 6, 1962, which documents Trans-Lux Vice-president Richard Carlton's challenge to the industry to accept responsibility for children's programming; "Into Their Minds: The Sell," *TV Age*, January 8, 1962; "No Room for Quality?" *TV Age*, April 15, 1963, which quotes ABC's Edward Bleier; and "Monday Memo," Cy Schneider, *BRD*, December 24, 1962, a commentary against "edutainment."

Newton Minow's concluding reflections on children's programming emerged from the author's March 6, 1986, interview.


## Notes to Chapter 8

The place of advertising in post-World War II America is considered in a great many social histories. Among the several reviewed for this chapter were *The Americans: The Democratic Experience*, by Daniel J. Boorstin (NY: Vintage Books, 1973); *The Unraveling of America: A History of Liberalism in the 1960s*, Allen J. Matusow (NY: Harper & Row Publishers, 1984); and *A Time of Passion: America 1960–1980*, Charles R. Morris (NY: Harper & Row, 1984).

The economic policies of the Kennedy administration are detailed in numerous scholarly and biographical works. The chapter "The Fight Against Recession" from Ted Sorensen's *Kennedy* (NY: Harper & Row, Publishers, 1965), was especially useful here.

The outrageous proposal by Harry Bannister, NBC vice-president in charge of station relations, to Robert Sarnoff is detailed in an October 17, 1961, memo, which is included in the files of the Bannister collection (SHSW).

A discussion of the cultural implications of broadcast advertising was offered in "Television USA: The Master Planners," by John Bartlow Martin, *Saturday Evening Post*, November 4, 1961. "The Individual in a Mass Culture," by George Gerbner, a consideration of broadcast advertising from a cultural perspective, was first published in the *Saturday Review*, June 18, 1960.

The text of Newton Minow's February 1962 address to the Advertising Federation of America, regarding the relationship between commercial judgment and artistic judgment in programming, is filed in the chairman's papers (SHSW).

The undated speech "Renaissance Man and Advertising Man," by George Gribbin, president of Young & Rubicam, Inc., which considers advertising and the growing youth culture in the early 1960s is filed in the Gribbin collection (SHSW).

The retrospective report "The 60s—Story of an Awesome Decade," *U.S. News & World Report*, January 12, 1970, briefly addresses the connection among America's population explosion, the resulting business boom, and advertising.

Advertisers' belief that their work served the national purpose was illustrated in "Advertising Getting Bigger and Bigger, Doherty Believes," *BRD*, February 18, 1963; in "Prosperity and Survival," the summarized remarks of Marion Harper, Jr., former president of McCann-Erickson, Inc., before the Sales Marketing Executives of Chicago, which appeared in *TV Mag*, February 1961; and in "Salesman's Decade," the summarized remarks of broadcast personality Arthur Godfrey to a Radio-Television Executives Society luncheon, also published in *TV Mag*, February 1961.

A review of the phenomenal success of several television advertising campaigns was included in "Successes This Year; Which Will They Be?: The Hot Campaigns of 1962 Set Marks for 1963 Advertisers," *BRD*, February 18, 1963.

A discussion of technical sophistication in the production of commercials at the beginning of the decade can be found in "Agency Video Tape Use Expands," *BRD*, December 5, 1960. Trends in casting television ads was the subject of "Household Products Commercials Feature More 'Realistic' Gals," *Sponsor*, March 18, 1963. Also, "The Creative Sell: TV's White Hope," *TV Mag*, March 1961, considered advertising strategy.

The impact of research on the development of broadcast advertising was a recurring theme in the trade press of the time. Among the articles considered in this category were: "To Strengthen Commercials, Do Research," *BRD*, December 12, 1960; and "Focus on Commericals," *TV Mag*, April 1961. The remarks of T. S. Repplier, president of the Advertising Council, regarding social science and advertising were delivered at the AFA-AAW Convention June 26, 1962. The text of the speech is filed in the Thomas D'Arcy Brophy papers (SHSW).

Erik Barnouw notes the 1960 introduction of the Clio awards in *Tube of Plenty* (NY: Oxford University Press, 1975). David Ogilvy's remarks on his philosophy of advertising appeared in "The Flag Bearer," the in-house newsletter of Ogilvy, Benson & Mather, Inc., dated February 9, 1962, and collected in the papers of Rosser Reeves (SHSW).

Among the sources consulted for information on proliferation of new products in the early 1960s were: "Surging Sales at Colgate," Morris J. Gelman, *TV Mag*, February 1963; "The Calculated Success of Procter & Gamble: TV's Amazing Buying Machine," by Jack B. Weiner, *TV Mag*, September 1961; and "Autos and TV: In the Throes of Change," by Albert R. Kroeger, *TV Mag*, March 1961.

Advertisers' efforts to associate corporate image with psychic satisfaction was addressed in "The TV Commercial: Window on Mass Culture," Fr. S. J. Hurley, *America*, January 5, 1963.

The data of Broadcast Advertisers Reports, Inc., which monitored all three networks and logged and indexed commercial announcements for its clients, are preserved at the State Historical Society of Wisconsin. This information provides the researcher with a catalogue of every nationally broadcast commercial on network television in the early 1960s and the programs in which they appeared.

LeRoy Collins's surprising stand on cigarette advertising was extensively covered in the trade press. Among the articles used in preparing this narrative were: "Collins Aims at $134-Million Customer," *BRD*, November 26, 1962; "Mutiny on the TV Bounty: Collins Flicks Ciggie Lighter," George Rosen, *VAR*, November 28, 1962; "Tobacco Ad Curb Plan Draws Fire, Praise," *Ad Age*, December 3, 1962; "How Deep the Trouble Collins Is In?" *BRD*, December 3, 1962; "Broadcaster Protests Mounting In Collins Cigarette Ban Controversy," *VAR*, December 5, 1962; "Showdown This Week on Cigarette Ads?" *BRD*, December 10, 1962; "Code Board Ponders Curb on Cigarette Ads," *Ad Age*, December 17, 1962; " 'Ban the Butts' Gaining Impetus; B&W Nixes Show," *VAR*, December 19, 1962; " 'Ban the Butts' Cues Another Cig Defection," *VAR*, December 26, 1962; "Collins Makes His Pitch on Cigarettes" *BRD*, December 17, 1962; "Where There's Smoke, No Fire," *BRD*, January 21, 1963; "NAB Agrees to 'Bury the Butt' As Collins Wins A New 3-Year Ticket," *VAR*, January 23, 1963.

The morality of cigarette advertising was also considered in "Would You Want Your Sister to Marry Rosser Reeves?" *Horizon*, July 1961. The correspondence from Senator Maurine Neuberger and Robert Kintner and Neuberger's note to Minow are filed in Minow's papers (SHSW).

A large collection of television advertisements from the early 1960s, including a great number of cigarette commercials, is housed at UCLA.

It should be noted that several years before the courageous stand of Governor Collins, a book entitled *Clear Channels: Television and the American People*, by Max Wylie (NY: Funk & Wagnalls Co., 1955) contained the chapter "Television, Cigarettes, Smoking and Lung Cancer"—a vituperative attack on cigarette smoking and television's promotion of the habit.

A description of Art Linkletter's exchange with black youngsters on his program in 1960 was found in "A Last Look At Television: 12 Noon to 6 p.m." by Helen Lawrenson, *Esquire*, October 1960. A discussion of black consumers and advertising was included in "The Negro Market—Business Courts Its 19 Million Customers," *Newsweek*, July 31, 1961.

The trade press of the period, notably in the following reports, also covered the subject of integration in advertising: "What to Do About Cementing a Public's Friendship," by Frederick H. Schmidt and Georges Carousso, *Public Relations Journal*, July 1962, which includes a discussion of locally produced television programs and commercials geared to black customers; "Agencies Blamed for Race Bias in TV," *Ad Age*, April 22, 1963; "Desegregate Ads, TV Lever Tells Agencies," Maurine Christopher, *Ad Age*, August 12, 1963; "Colgate Next Target in Integrated Ads Push," Maurine Christopher, *Ad Age*, August 19, 1963; "NAACP Is Listed in the Telephone Book: Broadcasters Told to Call and Discuss Integration," *BRD*, August 19, 1963; "Negroes Poised to Integrate Agencies," *BRD*, September 9, 1963; "CORE

Says P&G in Accord on Talent," *BRD*, September 9, 1963; and "TV Ads Intensify Negro's Drive for Rights, Harris Finds," *Ad Age*, October 21, 1963.

These articles appearing in the *Wall Street Journal* were also pertinent to integrated ads: "CORE Wants Negroes Used in Soap Commercials on TV," August 20, 1963; and "Colored Customers: Civil Rights Push Alerts Companies to Potential of Negro Market," August 19, 1963.

An article on integration in advertising, which detailed the CORE/Lever Brothers episode, appeared in *Pageant* in early 1964. The galleys of the article were found in the papers of E. William Henry (SHSW).

The August 19, 1963, issue of *Ad Age* carried the report "Yesterday's TV Ad-Viewing Tots Are Now Integration Activists: Hayakawa," which explained Senator Hayakawa's theory on TV advertising.

The acquisition of the Wisk baseball spot was possible due to the kind accommodation of Lever Brothers.

The Rapid Shave deception was extensively covered in the contemporaneous trade press. It was also the subject of a radio commentary given by Edward P. Morgan over the ABC network on January 4, 1962. The script of the broadcast can be found in the Minow papers.

The loudness of television commercials was the subject of "And Now, a WORD . . ." *Newsweek*, October 19, 1962; and in "Loud Commercials Blast FCC Ears, Too," the *New York Herald Tribune*, July 8, 1963. Jack Paar's annoyance over the high volume of commercials was noted in Jack Gould's column, *NYT*, February 18, 1962.

Overcommercialization of the television airwaves was the subject of "Admen Claim TV Is Too 'Cluttered,' " *Sponsor*, February 1963. Chairman Henry's effort to limit the amount of television advertising is covered in great detail in "FCC v. 'Overcommercialization,' " Freedom of Information Center Publication no. 115, School of Journalism, University of Missouri, Columbia, Missouri, January 1964.

Henry's campaign was also documented in "FCC Backs Minow Plan for Compulsory Time Limits on Radio and TV Commercials," Joseph W. Sullivan, *WSJ*, May 20, 1963; "FCC Chief 'Means It' When He Wars on Too Many Blurbs," *Daily VAR*, September 25, 1963; "News of Television and Radio Commercialization," by Val Adams, *NYT*, September 29, 1963; "Once 'Weak' FCC Now Called Usurper," by Laurence Laurent, *The Washington Post*, November 9, 1963; "Curbing Ads: Broadcasting Lobby in Congress Makes Effective FCC Action Difficult," by Jack Gould, *NYT*, November 24, 1963; "Retreat of the FCC," *Atlanta Journal*, January 20, 1964; and "TV Commercials: The Government Ducks the Issue," Desmond Smith, *The Nation*, March 23, 1964.

The testimony of W. Theodore Pierson of Pierson, Ball & Dowd, representing sixty broadcast clients before the FCC, on December 10, 1963, is filed in the Pierson papers (SHSW). The collection of the files of E. William Henry (SHSW) contains: the personal statement of E. William Henry, regarding overcommercialization, before the House Subcommittee on Communications on November 6, 1963; the statement of LeRoy Collins opposing the proposed FCC commercial time limitations dated August 26, 1963; and correspondence regarding the overcommercialization matter from Newton Minow and Professor Richard J. Stonesifer to the FCC chairman.

The advertising industry's hope of cultivating public acceptance of commercial inroads into American culture is documented in "Better Advertising Image: AAAA Goal," *BRD*, April 24, 1961. Consumer disinterest in the heated criticism of broadcast advertising is considered in "Growing Appreciation of TV's Commercials," *BRD*, June 15, 1964.

## Notes to Chapter 9

Absolutely critical to the development of this chapter was the valuable series of oral histories conducted by James Robertson in 1981 and 1982. Robertson, who was himself an active professional in the educational broadcasting field, followed a well-informed line of questioning in his interviews with key figures in the formation of America's educational television system. The transcripts, collectively titled "Public Television's Roots," are housed in the Mass Communications History Center of the State Historical Society of Wisconsin (SHSW).

Also vital to researching educational television during the New Frontier are the National Educational Television Records (SHSW). This monumental collection of documents (618 boxes) is divided into ten series, carefully catalogued and indexed to facilitate the researcher's efforts. The most valuable components for this study were Administration, Public Information, Research and Education, and Programming.

General background sources on the development of educational television include: *Channels of Learning: The Story of Educational Television*, by John Walker Powell (Washington, D.C.: Public Affairs Press, 1962); *The First Decade of the "Fourth Network": An Historical, Descriptive Analysis of the National Education Television and Radio Center*, by Donald Neal Wood (Doctoral Dissertation, the University of Michigan, 1963); and "ETV: Uncertain Trumpet," by Doris Willens, *TV Mag*, February 1964. "Educational TV: What It Is, Where It's Going," *Changing Times*, February 1963, also provided an overview.

Information on the early years of educational television was found in "1953: The Year of Decision in Educational Television," George E. Probst, *The University of Chicago Magazine*, January 1953; "If TV Moved Into the Classroom," by Robert Bendiner, *NYT Magazine*, March 8, 1953; and "TV Teaching Gets Set for a Boost," *Business Week*, December 22, 1956. A report of the Ford Foundation's 1960 promise of Ampex tape recorders was carried in "Foundation Aids Educational TV," Val Adams, *NYT*, December 19, 1960.

The complete text of Newton Minow's address to the National Association of Educational Broadcasters in October 1961 can be found in his papers (SHSW). John F. White's letter to President Kennedy offering NET's assistance in time of national crisis is filed in the National Educational Television Records, Series 5B (SHSW).

Sources specifically related to the Educational Television Facilities Act consist of the following: "New Frontiers for Educational Television," an address made by Professor Nicholas Johnson—who would become a controversial FCC commissioner later in the decade—of the University of California Law School-Berkeley, was presented to a local citizens group on May 14, 1962; the text of the speech that outlines the history and provisions of the Educational Television Facilities Act, was sent by Johnson to Chairman Minow, and is collected in the Minow papers (SHSW); a transcript of the *Prospects for Mankind* interview hosted by Eleanor Roosevelt is also included in the Minow papers.

A definitive source on the evolution of the All-Channel Receiver Bill is "The FCC and the All-Channel Receiver Bill of 1962," by Lawrence D. Longley, *JOB*, vol. XIII, no. 3, Summer 1969.

Contemporaneous articles in the trade press covering the All-Channel Receiver Bill include: "All-Channel Sets Minow's Goal," *BRD*, January 15, 1962; "FCC's All-Channel TV Set Bill Hits Snag in Senate," *Ad Age*, February 26, 1962; "UHF: A Status Report," *Sponsor*, March 18, 1963; "The Impact of All-Channel Sets," *BRD*, March 2, 1964; and "After April: Tail Fins on Television Sets," *TV Mag* editorial, April 1964.

The issue of all-channel television sets was naturally widely covered in the popular press. Among the reports reviewed for this chapter were: "A TV Law That Will Cost You Money," *U.S. News & World Report*, April 13, 1964; "U-Day and You: What the New 82-Channel Sets Mean to You," by David Lachenbruch, *TV Guide*, April 25, 1964; "Television: UHF + VHF = 82," *Newsweek*, April 27, 1964; and "FCC, TV Set Makers Clash Over Law That Calls for UHF Tuners," *WSJ*, May 1, 1964.

The complete texts of Chairman Minow's statements before the Senate and House hearings on the all-channel legislation, February 20 and March 6, 1962, respectively, are included in his files (SHSW), as are copies of correspondence from representatives of Admiral and Motorola sent to Senator John Pastore. Also valuable in understanding the development of the All-Channel Receiver Bill are detailed memos and correspondence from the Department of Commerce, filed in Minow's papers.

The direct quotations attributed in this narrative concerning the acquisition of Channel 13 for ETV were taken from Robertson's "Public Television's Roots" oral history series. Other sources include: "F.C.C. Head Gives Moral Aid To Citizens' Bid for WNTA-TV," *NYT*, March 27, 1961; "Bid Raised by $1.5 Million for Educational TV Here," by Terry Ferrer, *New York Herald Tribune*, March 21, 1961; "F.C.C. Votes Inquiry to Spur Educational TV Outlet for City," Jack Gould, *NYT*, March 30, 1961; "For Sale: One TV Channel," Frederick H. Guidry, *Christian Science Monitor*, April 7, 1961; "Educational TV Move Shows Growing Influence of Kennedy Outlook in FCC," Stanley E. Cohen, *Ad Age*, April 10, 1961; "WNTA-TV Sale to ETV Outfit Next Week," *Radio-Television Daily*, April 29, 1961; "ETV Takes a Giant Step," Newton N. Minow, *NYT Magazine*, September 16, 1962.

Reports covering the AFTRA-WNDT dispute include: "Union Gags Zero Mostel, Blow at Educational TV," by Richard K. Doan, *New York Herald Tribune*, September 6, 1962; "TV: Impasse at WNDT," Jack Gould, *NYT*, September 11, 1962; and "AFTRA Vs. 'Academic Paternalism'; WNDT Says Show Biz & Education Don't Mix, Quits Air After Premiere," *VAR*, September 19, 1962.

Information on the premiere broadcast of WNDT, and the controversy surrounding the BBC documentary, came from "Webs Steam at WNDT Preem: U.S. TV Blasted in Educ'l Debut," *VAR*, September 19, 1962; as well as the continuity script of the broadcast, which was filed among the papers of Newton Minow (SHSW).

A discussion of the attractiveness to corporate sponsors of underwriting NET programming appeared in "Educational TV 'Goes Commercial,' " *Sponsor*, June 17, 1963; and "ETV Gets Big Business Boost," *Sponsor*, June 18, 1962. Also consulted were "Commercialism: Guidelines Being Drafted on Commercial Backing of ETV," *BRD*, December 17, 1962; and "Educational TV: It Grows Rapidly But So Do Troubles; Some Stations Turn to Business Sponsors," Albert Karr, *WSJ*, December 19, 1963. The *Broadcasting* editorial "Fourth Network?," which complained of NET's encroachment into popular programming, appeared October 7, 1963.

Correspondence and memos pertaining to the Boeing company's proposal to NET for a program tentatively titled "Jet Age President" can be found in National Educational Television Records, Series 3 (SHSW). It is interesting to note that in 1985 a program entitled *Air Force One: The Planes and the Presidents* appeared on the PBS network. It was underwritten in part by Boeing; however, the company did not have creative or editorial control of the production. A report on the success of KQED's 1963 auction is in "An Educational Station's Five-Day Binge," Robert De Ross, *TV Guide*, December 7, 1963.

A comprehensive chronicling of the programming of NET in the early 1960s, including press releases and in many instances full scripts, is housed in the NET Records (SHSW). It was from this body of information that the discussion of NET's programming—including the civil rights coverage—was derived. Also found among these files were letters and memos between NET and station managers regarding the local broadcast of these programs.

The transcript of Minow's interview on *David Brinkley's Journal* was found in the papers of the program producer Ted Yates (SHSW). A copy of Minow's memo asking for the intercession of Arthur Schlesinger, Jr., was filed with the chairman's records.

## Notes to Chapter 10

A provocative academic discussion of international communication, including the potential of satellites, in the early 1960s can be found in "Newton Minow's Global View: Television and the National Interest," by Michael Curtin, Department of Communication Arts, University of Wisconsin-Madison, 1988. Another work by Michael Curtin, "ABC *Close-Up*: Documentary in the Corporate Interest," also considers the relationship between the Kennedy administration and international satellite communication (Master's thesis, Department of Communication Arts, University of Wisconsin-Madison, 1986).

"Space Communications—A Symposium," edited by Bernard Straussburg and Claude M. Blair, appeared in the Winter 1963 issue of *Television Quarterly*. It is a valuable document that chronicles the first year of satellite communication in the United States. An overview of satellite technology is found in "Switchboards in Space—A Look into the Future: Interview with David Sarnoff on the Revolution in Communications," *U.S. News & World Report*, July 5, 1965.

The BBC's Cable Film project was described in "Global Television—A Force for World Unity," an address by Sir Gerald Beadle, former president of BBC television, to the New York Chapter of the Academy of Television Arts and Sciences, October 5, 1961. The text is filed in the Minow papers (SHSW).

Minow's remarks on "The Satellite That Talks," May 6, 1962, are recorded in the CBS transcripts of *The Twentieth Century*.

Several AT&T public information releases and several NASA public information releases describing and detailing project *Telstar* are among the files of Newton Minow (SHSW). "Everybody in Instant Touch," by Arthur C. Clarke, in *Life* magazine, September 25, 1964, gives an overview of *Telstar* and provides an introduction to synchronous satellites.

The launch of *Telstar* and the first experimental transmissions were considered in "AT&T's Telstar Ushers in Global TV Age," *BRD*, July 16, 1962, and "First Space Telecast Comes in Clear to L.A.," by Cecil Smith, *LAT*, July 11, 1962.

A memo from Richard Salant clarifying CBS's position on the broadcast of *Telstar's* early experimental transmissions was sent to Newton Minow on July 11, 1962 (SHSW). The July 11th Europe-to-America transmission, which was included in the *Howard K. Smith News and Commentary* for that evening, was viewed at the Wisconsin Center for Film and Theater Research. A transcript of the Minow interview on *Meet the Press*, July 22, 1962, is preserved with his papers (SHSW).

The three-network broadcast and the European relay christening international satellite communication was detailed in " 'Go, America, Go! Go, Europe, Go!' and 2-Way Telstar Show's in Space," by Cecil Smith, *LAT*, July 24, 1962; "The Telstar Story," in *The Quill*, September 1962; and "Neutral Messenger," *Newsweek*, August 6, 1962. President Kennedy's press conference participation in the broadcast was recounted in "Telstarred Press Talk Held Dull for Reporters," by Robert Hartmann, *LAT*, July 24, 1962. The jubilant review by Gilbert Seldes, "The Telstar Programs," appeared in the August 4, 1962, edition of *TV Guide*.

Information on the hit tune "Telstar" was provided by pop music historian Joseph Moorehouse.

Some of the Telstar-relayed images of the opening of the Ecumenical Council by Pope John XXIII, in October 1962, were included as part of *A Television Album*, a CBS news special broadcast December 30, 1962. It was viewed at the MOB. The series *CBS Town Meeting of the World* was discussed in "Via Telstar: World Holds Its First Town Meeting," by Aleene MacMinn, *LAT*, July 7, 1963.

A chapter devoted to the legislation on communication satellites, which passed in 1962, is included in "A Descriptive Analysis of the Influence of Newton N. Minow Upon Major Issues in Broadcasting While Chairman of the FCC," by Emmett W. Lally, Master's thesis, Boston University, School of Public Communication, May 1966.

Newton Minow's oral history, as part of the Regulatory Agencies Panel, at the John F. Kennedy Library, includes his thoughts on the passage of the Communications Satellite Act of 1962. The chairman's May 18, 1961, letter to President Kennedy was a report on the FCC's activities and views on satellite policy (SHSW).

In a letter to Lyndon Johnson, date June 15, 1961, the President urged the Space Council to undertake satellite studies and make government policy recommendations without delay. On July 24, 1961, the White House issued "Statement of the President on Communication Satellite Policy," which outlined Kennedy's position. On February 7, 1962, the White House introduced the Communications Satellite Act through a letter from the President of the United Sates to the President of the Senate and the Speaker of the House of Representatives. Attorney General Robert Kennedy's statement before the House Committee on Interstate and Foreign Commerce, March 20, 1962, detailed the administration's beliefs and hopes regarding satellite communication.

The timing of *Telstar's* launch and attendant program specials during the Senate debate on the legislation was briefly considered in *The Unraveling of America: A History of Liberalism in the 1960s*, by Allen J. Matusow (NY: Harper & Row, 1984).

An editorial in *The New York Times* supporting the administration's policy of pooling public and private resources in a communication satellite system appeared on July 10, 1962.

The May 14, 1962, issue of *I.F. Stone's Weekly* carried a lead article critical of the administration's satellite policy, entitled "The Myths That Menace America's Future." The *New York Post* of August 4, 1961, included "Behind the Scenes Battle Over Giveaway to AT&T," by Milton Viorst, which detailed the bitter division over satellite policy. The rationale of proponents of a government-owned satellite system was set forth in the "Statement of Americans for Democratic Action to the Senate Committee on Small Business, Subcommittee on Monopoly" on November 20, 1961.

Newton Minow responded to the giveaway charge in a July 26, 1962, letter to Mike Mansfield, Majority Floor Leader of the United States Senate (SHSW).

"JFK Signs Satellite Bill," in *BRD*, September 3, 1962, was one of numerous reports in the trade press regarding the enactment of the legislation.

A discussion predicting the applications of satellite communication in future entertainment and news programming is found in "What Telstar Cannot Do," by R. W. Apple, Jr., *Saturday Review*, September 8, 1962.

Newton Minow's remarks to the International Radio and TV Society were documented in "Communications: Storm Warnings, Global TV, Broader Phone Service—All to Come From Satellites at Work," *Newsweek*, October 8, 1962. Minow's statement before the Senate Commerce Committee reviewing the development of the Space Communication Program on January 29, 1963, is among the chairman's papers (SHSW).

Information regarding Kennedy's November 20, 1963, White House Declaration on Communication Satellites was found in the January 1964 issue of *The Viewer*, the official publication of the National Audience Board, Inc.

The 1964 Summer Olympic Games from Japan were seen in the United States via the *Syncom III* communications satellite. The event was documented in "Satellite to Be Orbited Over Pacific as TV Relay for Olympic Games," by Marvin Miles, *LAT*, August 13, 1964; and "Syncom III a Success Relaying TV Program From Japan to U.S.," *WSJ*, October 8, 1964.

## Notes to Epilogue

Among the general sources consulted were *Four Days: The Historical Record of the Death of President Kennedy*, compiled by United Press International and *American Heritage* magazine—originally published in 1964 and reintroduced in 1983; and *The Torch Is Passed: The Associated Press Story of the Death of a President* (NY: Parallax Publishing, 1967).

Scholarly accounts include *Television and the Death of a President: Network Decisions in Covering Collective Events*, by Ruth Leeds Love (Doctoral Dissertation, Columbia University, 1969); and *The Kennedy Assassination and the American Public: Social Communication in Crisis*, edited by Bradley S. Greenberg and Edwin B. Parker (Stanford, CA: Stanford University Press, 1965).

References on the President's thoughts regarding television in the last weeks of his life were: J. Leonard Reinsch, personal interview with the author, July 1, 1987; *The People Machine*, by Robert MacNeil (NY: Harper & Row, Publishers, 1968); and, pertaining to the Volkswagen commercial, "When the Client Is a Candidate," by Pete Hamill, *NYT Magazine*, October 25, 1964.

The television industry's performance in covering the assassination and funeral was detailed in several accounts in the trade press including the following important articles: "The Four Days," Albert Kroeger, *TV Mag*, January 1964; and the Special Report entitled "A World Listened and Watched: Radio-TV Meets Greatest Challenge in Wake of JFK Tragedy; Dropping of Regular Programs to Cost About $32 Million," *BRD*, December 2, 1963.

Also informative were "America's Long Vigil: A Permanent Record of What We Watched on Television from Nov. 22 to 25, 1963," special section in *TV Guide*, January 25, 1964; and "Broadcasting's 'Finest Hour,' " *The Viewer*, newsletter of the National Audience Board, Inc., December 1963.

A special pictorial memorial newsletter sent to all CBS employees recounted the network's coverage and provided statistical data on viewership for that weekend. The introductory message from CBS president Frank Stanton was dated December 12, 1963. An NBC year-end newsletter to all network personnel included similar information.

Sources pertinent to the media coverage of Lee Harvey Oswald and the suspect's death include: "Lee Harvey Oswald and Radio and Television," Fred L. Casmir, *The NAEB Journal*, September-October 1965; "The Press Corps and the Kennedy Assassination," Darwin Payne, *Journalism Monographs*, no. 15, February 1970; "Media Raked Over the Coals for Oswald Play," *BRD*, December 9, 1963; and "Lee Oswald: TV, the Press And Justice," Joseph Carter, the *New York Herald Tribune*, October 4, 1964. Also, Dan Rather's account of his involvement with the Zapruder film is relayed in *The Camera Never Blinks*, Dan Rather with Mickey Herskowitz (NY: Ballantine Books, 1977).

The film produced by Drew Associates during the funeral of President Kennedy is called *The Faces of November* and was released as an independent short subject. It is now distributed by Direct Cinema Ltd. of Los Angeles.

The letters sent to Chet Huntley and David Brinkley are preserved in the personal papers of Chet Huntley (JFKL) and the papers of David Brinkley (SHSW).

Among the innumerable press accounts reviewed concerning broadcasting's coverage of the tragedy are: "Grim Lessons of Hatred," Harriet Van Horne, *New York World-Telegram and Sun*, November 26, 1963; "TV Told Poignant Story in Few Words," Laurence Laurent, *The Washington Post*, November 26, 1963; and from *NYT* columns by Jack Gould, "TV Personalizes Grief: Millions Feel Full Impact of Tragedy and Witness History's Grim Unfolding," November 24, 1963; "Government Praises Networks for TV Coverage of Tragedy," November 27, 1963; and "TV Risked Profits in Kennedy Shows: At First Many Advertisers Refused to Share costs," December 1, 1963.

Network adjustments in programming were detailed in "TV Will Continue a Sober Approach," Val Adams, *NYT*, November 24, 1963; "Networks Check Future Shows to Cut Works Offensive to a Mourning Nation," Val Adams, *NYT*, December 1, 1963; and "Route 66 Changes an Upcoming Show," Bernie Harrison, *Washington Star*, November 27, 1963.

Advertiser-network negotiations over missed commercial announcements were reported in "100 Advertisers Receive TV Plea," Jack Gould, *NYT*, December 3, 1963.

The change in regulatory climate from the Kennedy to the Johnson administration was covered in "Washington Outlook: '64," Jay Lewis, *TV Age*, January 6, 1964; "TV Industry Expects Less FCC Pressure," Larry Wolters, *Chicago Tribune*, December 16, 1963; "Toil to Inspire Confidence, Johnson Tells Agencies," *Washington Star*, December 4, 1963; "FCC: The New Mood," *TV Age*, March 30, 1964; and "The Johnson Wealth: How President's Wife Built $17,500 Into Big Fortune in Television," Louis M. Kohlmeier, *WSJ*, March 23, 1964.

The *That Was the Week That Was* tribute, Jacqueline Kennedy's televised thank-you address to the nation, and *John F. Kennedy, May 29, 1964* were reviewed at the JFKL.

# Index